**Make Money Online – Online Affiliate Guide**

**Building An Online**

**Cash Cow**

**A Complete Step-By-Step Guide To Affiliate Marketing**

**Antony Barlow**

# Table of Contents

# Table of Contents

# Table of Contents

**Table of Contents**

# Table of Contents

# Table of Contents

# Table of Contents

# Table of Contents

# Table of Contents

# Table of Contents

**Table of Contents**

# Table of Contents

## Table of Contents

# Foreword

Just over five years ago I was fighting a losing battle running a computer hardware business. Rapidly falling margins and increased competition from high street stores, online retailers and local businesses pushed my working daily hours up to an unacceptable level, which in turn put a great strain not only on myself, but on my relationship with my wife and children. As I was in my early forties, I knew things had to change before I burnt myself out going nowhere.

From personal experience I can tell you that it is not easy making a career change, especially for someone in their 40s. I can also tell you, with complete honesty, that taking the plunge to train myself to become an online affiliate was the best decision I have ever made in my life. In my experience, however, it was far from easy to convert the hours upon hours I dedicated each week into actual financial rewards. I wasted over a year putting far too much trust and faith into so-called proven techniques and systems, which were clearly designed to make money for the author, rather than for the sad buyers, myself included.

Was it a struggle to establish myself as a successful affiliate and create regular, reliable, passive income streams? Well of course it was! Not just a struggle, but indeed a tremendous struggle, although I was never going to be beat! In my favour was the tremendous support I received from my wife during the initial couple of years that I spent building my websites. As at first I was not producing any revenue, my wife had to take up a job as a care assistant, so was in effect wiping people's arses so that we could pay the bills and hang onto our savings. Without the support of my wife, I would not have succeeded. It's as simple as that! Without my wife's support I would now probably be doing my best to hang onto some form of dead-end IT job, struggling to build a pension and pay my monthly bills. Julie, from the bottom of my heart I thank you for the support you have given me, for having faith in me, even when I doubted myself. I realise I'm such a lucky man to have you as my wife!

Now five years on, as I start to write this book, my family and I have ditched the grey skies of the UK to start a new life in Spain. My wife is now happily retired and I only work during the mornings, which gives us the rest of the day to actually live. How times have changed! Taking the plunge to make a major career change, venturing into the world of online affiliate marketing, has indeed proved to be the best decision I ever made.

# Introduction

Although I had years of experience in the IT world, I had very little experience of the internet in respect to building sites and indeed internet marketing. Don't think that my IT background gave me a head start in my online affiliate career, because to be honest it did not. I started my journey into the world of internet marketing with no experience of Wordpress, zero SEO knowledge and very little knowledge of internet marketing techniques. I will, however, say that as I had worked for myself for over 20 years, I did have one skill that was indeed a great asset to my new career. This transferable skill was of course the ability to put in the hours, day in, day out, which I realise is a struggle for most. If you want to succeed, you will have to train yourself to avoid the distractions that occur on a daily basis. I realise that there are always better things to do than write another bloody article or build another link, but you must learn to apply yourself and keep on keeping on! Most people waste a large proportion of their lives watching TV, visiting social networking sites or simply doing nothing. In reality, for those who are motivated, even those with full-time jobs have at least a couple of hours a day they could utilise to build new, highly profitable, passive income streams. To build a profitable online cash cow you do not need to be an internet mastermind or SEO genius. You simply need to funnel all your drive and motivation to the project in hand. Once your site is up and running, if you can create quality daily content plus add a few links to your pages, each and every day, you can succeed. Yes, it is really as simple as that.

## About This Book

This book is designed for those who want to venture into the highly profitable world of online affiliate marketing. This book is by no means a "get rich quick" master plan, promising great rewards for little effort. Nor is this book crammed with jargon to confuse you and make me appear to be far more intellectual than I actually am. Before going to print, to ensure I have covered all aspects of a new affiliate's first year, I have re-edited this book twice after receiving many reviews both from trusted affiliates and from those with no experience of affiliate marketing. My main goal is to give the reader a concise, jargon-free, clear guide to exactly what is required to make money online. This book guides you through your first year of building a quality online cash cow! To get the most from this book simply read it first in its entirety and then work through the action plans over the course of a year.

## Internet Real Estate

If you have read wealth-creation books such as *Rich Dad Poor Dad* and *The One Minute Millionaire*, you already know that the main secret to "making it big" is simply to create multiple passive income streams. If you have not read these books, I strongly advise you to do so! Many such books advocate purchasing property or even stocks and shares, but of course venturing into these markets requires a substantial investment as a starting point. You may well dream of owning a portfolio of properties that generate a tidy sum in monthly rentals, but in reality building such a portfolio, if possible, could take a lifetime. Internet real estate, in the form of affiliate websites, can be far more profitable than property located in even highly sought-after locations. Better still, highly profitable affiliate websites can be built by anybody, no matter the size of their investment capital. Once you have read this book, you could actually start building affiliate websites with no initial capital investment.

One of my very first online affiliate sites, which targeted the online bingo niche, cost me under $200 to build. Just over a year later I turned down a six-figure offer for the website. Years on the website is still earning!

## Break Out of the 9 to 5 Rat Race

Are you stuck in a rut and sick of the 9 to 5 grind? Are you earning just enough to cover your monthly bills and cannot have a quality holiday each year?  By starting your own online business you could easily make more than your employee salary, perhaps much more! Better still you can run your own online affiliate business from your home at a fraction of the cost you would need to start a brick and mortar business. Many of today's successful affiliates started on a part-time basis, simply utilising their "TV viewing time" to do something far more profitable and rewarding. It is not easy, but those who apply themselves and stick to it are those who succeed!

I am not going to promise that you can easily generate a six-figure-plus income, because in reality only a very small percentage of affiliates achieve that. If you are dedicated and self-motivated, monthly revenue of up to £5000 is easily possible for full-time affiliates. If you intend to work as a part-time affiliate, monthly revenue of £1,000 to £2,500 is a realistic target. How would an extra £30,000 a year change your life?

## Why the 9 to 5 Grind Will Never Make You Rich

From a very early age we are all taught that the way to succeed in life is to study hard, perhaps go to university and then work our way up the career ladder. In my opinion this way of thinking is completely flawed.  I have played the role of an ambitious employee climbing the career ladder and although I did reap some financial reward, the quality of my life, due to an increased workload, actually declined. According to www.monster.co.uk the average salary for a UK male is just over £30K while the average female salary is just £24K. Only 5% of UK employees earn over £60K while a mere 1% earn over £100K. Perhaps worse still, many fall into the trap of tying up a large proportion of their earnings in brick and mortar, which in many cases becomes a financial burden for much of their working life. The simple truth is that if you think that studying hard and then working your balls off is going to make you decent money as an employee, let's say at least £60K a year, 95% of you are going to end up very disappointed, as you will be extremely lucky to surpass the £30K mark.

I realise now that being rich is only partly about money. True richness is having the freedom to enjoy your life, spend quality time with your family and do things you want to do when you want to do them. How many people actually achieve having the freedom to work where they want, when they want? I still have many friends who are trapped in the archaic council estate I had to endure during my school years. I can virtually guarantee that most will remain there for the rest of their lives because they have become trapped in the 9 to 5 rat race.

With the rapid rise of the internet there now is another option. Those who earn online have the ability to work anywhere in the world where they have access to a stable internet connection. They also can run a business at a fraction of the cost of a traditional business working the hours that suit them. Through my online affiliate business I was able to move my family to Spain. I now have the freedom to live and work in any country of my choice. Better still, I choose the hours I work, which enables me to put my family first. Long gone are the days when an employer ruled my life!

## How Creating Pages That Earn Just 10p a Day Will Make You Rich!

If you are employed, then once you have completed an hour's work, at a rate of £6 per hour, £16 per hour or even £26 per hour, that hour is gone forever. That hour of your life, in regards to earning potential, has simply expired. Working as an online affiliate, however, most of your working hours will have a much longer lifespan and far superior earning potential. To demonstrate this fact, let's work on the assumption that every page of content you create generates just 10p in revenue per day. If I gave you a choice of earning £20 an hour as an employee or 10p for each article you produce, which to simplify this scenario we will say takes one hour to write, which would you prefer?

If you opted for the £20 as an employee, working one hour a day over the course of a year you would have earned 365 x £20, which is £7,300. Over the course of two years you would have earned £14,600 in total. If you chose the 10p per article option then in the first year you would have earned £6,679.50, but by the end of the second year you would have earned £26,681.50! Even using such a miserly sum as 10p per article, each article would earn £36.50 per year from the day it is posted on your website, (10p x 365 days). In reality every article you post becomes another passive income stream generating revenue for you over and over again. You don't need to target expensive products to make extremely good money online as long as you are able to keep producing content which in turns keeps on generating revenue, even as little as 10p per day.

Imagine that you spent an hour creating a review page for a product that had a retail price of £100 and you received 5% commission for each sale. Generating clicks that resulted in just one sale a day would generate £1,825 per year, (£5 x 365 days). Imagine having 20 such sales pages, which would generate 20 x £1,825 or in real terms £36,500 per year! If you had 100 such pages you would earn £182,500 per year. Understand now why those affiliates that take the time to master the art of online affiliating marketing become so wealthy?

There are many online webmasters who have become extremely wealthy simply by earning just a few pennies a click from Google AdSense or by generating clicks for affiliate programs such as Amazon and Clickbank. You can become one of them simply by having the drive and motivation to create daily quality content.

## Devote Quality Time to Create Quality Content!

You are going to have to dedicate at least two to four hours a day to this project if you are going to be successful. The more quality time you devote, the greater is your chance of success. Those that build their site on a full-time basis can of course build their website and their revenue streams more quickly than those who build their website on a part-time basis. Remember your main goal should be to create quality unique content each and every day. If you take shortcuts, such as simply copying content from other websites, or produce shoddy, poor quality content, you are simply wasting your time. In addition, take note that if you quickly fall into the trap of "I'll do it tomorrow", then again, I am sorry to say you are simply wasting your time.

## What's the Master Plan?

Most online marketing type books insist that the best way to make money online is by creating a network of thin type affiliate sites that generate income from many different niches. By "thin", I refer to websites that comprise less than 100 pages and target just a handful of search phrases. The trouble with this strategy is that these types of website are the ones that have been hit the hardest by the latest Google algorithm updates. I take a completely different view with respect to making money online. I believe, and have actually proved, that the way forward is to build big brand type authority sites, that comprise at least 1000 pages. Build a brand and build it big is the way to go, in my opinion.

If you check the websites that currently dominate your favoured niche, you find that it is indeed the big brand type sites that are dominating Google's search results. Thin type affiliate sites that still rank highly are basically living on borrowed time. It is a fact that a site that has, let's say, 1000 pages, has far more internal SEO (search engine optimisation) power than 20 sites of 50 pages. You don't have to be the BBC or Amazon to build a brand in the virtual eyes of search engines. Most would-be affiliates, however, want the easy option, opting to build sites of 10 to 50 pages with the great ambition of getting their website completed in a couple of weeks so that they can sit back and watch the money come rolling in. Of course this simply does not happen! Remember, to build a 1000 page affiliate site you only need to add three articles a day over the course of a year. Sounds very easy, doesn't it? However, to keep producing three articles a day, day in, day out, is not as easy as you would think. At first, pumped full of enthusiasm, starting a potentially life-changing online business, most people find it easy to complete the daily tasks, even those who are still working 9 to 5. In most cases, however, within a few weeks the initial enthusiasm has died down from a raging fire to just a few embers. Remember those that succeed are those who accept from the very start that the project they have undertaken is going to take time to flourish. Don't expect any reward for your efforts during the initial 6 to 12 months as it simply takes time to establish a new online affiliate business.

## Get Rich Quick Affiliate Systems

I state again that this book is not another of those "get rich quick" guides that seem to be littered all over the internet. I cannot promise that you will make a five-figure monthly income, nor can I promise that you will be living the high life in a year's time. I can say, however, that if you follow the guidelines in this book and devote yourself to your site for at least a year, then you will indeed have a quality site with multiple revenue streams.

"Get rich quick" affiliate guides make only those selling the guides rich. Such guides still sell thousands of copies each week, as there seems to be an army of buyers ready to swallow the clever marketing spew. Don't be another victim! If you are following this guide while holding down a full-time job, then I will be honest and say that you have a really tough task to get through the first year. I will, however, also say that I know of many now successful affiliates who did build a successful affiliate site while working in the "real world" full-time. At the end of the day it all depends on how much you really want it!

Are you prepared to sacrifice a couple of hours TV viewing each day in return for multiple revenue streams that will continue to make money even while you sleep? Do you want your own profitable business from which you reap all the rewards and which you can maintain anywhere in the world where you have a stable internet connection? I was in my early forties when I jumped on the online affiliate bandwagon. If I can do it, anybody can!

## Online Sales Are Booming!

The way we shop, play and even gamble have changed a great deal over the last decade. I, like many, now buy many items online including the weekly shopping, electrical goods, books and music. Most of what I buy offline, I have at the very least researched online before purchasing. A large proportion of the world's population are now happy to buy online. Although we are in the grips of an economic slowdown in most of the western world, it seems that online sales are going from strength to strength. A recent survey published by Actinic stated that online sales in the UK for the third quarter of 2011 increased by 7% with the number of actual online orders also increasing by 7%. The UK company Marks and Spencer have recently announced a £15 million investment in IBM's Smarter Commerce technology with plans to increase their online turnover from £500 million to £1 billion in the next two and a half years. Another UK retail company, Debenhams, has recently launched a catalogue to boost online sales while retail giant Tesco seems to be increasing internet sales each month at a rapid rate.

While many simply blame the poor economic climate for the demise of the UK high street, with empty stores in many UK towns and cities, it seems clear that we now shop in a different manner. Dedicated online stores are able to undercut traditional high street stores as they have vastly reduced overheads in running their business. With many in the western world feeling the pinch during the poor economic climate, more and more shoppers are simply opting to seek the better prices available online. Times certainly have changed. Virtually everything can now be purchased online, from a bottle of milk to placing a bet on the 3.30 at Kempton.

## Increase in Internet Users

If we look back just over a decade, to December 2000, according to statistics published by www.internetworldstats.com there were a mere 361 million internet users worldwide, which made up just 5.8% of the world population. The latest report, published in June 2011, stated that the actual number of worldwide internet users had grown to a staggering 2,110 million, which equates to over 30% of the world population. What is even more staggering is that Cisco recently published a report that stated the number of devices connected to the internet worldwide would increase to more than 15 billion in the next 4 years, which is more than double the current world population. It seems clear that although the internet has grown to become part of our lives, for the next few years we could see even greater growth than ever before.

If you think that the internet revolution has passed you by and your chance of jumping on the online affiliate bandwagon has gone forever, nothing could be further from the truth. Now is as good a time as any to start building your own online cash cow!

# Chapter 1 – Online Affiliates

## Life as an Online Affiliate

Before we actually get stuck into the "nitty gritty" of getting an affiliate site up and running, I think it is only fair to let you know what you are letting yourself in for. Again I repeat that one of my pet hates is the "get rich quick" affiliate book, as most simply line the pockets of those who write them. It is fair to say that the online affiliate books and indeed the "get rich quick" eBook niches are extremely profitable. Part of my online affiliate education, just like many other would-be affiliates, involved looking for the secret methods of success with very little work. Looking back, perhaps the crappy eBooks I purchased actually helped me, as they made me more determined to succeed. If you take a few minutes to Google "Clickbank top 10 products" or better still visit cbengine.com, I can guarantee that you will find "get rich quick" and dieting ebooks in the current top 10 best-sellers, no matter whether you are reading this book a week after its publication, a year later or even 5 years on. The top Clickbank products always cater to people's main desires, such as instant wealth, the perfect body and, of course, finding the perfect soul mate. Naturally, these sales products have superb sales pages that entice you to buy. Take time out to read the top Clickbank sales pages, but avoid the urge to buy!

If you really want to establish yourself as a long-term successful online affiliate, then there are no shortcuts. I am not going to drip-feed you the pure bullshit you find in many other online marketing books. I intend to give you the facts, cutting out the crap. In reality, making money online is extremely hard work, especially during the first year.

Let me detail what a day actually comprised during the first year when I set out on my journey to build an authority type affiliate site. Each morning my wife and I would arise at around 6am, with the first task of my day being to check my Google analytic stats and my affiliate stats. During the first few months this was a soul-destroying task. Most of the products I was promoting had few clicks and zero sales. On the days when I actually did generate even a single sale, the buzz was incredible. Even generating just a few pounds overnight motivated me to work harder.

Once my son had left for school and my wife had left for work, my next task was to examine the click maps of my pages. Each day I compared page views with clicks in order to see which calls to action were actually working. Once a week I examined page views and clicks in far more detail and made changes to my calls to action to generate more clicks.

After the normally grim task of checking my stats and clicks, the next task was to check my emails, and then create at least three pages of content. For this content I searched the news sections of leading sites that covered my niche to get at least one news story to add to work taken from my weekly content creation list. Creating a weekly content list will be discussed in detail later in this book. Once the content had been written, I then posted each article and took a small break for lunch.

After lunch I worked on link building for at least an hour or two, before spending up to an hour reading quality webmaster forums simply to find out what was going on in the world of SEO (search engine optimisation). During my early days I spent far too much time on forums, on many occasions wasting much of the day, so please do not fall into this trap. I also took the time actually to visit the merchant sites I was promoting to see if there were any new offers etc. I am still amazed by how many merchant sites do not inform affiliates before they launch new offers and promotions, which is a real pain. Many times I have had to stop what I am doing to edit my sales pages to include new promotions that have simply appeared on the merchant sites without any prior warning.

After checking the forums and merchant sites, I then took a break for dinner, spending a little time with my son and wife before creating at least a couple more articles from my weekly content list, sometimes more if I had the time. Before bed I again checked my Google analytics and affiliate stats. This daily process was repeated day in, day out, for the first year.

At some point each week, when I had the time, I examined my Google analytic stats in far more detail to find keywords that were generating a little traffic with low rankings. Simply adding links for these phrases did, of course, improve their rankings and increase their daily traffic.

To be honest, after my initial "new site" motivation had died down, it was a real grind! All affiliate marketers experience this, as it is not easy doing the same mundane tasks day in, day out. You simply have to be inspired by the small sparks of success during the first few months, such as a little extra daily traffic, a few extra clicks and of course any actual sales. I can tell you that it is extremely hard to keep going during the first six months, as you see very little reward for all your effort.

Now it is much easier for me as I generate a healthy monthly income that enables me to employ quality writers who churn out dozens of quality articles each day, plus I have a virtual assistant who edits and posts all articles. I still, however, work three or four hours a day on my sites as I still have to create content lists and, of course, I have to keep an eye on all my stats.

## How Much Do Affiliates Earn?

To be completely honest, most affiliates earn nothing! The simple stark truth is that 90% to 95% of those who venture into the world of affiliate marketing quit within three months. I am sorry to say that many of those reading this book will also fail, as they will not apply themselves to the set tasks. The good news is that for the small percentage that keep at it, the rewards are substantial. Why do so many would-be affiliates fail? In my opinion they fail because they have been conditioned to take the safe approach in life, taking the monthly pay-cheque from an employer. For many, making the switch from being an employee to becoming self-employed is basically a step too far.

The sole aim of this book is to give you the knowledge so that you can succeed. It is not going to be easy, although you have already given yourself a great start by acquiring the book.

### *So How Much Do Affiliates Really Earn?*

The following screenshots are actual snapshots taken from affiliate program back ends.

### *Virgin Games Monthly Earnings*

As you can see from the screenshot below, for one of my Virgin Games accounts, generated in total 431 sign ups during a month, of which 217 made a real money deposit.

**Please select date range** (use presets or enter dates manually for custom period)

preset `Last month` ▼   from `01/10/2011` 📅   to `31/10/2011` 📅   **SUBMIT**

Snapshot report - **01/10/2011** to **31/10/2011**

### Traffic

| | |
|---|---|
| Views | 260212 |
| Click Throughs | 14077 |
| **CTR %** only displays if the impressions tracker is in use | **5.4 %** |

### Registrations

| | |
|---|---|
| New registrations (active) | 217 |
| New registrations (inactive) | 214 |
| **New registrations (total)** | **431** |
| Registration rate | 3.1 % |

For this month alone my total earnings from Virgin Games were £7,433.27!

| | | | |
|---|---|---|---|
| October CPA (192 x £30) | Oct 2011 | 5,760.00 | |
| October 2011 commission | Oct 2011 | 1,673.27 | |
| Commission Paid | Oct 2011 | | 7,433.27 |
| | | **Total owing** | £0.00 |

## *Market Ace Monthly Earnings*

Market Ace is actually a mini network comprising of several different gambling brands such as Jackpotjoy, Sun Bingo, Caesars plus others.

| Impressions | Clicks | Click-Through Ratio | Downloads | Download Ratio | Total Commission |
|---|---|---|---|---|---|
| 12610 | 4292 | 34.04 % | 313 | 7.29 % | £ 6,717.09 |
| 39706 | 523 | 1.32 % | 10 | 1.91 % | € 45.08 |
| 39706 | 523 | 1.32 % | 10 | 1.91 % | € 45.08 |
| 12610 | 4292 | 34.04 % | 313 | 7.29 % | £ 6,717.09 |

As you can see from the above, the total monthly earnings were £6,717!

## Sky Gaming Monthly Earnings

# AFFILIATE HUB

| Impressions | Clicks | Click-Through Ratio | Total Commission |
|---|---|---|---|
| 1809 | 2148 | 118.74 % | £ 4,088.13 |
| 1809 | 2148 | 118.74 % | £ 4,088.13 |

Sky Gaming which comprises of Sky Bet, Sky Poker, Sky Vegas and Sky Bingo is another great gambling brand to promote as the brand is held in high regards by UK punters. As you can see from the above my monthly earnings were £4,088!

### Net Play Monthly Earnings

Net Play, just like Market Ace is another mini network.

| Merchant | Impressions | Clicks | Registrations | New Depositing Acc | Total Commission |
|---|---|---|---|---|---|
| SuperCasino.com | 2434 | 173 | 30 | 1 | £120.42 |
| Jackpot247.com | 2458 | 99 | 92 | 22 | £3,401.15 |
| Total - | 4892 | 272 | 122 | 23 | 3,521.57 |

From promoting just Net Play two brands my monthly revenue was £3,521!

### Betfred Monthly Earning

| Merchant | Impressions | Clicks | Registrations | New Depositing Acc | Total Commission |
|---|---|---|---|---|---|
| Betfred | 114909 | 1298 | 84 | 30 | $2,315.60 |
| Total - | 114909 | 1298 | 84 | 30 | 2,315.60 |

MTD | YTD | Today | Yesterday | **Last Month**  | All Merchants ▼ |

Betfred, for some obscure reason, still use the currency of dollars in their backend. From the above you can see that from 84 monthly registrations, 30 made a deposit, generating monthly income for me of $2,315.

# Chapter 1 – Online Affiliates

Of course anybody can create realistic affiliate stats with graphic packages such as Photoshop. To ease your mind and to clarify that I am indeed a decent online affiliate, below are references from Virgin Games and Market Ace.

## *Virgin Games Reference*

*As founder and first manager of Virgin Games Affiliates, I've known Tony since 2007 when he signed up to our newly launched in-house program. He's been one of our top earners every month ever since, but in the wider context of this book that's just ancillary; it's how he did it that matters.*

*Starting off as a specialized Poker affiliate, he gradually shifted his focus towards the online Casino and online Bingo marketplaces. Not the easiest of migration: while under the same "gambling" umbrella, Poker, Casino and Bingo appeal to entirely distinct audiences; each requiring different tones and marketing techniques.*

*I've worked with thousands of affiliates over the years and an overwhelming majority owe their continued success to sticking to what they know and do best. In little more than 2 years, Tony's drive, hard work, his ability to gauge a new market, adapt to it, then innovate within it, have allowed him to secure a significant share of traffic in two very competitive online sectors.*

*At time of writing, one of his sites sits proudly in the top 5 UK online Bingo sites, amidst affiliate companies who have owned the space for the best part of 10 years. No mean feat.*

*Without even reading the recipe book, one just needs to look at Tony's sites to understand there is something special going on there. This is an affiliate business built on content, clinical and innovative call-to-action, all supported by a highly structured underlying SEO mesh.*

*These ingredients have been used and abused by online marketers for years, but it takes a special talent to stir up a blend elegant enough to shake an industry. I believe Tony has this talent.*

*Pierrick Leveque*
*Head of Acquisition*
*Virgin Games*

*Market Ace Reference*

*I have been in the online gaming market for a number of years and joined Market-ace in January 2010, with previous roles at Coral, Gala Bingo and Virgin Games.*

*The gaming affiliate market has evolved rapidly in the last few years with new affiliates entering the market to challenge established affiliates. These new affiliates entering the market are really well finance and count with an army of competent SEO professionals and agencies.*

*Online gaming is fast and furious industry which keeps changing and nowadays is almost impossible for an affiliate to match the industry's pace. However, Tony is definitely the one to look up for in the gaming affiliate market.*

*Tony's SEO knowledge is second to none which I personally witness myself in many occasions, the most notable of which Jackpotjoy Red or Black campaign when Tony demonstrated his SEO expertise by ranking page 1 in Google in less than 2 weeks, and most importantly retained it! It's worth mentioning that Tony challenged multi- millionaire budget from the likes of ITV.*

*If you are looking for a solid advice on the gaming affiliate market, I could not recommend highly enough this book.*

*David Volovici*

*Head of Affiliates*

*Market-ace*

## Just the Tip of the Iceberg!

Although I have only included screenshots from just a few of the affiliate programs I promote, I actually actively promote over 50 different programs in the gambling niche, all of which generate income each month. You may be surprised to learn that all of the accounts are from just two authority sites that cover the bingo and casino niches. My other accounts' revenue range from as little as £50 a month to a monster that generates a five-figure sum each month! With a high quality authority type site you really can branch out and promote dozens of programs, which is in stark contrast to thin type affiliate sites that usually only promote one or two programs. The screenshots posted demonstrate what sort of monthly revenue you can achieve in your first year. Of course once you have achieved such income, you can really kick on as you have the finances to hire quality writers to produce more quality content which in turn increase your monthly revenue further.

## Are You Really Cut Out for This?

Before we venture into creating your very own affiliate cash cow, I want to tell you a story of two affiliates. In the last few years I have coached a handful of people who aspired to become online affiliates. Coaching "would-be" affiliates has been a great aid for me, because it made me realise just how hard it is for most people to build a successful online affiliate website. As I have always worked for myself, I found it easy to adapt to working at home as an affiliate. I have years of experience of working for myself, driven by the need to get the mortgage and bills paid each month, plus of course putting food on the table for my wife and children. When I endured slow months, I simply had to generate more sales and work even harder to do so. Working for yourself is not easy! There are always distractions and better things to do. Working online it is so easy to get distracted and end up wasting days or even weeks achieving nothing.

From the people I have coached over the years, two of them are firmly entrenched in my mind. One was an accountant who took voluntary redundancy, while the other was a lorry driver. The former had a talent for writing top quality articles and a passion and indeed a talent for golf. Which one of the two would-be affiliates do you think has been the most successful to date? Well, within the first year the lorry driver completely astounded me by achieving monthly revenue of over £2,000, while the accountant failed to earn a single penny. What was even more astounding was that the lorry driver achieved the £2K revenue while still holding down his full-time job. The former accountant, wisely, quickly discovered that online affiliating was not for him and refocused on becoming a quality freelance writer, in which by all accounts he has gained a great deal of success.

The sad truth is that many who read this book are bound to fail. I am not going to lie to you. I can teach you how to build a quality affiliate site, I can teach you how to market your site, I can teach you how to gain great ranking in search engines, but I cannot give you the motivation and drive to succeed. That needs to come from you!

Over 90% of affiliates fail and abandon their sites within three months because they expect instant success. Those that succeed are the ones who have the drive and motivation to stick it out for the long term. Expect nothing for the first year, but simply build your site into a 1000 page authority site and you reap the rewards in the long term. It's far from easy, but of course if it were, everybody would be raking in the money online.

## Why Affiliates Fail

The basics of successful affiliate marketing are surprisingly simple. You build a website and drive traffic to your website, which in turn produces clicks, which in turn produces sales. Yes it is simple as that! Unfortunately, to build a website takes time, effort and a degree of drive and self-determination that many "would-be" affiliates lack. Again I repeat, do not expect instant success, as building a successful "online cash cow" takes time. From my experience of building many affiliate websites, covering many different niches, I know that you should in reality expect very little reward for your efforts during the first 6 to 12 months. It could be a year before your website starts to generate decent monthly revenue. The good news is, however, that those of you who do "keep on keeping on" have a great chance of generating highly profitable passive revenue streams, which could indeed change your life! Remember, every article you add to your site in effect pushes up the value of your site. Let me quickly tell you another story.

Last year, a friend whom I was coaching was to say the least disheartened, because after three months he had not made a single penny. I invited him round and took a good look at his site. In just three months he had over 300 quality articles, plus a dozen or so key phrases that had steadily climbed to page 2 of Google's search results. Yet I could ascertain from the way he was talking that he was on the verge of throwing in the towel.

Although he had no earnings, his site did have value, which was increasing with every article he posted. As his 300 articles were of high quality and he was in effect halfway there with his rankings, I valued his site at around $3,000 to $5,000. I use US dollars because in general the currency of the web for websites, domains and indeed links is commonly dollars. For the quality of his articles I would expect to pay around $10 to $25 per article from an online freelancer. In addition the site's rankings also had a value, as did its layout and quality. As he seemed extremely discouraged, although he was in the early days of his journey into the world of online affiliating, I told him to list his site for sale on an affiliate webmasters forum with a reserve of double my initial top estimate. This would give him the chance to see how other affiliates valued his work, with perhaps the option of cashing in if the reserve was met. Within 48 hours he removed the site from the sales thread after many bids with a top bid of $5,500. He had realised his site did have value and did not want to lose it. Although I was extremely frustrated by his initial lack of self-belief, I must admit I was delighted that he had seen the error of his ways. A year later his site ranks extremely well for a handful of competitive terms and is generating average revenue of over £4,700 per month, which gives his site an estimated value of at least £70,000. The site owner now works on his site full-time. The moral of this story is simply to have faith in what you are doing!

Out of the hundreds of affiliates I have spoken to over the years, most admit that it took them a year to find their feet in the industry. Remember it does indeed take time! Don't expect instant results. The affiliates who are the big earners are those who have the drive, determination and grit to stick it out for the long term.

### *Don't Build Too Many Sites*

I for one have been guilty of trying to build too many sites and I could name many other affiliates who also have fallen into this trap. As soon as you start to understand how search engines work, and as your keyword research skills improve, you stumble onto many other potentially good ideas for other websites. In no time at all you have several sites, thus diluting your link building and content creation. Until you start generating decent revenue, simply stick to just one site as described in this book. Once you start making money, then you can diversify with different sites. I do, however, strongly advise that you do not even contemplate building a second site until you have completed one full year as an affiliate.

### *I Will Catch Up Tomorrow Syndrome*

Once your site is up and running, you simply have to devote at least a few hours each day to content creation and link building. Of course if you have more time each day, that is even better. Most new affiliates start off full of good intentions but then fall into the trap of "I will catch up tomorrow". If you do not keep up with your daily schedule, you will never make any money. Always remember that in reality tomorrow never comes!

## Why You Must Build a List

I am still amazed by how many quality affiliate sites do not, in some shape or form, try to capture their visitors' email addresses. Let us imagine that you simply offer a monthly newsletter full of special offers that generates three new subscribers each day. Over a year that is over 1000 subscribers. Now let's say a small site offers you £150 CPA per sign-up. You are not keen to add this new program to your website, so you simply send out a mailshot to your 1000 members. Suppose that just 2% take up this offer. This would generate £3,000 in revenue for perhaps only 20 minutes work!

For my gambling websites and indeed websites in other niches, I prefer to generate subscribers rather than actual sign-ups and sales from clicks. Let me tell you why. It is a fact that many websites generate sign-ups and sales from visitors who only visit their websites once. Once they are passed onto the merchant website by means of clicking an affiliate link, they may never return. Subscribers to a list are a completely different matter. I can tell you from the thousands of subscribers I have generated over the years that many have purchased from my frequent newsletters time and time again. It is a fact that my subscribers are far more profitable to me than those who simply click my affiliate links, as subscribers are highly likely to generate income for the long term by simply responding to newsletters. Take note! Your website MUST include a list-building script which I will detail later in the book.

## Build a Brand and Build it Big!

The Google algorithm is changing and has been doing so for some time in a major way. Slowly but surely, thin type affiliate sites are vanishing from the top search positions, being replaced by authority type websites. There is no doubt that aged thousand page plus sites, structured in the correct manner, are far more powerful than thin type affiliate sites of less than a hundred pages. With Google rolling out a major algorithm change early in 2011, named as PANDA by many webmasters, plus further major algo tweaks during the first quarter of 2012, the rules for creating and ranking sites were changed in many ways. The roll-out of PANDA hit many webmasters extremely hard, with many losing their Google traffic overnight. Long gone are the days when crappy thin affiliate websites could dominate competitive high-ranking positions in Google. Long gone are the days when webmasters could simply "spin" other webmasters' quality articles and gain great ranking. Many leading SEO experts have started to express the view that the rules of SEO have completely changed. Quality fresh content really is now worth its weight in gold for webmasters in the know!

## Don't Put All Your Eggs in One Basket

As soon as your first site is established and starting to generate revenue, add another section to your website that covers another aspect of your chosen niche. Remember the name of the game is to "build it big" which, with the correct structure, will give your website even more SEO power. The way you structure your website is of paramount importance, especially with Google PANDA updates occurring most months. As you will be building your website using multiple subdirectories, you are in effect isolating each section from possible search engine penalties. If one of your sections is penalized, the other sections of your site remain penalty free. Most online affiliates have yet to harness the power of using subdirectories for authority type sites, which is a big mistake. We will cover this topic in much greater detail later in the book.

For those thinking about branching out into another niche, again I say do not even contemplate this until either you have a year's experience under your belt or you have generated £3K in monthly income for at least 3 consecutive months.  Many novice webmasters simply end up with a dozen or more affiliate sites none of which have actually generated any revenue. If you are working solo, building one authority website in a year is a tough enough job, so don't dilute your efforts unless you are generating enough revenue to outsource the content.  Stay focused and you will be rewarded!

# Chapter 2 - Affiliate Basics

Surprisingly, one of the most frequent questions I am asked is, "What is affiliate marketing?" Firstly let me say that in my time as an online affiliate, although I have sold a wide range of products, from chicken-coop plans to high definition TVs, I have never actually had any responsibility for either stocking products, despatching products or payment processing. For some reason many think that an online affiliate is some form of online "Del Boy" character with rooms crammed full of products ready to be shipped around the world. Nothing could be further from the truth.

## So What Is Affiliate Marketing?

In real terms affiliate marketing is a means of making money by sending traffic to merchant websites. Trackable links are placed on affiliate website pages (your website) with commission earned for each click, sale or lead depending on the actual affiliate program. For example, let's say you have a blog that reviews movies. You could monetize your blog with perhaps an affiliate deal with an online DVD store. In each movie review that you publish you include a link for the reader to buy the movie reviewed. Every time a reader clicks your link, enters the store and makes a purchase, you are rewarded with a set commission or payment.

## Affiliate Program Types

Online affiliate programs vary a great deal. For example, pay per click (PPC) affiliate programs range from just a couple of cents per click to several dollars per click or even in some cases much more. Commission-based affiliate programs can range from as little as 1% per sale, from companies such as Del Computers, to up to 50% for the very competitive online gambling or finance niches. Other affiliate programs pay a fixed amount per sale, which is commonly known as Cost Per Acquisition (CPA). For any niche you will find a great selection of affiliate programs. Your job is to find the best converting products with the highest payment.

## Great Aspects of Affiliate Marketing

There are many great aspects of affiliate marketing, mainly revolving around the financial rewards, plus of course the freedom that becoming a successful affiliate affords you. Let's take a look at the best aspects of becoming a successful affiliate.

## *Earn While You Sleep*

Once you have established your website and are generating healthy daily traffic, you are generating revenue even when you sleep. There is nothing better than waking up in the morning and checking your stats to find out how much you have earned overnight. Each and every morning, the first thing I do is to check how much I have earned while I have slept. Even after six years I still get a buzz from seeing new sales and of course new commission and CPA payments in my affiliate accounts. Remember the internet never sleeps!

## *Be Your Own Boss*

Working for yourself is so rewarding. You get all the rewards rather than just the small slice of the pie that you would earn as an employee. The harder you work the greater is the reward! There are of course downsides to working for yourself. Firstly the buck stops with you. If you are ill and unable to work, your online business stalls. It is always a good idea to have a stash of content for times you cannot produce new content due to illness or other reasons. In addition, if you have a bad month in regards to revenue, you aren't paid. It is common sense to put aside funds when you have great months to cover the months that are disappointing.

Working from home might sound ideal although in reality it can be a daunting experience. Many miss the banter from the workplace while others find it hard to stay focused due to the number of distractions. If you have children under school age, it is an even more difficult task. You can of course work the hours of your choice, so simply work the hours when there are fewer distractions.

## *Work When You Want Where You Want!*

Working online you are no longer shackled to a 9 to 5 routine. You can simply work when you want, where you want! As soon as my online business was established, generating a good stable monthly income, my family and I moved to Spain. One of the great aspects of working online is you can work anywhere in the world where you have a laptop and a half decent internet connection.

## *Give Yourself a Chance To Make It Big!*

Most people go through life with no chance of ever making a fortune. Stuck in a boring job with just enough to pay their mortgage and bills and perhaps the odd holiday each year they have no prospects of anything better. I am not going to promise that you will make a fortune but at least you will be giving yourself a chance of doing so. I believe most of us become so wrapped up in our working lives that we forget about the actual quality of our lives. Do you work to live or live to work?

Imagine if you earned just enough as an online affiliate to match your existing salary, but you did so by only working a few hours each day. How would that change your life? What freedom would you achieve? Remember, however, that you have the chance to earn much more!

## Revenue Share v CPA v PPC

Another question I am frequently asked by new affiliates is, "What type of affiliate program is best, revenue share, CPA or PPC?" There are so many variables it is a very difficult question to answer. As you may already be aware, I nowadays work in the UK gambling niche. UK gambling affiliate programs offer revenue share, CPA or sometimes hybrid deals that comprise CPA and reduced revenue share. UK gambling brands, on the whole, do a great job of customer retention and offer sports betting, casino games, poker games and even bingo. I have generated many sign-ups who simply deposit a few pounds to play a few casino games or even a few hours of bingo. They disappear for weeks or months on end but return to bet on major sporting events such as the Grand National and the FA Cup. They also return during bank holidays and during the winter when there is little else to do in the UK. I have many such sign-ups who have been earning me money for over five years. Some have earned me hundreds of pounds over the years, some much more. Taking a CPA payment of even £200 for these sign-ups would in my opinion be a bad move and cost me money in the long term, so I always opt for revenue share from UK gambling merchants.

For those who promote US gambling merchants, it is a different ball game. Firstly there is no guarantee that any of the brands that currently accept US deposit will be around in a year's time or even less, due to current online gambling laws in the US. In real terms, according to US law, such sites are operating illegally. Those who choose to promote such sites have the option of CPA or revenue share. It is no surprise that most opt for CPA.

Many new affiliates opt for CPA during their early affiliate career as they can earn more during the first year, which in turn helps them to build their sites. For example, let's say a gambling affiliate manager offers you either £100 CPA payment for every new sign-up who makes a deposit, or 30% revenue share with the average player worth, in this case, just £10 per month. Suppose we are generating just five sign-ups a month. The table below shows the earnings for CPA and revenue share for the first six months.

**5 x Sign Ups Per Month - £100 CPA v Rev Share @ £10 per month per Players**

| Month | CPA @ £100 per player | MGR @ £10 per player per month |
|---|---|---|
| January | £500 | £50 |
| February | £500 | £100 |
| March | £500 | £150 |
| April | £500 | £200 |
| May | £500 | £250 |
| June | £500 | £300 |
| July | £500 | £350 |
| August | £500 | £400 |
| September | £500 | £450 |
| October | £500 | £500 |
| November | £500 | £550 |
| December | £500 | £600 |
|  |  |  |
| **Year Total** | **£6000** | **£3900** |

As you can see from the above table, taking CPA actually gives the best return for the first year. It is not until month 11 that MGR becomes the more profitable monthly option. The extra return for opting for CPA, especially for the first year, can be very beneficial for those new to the online affiliate world, especially if they are struggling to produce content. The extra income could be used to purchase hundreds of articles or even to fund a new section targeting a sub-niche. Although in this instance I am referring to the online gambling niche, many other niches give the affiliate the choice of revenue share or CPA. At the end of the day what is best for you is your decision.

## Tenancy Agreements

A tenancy agreement is a fixed amount that is offered by a merchant to a website owner in return for displaying the merchant site on their website, usually in a prime spot above the fold on the homepage. Tenancy agreements in general are few and far between and in my opinion are in most cases heavily weighted towards the merchant, although there are exceptions. Tenancy agreements can be a great way for merchants to gain top placements on affiliate websites, and in doing so, take new customers away from their competitors.

As a general rule, a merchant offers to pay a fixed amount per month instead of paying you revenue share or CPA payments. Sometimes, however, a merchant may offer you a tenancy agreement with either a reduced CPA or reduced revenue share. As an affiliate you have to weigh up whether you would receive more from CPA or revenue share or from the tenancy agreement offered.

For example, let's say that the merchant affiliate manager offers you £1,000 per month for prime placement on your site. You check the merchant's affiliate program and find that they offer £50 CPA per new acquisition or 30% revenue share. You should already know from the data from your existing ads how many clicks and sales an ad in the spot requested generates. If you know that the ad will generate more than 20 new acquisitions, you will be losing money as you could earn more from a CPA deal. Estimating revenue share for a new merchant program is a little tricky, as all programs do not convert in the same manner. I would rather work on either CPA or revenue share for at least a month, perhaps listing the merchant on a decent spot on my site, although not a prime spot, so that I could evaluate how the merchant program performed.

I have been offered a dozen or so tenancy agreements over the years and all but one I turned down. The one that I accepted was simply too good to refuse. I was offered a sum above the merchant's normal revenue share rate plus a four-figure monthly payment, so had nothing to lose.

In addition you have to add into the equation loss of revenue from the current ad that occupies the requested spot on your site. Would removing the current ad really be a profitable move?

Merchants usually only offer tenancy agreements for a short period at first. They want to ensure that they are getting their money's worth. Most tenancy agreements are only offered for a month or two initially. If after the initial period a merchant is ultra-keen to commit to a long-term deal, you had better try to find out how the ad is performing, as you can virtually guarantee that the ad is generating many new acquisitions for the merchant. You can bet your last dollar that if the ad had proved more costly than standard CPA or revenue share, the merchant affiliate manager would either try to reduce the cost of the agreement for future months or simply terminate the agreement after the initial period is over.

## Affiliate Programs

Virtually every niche has at least dozens of affiliate programs, although they are not equal. Finding the best performing affiliate programs for your content is going to take time. One tip I can offer you now is never to fall in love with any affiliate program. Even if an affiliate program is making you a four or five figure sum each month, don't be afraid to try another affiliate program in the same spot for at least a week, because you may find the new program actually generates more revenue.

## Researching Affiliate Programs

Finding quality programs to promote will ultimately be the key to your long-term success. I like to build my sites around quality programs offered by well-known quality brands. I prefer to opt for revenue share working with well-known UK brands. You should never simply select a program to promote just because someone tells you so. You should spend at least a little time doing your own research, not from just an affiliate's point of view but more importantly, a customer's point of view.

Here are the processes I go through when testing out a new program.

### *Program Landing Page*

As an affiliate my job is to push my visitors to the merchant's landing pages. The merchant's landing page should be well designed, have great calls to action and do its utmost to entice the reader to buy, with perhaps special offers for new customers. If the landing page is poor, it is going to affect my conversions. Take time to study merchants' landing pages as a customer.

### *Sign Up / Initial Contact*

I always sign up to the program / store as a customer so that I can check out the sign-up process. The sign-up process should be smooth and easy. At this stage, however, I will not make any purchase. A good merchant targets subscribers with tempting offers or even special discounts in an attempt to convert the subscriber to a customer. Take note of the emails you get from merchants and what they offer you. If the merchant fails to send you tempting offers, I would advise you to try other merchants, as the conversion rate is bound to suffer.

How the program handles new customers is of great importance to me. I would expect a welcome email but perhaps also a great offer to entice me to make my first purchase. I also expect the program to email me again within a couple of days if I have not made a purchase. I do not want the program to bombard new sign-ups with daily emails, but I do expect the program to do their utmost to tempt them to buy. Great programs send an email to inactive new sign-ups at least on a monthly basis to entice them to become active customers.

## Would You Buy?

I always log in to a merchant site that I am thinking about promoting, simply to see what the site has to offer. There is of course no point in opting for a merchant that has limited stock or that has sales pages that do not look professional. Take time to see what the merchant site actually offers potential customers. In addition do a little market research to ascertain if the actual prices of the goods are competitive. Remember that internet users shop around for the very best deals.

## Test the Shopping Cart

Take the time to test the actual shopping cart. Is it easy to add and remove items? Beware of shopping carts that are overly clumsy to use, as you will find that many of your potential customers will simply abandon their orders and move on to a more user-friendly store.

## Make a Purchase

A week or two after signing up to the store, provided I am happy with the initial email contact, I actually make a test purchase from the merchant. I simply purchase a small item so that I have a full understanding of the complete checkout procedure and the payment types accepted. I also gain valuable information regarding the merchant's delivery process. Taking the time to carry out all the above checks on merchants gives me valuable information which I can add to my sales pages, a benefit that many affiliates don't even consider.

### *On-going Marketing*

A good merchant does a great job of marketing to existing customers for the long term. I would expect that at least once per month the merchant would email all customers on their database informing them of new promotions. As I am an active customer, I too receive these promotions. These emails are a great source for creating new content and when posted on the site ensure that my website is always up to date.

### *Offline Marketing*

When any of the merchants that I promote runs a TV ad campaign, this always results in increased traffic, which of course leads to increased conversions and revenue. One of the sites I promote ran a two-week TV ad earlier this year. My sales for that merchant program alone increased over 200% for the two-week period. In general, the more advertising and brand building a merchant employs, which can be in the form of TV advertising, radio commercials, newspaper and magazine advertising, the easier the merchant becomes to convert. Quality advertising creates trust among consumers, which in turn makes selling the merchant's products much easier.

### *Account Managers*

I will be honest and say that many affiliate programs have poor support. Ask any affiliate and they will tell you that they have been frustrated time and time again trying to get hold of their account manager. Great account managers are few and far between. The turnover of staff on some of the smaller programs can be extremely frustrating. You build up a great working relationship with one account manager only to find that he / she has moved on elsewhere. Great account managers, however, are not going to be leaving the industry so I tend to follow them as they progress up the ladder. I am very loyal to both great affiliate programs and account managers as I realise just how much they are worth to me.

Another important factor to check out before deciding on a merchant to promote is what charges will be made against your revenue share or CPA payments. Always take the time to read the terms and conditions in full. If there are parts of the terms you do not understand, simply email the merchant and ask for clarification. If I am unable to contact my account manager, alarm bells start to ring. I realise that account managers have a tough job looking after hundreds or even thousands of affiliates, but it only takes a few seconds to send an email stating that they are busy and will get back to me later. I have a great solution for account managers that are difficult to get hold of. I simply don't work with them!

As you can see, I am very picky about which sites I promote. If a merchant does a poor job emailing their client base, I will lose money. If the merchant's landing page is not 100%, I will lose money. If the merchant's shopping cart is too complicated or clumsy a process, this results in customers abandoning their orders and moving onto another online store, so again I will lose money. If the merchant has a poor marketing strategy, I will lose money. I am looking for the maximum return on every click possible, so I do not want to throw money away working with less than quality merchants.

Smaller programs may offer me a higher revenue share deal but in the long term the big brands always make me more money!

So before even building your site, do your research as a customer and as a potential affiliate. Good affiliate managers will be happy to answer your emails before you sign up to their program.

## Affiliate Applications

Before contacting online merchants regarding affiliate partnerships, ensure you are happy with your site. Make sure all your posts have been spell-checked. If you have any technical problems with your site, you can always advertise on Digital Point or better still Elance to hire someone to correct them. Once you are happy with your website, you should contact merchants about setting up an affiliate partnership. The reason we have waited until the site is up and running is simply because most quality merchants like to take a look at your site before they approve you. It would be very foolish to apply when your site is only half built.

## Payment Methods

The most popular methods that affiliate programs use to pay affiliates are bank transfer, cheque, PayPal, Neteller and Moneybookers. You should also ensure that you read the full terms and conditions of each affiliate program to which you sign up. Most have a minimum payment amount, which can range from £50 to £500. Most affiliate programs also have a set payment date. As a rule affiliates that receive their payments into online wallets such as Neteller and Moneybookers receive their payments first. I always prefer to receive my payments direct into my Neteller account and then simply withdraw to my bank account each month. In doing so I avoid the terrible phrase, "The cheque is in the post."

## Affiliate Networks

Many merchants run their own affiliate programs while some, including some of the biggest brands, run through affiliate networks such as TradeDoubler and Affiliate Window. One of the later chapters of this book is devoted to Affiliate Networks, listing the very best of the best.

# Chapter 3 – Setup & Running Costs

## Quick Costing Overview

Another question that I am frequently asked is, "How much does it cost to set up an affiliate site?" You may be very surprised to know that in real terms the actual setup costs and indeed running costs of an affiliate site are minimal. As a new affiliate I strongly suggest you keep costs down to as little as possible during your first year, which is good business sense. If at first you can produce your own content, your initial outlay can actually be as little as $100. As we run through the process of creating your site, I am sure that you will be amazed at how little, in real terms, the costs actually are.

### Setup Costs

- Aged Domain: $20

- Monthly Hosting: $10

- Logo / Header: $25

- Wordpress Theme: from $30

### Recurring Monthly Costs

- Hosting: max $10 per Month

- Internet Connection: $30 per month

As you can see from the above, you can be up and running with a professional looking affiliate site for less than $100. After the initial setup costs your only recurring costs are hosting, which can be secured for $10 or even less per month, and most importantly a stable internet connection. In respect to an internet connection you do not need a dedicated internet connection for your affiliate website but can just use your existing home internet connection. If you don't have $100 to get up and running, you can simply set up using a blog host such as www.wordpress.com or www.blogger.com completely free, although having your own domain and hosting is more beneficial in the long term. Although you can start up using free blog hosting with Wordpress and Blogger, I strongly advise you to go the paid route and purchase your own domain and hosting. Your other big investment is of course your commitment. If you cannot commit for the long term, I will tell you now that you will fail.

## Hosting & Domains

### *Finding the Right Domain Name*

Before you start to set up your affiliate site you are going to need a domain name. In my, possibly subjective, opinion new domain names can take much longer to rank in Google than aged ones. I believe that to give yourself a good start you need a domain name that is at least two years old and has never been dropped. For those that do not understand, let me go into more detail. Firstly the best place to purchase an aged domain name is the Godaddy Auction site. Let's say we are looking for an aged treadmill domain name.

Go to https://auctions.godaddy.com/

Type "treadmill" in the search box.

After a few seconds a list of domains is displayed. This list is updated every day so don't rush into buying the first domain you see!

For our example, the domain that interests me most in the list is treadmilltoday.com.

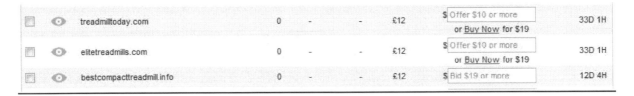

As you can see the domain is available for only $19. Let's check how old it is.

### *How to Check Domain Names*

Go to http://whois.domaintools.com/

Enter the domain name "treadmilltoday.com" in the search box.

# WHOIS Lookup at DomainTools.com

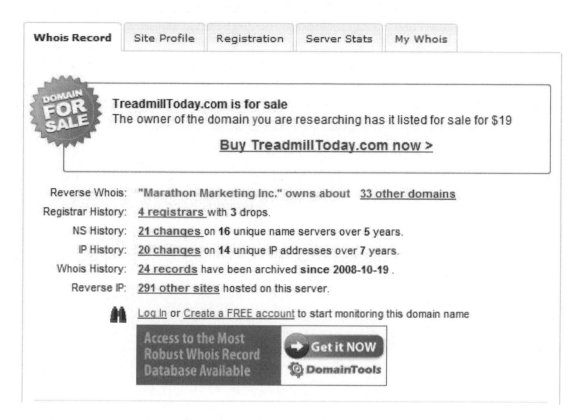

As you can see from the above the domain is seven years old but has been dropped three times. I'm not keen on using aged domains that have been dropped, especially those that have been dropped multiple times. Although I do indeed like this domain, I would search for another with age but without any drops. Let's though do further research on this domain name.

### *How to Check a Domain's History*
Go to http://www.archive.org/index.php, then type www.treadmilltoday.com into the search box.

If this domain had a site at one time, it will be listed. Most you will find are not. Over the years I have found some real gems by simply taking the time to run an aged domain through the archive. You can also check if the domain has any backlinks. You will understand more about backlinks as you read through this book, so don't worry. To check for existing backlinks simply follow the instructions below.

### *How to Check Existing Backlinks*
Go to www.opensiteexplorer.org

In the search box again type "site: www.treadmilltoday.com"

In most cases the domain will have no backlinks. For a good domain with a decent name that used to be a site and has existing backlinks you have to pay more, sometimes much more, although you may get very lucky as I have done over the years. However this is not essential. As this is your first site, simply go for an aged domain that costs under $50.

### Don't Rush into Buying a Domain

Take the time to choose a domain name that you can brand. If possible try to find a domain with age and at some time had a site and a few backlinks if possible. Make sure the domain you purchase is at least two years old with no drops and is brandable. In the past I have purchased domain names up to eight years old with existing backlinks for only $10.

## Hiring Graphic Designers

One of the biggest costs associated with setting up a new site is often the design of the site's logo and header. For my first site I was quoted a price of just under £1,000 for just a header and logo from a UK graphic design company. After searching around online, I eventually ended up paying only $50 in total for both the logo and header and had over 20 designs from which to choose.

My first port of call for any graphics is now the Digital Point Forum. You can get a custom banner designed for as little as $5, a logo for as little as $10 or even a complete header for as little as $20. Take 10 minutes out and visit the Digital Point Forum and scroll down to the Buy, Sell or Trade section and click on Contests. This section should be crammed with users who have posted graphic design contests.

Unfortunately you cannot just sign up to Digital Point and post a contest. You have to have a certain number of posts in order to build up trust before you can post a contest. Simply sign up and make one or two relevant posts a day. Do not post for the sake of it or you will be quickly banned. Try to post something with value or even ask a question or two. Ensure that you build quality posts and not just spam posts like many newbies to Digital Point.

### Posting a Graphic Design Contest

Before posting your contest at Digital Point, take the time to examine many other contests and specifically how the contestant holder has specified their requirements. When you post your contest, you must ensure that you detail a full brief of what you actually require. Remember graphic designers are not mind readers so you must post full details of your requirements including the following:

- Size in pixels

- Colours Required

- Text Required

- Theme of Design

- Closing Date

- Payment Method

I also strongly advise you to request that all designs submitted must be watermarked. Having designs watermarked stops others viewing your contest and stealing the designs submitted, of which I am sorry to say I have been a victim. Digital Point is a great resource for webmasters but is also a haunt of many scammers.

## *Running Your Digital Point Contest*

For some reason I have found that the initial entries are in most cases from those who have the same design skills as myself. Yes, I admit my design skills are limited to matchstick men alone. Don't be harsh with the initial entries but thank them for their time and politely explain that their designs are not what you are looking for. As you get better entries, take the time to post good feedback. Tell the contestants what you like about their designs and what they could change to make their designs even better. Checking the contest thread at least a couple of times each day and posting good feedback encourages the better designers to enter. I have also found that the quality designers enter design contests during the last couple of days, once they have studied your feedback and have a better understanding of what you are looking for. Don't be too hasty in picking a winner and also give the designers plenty of scope to be creative. Many times I have been astounded with what the designers have come up with, which in many cases was far better than I had initially had in mind.

## *Digital Point Feedback Scores*

All those who post contests, sales and even those who purchase goods from Digital Point have a feedback score. For every contest that you post you should post feedback for the winning designer, assuming that you select a winner, and encourage the designer to post feedback for you, once he has been paid and you have received the graphics file. I am sorry to say that many of the contests posted on Digital Point result in no actual winner even though many of the designers have spent hours on the designs. If you post a design contest on Digital Point, and for no reason do not select a winner, then the chances of the best designers entering future contests you post are extremely remote.

## *Paying Designers*

The best method to pay those who win your contest is by PayPal. Once you have selected a winner, simply send a message to the winning designer and ask for their PayPal address. Send the contest amount to the designer and then contact him again, telling him the payment has been made and forwarding your email so that he can send you the design. Add his email address to your contact lists for future reference.

### *Other Graphic Design Sources*

As you are building your very first affiliate site, I would strongly advise you to keep the actual costs of building your site to a minimum. Posting a contest on Digital Point is a great way to get a logo or header designed for next to nothing. If, however, you have a bigger budget to get your site up and running, you can use other sites, but be prepared to pay a lot more. Sites such as Design Crowd and 99 Designs also run contests, but for much higher awards. Take time out to visit both these sites and once again study the design briefs and the entries submitted. You may even find a design style you like, although you must NEVER copy a design.

## Hiring Writers

Once you get into the swing of things and have had your site up and running for a month or so, I can virtually guarantee that you will find the task of creating quality daily content a tremendous chore. During my early days as an affiliate I created all my own content, sometimes up to 30 articles a day. As my first site started to generate income each month, I simply hired writers, which gave me more time to concentrate on other aspects of my site such as link building and key phrase research. From experience I can tell you that finding a quality, affordable, reliable writer is no easy task.

When you get to the stage where you need to hire writers, your first port of call should be outsourcing sites such as Elance. My favourite outsource sites are as follows:

- Elance.com
- Guru.com
- Odesk.com
- Freelanceswitch.com
- Getafreelancer.com
- Ifreelance.com

There are many more freelance sites that have a directory of content writers but the websites listed above are considered the best by most. My personal favourite by far has to be Elance.

## *How Does Elance Work?*

You can have your very first job posted on Elance in minutes, with writers applying for your job just minutes later.

Firstly you need to sign up to Elance by creating a new account and selecting the option "I Want To Hire". Once you have created an account, you simply click the confirmation email that is sent to your inbox and are ready to post your first job. The great news is that for those seeking content writers, the service is 100% free!

## *Understanding Elance Trust*

Those that advertise jobs and indeed those who apply for the jobs have a rating. After each job you post is completed, you are asked to rate the writer. In turn the provider is also asked to rate you. For every completed job you are requested to rate the provider from 1 to 5 stars for the following:

- Quality

- Expertise

- Cost

- Schedule

- Response

- Professional

All online freelance sites have a range of providers who range from superb to downright dire. Before offering any applicant a job, ensure that you take the time to research their review pages and feedback. I only hire writers who have completed 20+ jobs with an average rating of 4.8 or higher. I have sometimes taken a chance on those new to Elance but many times have been left very disappointed as either the standard of writing was poor or the writer took much longer to finish the job than I requested.

## *The Cost of Hiring Writers*

The cost of hiring writers varies immensely. You can pay as little as $1 per 100 words up to $10 per 100 words, or much more. As a general rule for news type articles, where the writer can simple source news to rewrite with their own spin on the story you should expect to pay only $1 or $2 per 100 words. I know of many affiliates who will not pay more than $4 or $5 for a 500-word news article. I would suggest that before posting your first job you take the time to look for existing writing jobs posted at Elance, make a note of the cost for 100 words and budget accordingly.

## *Avoiding Scammers & Cheats*

During my early days of being an affiliate I did, through lack of experience, have one or two nasty experiences with writers. All freelance type sites do, I am sorry to say, have at least a small element of those looking for easy money. As a new affiliate you are on a steep learning curve in many different aspects of the affiliate world. Listed below are a few common scams employed by some dishonest writers that you should avoid.

## *Duplicate Content Check*

I was once stung by a writer who completed a large batch of articles for me, only for me to find out that they were also sold to at least three other affiliates. This is a common scam employed by some writers. When posting any job on any Freelance site, ensure that your job description states that you will own the copyright to the completed articles. Also ensure that you check all the completed articles with Copyscape.com. I always state in my article job descriptions that all articles must pass Copyscape 100%, as otherwise I will not accept them. Copyscape simply allows you to automatically check if any part of the article has been "copied" from the internet. Any copied sections of the articles are referenced to the page from which they have been copied.

## *Content Quality Control*

Some writers on sites such as Elance do from time to time, when they are busy, subcontract work out to other writers. You may have done your homework by checking the writer's reviews, but find that the quality of work done is to say the least poor. I have experienced this a good few times over the years and simply contact the writer as soon as possible to tell them exactly why I am not happy. The writer does not want bad feedback, so will in most cases either rewrite the poor quality articles or even write new ones to the standard required. With this in mind I always state that the articles I require must be completed by the writer and not subcontracted out to other writers.

## *Elance Payments*

Although you pay for each job before the writer actually starts the work, Elance holds the funds paid. You have full control over when the funds are released to the writer and you should never release funds until the job has been completed to a satisfactory standard. For large volume jobs the writer sometimes asks for the job to be split into batches with payment made when set batches are completed, which is fair enough. Never release funds to a writer until either the full job or agreed batch has been completed, no matter what sob story they may give you.

### *Building Your Elance Rating*

Just as writers have to build their review ratings to secure work, you too have to build your own rating to secure applications for the jobs you post. Those who apply for jobs have to pay a small fee to apply to do so on some freelance websites, so they will not apply for jobs from contractors who have a history of posting jobs and not awarding the job to applicants. I have spoken to many writers who are members of Elance, and virtually all said they would not waste their time and money in applying for jobs where the contractor has a low award ratio. Always ensure that you are committed to the jobs you post and are not simply posting to see if you can get a very low price. Specify in the job description the actual price for 100 words that you are happy to pay. There will of course be some jobs you post where the standard of applications is simply not up to the standard you require. A good contractor, however, should have an award ratio of over 90%.

### *Securing Quality Writers for the Long Term*

As you use more and more writers you will understand that actual quality writers are few and far between. I have found that most of the writers that have worked for me have done a great job for the first few assignments, but in time become less reliable and don't stick to deadlines. For the real quality writers I have stumbled upon, I do my utmost to hang on to them. If you are in the early stages of building your site, do all you can to hang on to quality writers. Be 100% honest with them and tell them if you cannot afford to hire them every week. Tell them that when you have writing work, you will contact them first. Try to get other contact details from them such as their email as many quality writers end up moving away from freelance sites as they generate enough work from existing customers and by word of mouth. Adding at least a few quality writers to your contact list is a very smart move for any affiliate.

## Outsource Your Way To Riches!

One of my biggest flaws is that I am a control freak. I am never happy letting anybody do something for me that I know I could do even 0.00001% better myself. This of course is a major flaw, especially for an affiliate. Over the last five or six years I have worked my bloody balls off. I have, however, built a good network, which includes leading poker, casino and bingo affiliate sites.

Looking back, it now seems clear to me that being unable to delegate has hampered me and perhaps cost me a small fortune. One tip, perhaps the best tip I can give anybody who wants to be a successful affiliate, is that you must learn to outsource. Over the years, even after building my first profitable affiliate website, I wasted far too much time producing my own content. There is no doubt in my mind that I should have sourced quality writers two years before I actually did so!

The internet has created a new global workforce to which all affiliates have access. Sites such as Elance and Freelancer plus hundreds of others are packed with writers, coders and graphic designers ready and willing to carry out your tasks at competitive rates. For some crazy reason my outsourcing was restricted to hiring writers, although even then I wasted too much time giving them detailed instructions and research material far beyond what they required. Once they had completed the ordered content, in most cases I would rewrite the articles anyway, which meant that I had not only wasted my money, but more importantly I had wasted even more time.

In the last few years I realised I needed someone like me. Someone who would simply do the tasks I carried out just like me. I spent some time researching Virtual Assistants, took the plunge and posted a job vacancy. I will be honest and say that 95% of the applicants were not even close to the standard I was looking for. I nearly gave up but knew this was something I had to do.

After three weeks sifting through applications, many of which were so bad that it was unreal, I had a handful of applicants with possible potential. These applicants were given a research and written test with the promise that the top three would receive an interview. As all three applicants on my shortlist were based thousands of miles away, the interviews were carried out through Skype. A few days later I hired a Virtual Assistant.

The person I hired was in reality a rough diamond. I knew that to get him to work like me, I would have to take the time to train him. Each of the tasks I carried out on a daily basis I videoed using a free app I found online. I simply uploaded each video and urged him to contact me if he had any questions. Over the course of a few months or so he learned how to carry out my daily tasks just like me. He now writes articles, posts articles, installs Wordpress, edits image files, uploads and downloads files using FTP and carries out dozens of other tasks, just like me. The more he learned, and of course, the more money he made for me, the more I paid him. I just wished I had hired somebody years earlier!

Through working with many new affiliates I can tell you that most affiliates are simply not capable of creating even three pages of content a day. Most start off with a wave of enthusiasm, but in most cases this subsides after around a month. I guarantee that many affiliates reading this article will agree and have sites that are crying out for content. The simple truth is that most new affiliates fail to stick to a regime of churning out content, day in, day out. As I have said, there is a global workforce available to help you. If you plan to become a successful affiliate, one of your very first tasks, once you start making money, should be to delegate the task of creating content. Where though do you start?

Your first port of call should be www.elance.com.  Using Elance you can post a job for a set of articles and get dozens of writers applying to write for you for as little as $5 per article. You can check the feedback of each applicant and even ask him or her to supply a sample article based on the topic of your choice. If you have a bigger budget, you can offer $10 to $20 per article, which will attract the very best Elance writers. Of course the actual skill sets and abilities of the applicants vary immensely so you will have to devote some time to finding a writer who is right for you. For new affiliates I strongly advise you to post at least a couple of jobs on Elance. Doing so will put you in contact with at least a few good writers whom you can call upon when you are struggling.

Another great source for online help is www.onlinejobs.ph. This site is used by thousands of Filipinos looking for work. From experience I can say that 95% of the applicants will not be suitable as I found that their English writing skills were simply not up to scratch. If, however, you have the time to persevere, you will find a few rough diamonds. I have hired Filipino writers and virtual assistants and have been amazed at how good they have been. If you are willing to invest some time teaching them how you want things done, then in the long term you will end up with a quality, loyal writer or assistant. I have one Filipino who works for me who runs one of my sites on his own. He writes articles, post articles, edits images and even link builds so that I can get on with other things. Filipinos on the whole expect much lower wages than their US or European counterparts. My approach has been to start them on a fair Filipino rate and as they improve reward them on a regular basis.  I don't have a problem rewarding Filipinos with European / US rates once they have proved to me they are worth it.

Just a few weeks or so ago an account manager gave me a tip about a special promo his company would be running over the weekend. I was too busy so I simply forwarded the email to one of my writers, added a few comments and asked the writer to create an article for me giving my VA a set time to post it. If I had not had writers available to me, then in all honesty the article would not have been produced as I was simply far too busy. The article generated over 30 RMPs during the course of the weekend, making me over £1,000 which is not bad as the article only cost me a mere $15!

I thought it would also be beneficial to you to understand freelancing from a writer's point of view, so I have included a short article from a well-respected freelance writer, AndyRe.

## "How To Be A Freelance Writer And Stay Sane" (Author: AndyRe)

With eight years experience of freelance writing and four years experience of using the Elance site, I'd like to think that I have learnt a thing or two about using freelance sites to find work. I know for a fact that there are plenty of things that I have yet to learn and will probably never learn. In fact, I still need to finish off my profile page properly! My provider name is AndyRe if you want to have a look but that isn't really important. What is important is how you get involved with and then get ahead in the world of freelance sites.

When I started out, I had been writing music and football reviews for magazines and blogs for a number of years. That was great fun, but I was looking to make some more money and decided that I had to branch out into other areas, which led to me searching for writing jobs online. After being bombarded with all the spam "make money online" sites and articles, I started to notice a few freelance sites being mentioned regularly, which led me to Elance. I have used that site ever since.

When I first used the freelance writing site, I was writing 7-10 hours a week, an hour or two for a night or two and then some time at the weekend. It was a good way to make some extra cash and I could be flexible, working when I wanted. If I had other plans, I could work less; if I was free, I could work more; and it was always very handy to have additional money coming in.

Circumstances change and at the end of 2010 I had to make a decision about my career prospects in my place of work, so I bit the bullet, went full-time with the freelancing aspect and this is where I am today. The average working week consists of over 50 hours, which can seem a lot but when you factor in the commute-time from my old job, it leaves me with the same amount of leisure time. There is a bit more flexibility with being a freelancer, but you always need to tell yourself that if you don't work, you don't get paid, and that tends to keep you on the straight and narrow!

### *Be confident and enjoy your work*

The first thing is to make sure you are confident and happy with the way that you write. Obviously you need to be happy with what you write but in this line of work, you need to be able to please others as well. You aren't going to please everyone and you will get rejections for projects because clients don't like your style of writing but that is fine. If you can write well and get your points across, there will be people who like your work and there will be people who are willing to pay for it. It's important to be sure of yourself and not be overawed when you enter a freelance site. Yes, some writers will have a wealth of experience but everyone has been in your position at one point so just relax and focus on yourself. Worrying about the competition isn't something you need to spend too much time on.

Finding the right price to apply for jobs is difficult and even after a couple of years it is hard to say if I'm using the right tactic. It's important to remember that you're not competing on the same level or surface as other people so if you spend your time trying to be competitive, there will be times when you get seriously burnt. You may get more projects but if you are over-worked and under-paid you are only going to be worse off in the long run. This is why when it comes to setting your tender price for bids, think about your own costs and your own life, and don't worry about anyone else.

Firstly, you need to know how long it will take you to write the article and this includes your research time. If you are researching a topic to write your article, you're still working, even if you aren't typing or writing away so you need to factor this time into your overall equation. It is best to calculate what you want to earn an hour and use this as your base. If you know your typing skills and how long it takes you to write 500, 1000, 2000 or x amount of words, you can make a more informed bid based on covering your costs and making the project worth your while. If you are serious about being a freelance writer, give yourself tests and dry runs before you start submitting bids.

### Focus on you, not other writers

It can be helpful to look at projects, but even although the bids placed by other writers may give you a cost guide, don't look at these bids for now. Find a project that gives you the project title, rough outline and how many words it will take you to complete it and then do the project. Don't bid on it; just go and write it and see how long it takes. This will help you to start getting a rough guide to how long a project of x amount of words will take you to complete.

If you have a subject or subjects that you know a lot about, there is no need for as much research time but you will find that these projects will come up less frequently. If you are looking to bid for a wide variety of projects and topics, you will have more projects to choose from but you will need to do more research time. It is always going to be a case of give and take, so try to find the compromises you can live with and then take that as the basis for your project. You won't always get it right; no one does, not even long-term freelancers, but if you find your average speed and time taken for projects, you will be in a far better position to tender properly.

The benefits of using a site like Elance is that it completely opens up the global market and you can bid for projects based all around the world. This is great for a writer because it gives more options but it also means that you will be competing against writers from all over the world as well. This can cause problems if you live in a country with a reasonable standard of living because basic economics will tell you that writers from developing nations will be able to undercut your price. This may lead to some writers bidding at a price lower than they are happy with to be competitive, but you need to have some limits. Underbidding is not a great tactic but when you are starting out and looking for feedback and working history, it is a tactic that can be too good to ignore.

***You shouldn't sell yourself short***

Again, it is all about compromises and trade-offs when you are looking to find work on these freelance sites but if you show your quality with a strong portfolio and you are fairly priced, you will be in with a shot. There are a growing number of freelance sites setting up with extremely low prices and it is easy to see why this is just not suitable for many writers. The thing is, not every client is looking for high quality content; some just want content stuffed with keywords and as a client, that is their right to look for that. The only thing is, search engines operate very differently these days and websites filled with poor quality content don't appear on search engine result pages anymore. This means that some jobs and projects won't be for you so you need to know what jobs are of interest and relevance to you and how to look for them.

This can be a tricky prospect so be prepared to spend a fair bit of time trawling through projects. Over time you will start to find consistency in which articles to look out for and which articles to run away from. Elance has a number of filters in place that are very useful and can help you hone in on what you are looking for. The number of writing and translation projects on Elance is usually around the 2,000 mark at any one time. This is a lot of jobs but these projects are broken down into smaller sections, allowing you to have a greater degree of focus on what you are looking for. Some writers are of the opinion that writing is writing and that they can turn their attention to anything, but that isn't the sort of attitude that will help you gain a lot of repeat projects.

### How many writing skills do you possess?

If you are naturally skilled across the many different writing disciplines, congratulations! You will find life on a freelance site to be a lot easier than it is for many other writers. If you are not immediately blessed with all-round writing skills, selecting the sections that you have an interest or experience in is a definite starting point. Article writing and web content are the most popular of the writing sections and it is likely that most people will have an interest in writing in these disciplines so if you are carrying out a filter, include these. Translation work is another popular section on freelance sites but it is clear that you need to have genuine skills in this chosen field. You may feel that you can flip between web content and writing a report easily but the same can't be said for going between web content and then translating an article from English to Japanese! That is the most extreme example but with other sections including children's books, newsletters, press releases, how to manuals, academic writing, proofing and editing and much more, there are a lot of things to consider. Don't do yourself or your work a disservice by thinking that all writing is the same. There are different needs and aims from different writing projects and not every writer will be able to successfully write them all. This isn't a concern or a failing. Focus on what you are good at and if you have time, try to improve your skills in the areas where you are currently lacking.

The type of writing is one filter but other filters include the job type (is it a fixed price or hourly rate), the budget (where you can set a minimum or maximum price filter for projects), the hourly rate and even if jobs have been advertised with a premium sponsorship or if the client has a verified payment method. If you have concerns that the client will take your work and not pay for it, using these filters can give you an added level of protection. There will always be horror stories about clients disappearing after the work is complete but before payment is made but on the whole, the respected freelance sites are respected for a reason. The vast majority of writers and clients are honest people looking for work / workers but there are some clients to be wary of.

### Study the client's history

If you have concerns, you can look at the client's history; one important place to look is their job posting history. If you come across a client who has a low percentage of awarding projects to writers, you may want to consider if it is worth your while submitting a bid. After all, bids come at a price, financial or the opportunity cost of losing a bid that could have been used on another project so this has to be considered. There are a number of clients who have a very low awarding record for the amount of projects they submit on Elance and this is definitely a concern.

This issue comes up quite regularly with clients claiming to represent a magazine looking for writers, usually with a fairly attractive price per article. As you would expect, the client requests the writer to send a few examples of their work to examine, which, with some projects attracting upwards of 20, 30 or even more bids, means there are a lot of articles being submitted to the client. For example, if over 30 writers submitted on average three articles for a project, this would amount to around 100 pieces of work. An unscrupulous client may then decide to take all these articles and not award the project to anyone. This isn't something that is discussed too often on the forums at Elance or other freelance sites but it has happened too often to be a coincidence over the years. Not saying that every project that claims to be a magazine looking for article submissions is suspicious but please do some research on the client and their project history before wasting your time and submitting good work.

There are other projects to rule out and with a bit of luck, you can spot these early on in the process. Some projects that have bad spelling and grammar will immediately have you on edge and again, past experience dictates that you should tread carefully when submitting projects for these sorts of posts. Given that the client is looking for a writer, it is fair enough that they may not possess the best written skills but are they going to be the best judge of your work or its relevant quality? You may find that these clients are looking for quantity over quality and at a price that suits them. Depending on your circumstances, this may not be the sort of work you are looking for.

It is also worthwhile considering the country of origin of the client when considering projects and placing bids. It may be that the cost of living and local price of work in that country will see a standard bid for yourself being considered too high by the client. Again, this may seem frustrating but there is not a lot you can really do about it and it isn't worth worrying about.

### Not every writer is who they seem to be

One of the biggest bug bears for a writer is being underbid on a project and then finding the exact same project being re-tendered by whoever has won the bid. There are a number of writers / firms operating on freelance sites who are getting through a lot of work by working in this fashion. This means they are getting money for being the "middle man" and possibly a small bit of editing, which is obviously great for them but not so good for everyone else. This style of working isn't really permissible on freelance sites but it can be difficult to prove or complain about and it means a lot of writers or firms are able to build up a strong portfolio in a short space of time. It is not good for the client because they are not communicating directly with the writer and the writer will be working for a smaller fee than they would have obtained if they were working for the client directly. The writer is hopefully earning enough money to make the project worthwhile but they are not earning as much as they could do, which is always a bad thing in the long run.

Again, the global market place and some writers' ability, for whatever reason, to undercut other writers creates this potential in the market place. A writer or writing firm with great feedback will find it easier to win more work and a cyclical process takes place where this "middle man" starts to earn a great deal of money for very little work. There will be frustrations in the freelance industry so prepare yourself for times when you feel like punching or kicking the wall. Not all days and projects are like this, so don't panic but please be prepared for some bad days!

If you are submitting but feel as though you want more information about the project, feel free to ask questions. If the client doesn't want to answer, is he or she likely to be the best client to work for? In an ideal world, you would find clients you like writing for and you can forge a longer-term working relationship with. A large number of clients on these sites have repeat projects or other sites / books / reports they need written so they would be happy to find a writer they have a rapport and good working relationship with too. This may mean a little bit of give and go is required in the early stages which can be frustrating if you want to get on with the project but if you want to write long-term, this can really help you.

Writing for clients is no different from any other customer service so remember to be courteous, respond as quickly as you can and do your best. You can sometimes forget about these business essentials when you freelance but it is your name and reputation on the line with every project so do yourself justice. There will be some people who don't take to you or your work; that's just life but if you give the best possible service you can, you'll do well in the long run.

### *Freelance life doesn't have to be difficult*

One of the most important things for a client to do when they are creating a post is to remember that if they want something, they should ask for it. Many clients probably think they are helping the writer by providing an open proposal but if there is something that a client has in mind, it is best to ask for it up front and let the writer work to that goal. It doesn't matter if it is word count, keywords, tone or style, if the client wants the writer to come back with a specific article, it is always better to make that clear. Writers aren't mind-readers and as you will gather one writer's opinion on how an article should pan out can be very different from another writer's.

Even when the work is done, there can still be a prickly moment when it comes to the payment. If you ask a writer when they want paid, the answer will be NOW, if not sooner! There has to be an acceptance that the client needs to read over the articles and proof them before paying, and the vast majority of writers accept this. However, if a job has been completed satisfactorily or the client doesn't get back to the writer within a day or two, you would expect the payment to be forthcoming.

There is nothing worse than the thought of doing a lot of work and not getting paid and it is understandable why some writers will get a bit tetchy after a few days. There can be reasons why payments are delayed and as long as clients are honest and up-front about the on-going situation, most writers will give them a bit of leeway.

For larger projects, it may be advisable to put in milestones where payments can be made after a percentage of work is carried out. For really big projects like ebooks or on-going projects, some writers will ask for a level of payment up-front or for a sizable amount of money to be put into escrow or holding for the job. If a writer and client haven't worked together before, this sort of agreement can be a good way to develop trust and to ensure that both parties are committed to the project.

Once you start working, there will hopefully be a good level of give and go between the writer and client and this is where the start of a longer-term working relationship can begin. Some relationships between client and writer are a one-job deal, get in and get out and they are fine. However, it may be that working together on repeat projects can be of benefit to everyone. The writer gets regular work and they will be working with a client that likes their style and their customer service. A client doesn't have to go through the recruitment process and they get to develop consistency in their written work. When it comes to thinking about working with someone long-term, base your opinion on whether you like the work, the price, the service and the interaction you have. If all these elements are present, do clients need to go looking for other writers and do writers need to spend time looking for other clients?

I've been fortunate enough to have gained a number of repeat clients and it's not as if I provided anything special or different with these clients. They had other work needing done, they obviously liked the work and service I provided and I was happy to take on more work. It sounds simple and in reality, it is, so just do your best, be yourself and you will hopefully find that other work follows on.

That should be enough to give you grounding in the perils of freelance writing but there is often one piece of advice that is overlooked by people trying to start out in freelance writing. Have fun! Yes, you need to keep working to bring the money in but you obviously have a passion for writing, so engage that passion and let it flow into your work.

AndyRe

# Chapter 4 - What's Your Niche?

Before you go any further you need to decide on a niche for your affiliate website. If you can find a niche in which you have a genuine interest or indeed a passion, you will find that creating quality content is a much easier task. Many so-called internet marketing gurus take a completely different approach to the niche selection process. They advise that you should simply find an uncompetitive niche; with no mention or indeed thought as to whether you have any knowledge of the chosen niche. Common sense tells us that this method of selecting a niche is flawed as it results in affiliates creating websites with poor quality content because they do not understand the selected niche. This is exactly why a large percentage of affiliate websites consist of copied or rewritten content, which the latest Google PANDA algorithm updates are happy to penalize by sending to the depths of search results.

Remember that your articles should ooze authority, quality and passion! Utilising your existing long-term interests should in most cases give you thousands of ideas for potential articles. I believe that everybody has at least one niche in which they could excel. For example, a young mother could create a diary of her child's development, chronicling the joys and perhaps even the pitfalls of motherhood. The blog of course would also include product reviews of the hundreds of children's items that are purchased, such as nappies, clothes, toys and pushchairs, which would be an invaluable source for mothers-to-be. The product reviews would, naturally, contain affiliate links.

A school leaver with a great interest in online gaming could create a website that reviews the latest Xbox game releases and new gaming equipment, while an avid football fan could create a website devoted to his or her favourite team.

Even someone who simply slumps in front of the TV set each night could set up as an online critic, selecting a niche such as UK soaps, with sections such as spoilers, catch up, future story lines and soap actors etc. Finding products to promote for this kind of niche would be easy, as you would just make a note of what products were advertised during the commercial breaks. If the advertisers are happy to part with hundreds of thousands of pounds to pay for commercials during the show, then you simply target the same types of product on your pages. If you build it, they will come, as Kevin Costner once said.

Your main objective should be to create an authority site that covers all aspects of your chosen niche. Google simply loves brands, so you should opt to create a brand for your affiliate site, a process that we will cover in greater detail in later chapters.

Don't rush into selecting the niche of your affiliate site. Take your time! Do you know enough about your chosen niche to keep producing fresh quality content on a daily basis? Take the time to jot down the titles of potential articles and reviews. If you struggle to jot down a hundred article titles, perhaps the niche is not for you.

As I said in the Introduction, in your first year you should aim to write three articles each day. Three articles a day over a year is (3 x 365), which equals 1095 articles a year. You could of course "pad out" your affiliate site with a news section, video reviews and even readers' reviews. Even so, you need to ensure that before you venture into setting up your affiliate site, you are 100% sure that you can produce three articles each and every day. If you intend to create your site as a part-time affiliate, you can cut the daily number of articles down to two, although this will have the effect of taking you longer to build your site.

In addition, you need to find quality affiliate programs in your chosen niche. For example, let's refer back to the young mother's baby diary. What products could she promote on her website? She should simply seek out online stores where she could purchase baby products by typing phrases such as "Mothercare affiliate program" and "baby products affiliate program" into search engines such as Google. A quick Google search instantly reveals affiliate programs such as Mothercare, Pampers and Ababy.com.

You should aim to start with at least five different affiliate programs / products. If you are struggling to find more than just a couple of products for your niche, you either need to expand your niche or switch to another niche. Once again I say, take your time selecting a niche.

## Utilise Your Existing Knowledge & Interests

You don't have to be a gambler to run an online affiliate gambling site or a fitness fanatic to run a treadmill affiliate site. You do, however, need a great working knowledge of your chosen niche because your main goal must be to generate content that oozes authority. Produce poor quality content that is filled with factual errors, and you will soon be found out by your readers.

If you truly believe that your existing interests are not suitable for an affiliate website, you have a much harder task. When I decided to diversify into the online bingo niche, I knew absolutely nothing about online bingo. Yes, of course I had played the odd game of bingo as a child, but I was at a complete loss as to what content I could create. My actual knowledge would have produced a maximum of 10 articles, which would not have been even close to enough content for a week. To gain knowledge, I immersed myself in the world of bingo by visiting local bingo halls, signing up to online bingo sites and actually talking to those who played the game. During the course of six to eight weeks I acquired valuable knowledge that enabled me to build a quality online bingo affiliate portal that in just over a year was challenging the market leaders.

Even now I still take the time both to visit online bingo rooms and to talk to players who frequent UK bingo halls so that I keep in touch with exactly what is going on in the world of bingo. I also monitor new games and developments from all bingo software providers, and frequently talk to bingo affiliate managers about new developments in the online bingo world. Other affiliates that target the online bingo niche simply rewrite hundreds of existing articles and then wonder why they cannot generate healthy monthly revenue. Be warned! If you intend to tackle a niche that is new to you, then ensure you take the time to immerse yourself in the niche, because doing so will give you a great advantage over other affiliates.

## What Websites Exist In Your Chosen Niche?

Once you have narrowed down possible niches for your website, do take the time to see what websites for the niche already exist. Can you do better than the existing sites? Can you offer something new to your chosen niche? As a general rule, but not always, the most profitable niches are heavily targeted by affiliates. For example, all forms of online gambling, including poker, casino, sports betting and even bingo are highly profitable but extremely competitive. There are literally thousands of affiliates from around the world targeting gambling affiliate programs. For your first venture you really need to find a niche that is not heavily targeted, as you will vastly increase your chances of success. Gambling, dating, making money online, insurance & financial niches are very lucrative but extremely difficult to master, especially for those new to online affiliating. It is far better to start with a less competitive niche to build your experience and financial bankroll. Once you have excelled in a less competitive niche, you will have the experience and indeed confidence to tackle more competitive niches.

The good news is, however, that many niches are lightly targeted, so do take your time over your initial niche selection. Many affiliates make the basic mistake of not researching their chosen niche and not researching the programs they will promote for their chosen niche. Take your time to carry out detailed research!

## Finding Profitable Niches

A profitable niche is a niche that has a decent amount of search queries, indicating both that people are searching for key phrases related to the niche, and that there are affiliate programs catering to the niche. There is of course no point in creating an affiliate website for which there is either no demand, or very little demand. Even where there is high search traffic, there is no point in creating a website if there are no products that target the traffic.

## Researching Niches

The process of setting up your very first affiliate site can be a mind-blowing ordeal. To simplify things a little I have broken the process down into the flowing stages.

1. Brainstorming – What Existing Knowledge Can You Utilise?
2. Key Phrase Research
3. Existing Competition Research
4. Trend Research
5. Monetization Research

Remember that taking time to plan and research your site pays dividends in the long run.

Returning to my own niche; many niches within the gambling industry are saturated while some niches are more profitable than others. For some reason many new gambling affiliates seem to want to jump into the very competitive niche of online poker simply because they know of others who have made a small fortune from this niche in recent years. For now the online poker boom is well and truly over. Many European sites are reporting reduced turnover and many more of the smaller online poker operators are struggling. Many believe that online poker is the most profitable niche in the gambling industry but this is simply no longer true.

In respect to online gambling there are many new niches that could prove very rewarding and profitable. I have a friend who wanted to set up his first affiliate site last year. He was a keen follower of football so was eager to set up an online football tipping site. As he was an Arsenal fan he wanted to target the English Premier League. This of course would have been a bad mistake as there were already dozens of quality websites targeting this niche.

You simply have to start by making things easier for yourself. If you start with a site targeting Premier League football, you are virtually committing yourself to failure as the niche is simply too competitive. If you are determined to target a competitive niche, you need to find a less competitive sub niche within the main niche.

If you use Google to search for "Premier League Football" or "Premier League Betting" you will quickly see that this is a very competitive market. However, if you search for the lower leagues of English football, you will find these are far less competitive and simply waiting to be tapped. Find an uncompetitive sub niche!

Again I say, take your time, there is no rush. The planning and research stage is perhaps one of the most important stages of setting up your affiliate website. Poor planning and research in most cases damages your chances of long-term success! My friend opted to create a site targeting lower league English football, with which I'm delighted to say he is doing rather well.

## Case Study – Treadmills

Choosing the right niche is in my opinion the most important task you carry out as an online affiliate. Choose a poor performing niche or one for which you struggle to create quality content and you are doomed from day one.

To help you with your initial niche research let's run through the complete process I go through when starting out with an idea for a new site.

### *Is the Niche Popular?*

My first step is to carry out just a little keyword research to find out if the niche, in this case "treadmills", is indeed popular. Firstly I simply type "treadmills" into Google and check that there are plenty of Google ads as shown on the following page.

As you can see from the above Google screenshot, there is plenty of advertising activity for the search phrase "treadmills"; so far so good. If we take a look at the bottom of the Google search page, Google shows us other popular "hot" treadmill searches.

Searches related to **treadmill reviews**

**nordic track** treadmill reviews      **proform fitness** treadmill reviews

**reebok** treadmill reviews      **horizon** treadmill reviews

**roger black** treadmill reviews      **trackspeed5000** treadmill reviews

treadmill reviews 2010      **fuel** treadmill reviews

## *Understanding the Different Types of Search Queries*

As with most things, search queries can be broken down to more definite categories. Typically the queries can be defined as belonging to one of three major sectors based upon the desired result of the user's search. The categories we shall focus on are navigational, informational, and transactional searches.

### *Navigational Queries*

A Navigation Query is fairly straightforward; the searcher knows a specific location where he intends to arrive. These could be searches for a company or brand name. If the user wishes to find the corporate website for your company, the odds are that he will search your company's name with the intention of navigating towards your site (e.g. John Doe Construction Ltd.).

### *Informational Queries*

These searches are performed with no predetermined destination or source in mind. The user has a question or topic of interest and is in search of information to satisfy his needs. The user's query reflects this search for specific information, with a general topic being run through the engine. The results of the search may come from a variety of sources, and the final destination is not of as much concern to the person performing the search as the information contained within it (e.g. poker strategies).

### *Transactional Queries*

When a person types in, for example, "Surround Sound Speakers", there is a pretty good chance that they are in the market to buy them, but it is also likely that the intention of the search is to research a future purchase rather than to buy outright. They probably don't yet know exactly what it is they want to buy. This search is an example of what can be defined as an Initial Transactional Query, with this session of searching evolving in stages through the user's research process as a number of separate queries are submitted to the engine.

### *Key Phrases Tools*

Once we have understood the different types of search query, we next need to get some idea of the numbers of searches the niche produces each month, as we don't want to target a niche in which there is little interest. For this task I prefer to use a purchased key phrase tool, the Niche Finder Tool, although you can use the Google Keyword Tool to carry out the same tasks completely free.

Simply typing "treadmills" into the tool brings up the following screen.

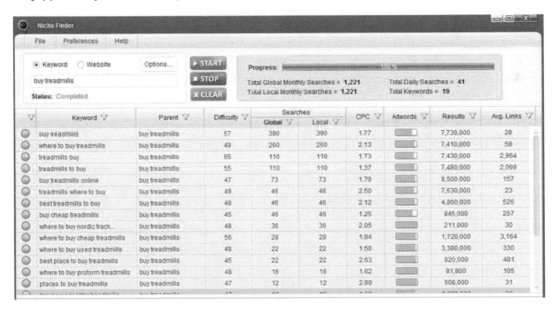

Next let's take a look at key phrase volume for some good treadmill buying phrases, simply running the key phrase "buy treadmills" into the tool. You can find out more about using this invaluable tool by watching this YouTube video:

http://www.youtube.com/watch?v=m1PZNIkCv30

Already, by running "buy treadmills" through the Niche Finder, I can see the potential of the treadmill niche. Although many of the key phrases are very competitive, I can also see many that have less than 50 links, with a difficulty level of less than 50 and with less than 100,000 results.

The initial Google search for "Treadmills" also gave us some "hot" key phrases for the niche, all of which included the word "reviews". Such key phrases are the golden long tail key phrases that often lead to a sale.

At the start of a search, users often begin by searching for "treadmills" and then refine their search to more specific long tail search phrases during the search session to match their exact needs. For example, a user searching for a treadmill to purchase could take the following route.

- Search 1: Treadmill
- Search 2: Folding Treadmill
- Search 3: Nordic Folding Treadmill
- Search 4: Nordic Track Folding Treadmill
- Search 5: Nordic Track C2500 Folding Treadmill Reviews

As a rule it is the long-tail key phrases that are most likely to be at the end of the search session, and so lead to sales.

Let's also take a look at "treadmill review" key phrases.

| | Keyword | Parent | Difficulty | Searches Global | Searches Local | CPC | Adwords | Results | Avg. Links |
|---|---|---|---|---|---|---|---|---|---|
| | treadmill review | treadmill review | 63 | 1,900 | 1,900 | 1.78 | | 3,040,000 | 5,821 |
| | proform treadmill review | treadmill review | 42 | 1,000 | 1,000 | 2.03 | | 292,000 | 109 |
| | horizon t101 treadmill review | treadmill review | 40 | 480 | 480 | 1.67 | | 126,000 | 29 |
| | lifespan treadmill review | treadmill review | 39 | 390 | 390 | 1.18 | | 79,200 | 30 |
| | nordictrack t5 zi treadmill review | treadmill review | 44 | 320 | 320 | 2.39 | | 4,720 | 28 |
| | weslo treadmill review | treadmill review | 42 | 260 | 260 | 1.20 | | 108,000 | 30 |
| | manual treadmill review | treadmill review | 43 | 260 | 260 | 1.46 | | 345,000 | 32 |
| | proform 605 cs treadmill review | treadmill review | 51 | 210 | 210 | 2 | | 1,430 | 27 |
| | proform zt5 treadmill review | treadmill review | 45 | 210 | 210 | 1.76 | | 6,730 | 27 |
| | smooth 5.65 treadmill review | treadmill review | 48 | 210 | 210 | 4.21 | | 9,570 | 74 |
| | freemotion xtr treadmill review | treadmill review | 41 | 210 | 210 | 1.98 | | 4,650 | 30 |
| | proform 705 cst treadmill rev... | treadmill review | 44 | 170 | 170 | 1.60 | | 13,400 | 30 |
| | weslo cadence g40 treadmill... | treadmill review | | 170 | 170 | 1.90 | | No Data | |
| | horizon treadmill review | treadmill review | 41 | 170 | 170 | 1.58 | | 191,000 | 93 |

## *Estimating Potential Site Traffic*

As you can see from the above, the actual search volumes for "treadmill reviews" are vastly reduced from the general "treadmill" key phrases with which we started. The average per search is only around 200 a month. Imagine, however, that after a year we had a hundred treadmill review pages targeting exactly these types of search phrases. I always prefer to be pessimistic when trying to calculate potential daily traffic, so let's say each of our 100 review pages generates on average just two unique visitors each day, with our non-review pages also pushing another unique visitor a day to each review page. Our 100 review pages would therefore generate 300 unique visitors each day. From experience, I can tell you that some of your review pages will generate much more than three unique visitors a day, while of course some will generate less. In reality though, an average of three uniques a day per review page should be the absolute minimum of daily uniques you should expect.

## Search Volume Explained

Another question I am frequently asked is how accurate the search volume data is from online tools such as Niche Finder or even the Google Adwords External Tool. If a key phrase has an estimated search volume of 10,000, how much traffic would you expect if you managed to rank 1st Position in Google for the search phrase?

Up until 2006 there was not much solid data to help us to analyze search volume results. During 2006, AOL leaked information on more than nine million searches that generated fewer than five million clicks. Members of Earners Forum spent a great deal of time and effort analyzing the data and later published ground-breaking results. For some reason the AOL data leak is not mentioned on many SEO or Webmaster forums. This amazes me as the work done by members of the Earners Forum is of benefit to us all.

The first thing that struck me about the results was the percentage of actual clicks to searches. Out of 9,038,794 searches there were only 4,926,624 clicks. From this data we can say that from a given search we should only expect 54.5% of the search volume to generate clicks. So if a key phrase has an estimated search volume of 10,000, we should expect 5450 clicks (10,000 * 0.545) from organic search results in total from all positions. We know that a site ranked 1st for the search phrases generates more clicks than a site ranked 7th, but how much more?  Well let's simply use the AOL data to take a look at the clicks received for the top 10 positions.

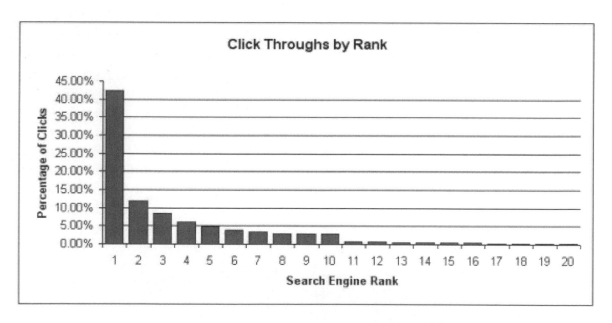

The total of clicks for position 11 and greater was 501.397 (10.18%)

Using the data above you can now get a much better understanding of expected traffic from any key phrases using key phrases tools. Going back to our expected 10,000 search volume, let's say we are confident we can rank 1st position.

The traffic we could expect could be calculated as:

Expected Clicks (traffic) = (10,000 * 0.545) = 5450

Expected traffic for 1st position = 42.13%

(5450 * 0.4213) = 2296 monthly visitors

For 3rd position we could only expect 8.5%

(5450 * 0.085) = 463 monthly visitors

The above explains why many are disappointed by the number of clicks generated from high-ranking key phrases.

### Google Trends

I also like to spend at least a couple of minutes testing the niche in Google Trends. Google Trends is extremely easy to use. Simply go to http://www.google.com/trends/ and type in the name of your potential niche. With a niche such as treadmills it is of course a "no brainer" that the western world is in the grips of an obesity overload, so the treadmill niche should be popular and indeed popular for the long term.

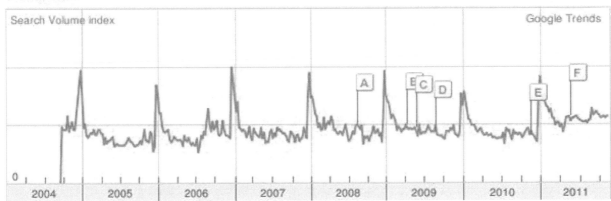

Notice the season peaks at the end and start of each year. I would suggest that treadmills are a popular Christmas present and are also an impulse buy for many people who set New Year resolutions to get back into shape. Also note that throughout the year interest in treadmills is steady and there has also been a gradual increase in general interest through recent years, from the 2005 level to the higher level of interest in 2011. Let's now take a quick look at a niche that would not be ideal to target. Remember the UK brand Amstrad? Just have a look at the drop in interest in Amstrad shown in the following chart.

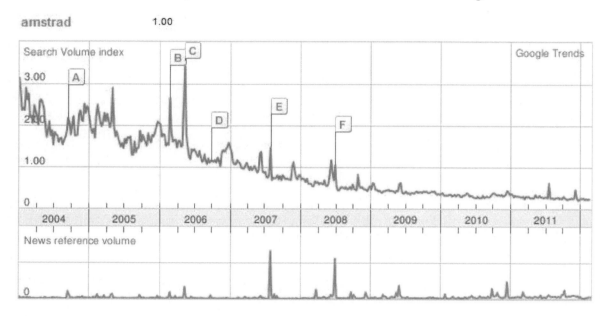

## Estimating Niche Value

Now that we have a good idea of the daily traffic we should be able to generate for our review pages on treadmills, taking a fairly pessimistic view, what comes next? Well, now we need to see if we can monetize the treadmill niche.

During our initial search for treadmills to determine if there was a demand, you should have noted Amazon and Argos ads on the search page. Let's now take a look at the treadmills on offer at Amazon to get some idea of the price of treadmills and of how much we can earn per sale.

The treadmills on offer at Amazon range from a basic model for just over $100 to many over $2000, with some costing much more. For now, let's again be a little pessimistic and work on an average sale price of just $500. Amazon's commission starts at just 4% a sale, although it rises the more sales you have each month. Selling one treadmill at our average price of $500 would earn us $20. If we refer back to our daily unique visitors per day calculations of 300 unique visitors a day for our review pages, and use a relatively pessimistic conversion rate of 2%, this would equate to six sales a day. Six sales a day earning $20 per sale would generate $120 a day, $840 a week, and $3,600 for a 30 day month. But before we rush to sign up to Amazon, let's see if we can get a better deal.

Let's go back to Google search and this time search for "treadmill affiliates" in order to take a look at other affiliate programs.

www.treadmillscentral.com offers affiliates 8% commission and has a great range of treadmills while www.mytreadmilltrainer.com offers treadmill training programs and pays affiliates 50% commission – that's anywhere from $8.50 to $98.75 per sale (depending on the program or package purchased)! www.treadmillfactory.ca only pays 3% commission, www.workoutwarehouse.com pays 8% to 11% depending on turnover and www.connection-fitness.co.uk offers 5% to 7%, again depending on total sales. Another good way to seek out good affiliate programs in your chosen niche is simply to visit other affiliate sites and see which affiliate programs they are promoting.

We can also search for affiliate programs for our niche by visiting www.offervault.com although the search option could be a lot better.

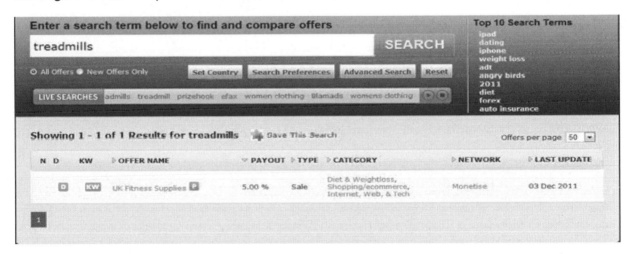

A quick search of Offer Vault gives us another affiliate program to promote, UK Fitness Supplies, listed on the Monetize network.

## *Existing Affiliates*

More research should also be undertaken regarding existing affiliates. If there are dozens of quality affiliates already operating in the niche, then in many cases it would be wise to give the niche a wide berth. Take time out to search for popular products in the niche. Make a note of what sites rank highly for the products. Another good tip is to find out how many pages each of the leading sites in the niche have indexed in Google. You can easily do this by typing the following into Google:

site:www.nameofthesite.com

For example, if we wanted to find out how many pages the Derby County website had indexed in Google we would simply type:

site:www.dcfc.co.uk

As you can see from the above Google screenshot, the dcfc website has 14,900 pages included in the Google index. To simplify matters, we will classify any site that has over 1000 pages indexed in Google as a quality site and note that it will be one of our main competitors.

For your potential niche you want ideally to find that most of your competitors have thin type affiliate sites with less than 200 pages indexed. With most niches you will find a small number of authority type sites with 1000 plus pages indexed, but with the bulk of affiliate sites having less than 100 indexed pages. Remember your goal over the coming year is to create a 1000 page authority site. Once you have achieved this, the internal SEO power of your site will easily help you to outrank the "thin" type affiliate sites.

## Can You Really Provide The Content?

Now we have chosen a niche, which is indeed popular and profitable, we have to take the time to be honest and work out if we can actually provide the volume of quality content required. Remember the aim is to produce 1000 articles for our first year. Firstly let's break the content down into five or six sections.

### Home Section

This will be the virtual front door section of our site. It will contain the latest news in the treadmill world, treadmill buying advice, special offers and new treadmill products.

### Treadmill Reviews

This section will be the home of all our treadmill review pages. From doing a little research I have found over 400 different treadmill machines, although there are hundreds, if not thousands, more.

### Treadmill Training

This section will contain advice about different treadmill training guides and products

### Treadmill Gear

This section will contain information about treadmill accessories such as footwear, clothing and timers etc.

### Used Treadmills

This section will contain information about buying used treadmills. It will cover popular makes with details of prices and the specifics of which models are the most reliable etc.

Even before I even think about purchasing a domain for a new site, I will take the time to start jotting down article titles. The last thing I want is to have my site online and ready for content, only to find that I can't actually produce the content. Take the time to make a list of article titles for each section. Again, ensure that you will be able to create 1000 articles over the coming year.

# Chapter 5 - Wordpress Rocks!

## Why Wordpress?

For anybody thinking of setting up an affiliate website another difficult decision is which software platform to use. You could of course hire a programmer to create a custom website using html or php but this would prove extremely expensive and could take weeks or even months to create. Worse still, in many cases adding new content to a custom html or php website would require programming knowledge, so either you would have to develop your programming skills or pay for a programmer to add content for you.

Many affiliates opt to take the easy route by using a content management system (CMS), such as Drupal, Joomla or, my favourite by far, Wordpress. If you use a CMS, adding content requires no programming expertise as you can simply add a new page by copying and pasting articles from Microsoft Word and other Word Processing software packages.

But why do I prefer to use Wordpress and why, more importantly, do I strongly suggest you opt for Wordpress too?

***Wordpress Cost*** - Wordpress is open source and is 100% free!

***Easy to Install*** - Wordpress is a breeze to install. You can simply log into your hosting account and load a new basic install of Wordpress in under a minute with no technical expertise, using Fantastico. Take a look at how easy it is to install Wordpress on a Hostgator hosting account:

- http://www.hostgator.com/apps/wordpress-hosting.shtml

***Professional Design*** – I would agree that if you use the Wordpress default theme, it looks a little naff, but you can purchase a professional theme for less than $30 in many cases. Simply visit a Wordpress theme website such as Themeforest.net, and purchase a theme from the Wordpress section: http://themeforest.net/category/wordpress. Install the theme, which takes just a few minutes, and you will then have a professional looking website waiting for your articles.

***SEO Friendly*** - Search engines seem to love Wordpress and you can make your Wordpress install even more search engine friendly by adding the free search engine plug-in All In One SEO Pack - http://wordpress.org/extend/plug-ins/all-in-one-seo-pack/

***Superb Support -*** As I write this chapter, nearly 72 million websites are using Wordpress with the result that there are tens of thousands of websites that offer advice on different aspects of running and using Wordpress. Youtube is a great resource for free Wordpress "how to" videos, and many quality webhosts, such as Hostgator, have a great range of Wordpress help videos.

***Frequent Updates -*** Wordpress is constantly evolving with updates released most months, not to mention the thousands of themes, plug-ins and widgets that are also available and constantly updated.

## Wordpress Essential Plug-ins

One of the many great features of Wordpress is that there are many plug-ins available which cover a multitude of tasks. For some reason those new to Wordpress go plug-in crazy, ending up installing dozens of plug-ins onto their Wordpress install, which reduces the overall security of the install and in most cases increases page load time.  This is yet another basic mistake that new affiliates seem to make.

As a general rule, keep the plug-ins you install to a minimum. Installing dozens of plug-ins will not only slow down your website, but will also cause you many problems when you run the frequent Wordpress updates. Many plug-ins become incompatible when Wordpress rolls out updates, which can cause you severe problems, to the extent that your website may not even load. Keep Wordpress plug-ins installed to a bare minimum and only use Wordpress plug-ins that are supported with constant updates!

Some Wordpress plug-ins are however essential, so let's take a look at the plug-ins you should have installed.

### All in One SEO Word Press Plug-in

This is a great little plug-in, which in effect gives you an easy way to add meta data to your posts and pages.

### Remove Category Base

By default Wordpress adds "category" to the URL of each category you create. For example, let's imagine that you add a post entitled "best widgets" to a widgets category. Wordpress would generate the following URL for the post.

http://www.yoursite.com/category/widgets/best-widgets/

By simply installing the Remove Category Base plug-in the word "category" would automatically be removed from the URL, giving the URL below.

http://www.yoursite.com/widgets/best-widgets/

### *Wordpress Google Sitemap*

This again is a great little plug-in that in effect automates the creation of a sitemap. The URL of the sitemap should be added to Google Webmaster Tools so that Google can locate every page of your website.

### *Wordpress Google Analytics Plug-in*

This plug-in helps you by adding the Google Analytics code to every page of your website so that through the use of the free Google Analytics software, you can see exactly how many visitors you have attracted to your site.

### *How to Install Wordpress Plug-ins*

Wordpress plug-ins are a breeze to install. Simply log in into your Wordpress install by typing your site name and wp-admin, such as www.yoursitename.com/wp-admin. Once logged in, hover over the "Plug-ins" option, which you will find on the left hand sidebar. Select "Add New", and enter in the search box the name of the plug-in you would like to install. The search may well list several versions of the plug-in. Simply select the latest version.

### *Always Update Plug-ins*

Another great feature of Wordpress is that you will receive a prompt when a new version of either Wordpress or plug-ins are available. Always ensure that you are running the very latest version of Wordpress and any plug-ins that you have installed on your website.

## Wordpress Housekeeping Tasks

Wordpress is a great content management system but you should always ensure that your current install is looked after in the correct manner. Going back to my days running a computer hardware business, I lost track of how many times my customers lost data, simply because they did not take the time to back up their data, even although I warned them, time and time again. The same is also true for your Wordpress install. You must ensure that you make a backup at least once a week. If you have some form of disaster, then the most you will lose is one week's work. I take things a step further and ensure all of my sites are backed up daily.

## Wordpress Backups

With Wordpress you have in effect two elements. You have the actual php files and a database. The php files consist of the actual Wordpress install, plug-ins and of course a theme. The database is a SQL database. Every time you add a new post, or indeed edit a post, your Wordpress SQL database is updated. The actual php files do not change when posts are added or edited. Most basic hosting packages do not include backups so you should ensure that you have some form of backup that is run at least each week, although I would recommend every couple of days. If you have Cpanel with your hosting package, you can simply download the sql database to your home computer. If you are unsure of how to do this, contact your host. I prefer to download the full SQL database to my computer, rather than doing this task by means of a plug-in. The link below details how to perform a Wordpress SQL backup.

http://codex.wordpress.org/WordPress_Backups#cPanel

Regarding the actual php files of your Wordpress install, you can simply use a free FTP program such as FreeZilla to download all the files to your computer. You only need to back up when you update either Wordpress or any of your plug-ins, or of course if you update your theme.

## Wordpress Updates

Wordpress is frequently updated and it is essential that as soon as a new update appears on your Wordpress dashboard, you run the update. Plug-ins are also frequently updated so you must also ensure that when upgrades become available, you run them. Wordpress, like any software package, does to some degree have its drawbacks, and in my opinion is one of the most hacked content management systems. I have been hacked several times, mainly due to my own fault in not ensuring my Wordpress installs were up to date. Those running older versions of Wordpress are at a higher risk of being hacked.

A common problem with running Wordpress updates is that sometimes plug-ins are incompatible with the latest version, which is a prime reason you should keep plug-ins to a minimum. Also, from time to time, some Wordpress updates open security holes in Wordpress, which is why you should have some form of security install on your site.

## *Wordpress Update Problems*

If you are unfortunate enough to find that your site is not functioning correctly after you have run a Wordpress update, your first action should be to disable your plug-ins one by one to see if this fixes the problem. If you find that a plug-in is not compatible with a new version of Wordpress, visit the website of the plug-in and report the problem. If you use plug-ins sparingly and stick to the ones I have listed, you should not have a problem. If you install dozens of plug-ins, I can guarantee that in time you will run into problems.

## *Delete Comment Spam*

Another major problem with Wordpress is that there are many automated tools that seek out Wordpress sites and automatically post crappy comments complete with links. Ensure that each day you trash comment spam posts and don't leave them to build until you have thousands of comments awaiting moderation.

# Wordpress Security

As stated in the Wordpress Housekeeping section, Wordpress is highly targeted by spammers and hackers. Hundreds of thousands of Wordpress installs, if not more, have at some time been hacked. The most common hack is a php injection, which  embeds links into posts and pages. If the hack is done well, the first you may know about it is when you lose all your rankings in Google search results.

If you think your Wordpress install may have been hacked, firstly check your php files on your server using a FTP program. Look to see if the actual file stamp dates have been changed. Also check your index.php files by opening them up in a file editor such as notepad and search for embedded code. If you are using Hostgator as your host, ask them to check your hosting package for malware and php injections. I have suffered from this several times and have always received great free help from Hostgator.

## *Making Wordpress Secure in 10 Easy Steps*

The fact that Wordpress is open-source is generally regarded as a very good thing, but this security aspect of it is certainly not.  Although you can take the steps outlined above if you find that your Wordpress install has been hacked, obviously prevention in the first place is far better.

To protect your Wordpress install, I can recommend highly the free Wordpress plug-in, Bulletproof. I strongly advise you to install and run this plug-in as soon as you set up your site. Once it is loaded, ensure you run through the full setup, which thankfully includes full instructions.

There are other steps that you can take in order to ensure that both your site and your traffic are protected from unscrupulous hackers. I outline a ten-step plan below:

## 1. Delete the Admin Superuser

Everyone using Wordpress, or even with just a modicum of knowledge regarding it, will know that 99% of the time there is a superuser, who will have all the top-level clearances. What's more, most of the time this superuser has the username "Admin", which means that all the hackers have to do is find out the superuser's password. Therefore, you should take away the original admin account and replace it with a different one, but this time changing the username to something less obvious.

My alternative, and favourite technique here, is to have two accounts – one with administrative clearance and one that simply allows you to make posts and conduct other basic activity. You can then have an extremely complex username and password for the admin login – which you would store somewhere safe and only rarely use – and have an author/contributor account with an easy password, where you can update the site's posts and add new ones. This means that there is virtually no chance of you having your admin account hacked and that you also don't have to go through the problems of typing in huge passwords every time you login!

## 2. Create a Secure Password

By a "good" password, I mean one that is very strong and contains a mixture of letters, numbers and at least one symbol. Your site could run the risk of being attacked by what is known as a "brute force attack" and, although Step 1 above, deleting the admin superuser, deters 99% of those attempting this, the remaining 1% can still cause lots of damage and are also, more worryingly, very persistent in their attempts to gain access. So, you must make sure that you pick a password that is secure and tough to hack. There are two ways to do this. The first is to use a password generator to make a password that is completely random. The second is to log on to www.passwordmeter.com and use them to check the strength of your password for you. Of course, these methods can be complementary, checking your random password with passwordmeter.

## 3. Block Continued Hacking Login Attempts

Just having a strong password is not always enough, however, so it is also prudent to block as many attempts at false logins as possible. There are many different plug-ins that can be downloaded that assist with this, but the one that I use is called Login LockDown, which keeps a log of any failed attempts that are made to login to the site. Should it detect a significant number of failed login attempts to the site from a specific IP address, it will ban logins from that IP address from occurring. You will find that most hackers get bored if they are continuously blocked, so it can be very helpful.

### 4. Keep Wordpress Up-To-Date

When you receive a message saying that there is a Wordpress update ready to install, you should carry out this action straight away; after all, it only takes about five minutes, and that is for a particularly big update. Each update tells you about the security flaws that have been fixed, which means that hackers then also know about these security flaws and prey on sites that have not updated yet.

### 5. Hide Your Version of Wordpress

If you have not got around to updating your site to the latest Wordpress, or if you simply know that you always forget to, then hiding the version that you use is something that you should certainly do.

To take out the Wordpress version details from your site's code, making it harder for hackers to determine which version you are running, simply open up the functions.php file and add the following code:

**<?php remove_action('wp_head', 'wp_generator'); ?>**

If you are using a premium theme, the chances are that this has already been done, but there is no harm in pasting in this code just to make sure.

### 6. Change the File Permissions

File permissions are vital when trying to secure your site and I always try to ensure that file permissions are as restrictive as possible. This means that the folder CHMOD values should be at 744, which means that everyone other than you can only access the site as read-only.

To do this you simply need to go into your FTP program and then select "File Permissions". You should then change each folder's value to 744. If it is currently set at 777, you should count yourself as very fortunate that you have not already been hacked!

### 7. *Utilise an IP Whitelist*

A whitelist is basically something that controls who can access the different areas of your website, so that you can completely protect your vital admin folder from anyone else. The easiest way to do this is by making use of the file called .htaccess.

Firstly you need to go to your /wp-admin/ folder and then locate the .htaccess file. If there isn't one, simply make one there and then. If there is one, make sure that you back it up before you start editing it. One incredibly important thing I must stress is that you must **make sure that you are using the wp-admin folder – not the similar root folder!**

Now you need to paste the following code into the file, making sure that you place your IP address in the places where there are xx. You can find out your IP by going to www.whatismyip.com.

AuthUserFile /dev/null

AuthGroupFile /dev/null

AuthName "WordPress Admin Access Control"

AuthType Basic

<LIMIT GET>

order deny,allow

deny from all

# Whitelist Your IP address

allow from xx.xx.xx.xxx

# Whitelist Your Office's IP address

allow from xx.xx.xx.xxx

# Whitelist Your IP address While Your Traveling (Delete When You Come Back Home)

allow from xx.xx.xx.xxx

</LIMIT>

One thing to bear in mind is that when you want to log in from somewhere other than your usual IP, you need to make sure that you change the IP in this code before you try logging in.

### 8. Frequently Back up Your Site

Even if your Wordpress site is akin to a digital version of Fort Knox, it is still good practice to back it up. There are three ways that you can do this, with the first being to use cron jobs, if your host offers this service. If you have the expertise, then simply use the following commands ensuring that you replace DB_NAME, DB_PASSWORD and DB_USER with your actual values. If you lack the expertise to complete this process don't worry as it is not essential although you could easily hire somebody from Elance.


DBNAME=DB_NAME

DBPASS=DB_PASSWORD

DBUSER=DB_USER

EMAIL="you@your_email.com"

mysqldump --opt -u $DBUSER -p$DBPASS $DBNAME > backup.sql

gzip backup.sql

DATE=`date +%Y%m%d` ; mv backup.sql.gz $DBNAME-backup-$DATE.sql.gz

echo 'BLOG BACKUP:Your Backup is attached' | mutt -a $DBNAME-backup-$DATE.sql.gz $EMAIL -s "MySQL Backup"

rm $DBNAME-backup-$DATE.sql.gz


The other options are either to use Vaultpress, or simply to go into the admin panel on Wordpress and export the data. Again if this is beyond your expertise then hire someone to help you, because regular backups are vital.

### 9. Hide Your Wordpress Plug-ins

Most of you probably think that hiding plug-ins is not needed when it comes to security – after all, why would letting people know the plug-ins you use help them to hack your site? Well, plug-ins are in fact a great way for hackers to discover two things: whether your site is hackable and then, if it is, how best to go about hacking it. Remember, I have already said that there are lots of security flaws in Wordpress plug-ins, so hackers are able to see which ones you have, including any with possible exploits.

Plug-ins can be found whenever someone visits the /wp-content/plug-ins folder on your site. The way to protect yourself is to add a blank file called index.html to the plug-ins folder. Although this will not deter every hacker, it will dissuade many. It is essentially like having a "Beware of the Dog" sign on your front door, even although in reality you only own a cat and a hamster.

### 10. Look at Your Server Logs

With all the technical and powerful security solutions available, there is still one thing that beats them all when it comes to protecting your site – your brain. This means that you should make sure that you regularly check your server logs and the data on Google Analytics to see if any odd behaviour is occurring. To give you an idea of how important this is, I tend to look at least once a day. If strange key phrases start appearing in your Google analytic stats or you find repeated login attempts from an IP address that is not yours, then seek advice from your host.

## Warning - Wordpress Sucks!

Yes Wordpress really can suck! After reading my glorious praise of Wordpress you may now be a little confused by this statement. One of the downfalls of Wordpress becoming so popular is that many hackers actively target weak Wordpress installs. By weak I am referring to Wordpress installs and plug-ins that are not updated as soon as new versions become available. Many hackers are happy to spend a great deal of time searching the Wordpress open source code, themes and plug-ins for vulnerabilities. Once vulnerabilities are found, they simply run bots that find active Wordpress installs that are vulnerable and attack them. In recent times many Wordpress blogs have been infected with malware, which results in Google and other search engines black-listing the infected sites.

I would say that 90% of the webmasters I know have suffered a hack attack at least once, myself included, although many have been hacked repeatedly. Most, however, do not lock down their Wordpress installs by completing the steps I have just given you to secure Wordpress.

Recently I suffered a major custom hack that inserted unique code into some of my php and java files even although I thought my Wordpress installs were secure. I have now taken my Wordpress security to a higher level using the services of Securi.net and Codeguard.com. Securi.net is a great service which not only monitors my sites with deep daily scans, but if any files are infected, Securi.net removes the infected files and offers advice on how to stop a similar attack. Codeguard.com monitors all files and runs a daily backup. With Codeguard.com if any files are changed, I receive an email informing me of the changes. You simply have to admit that no website is 100% secure from hacks. Employing systems that spot hacks straight away is a smart move in my opinion since hacks can be quickly spotted, cleaned and blocked.

# Chapter 6 - Structure, Design & Layout

## Structure, Layout and Design

The structure, layout and design of your site should lead your visitors towards the conversion goals that you have set. For example, conversion goals could simply be that your readers click a link to a merchant site or even subscribe to a newsletter. The most important elements of structure, design and layout include:

- Structuring the navigation of your site to benefit your visitors.
- How the design of your site will affect the number of conversions that you get.
- How colour can be used both to draw attention to your site and also to elicit different feelings in the minds of your customers.
- How different people usually look through a website and therefore how to build your site to appeal to all types of visitors.

Basically, the above points are all ways of getting your visitor to the conversion goal, but the big bonus is that you control them, not the visitor. Therefore, you should ensure your website is designed to maximum effect to help your visitors, and not hinder them, meaning that there is more chance of them converting. So, let's jump in and look at the important elements of website usability design!

### *Keeping Visitors Happy*

How many times have you visited a website and then left abruptly, annoyed that you could not locate exactly what you were looking for? You are not alone in this, as the main reason that people leave a site is because they cannot find what they are looking for. This means that it is up to you to provide your visitors with the information that they need – or a link to the information that they need – as soon as they land on your site. Part of the new Google PANDA algorithm update actually tracks those that visit your site and instantly return to Google to search again. Each visitor who quickly leaves your site and returns to Google search is in effect a negative vote for your site. Many believe that the PANDA algorithm is using such data to determine the quality of webmaster pages. If so, you don't want a large proportion of your visitors instantly leaving your website or you will be dealt a dreaded Google PANDA penalty.

Four extremely important aspects to be considered in order to keep your visitors happy are:

- Navigational structure.
- Your site's load time.
- Layout.
- The quality of the information.

Much of the time you might find yourself wondering what a visitor's problem is when they cannot navigate your site easily, as you are perfectly able to navigate around quickly and without barriers. For example, you might get an email from someone saying that they are unable to find information on Product XYZ, but you know exactly where to look and so think that they must either be stupid or simply not looking properly. However, if one person who bothers to email you cannot find the information, then many, many more people are probably in the same situation. This means that you should take note of any negative feedback you receive from your readers, as it is probably a symptom of a much bigger problem.

The basic way that you should treat your visitors – and it sounds like a horrible thing to say – is that all the visitors there are stupid.  Never underestimate the stupidity of some of your website visitors; if you cater to the lowest common denominator, you will have made the site easy for everyone to navigate.

### *Understanding Navigational Structure*
You could be forgiven for thinking that navigational structure refers solely to the navigation bars that are found at the top and on the sides of your webpage, but this is not the case. It also refers to the way that visitors can navigate through a specific page on your site, or between different pages.

Navigation can therefore encompass something like the links found within the text of your articles, not just the links in main menus and sidebars but also text links that you have included on the page. Basically, navigation encompasses anything that a user can use to find other articles on your website. For example, if you refer to another topic or product in an article, make sure to create a link to it. This will ensure that your visitor can find the referenced article with just one click.

The important question that you must bear in mind when designing your website is this: when a user lands on the page, can they see exactly what they are supposed to do? This means that you should be making the path that they need to follow a clear one, which is obvious to them and completely free of obstacles.

While you and I might spend a little longer on a site looking for a specified article if we cannot find what we are looking for, most people will not. People, especially when surfing online, are impatient and if they cannot find the order button, or the button to take them onto the next stage of the purchase or subscription process, they will simply abandon the process and look elsewhere, which of course will lose you a conversion.

Information pages on your web site are incredibly important. The basic rule is this: a visitor should never be more than two clicks away from an information page. This means that even if someone heads deep into your website, enthralled by the content that you have provided, they should still be able to return to the basic information on the product or service easily and quickly.

Although the above rule of two clicks still applies, it is even more usual for people to be only one click away from the information page, because the key information pages should form a part of your navigation bar that appears on every page throughout the site. This is not always the case, however, as there might be some pages that do not contain your main navigation bar. In these cases you should follow the two-click rule, although it would be extremely foolish to have a great product review article without containing at least one link to the actual product so that users could reach it by a single click.

Once you have started to generate content for your website, take a look at the way your site's navigation works. Is it funnelling people through your site to your desired goal – the conversion – or is it providing a number of opportunities for them to spill out of the funnel and therefore be lost as possible conversion targets?

The funnel is basically a prompt for people to follow the path that you want them to take. This means that if you are clever about it and do it correctly, you will be able to cater to all the different types of visitors on your site without losing any of them in the process.

So let's look at the difference between a good navigation and a bad navigation, starting with how a good navigation should go. The basic process for good navigation is this:

- The visitor lands on the homepage and thinks, "What is the product all about?"
- To answer this question, they have an easily visible "What Is It?" page, which they then click on.
- From this page, they are able to click onto a page such as, "What Will It Do For

You?" thereby giving them more interest and desire for the product.

- Now they can go onto a page such as "How It Compares To Competitors", which will allow them to evaluate the alternatives and come out with a positive view of the product that you are selling.
- After this you move to the business end of the process, where you can guide the visitor to details of any special offers that you have and ultimately to the "Buy Now" page.

This process means that everyone coming to your site can easily find something that is relevant to their own individual needs, regardless of where they are on the site (assuming that all the above navigation links are in place).

So what could make a bad navigation instead of a good one? Well, a few different aspects could be:

- Poor ordering of pages. For example, having the "Buy Now" page in the funnel before the information would immediately put people off. This will only work for people who buy impulsively, and the majority of visitors do not fall into this category. This means you have to explain to them the features and benefits before going in for the conversion.
- Some sites split off too much once you get further into the site, meaning that there is no clear path. Visitors can become confused and lost – something that is remedied by having simple and easy to use paths.
- Navigation menus on some sites are often not very clear. Ideally you want them to be on the left or right, in view and easily visible to people as they browse every page, not hidden away at the bottom or in a tiny font at the top of the page.

## *Good Layout Techniques*
Listed below are some of the good layout practices that you should always try to follow:

- Style over substance is not usually a good thing, so don't get too obsessed with making your site look pretty. This is a mistake that many people make, which often causes them to end up with a beautiful website that doesn't convert at all.
- Keep the header and the logo small, so that they do not take up too much space. To get an idea of how big your logo should be, head over to some of the world's biggest sites, such as Amazon, and see just how small their logo is in comparison

to the rest of their site. This is also done because, sad as it might seem to you, people don't care what your website is called. They most probably found you by going through Google or some other search engine, so they know the name already.

- The navigation bar is important, but where you place it on the site is not. I have looked into this in huge detail in the past, taking in the theories of a number of different people, and my tests have shown that there is no disadvantage to it being on the left, right or the top. The thing to worry about is the style that your menu has and the colours that it contains. These can be used effectively to draw attention to the pages that you want people to click on, therefore increasing your conversion chances.

- White space is not always bad, so don't be afraid of it. It allows visitors to rest their eyes and also means that you can draw attention to other things far more easily. The basic rule is that cluttered websites are much worse than simple websites, so white space is not bad at all when put in this context. Of course large areas of white space can be a bad thing as for user experience because your website could be perceived as not finished or users may feel some content has not loaded.

## *Website Clarity and Load Time*

The use of colours on a webpage, and more specifically how contrasting colours can really help to draw a visitor's attention to a specific part of the site. You must remember, however, that too many colours can cause confusion and give the site much less clarity – something that will cause visitors to leave incredibly quickly. We deal with colours in much more detail in the next section.

When it comes to the time it takes your site to load, you must make sure that the page load time is as quick as possible – remember that visitors usually give a site only seven seconds to get their attention, including the time taken to load. To optimize the page load time, make sure that all of your images are optimized and that the code of your site is as clean as possible – if you are not confident about the code, get a pro from Elance to quickly look over it for you.

There is always the temptation to include eye-catching elements constructed through the use of a non-standard form, such as Flash or JavaScript. While these undoubtedly look great, you must remember that many of your visitors will not have the software (plug-ins) or even in some cases, the processing power to view such elements. I would advise you to limit such elements on your site to those that are absolutely essential.

A good example of the above would be a header on your site in the form of a flash animation. This header could have all the benefits of the product you are selling, which will look great to 80% of your visitors but for the remaining 20% all they would see would be an error message.

## *Website Design Summary*

If you only take one point away from this section, it should be this: always make sure that your site has a clear structure to its navigation, which allows people to return to relevant pages regardless of how deep they get into your site. The structure of the navigation should have a clear aim – getting people to the conversion page – and not just be a jumbled mass of different links leading them in circles.

Keep your site simple, as simplicity breeds less confusion for the visitor. This simplicity will allow you the chance to get visitors' attention easily with different aspects of the site, and then to guide them through to the pages that they need to see.

# The Power of Colour

Colours play a massive role in any website, as colours can evoke different feelings in visitors and ultimately help to dictate to them exactly where they will go on your site, and the actions that they will take. This means that the colours you decide to incorporate are another very important aspect of website design.

## *Understanding The Importance of Colours*

The first thing that you should always bear in mind is that the best colours for the job do not always follow the best design principles; we have already established that what looks good to the eye is not always the best thing for conversions. So, for this reason, do not look on your site as a design project – always stay focused on the end goal, which is to get as many conversions as possible.

Colours are about so much more than making your site look pretty. They can draw a visitor's attention to a specific area of the site, they can help you control the flow of information that visitors read and they can also help to control where a user clicks next on the page. Colours can also be used effectively to evoke different feelings in people, although you must understand that different cultures have different views on certain colours. For example, the colour red is lucky in China, but in some parts of Europe it is commonly considered to signify danger.

## *Using The Power Of Colours*

Different colours will ignite different feelings in your visitors, and even although colours can be seen differently by different cultures, there is generally a consensus on the way that they are viewed, especially in the USA and in Europe – the two areas that are likely to be your main source of traffic. What is important is that you put your own personal feelings about colours aside and do what is best for your conversion rate, meaning that sometimes you will find yourself using a colour that you do not personally like. Also make sure that you are aware that every colour has both a positive and negative side, so there is no such thing as "the right colour". You just need to know what the impact of each of these colours is and how to make sure that the colours fit in with the message that you are trying to convey.

So what are some of the different colours and how can they influence your site, both positively and negatively?

- Blue – Blue evokes the feeling of calm and tranquillity, as well as cleanliness and strength. On the other hand, it can represent depression and iciness, as well as fear.
- Red – Red is intrinsically linked with passion and love, and with power and femininity. This means that it could be the perfect choice for a site dealing in something like dating. On the flip side, it can also conjure up feelings of evil and danger, which would be entirely wrong for a site dealing in children's products, for example.
- Green – Green is a very natural colour – just look at the amount of organic companies that use it – and also indicates wealth and safety. It can represent illness, however, or envy and greed.
- Purple – Purple is a regal colour, and also conjures up feelings of sensuality and mystery, but can make people think of mourning, profanity and confusion.
- Black – Black is a very powerful colour, and can convey style, modernity and power. It can also be incredibly depressing and bring about images of death – for example, the black suits and ties that are always worn to funerals.
- Orange – Orange is a vibrant colour that is warm and has a huge amount of energy to it, which can be great for sites looking to promote exercise or other such activities. It can also denote a feeling of arrogance, fire or aggression if it is not used properly, however.
- White – White is the ultimate colour to represent purity and feelings of peace and innocence, but it can also look unimaginative and convey a sense of coldness to

visitors.

- Yellow – Yellow, like orange, can be a vibrant colour, and can inspire the visitor to feel happiness and warmth within themselves. It is also the colour of cowardice however, as well as dishonesty and greed.

## *Using Colour For Maximum Effect*

It is very important that you understand the colours that are going to be appropriate for your website (e.g. green for a site promoting natural products), and you also need to make sure that you understand the positive and negative feelings that the colours could evoke in your visitors. At the same time, do not design the whole site around whether you can use specific colours. Even if you don't want to use red, for example, because it promotes danger to people, there is no reason why you can't have splashes of this colour on the site; just don't use it as the primary colour.

## *Using Colour Effectively*

As well as the above points, you must also understand the different ways that colour can be used effectively to catch people's attention. A great example of this is the colour red, as it is a bright colour that immediately draws people's eyes. This means that many sites will use red for the most important information that they have, such as "Buy Now" buttons and information relating to low stock or other tactics to illicit a sense of urgency among potential buyers. However, you must also consider that red can be seen as a sign to stop, so you need to test whether this has an impact on how people react when the "Buy Now" button is red in colour.

On the other hand, green is seen as meaning "go" in the vast majority of cultures throughout the world, so this colour could be used as an alternative to the red "Buy Now" button. Although red is better at getting the attention of readers, green can be a better colour for the order button due to the calm feelings that it evokes. Basically, the point I am making is that all calls to action should be created in a strong colour that stands out, so that they are easier for the visitor to find. Contrasting colours also help with this, and they can be used throughout the page, such as in the header and in the menu, as well as in the copy and the images. Make sure you don't go over the top with contrasting colours however, as this will simply create confusion amongst your visitors. Therefore, use them to enhance the main parts of the page – not the whole page!

The above screenshot is of a site that I know converts extremely well, for a number of different reasons. One of the main reasons that it converts well is due to the use of colour that it employs. Firstly, your eyes are immediately drawn to the red parts, because they contrast well with the white background. You will notice that everything in red is something that the site wants you to see straight away, and therefore by highlighting these areas the site gives you all the important information within the first seven seconds of your visit.

The call to action button – the red button stating "Click Here Now" – also makes great use of colour, as it contrasts perfectly with the background and the text/images around it. This means that a visitor to the site never has to look for very long before finding out how to buy the product being sold. The red is also used well on the part that says "Buy One – Get One Free", which means that the site easily creates desire for the product thanks to the value that it provides.

The white on the site also works perfectly, for a couple of different reasons. Firstly, white is associated with purity and cleanliness, which are two very important aspects of any diet site. White also creates a certain element of trust, thanks to the professional look it gives the site. Moreover, white provides the perfect base for the rest of the site, which is mainly coloured in red and black. The contrast allows the important information to stand out in a way that is beneficial to the conversion rates.

Just imagine if this site was all in one colour, or had colours that blended into each other. You would never be able to scan the page and pick out all the information that you need quickly. This would cause many people to leave, fed up that they actually have to put in some effort to find what they are looking for.

### *Colour Summary*

To summarise the important points that you should have learnt from this section:

- Know what the different colours can represent and, more importantly, how the visitors to your website could perceive them.
- Bright colours that contrast with other parts of the page are a great way to draw attention to a section of the page that you want people to notice easily.
- Ensure that you do not go over the top with your colour on the site, as this will detract from the impact and instead cause people to be confused and not know where to look on the page to find the most pertinent information.
- Dark backgrounds can help to make light content easier to read, while light backgrounds work well for dark-coloured content.
- What looks good to you might not be the right choice. There is a clear line between the aesthetics of a site and what converts the best – make sure that you always look at your conversions and not at how the site looks overall.

## The Importance of Scannable Pages

### *Understanding Scannable Pages*

Understanding how to create pages that visitors can scan is another extremely important element of web design. The first thing you probably want to know is what I mean exactly by "scannable pages"! Well, consider how you usually read a website. You do not read every last piece of content; instead, you scan through until you reach the bottom, before then going back up and revisiting any areas that have jumped out at you and caught your eye. Your website visitors only really notice a few parts of the webpage – parts that when revisited they either read properly, or click on the link to take them through to another page on your site.

This means that you must format your webpages with this kind of visitor behaviour in mind. There are a variety of different ways that this can be done, but perhaps the most important of these is to make sure that you are selective about the parts of your page that stand out from the rest, meaning that you must work out which parts of the webpage content are most important to your readers. Just remember – formatting is an essential part of getting good conversion rates, but it is an area that so many affiliates neglect. Even if you have the best content in the world, you will struggle to get conversions without good formatting.

## *The Golden Triangle*

Most websites exhibit something that we call the Golden Triangle, which is the area in the left hand corner to which peoples' eyes are most drawn when they browse a website. Of course, this triangle can differ in its size and sometimes is not even a triangle, but the basic thing to remember is that there is nearly always an area in the top left of the page where people view the most.

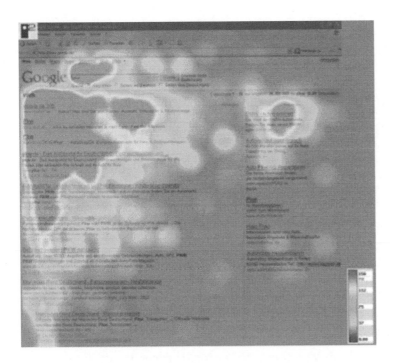

The above image is from a study compiled to see exactly where people look on a webpage – in this instance, the results page from Google. They have used eye-tracking devices to monitor where people look, with the brighter colours, such as red, indicating the areas where people look the most. Conversely, the duller colours – such as the blue – show the areas to which people do not pay too much attention when they are browsing this particular page.

What this picture shows is a clear triangle at the top left, which is made from the red, orange and yellow parts of the image. This is what is known as the Golden Triangle, and as you might have already guessed, we should always strive to place the most important information in this area. At least you should make sure that the content in this area points people towards your conversion pages, but only if you can't get links to the conversion pages in the triangle itself. For an even more in-depth review of how people look through your website – even how you subconsciously look through it – you can use a program called QuickTale. This allows you to see how people scan through your website, starting from the top, then going down, before then returning to the areas of interest that they noticed. For now, just trust me when I say that the Golden Triangle exists and that it is extremely important to the way in which your site is laid out.

### *Techniques To Make Scannable Pages*

The key to ensuring that people go back to the areas of the page that you want them to is to make your page scannable. There are a number of different ways to do this…

- Ensure that your paragraphs are short – ideally no more than three to four lines on a page. Short paragraphs create the illusion of there being less to read, even if it means that you simply have to include more paragraphs to get all the information in. The paragraphs now seem a lot easier to read and absorb, therefore making people more likely to return to them after they have reached the bottom of the page.
- Make use of subheadings as much as possible, as this breaks up the text and provides handy markers for people to use that tell them exactly what the following paragraph will be about. It also means that people can find the part of the page they are looking for easily, as we know by now just how impatient visitors to your website can be!
- Try to break up the text by including images on your page, as this will provide a nice variety for people when they are scanning through. Images are also much easier to absorb than text, so they will allow the visitor to absorb information a lot quicker.
- Bullet points – as I have done here for you busy readers – are an excellent way to get across a number of points in a short space. It is best to use them as high up as

possible on your index page, but also throughout the whole site as well. Make sure that you do not include too many bullet points, however, as this will put people off reading any of them. Three to five different points are probably best for most websites.

- Make the most important phrases in your webpage stand out by putting them in bold type. If you know about SEO, you will know that putting your keywords in a bold font can help with the promotion of them to search engines. When you are trying to get conversions, however, it is the most important points to the reader – not the search engine – that you want to place in bold type. Basically, somebody should be able to read only the bold text on your site and understand exactly what you are trying to say throughout the page. It is prudent to use bold only about once every paragraph, however, as otherwise it loses its effect.

- People don't like reading long sentences, so keep them short. The average sentence on your site should only be about 10-15 words long, although obviously it is sometimes necessary to increase the length. Essentially, you want your content to be as digestible as possible for your visitors, and short sentences help this enormously. Make sure that you don't simplify sentences too much though, as you could come across as patronising, which is never good!

- Try to place links intelligently at the end of each mini-section of the page. This means that whatever section of the site the visitors scrolls back up to once they've finished scanning the site, they'll find a link there that will allow them to find out even more information about the product or service that you have. In fact, it could even be a link to the order page, as you try to get visitors to convert. Essentially, you need to give them a link that moves them further down their decision-making process.

## An Example

The best way to look at the points above is to go through an example with you, and show you exactly how implementing at least some of them can drastically change how a piece of text reads. So, first off, take a look at the paragraph below:

"Always make sure that all pages are optimized so that the content is scannable and easy to read by your visitor. Make sure that the paragraphs are kept as short as possible, use sub-headings to break up the text and use bullet points to make the text seem like it is easier to read. This is because people looking at your site are usually going to be busy or lazy, or perhaps both at the same time. It is also a lot harder to read text when it is on a computer screen, so you need to work for your visitor in order to make their life as easy as possible. If you can ensure that your text is easy to read, then you will have a much better chance of getting a good conversion rate for your site and therefore earning yourself more money. More money means that you can live your dreams, so don't ignore the information that is contained within this paragraph, even if you feel like it is too much work!"

Now, imagine you saw the above paragraph on a website. Would you read it? I'm sure I wouldn't, as it just looks too indigestible. However, take a look at what injecting just a few points from those recommended above can do:

### *"How To Improve Your Conversion Rates"*

Always make sure that all pages are optimized so that the content is **scannable** and easy to read by your visitors. are clear to visitor. Make sure that:

- The paragraphs are kept as short as possible.
- You use sub-headings to break up the text.
- You use bullet points to make the text seem like it is easier to read.

This is because people looking at your site are usually going to be **busy or lazy**, or perhaps both at the same time. It is also a lot harder to read text when it is on a computer screen, so you need to work for your visitor in order to make their life as easy as possible.

If you can ensure that your text is easy to read, then you will have a much better chance of getting a good conversion rate for your site and therefore earning yourself more money.

**More money** means that you can **live your dreams**, so don't ignore the information that is contained within this paragraph, even if you feel like it is too much work!"

As you can see, apart from a couple of tiny changes to the text and the addition of a header, the second example gives exactly the same info as the first, but in a way that is much easier to read. There have been a few different changes to the second – see if you can spot them before reading the next paragraph!

Okay, so how many did you spot? Well, the most obvious is that the text has been broken up into small paragraphs, all of which are shorter than four lines. There has also been a header added, so that people can scan easily and see what it's about. Bullet points have been added, as have bold words, and the text is now not "justified" – there's more on this in the "copywriting" section of the book. All these add up to create a piece of text that's much easier to read. To further enhance it, you could even add a relevant image somewhere in the middle of the text as well.

### *Scannable Page Summary*

There are a number of different aspects that you need to understand from this section. In keeping with the theme of making things easier to read, I'll list them in bullet points below!

- If possible, you should include the most important information within the "Golden Triangle" on your site. This will take up some of your navigation space, but it will allow you the luxury of knowing that the vast majority of visitors are digesting the most important info.
- The format of your content should be easy for people to scan. Remember that people rarely go onto a site and begin reading straight away; instead, they scan the page and then return to the parts that they find the most interesting to them.
- Make each section of a page obvious and distinct from the others. To do this you can use such things as bullet points, short paragraphs and images, as well as white space.
- Make sure that each section of a page includes a link, so that the reader can have access to more information and be moved further along your funnel.
- Test your site yourself, to make sure that your eyes are drawn towards the most important aspects. Even better would be to ask friends and family to do the same, so that you can get a rounded opinion of how your site functions.


Just remember, the formatting of your site is absolutely essential when It comes to gaining conversions. If you find that your site is not converting in the way that you want it to, then you should begin by looking at the format before anything else, as this is the area that most online affiliates neglect. Check your site against the info provided in this chapter and see if there is anything that you can improve on – there almost certainly will be!

## Conversion and Funnels

### *Understand Funnels?*

In really basic terms, a funnel or conversion path is the route by which a visitor goes through your site from when they first land on a page to when they reach the conversion page – at which point we hope they turn into a successful conversion for you! It is imperative that you are in control of this funnel, as it means that you can control exactly what visitors see and in what order they see them. At the same time, you must ensure that you are catering to the visitor's needs throughout the visit to your site, as otherwise they will probably leave very quickly.

Later we shall analyze the different types of visitor to your website, dividing them into information seekers and buyers and into people who are in a hurry and those who are more cautious. The types of visitor are important because you will need to make sure that your site caters to the needs of all them.

To cater successfully for all these different types of visitor, you will need to have more than one funnel on your website. Not only do your visitors belong to different types, but they also enter your site at different stages, so you must ensure that they all have a route to go down that appeals to them. By having multiple funnels, you can cater for everyone's needs perfectly.

### *Initial Steps*

One of the first things that you will need to do when you first start to think about your funnel is to establish what questions visitors are likely to be asking themselves when they visit your site. To illustrate this, it is best to use an example.

In this example, we have a scenario where three different types of user are looking to buy a new computer. There is the uneducated person, a partly educated person and a person who is educated to a high standard. Let's start with the uneducated customer first.

We shall assume that the uneducated customer is at quite an early stage in the buying process, and is therefore still looking for information on the different options he has. This means that his first question is likely to be, "What computers are there out there that I can buy?" We need to ensure that he has this information straight away, which will allow him to get into the funnel that we have created. Make sure, however, that the page that he goes to is relevant to the different types of computer as otherwise he'll simply click away.

Now that you have the uneducated visitor into the funnel, it is a case of keeping him there. He has seen what types of computer are available to him, and now we need to give more interest, as we already have his attention. You could perhaps have a link that is very noticeable relating to comparisons between laptops and PCs, for example. After all, now that he knows what sorts of computer there are, he is going to want to take a further look and get a little more specific.

So he is now on the comparison page, and let's pretend that he has decided that he wants a regular PC and not a laptop. The next question that he has is about the different types of PC's there are out there – something to which we can provide the answer by giving him links to different manufacturers and the PCs that they produce. Therefore, you could have sections for Dell, Toshiba, HP and any other company that makes PCs. This is where the multiple paths rear their head – by giving him the option to look at all these different companies, we are creating multiple paths for him to go down. When he gets onto the review page for a specific model, we need to create the desire in him to buy, which can be done with a conspicuous link to the purchase page. It is imperative that all our different funnels – i.e. the different brand and model reviews – have in them this next step of the funnel, to the purchase page.

What you can now see is that we have constructed a funnel for the uneducated customer, which allows him to arrive at the site and obtain all the information that he needs by pre-empting his questions and then takes him to a page where he can become another conversion. As long as you answer the questions properly and provide answers to the correct questions, you will have a robust funnel.

Let's now consider the partly-educated visitor to the site. The basic principle is the same as the uneducated customer, but the partly-educated visitor will be further on in the buying process. He has already decided before coming onto your site that he wants a specific type of computer, but has not decided on an exact model. This just means that he is entering into the funnel a little later than the previous example, but we will still need to give him much of the information that the uneducated customer received. We give him the information on laptops vs. desktops, and all the pages after this in the funnel as well. Remember however, that this customer should, by the time he has reached the end of the funnel, be on a page where he can buy the item!

The final type of customer is our well-educated one, who already knows everything he needs to know – he simply wants to make a purchase. He knows that he wants a Dell Desktop PC, and therefore all we need to do is reassure him of his choice, before then leading him to a payment page. As you can see, he comes into the funnel at a very late stage.

**So...**

You can see that the first customer joins in the process right at the beginning of the funnel, whereas the other two come in later on. This means that, in this example, we could easily make just one funnel; a funnel that will provide all the necessary information and reassurance to all the different customers that visit your site, with the end result being that they all turn into conversions. This is an incredibly basic view, however, and also quite an unrealistic one.

I mentioned briefly how you can create multiple funnels leading to the different models and brands that your website offers. Well, it is also possible to funnel people towards a product that you want to promote the most, perhaps because it provides the largest amount of commission. At the same time, however, there are always going to be people who are not interested at all in this number one product that you have, so you must provide funnels for them as well. This means that multiple funnels are being created – all with a different weight to them in terms of promotion. You have to look at your site and decide whether to have funnels in your site at all, or whether the ones that you do have are good enough to generate conversions.

## Utilising Conversion Paths

Many of you are probably very curious about how we can create these conversion paths and funnels. Well, in my opinion, there are two different methods that work very well indeed.

- Firstly, you can ensure that your menu/navigation is structured so that every customer to the site can see exactly what he is looking for – i.e. information that is relevant to the stage that he is currently at in the buying process. Following on with the computer example, you could have links on your menu for "What type of computer?", which would immediately appeal to the uneducated visitors to your site and get them into the funnel straight away. Make sure that it is easy for the visitors to find by having it stand out – remember our discussion of colours earlier – so that the uneducated person doesn't miss it and feel that his question hasn't been answered.

  For the "partly-educated" customers, we also need to create a link on the menu that is noticeable and will appeal to them straight away. They came onto the site already knowing what type of computer they want, but we could have a link entitled "Top Ten Laptops" or even "Top Ten Desktops" to provide them with quick access to what they are looking for. Once again, we have led them into the funnel. If you want them to purchase a specific laptop or desktop, you can obviously write the review in such a way as to influence their decision. You will not necessarily set your site up exactly in this way in order to get different customers into the funnel since you will have a website in a different niche selling different products, but the principle is likely to be similar. The idea behind creating funnels is to appeal to different types of customers. We can also manipulate these funnels to ensure that visitors click-through to a certain page or get a bias towards a certain product, all with the intention of increasing the amount of money you make through conversions. You should always remember that your main funnel should not be your only funnel, as you need to cater for all your visitors' requirements.

- The other way that you can get people straight into funnels is to make a homepage that deals with all the different questions that they have. Obviously you will not be able to provide detailed answers on the home page, but you can provide a brief summary, before encouraging them to click on a link to find out more on the topic. This technique works very well because all the information is in one place, so when people scan through they find what they are looking for – as long as you have presented it correctly!

### What Is The 3 Step Image Technique?

One of the best ways that you can create a funnel is by using the "3 step image technique" which, as you probably can guess, has three images at its core!

These images actually take the form of buttons, and these three buttons are displayed in an extremely prominent position, above the fold, so that all visitors can see them. Let's imagine that we are running a site dedicated to trading on the stock exchange. We might have three buttons displayed that read "New To Stocks?", "Need Extra Training?" and "Looking For A Stockbroker?". These buttons are specifically tailored for people at different stages of the funnel and are a great way to get them into the funnel in the correct place.

Using these three buttons gives the readers the chance to get into the funnel regardless of what they want. This means that people won't spend ages looking for the information that they want, before then getting bored and heading to a different website instead.

## *Why You Must Keep Visitors In The Funnel*

Once the visitors are in the funnel, we have to work hard at keeping them in the funnel. This means that every single page should catch their attention, give them an interest, and then produce desire in them.

The desire part of this thought process is an interesting one, because most people assume that it relates to giving the visitor the desire to purchase the product, which is not true at all. Most of the pages that you have will be helping to build the desire for a product, but their individual aim will be to get the reader to have the desire to move onto the next page in the funnel. This desire to keep going needs to be maintained all the way through to the purchase / decision process.

Another very important aspect that you must remember when it comes to keeping people in the funnel is that you must make it easy for them by creating a clear path, as otherwise they will drop out of the funnel. Remember that there are a number of different funnels, which means that you have to make them all easy to navigate, not just the one you are most interested in. All these funnels should end in the conversion goal, because if people can't find how to buy a product easily, they will simply take the information they have learnt and buy from somewhere else instead.

Relevance is the last point that needs to be made when it comes to keeping people in the funnel. All content must be completely relevant to the subject in which the visitor is trying to gain information, as otherwise they will simply get bored and leave to find the information they require on another site.

## *Conversion Funnels Summary*

The most important thing to remember from this section is that you can use funnels to control exactly what your visitor sees and how they behave while they are on the site. All your customers will be different – they will have different needs, or be at a different place in the decision / buying process, – but you can cope with this by creating multiple funnels, each of which provides relevant information. It is easy to get visitors to enter into the funnel at the right time, through using navigation menus or the "3 step image technique", for example, but it is not as easy to keep them in the funnel throughout the whole process. Although we have already gone through some tips about keeping them in the funnel, we shall go through a lot more as we progress through the book.

We already went over scannability, which is incredibly important when it comes to your funnels. The easier the website is to scan, the easier visitors find it to get the information that they are looking for. Once they have found this information, they have entered into the funnel. Being able to scan-read pages easily also means that your visitors are more likely to stay on the site for longer – and progress further through the funnel – as they won't get bored as easily.

# Chapter 7 – Building Your Online Cash Cow

## Website Structure Essentials

How you structure your website is of paramount importance, especially since Google updated its algorithm with what many webmasters now call the PANDA or Farmers Update in February 2011. For thin affiliate type websites the actual structure will make little difference compared to the thousand page plus authority type site you will be building.

When Google rolled out its PANDA update, many websites were hit hard. Not just thin type affiliate sites but even some major sites suffered a severe drop in Google search traffic. One such site was http://hubpages.com/. See the graph below to see just how hard Hub Pages was hit by the first PANDA update:

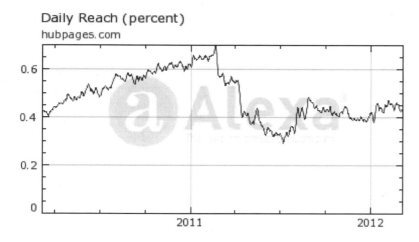

As you can see from the above graph, the initial Google PANDA algorithm update hit the website extremely hard as did later algorithm updates that occurred during April 2011, May 2011 and June 2011. From July 2011 Hub Pages actually recovered to some degree and since this recovery is of prime importance to you, let me explain it.

Firstly you have to understand why Hub Pages was hit so hard. The Google PANDA algorithm update was introduced to remove poor quality content from Google's search results. Breaking down the algorithm to its very basics, it learns to detect low quality content.

Many have suggested that one metric the PANDA algorithm employs is the click-through rate from Google's search results. It makes perfect sense that if a user clicks a Google's search listing and then quickly returns to the initial search listing, it means that the initial page served to the user did not fulfil the user's requirements since the user has returned to the search listing to try elsewhere. If the same page receives the same response from users over and over again, the Google algorithm can class the page as a low quality response for the specified search query.

Using SERPs click-through rate and other metrics Google was able to detect low quality pages. It seems that if a site had even a small number of "poor quality" pages, the whole website lost rankings with Google.

Hub Pages content is created by its users, who claim to be experts in the niche they write about, although of course many are not. The quality of articles on Hub Pages varies from superb to extremely poor. It seems clear that the poor quality content produced by some of Hub Pages' so-called "expert authors" caused the whole site to be penalized.

So what did Hub Pages do to reverse the penalty? From reports posted online we know that Google contacted the Hub Pages CEO Paul Edmondson directly, perhaps as many have claimed because prior to the penalty Hub Pages were generating $10 million in Google AdSense revenue.

The Wall Street Journal reported…

*In June, a top Google search engineer, Matt Cutts, wrote to Edmondson that he might want to try subdomains, among other things. The Hub Pages subdomain testing began in late June and already has shown positive results. Edmondson's own articles on Hub Pages, which saw a 50% drop in page views after Google's Panda updates, have returned to pre-Panda levels in the first three weeks since he activated subdomains for himself and several other authors. The other authors saw significant, if not full, recoveries of Web traffic.*

The Wall Street Journal also stated…

*A subdomain can be useful to separate out content that is completely different. Google uses subdomains for distinct products such news.google.com or maps.google.com, for example. If you're a newer webmaster or SEO, I'd recommend using subdirectories until you start to feel pretty confident with the architecture of your site. At that point, you'll be better equipped to make the right decision for your own site.*

Hub Pages acted on the advice and created subdirectories for each author. A few weeks later quality authors reported a return of traffic for their articles. It seems that if a large site utilises subdirectories and one of the subdirectories contains poor quality articles, only that directory will be penalized, with the rest of the site retaining its Google rankings.

Building a thousand page plus site it would be very foolish to put all our eggs in one basket, or should I say all our articles in one directory. Let's think again about a treadmill affiliate site that has the following content types:

- Treadmill Sales Pages
- Treadmill Accessory Sales Pages
- News Pages
- Treadmill Training Page

Rather than just using one directory comprising just one Wordpress install, the smart approach would be to use multiple Wordpress installs. For example, let's say your site is acetreadmills.com. In the home directory we will have our first Wordpress install (acetreadmills.com), which contains all our main Treadmill sales pages and introductory articles. We then have another Wordpress install for accessories (acetreadmills.com/treadmill-accessories/). We also have other subdirectories for news pages (acetreadmills.com/treadmill-news/), and of course for treadmill training (acetreadmills.com/treadmill-training/).

Google will to some degree treat each subdirectory as a separate site, although I have found that it seems much easier to pass authority from the main directory to the sub-directories, which have other SEO benefits. For example PageRank will pass from the main directory to subdirectories as will page authority. I strongly believe creating a site with this structure generates far more SEO power than just using one Wordpress install. So the structure of your authority site MUST include sub-directories.

### *Site Wide Links*
Site wide links are simply links that appear on every page of a website. With Wordpress, site wide links are normally placed on the sidebar, header or footer. For example, take a look at the header from the Marks & Spencer website.

Site wide links on the header include Women, Lingerie, Men, and Mother's Day etc. No matter which page of the Marks & Spencer site you visit, you will always see the same links with the same text (anchor text) in the header.

Your header site wide links should link to the other sections of your website, which of course are in subdirectories, each using a separate Wordpress install. You should ensure that for each of your Wordpress installs you use the same header titles with the same header links so in effect the header of each of your multiple Wordpress installs are the same, giving the appearance that your multiple installs are actually one big site.

### *Sidebar Site Wide Links*

Sidebar links are links with anchor text that are displayed on the sidebar of websites. If you look at the website below, the sidebar site wide links appear on the left hand side of the website.

Site wide links have in effect three main functions.

- Firstly they aid user navigation as the links and indeed anchor text appear on every page.
- Secondly they boost click-through rate: users may enter your website for one search phrase and be attracted by the descriptive anchor text of your site wide links, resulting in the user clicking one or more of the links.
- The third function of site wide links is to give the actual pages linked to the site wide links more SEO power. As the links appear on every page, authority and indeed PageRank will be passed through the site wide links to the pages.

Don't worry about PageRank and page/domain authority for now as they will be covered in detail in later chapters. Many authority type sites can easily rank for competitive key phrases with the power of their very own site wide links alone. As your website ages and gains authority and PageRank, you will notice that you start to gain increased rankings for the anchor text used on your site wide links. For example, if your site wide links included treadmill review anchor text such as "Nordic Track C2000 Treadmill Review", linked to a page with the same title, and the content of the page optimized for the same long tail key phrase, in time you would notice that you increased your ranking for that exact phrase from your internal links alone.

As we will be using multi Wordpress installs, you must ensure that you use different sidebar navigation links for each install. Using the same sidebar navigation links for all installs could very well result in a penalty. Take the time to ensure that on each of your Wordpress installs you select 25 different top buying key phrases that relate to each section. Remember that each new page you add to each section of your site will give your site wide links a little boost. Build up each section little by little over the course of a year and you will gain great rankings!

### *Footer Links*

I have to admit I am not a great fan of footer links. Many affiliates choose to add their navigational site wide links to the footer of their website, which I believe is a big mistake. Firstly users may not actually scroll down the page so may not even see the links in the footer. Secondly I strongly believe that Google and other search engines treat footer links as lesser links since over the years they have been highly exploited, especially on Wordpress sites. Years ago many gained great rankings from simply purchasing footer links in free Wordpress themes. Some of the popular free themes had thousands of downloads, which resulted in those who had links on the themes generating thousands of links in record time and ranking quickly for highly competitive key phrases. It did not take long for Google to catch onto this form of link building, which is against the terms set by Google. Many who employed the Wordpress theme footer links tactic found that they lost all rankings, with their websites banished from Google search results.

## Planning Your Website Structure

Before deciding on a Wordpress theme or even multiple themes for your affiliate site, ensure that the theme has a sidebar and of course has the option to edit and add header menu options manually. If you are using multiple themes, you will have to edit the themes so that they all have the same header and menu links. Take a look at the demo treadmill site at www.onlinecashcow.com.

Notice how different themes are used for each section but the same header is used for each different theme. Unless you have some knowledge of Wordpress coding, this is going to be beyond your current expertise. I would advise you to get your main Wordpress install set up and loaded with all the header menu options added. Next add your other Wordpress installs, and then simply hire someone from Elance to copy the main header to your other Wordpress installs. If you are using the same theme for each Wordpress install, then of course you will not have any problems.

Take time to plan your website structure because making major changes to site wide header and sidebar links after your site has been indexed in Google can often result in at least a temporary penalty.

## Common Site Styles

The way that your website is set out and its overall style can also play a massive role in the success of the conversion rate as a whole. For example, a common type of website is what is known as a *multi-sales pitch,* which essentially means that it is a site with a number of different pages, all geared towards getting conversions. These pages could include a homepage, testimonials, an order page and a FAQ page. The basic premise is that visitors land on the homepage and are then linked through the various pages – learning more and more as they go – until they reach the order page, by which time they are informed enough to make an order. They are popular among UK visitors to sites, who are generally more cautious than their US counterparts – making them cautious information seekers.

Another example is the *one-page sales pitch,* which is essentially one long page comprising the different pages of a *multi-sales pitch* site. This means that the page still has all the information included, but the need for navigation is cut out almost entirely. They are particularly popular with American websites, who are usually more likely to be busy information seekers in a hurry. The main advantage to this type of website is that there is only a small chance of a visitor leaving because they find the process too long; on the flip side though, visitors can be lost if the information isn't presented in exactly the right order.

Yet another type of website is the *email-capture page,* which is a page designed simply to collect people's emails and not actually to sell them anything at that specific time. When the site has collected email addresses, it uses them to advertise their products through emails and to try to convert leads in this way. The basic premise of the site is no different, however, whether they are be multiple pages or one page, and they have the same advantages and disadvantages.

The style of the content and graphics can also be important when trying to connect with visitors, as different visitors prefer different methods. For example, a multi-sales pitch will usually be soft and subtle and try to portray the look of an authority site, whereas a one-page sales pitch will usually be loud and in-your-face. The soft approach is usually good for those looking for information and who are cautious in their approach, while load pages work especially well with US visitors.

There are a number of different types of affiliate website that you can set up. These include:

- **Review Websites.** These, as you might expect, provide reviews of different products and provide links that the visitors can use to navigate to the site selling the specific item. Because many people are already searching for specific brands when they visit this type of website, they are often almost ready to make a purchase and all they require is a little bit more information - information that it is your job to supply.

- **Informational Websites.** These provide a large amount of information on a topic and then try to use this info to persuade people to buy certain items or complete certain actions. They provide information for those without much knowledge of the subject and are usually frequented by information seekers who are only at the beginning of the buying/decision-making process (something we will cover later in Chapter Eleven).

- **Authority Websites.** These types of sites try to portray themselves as knowledgeable and trustworthy on a specific topic, much in the same way that a site like Wikipedia is. Unlike Wiki however, they will then try to use this trust to persuade people into completing one of their conversion goals, whether this is signing up to a newsletter or buying a product.

- **Personal Experience Websites.** As the title suggests, these are websites where someone has had "personal experiences" with a service or product and has decided to create a website extolling the product's virtues.

- **Email Capture/Squeeze Pages.** Sites that have the primary goal of collecting email addresses and not actually making sales at that specific point.

As can be seen, choosing the correct site style is important, but so is the type of copy and layout that you use within it, as they will influence the way in which a visitor behaves on your site. The different aspects will all intermingle with each other as well, which means that you must be careful how you approach those different aspects. For example, if you have an authority website that is designed poorly and looks amateur, you will never gain any trust from your visitors as your site lacks authority. On the other hand, a personal experience website that has been designed by a pro will not convey the same personal touch that a more amateur looking website would. Therefore, you must decide on the type of website that you need in order to be able to piece together effectively all its constituent parts.

You must understand the different types of visitor that may visit your website and you must also ensure that your site is catering for them in the correct manner. Don't be overly worried about this yet, however – after all, that is what a large proportion of this book is dedicated to!

You need to decide what style of website will work best for your chosen niche and of course will be the best for you in the long term. Take time out to have a good look at other websites in your chosen niche and determine in each case which style has been employed. Could you use a different style, such as an authority site, to make a better impression on visitors to the site?

Are you engaging with the visitor and creating trust? Regardless of the type of website that you have, the visitors must trust you if they are to complete the conversion. Make sure that both the layout of your site and the copy are geared towards this and that it is consistent – i.e. authority sites should look professional, personal experience sites can look more amateur etc.

By this stage you should know – and need to know – who your visitors are and which different groups of visitors may visit your website so that, as you work through this book, you can adapt the teachings to suit your own website's needs and conversion goals.

As with choosing a niche, you should take time to plan your actual website design and structure. Rushing to get your affiliate website online and then having to make structural and design changes a couple of months down the line could very well result in a penalty from search engines such as Google.

## Choosing Wordpress Themes

As I said back in an earlier chapter, although Wordpress is completely free, in its natural state using its default basic theme, it is fair to say it looks a little naff. Take a look here to see exactly what a fresh install of Wordpress looks like – http://wordpress.org/extend/themes/default. Most people are, to say the least, a little underwhelmed when they see a standard Wordpress install. The good news is, however, that Wordpress is highly customizable, and there are literally hundreds of thousands of free and commercial themes available that can give your Wordpress install a professional look. Take a look here at some great Wordpress themes and note how Wordpress has been transformed to give a professional appearance - http://www.topdesignmag.com/top-100-most-beautiful-wordpress-themes/.

Even quality Wordpress themes only cost around $30, which in my opinion is an investment you must make. I strongly advise you to visit themeforest.net and search through the thousands of themes available to find a professional looking theme that you feel would be ideal for your niche. Remember that it is essential that the theme you choose has a sidebar either on the left or right, as you will be using this area of the theme for navigation. Also remember your affiliate site must have multi Wordpress installs to aid SEO. If you are going to use different themes for each section, you will have to "mod" the header and sidebars of each theme, although you can hire the services of a decent Wordpress coder from Elance. Some of the themes you will find listed for sale at Theme Forest actually have the option to change the general layout, so you may well find that buying such a theme is ideal for all your Wordpress installs. The theme(s) you choose, however, depend on your chosen niche and your actual proposed site style, so at the end of the day the choice of theme is down to you.

Choosing Wordpress themes is another area that you should not rush. Hastily choosing a theme, only to find out a month or so later that the theme is not suitable could prove to be a major setback in the development of your affiliate website. Before buying a theme, take the time to contact the theme developer with any questions or concerns you may have. All themes listed for sale at Theme Forest have user feedback. Take the time to read the buyers' feedback in full and beware of negative feedback.

When you have purchased your theme(s), simply follow the Wordpress install action plan, which you will find at the end of this book, to ensure that you install Wordpress in the correct manner with optimized settings together with all the plug-ins you require.

# Chapter 8 – Conversion Techniques

## Introduction To Conversions

Many affiliate webmasters simply do not apply good conversion strategy to their websites. I would say that conversion techniques are the most important techniques that you require. In real terms it is easy in the long term to generate visitors to your website, but converting even a steady stream of daily traffic is not so easy.

### *What Exactly is a Conversion?*

A conversion can be defined as:

"The percentage of people visiting your site who go on to perform a specific action while they are on the site, or after they have left it."

The most important part in the above quote is without doubt "specific action". You will possibly have expected it to say "sale" instead, but many affiliate websites are looking for goals other than sales, such as visitors inputting their email, visiting a specific page or even downloading a PDF brochure. So it is important to remember that a "conversion" is not always a sale – it can be a whole range of different actions performed by the visitor.

One very important thing to keep in mind is that visitors decide *when* they leave your site, but it is for you to decide *why* this happens. It is down to you to provide the information that someone needs in order to stay on your site, and it is down to you to ensure that your site is intuitive and easy to navigate. For this reason, it is important to understand why visitors are leaving and then to rectify this – this is the core of conversion optimization.

### *Understanding Conversion Goals*

To understand why people leave your site and to ensure that they have the best possible chance of completing the desired goal, it is essential that you understand exactly what your conversion goals are. So how do you do this? Well, take a look at your site and decide what exactly it is there for. Are you trying to gain sales as an affiliate? Are you trying to encourage people to sign up to a newsletter? Are you trying to provide information that will peak the visitors' interest and get them to go ahead and buy the product that they are researching?

If you are still unclear about what your conversion goals are, take a look at the way that your website is designed to make you money. After all, the vast majority of websites out there are designed to make their owner richer, regardless of whether it is Amazon or a small affiliate site promoting lawnmowers, treadmills or even computers.

For your affiliate website you should of course have conversion goals of getting people to click on the link taking them through to merchant websites, where they then need to complete a specific action in order for the affiliate site to make its commission. So identifying the exact way in which a website helps you to make money is important when establishing your conversion goals.

Although I don't want to confuse you, it is important to remember that a site can have more than one conversion goal, so you need to understand each of them individually. I have already covered how you go about making it easy for your visitors to be 'funnelled' into your conversion goals. The first conversion goal might be to get the visitor to navigate to a specific page on your affiliate site, and to use this first page to visit another page on the site, before then using this second page to navigate to the merchant site. As can be seen, we already have three different conversion goals, all of which follow one after the other.

The three goals above all lead up to the fourth, and final, conversion goal, which is to get the visitor to complete the desired action on the website he has been sent to, whether this is buying a product, signing up to a newsletter or downloading a free piece of information. So that is four conversion goals, all of which are linked to one action completed by the visitor. This means that you need to look at your website and understand the process by which people end up at the final action. Once you are clear about the process, you can break it down into goals that you can work on.

### *The Importance of Conversions*

As this whole chapter is dedicated to introducing conversions, you will assume that conversions are extremely important, and in this assumption you would be completely correct! Conversions are the way in which you can measure how successful your site is in terms of both how much money you are making and how many visitors you are getting. Web traffic is neither easy nor cheap to come by, so you want to ensure that you are making the most of the traffic that you do generate. Think about it; even organic (traffic from search engines) traffic has been paid for with your time and effort, so it would be a terrible mistake to let this time and effort go to waste. To ensure that it doesn't, you must optimize your conversion rate, so as to get as much of this hard-earned traffic through to the ultimate conversion goal as possible – a process that will reward you with increased amounts of commission and profit.

One thing to remember is that a tiny increase in your conversion rates can have a massive impact on the amount of money that you earn. Just take a look at the example below.

For this example we are going to look at a website before and after optimization. Let's assume that the website is currently working on a poor conversion rate of 1/200. This means that one sale is generated from every 200 visitors.  For the sake of this example, let's say the average order is worth $20 in commission and the website generates 10,000 visitors every month. Just by doing some simple maths, we see that this site should generate 50 sales each month (10,000 divided by 200) which in turn would generate monthly revenue of  $1000 (50 x $20) and annual revenue of $12,000 (12 x $1000).

Now imagine this site was able to optimize its conversion rate to four sales being generated from every 200 visitors, which is one sale from every 50 visitors. With the site's 10,000 monthly visitors, this would have the effect of 200 sales being made each month, giving monthly revenue of $4000 (200 x $20) and annual revenue of $48,000 (12 x $4000)

Just by looking at the example above you can see how important it is to work on your conversion rates, even if they only go up by a small amount. A small increase in conversion rates will lead to a healthy increase in profit. Surprisingly, many affiliates neglect conversion optimization, believing that to increase their earnings they simply need to generate more traffic, which of course is a big mistake.

## *Optimization Variables*

As with every other business, common sense does play a large role, but often you will also find that the best ways of doing things aren't always the most logical or the most obvious methods. This means that common sense has a place, but it is not the only factor in optimizing your site. Just remember that what you like and respond to is not always the same as what 99% of the world likes and responds to. As importantly, your liking or dislike for something might not dictate the way in which you act after seeing it. To optimize your conversions fully you must be able to put aside any preconceived notions of what looks good, what is right, what is wrong and what is effective, and be prepared to make changes to a site that you don't necessarily like much.

There are a huge number of different variables when it comes to setting up different websites. These include the quality of traffic, the type of traffic, the layout of the website and the action being promoted. Just because something works on one of your sites, it might not necessarily work on the new one you are creating. In fact, even if your two websites are targeting a similar market, you might get massively different results. This means that the only way that you can judge the impact that a change has had on the site is to perform a split-test, as the effects of a change you personally liked – and that you believed was simply common sense – might not have a good impact on the way others use your site.

## *Summary of Conversion Principles*

So, let's go through a brief summary of this section, starting with the highly important point that *you* control how visitors use your site. This means that the responsibility falls firmly on your shoulders when trying to get them through to a conversion goal. You must first decide what your conversion goals are, and then you must take action to make changes that will improve the number of conversions that you get.

When making these changes to your site, it is imperative that you split test any changes, as this is the only way in which you can judge how well a change has worked. Split-tests can be completed using specialist software, but it is also possible to do it simply by analyzing figures yourself, which is undoubtedly the cheaper option. Whatever method you choose, the important thing to understand is how your website was performing before the change, and how it is performing after it. Only by learning this can you know if a change is beneficial.

One important thing to mention quickly about split testing is that you should only ever change one thing at a time. If you rush in and make 10 different changes, conduct a split test and find out that, for example, your site has higher conversion rates, you won't know which change had the biggest effect! In fact, it might be the case that one change had a huge effect, and that the other nine are actually hampering it. Be patient – change one thing at a time. Don't worry too much about split-testing at the moment however, as we will be going over it in detail.

Before starting any form of conversion optimization on your site:

- Work out your current conversion rate.
- Work out the profit you are making on your site.
- Work out how much more money you would make if your conversions went up by just 1%.

# Understanding Different Visitor Types

This section helps you to understand In a nutshell exactly who your visitors are and, consequently, how you can offer them exactly what they want in a bid to ensure that your conversion rate is as high as possible. This is incredibly important because if your website

105

is not giving the visitor what they need, you will be facing an uphill battle to get a good conversion rate. Therefore, this is the first step in making sure that your website is getting the maximum results possible.

It is generally accepted that there are four different types of visitor who are likely to come to your website. These are:

- **The Cautious Information Seeker.** Generally speaking, this type of visitor is not likely to make a purchase straight away. They are still in the process of researching the different options open to them and therefore deciding what the best purchase would be for their own personal circumstances. On top of this, they are cautious, meaning that they want to see lots of information and be given a lot of reassurance that what they are researching is a good deal and the best option for them. To ensure that your website is effective for this type of visitor, you must make sure that you are providing as much information as possible and pre-empting any questions that they have, answering them with detailed responses on your site.

- **The Busy Information Seeker.** Just like the above category, these people are also not ready to make a purchase. The difference is, however, that they do not have the time to commit to as much research as the cautious information seeker. Therefore the information that you provide must be easy to access and to the point. Essentially they want to see as much information as possible, but in a form that is easy to read and digest. This means that you should consider things such as bullet points and short paragraphs for this type of visitor.

- **The Cautious Buyer.** This is the next step up from the cautious information seeker, as they have moved up to the next level and are now ready to make a purchase. They are not looking to commit quickly to a purchase, however, – they want to be reassured every step of the way and told that the decision that they are making is correct. You can appeal to them with testimonials and reassuring quotes about security and by pointing out how reliable the order process is. Most importantly, they need to be constantly reminded about why they are making a purchase and how it will make their lives better.

- **The Busy Buyer.** These people want to make a purchase and they want to make one quickly, because they are busy and do not have the time for a long sales process. This means that you need a streamlined order process and an intuitive site, so that they can complete the conversion as quickly as possible. If they find that the process takes too long, they could well click away and buy from a different site.

You will notice that I have used words like "buy" and "purchase" in the above descriptions, but these can obviously be substituted for other conversion goals. I have used these words because they are the most common conversion goals, but you could be looking for email signups or subscribers, for example. This means that the first two categories would stay the same, but the second two would change to "cautious subscribers" and "busy subscribers", for example.

So, the basic rule is that you need to understand the different nuances of the four different types of visitor described, You also need to look at what you are promoting and understand exactly what it is, the competitiveness of the price and whether it is a purchase that someone would make impulsively or not. Another important action to take is to look at the source of your traffic, and in particular the keywords that they are using to access your site. If you are getting a large number of visitors coming to your site after typing in search terms containing "buy" or "purchase", the chances are that you are attracting either cautious or busy buyers. Conversely, if the search terms contain words like "review" and "compare", you are probably getting the information seekers. Although you will get a mix of both, it is important that you understand to which type the majority of your visitors belong, while at the same time ensuring that your site caters for all the different types. So how can we do that? Below is a rundown for each of the four different types of visitors.

- *The Cautious Information Seeker.* The most important fact to remember about the cautious information seekers is that they crave information, so ensure that your site has lots of it. It is essential that you understand how information should be presented so that you appeal to the cautious information seeker and the busy information seeker at the same time.

- *The Busy Information Seeker.* The busy information seekers want information as well, but they want it in a way that can be read easily and quickly, such as in bullet points, short paragraphs, lists and easy to find links. If you ensure that you include as much information as possible, but make sure that all of it is easy to read and digest, you will be able to appeal to both sets of information seekers.

- *The Cautious Buyer.* The cautious buyers, as already stated, need lots of reassurance. This means that your buying process (or other process) needs to include reminders of why they are buying plus reassurance in the form of buyer testimonials. Don't clog the process up, however, with too much reassurance, as this will put off the next set of visitors.

- **The Busy Buyer.** Too much reassurance in the process will cause the busy buyer to become frustrated, so you need to make the process quick and easy, but with options to receive reassurance if needed. The busy buyer can then bypass these reassurances, but the cautious buyer can use them as extra motivation and encouragement.

It is important to understand all these different types of visitor as you will be making changes and learning techniques that apply to each of these different types. We shall go through lots of different ways of making these visitors more likely to reach the conversion goals on your site, such as navigation paths and order processes, in order to make your site a more profitable one. For the moment however, just make sure that you are aware of the different types of visitor and the type of visitor that your site is most likely to receive.

## The CBDM Model

CBDM stands for the **C**onsumer **B**uying **D**ecision-**M**aking Process, and is the thought process that most people go through before they make a purchase of any kind. Therefore it is extremely important that you are familiar with it if you want to maximize the effectiveness of your site. If you understand the process, you can adapt it to fit your own individual needs on your website, and therefore see your conversion rates increase.

In this section we are going to look at all the aspects of the CBDM model, all the way from the initial stage visitors are at when they navigate to your website, through to the stage whereby they complete the action that you want them to. So, let's look at the CBDM process in a bit more detail…

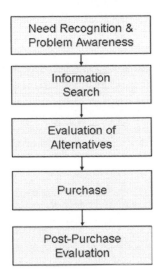

The above graphic shows the process that people go through when they make a purchase. You will notice that the initial stage is called "Need Recognition". This is basically the stage at which an individual decides that they either need or want something, even if they don't know exactly what the product is yet. For example, someone might decide that they need to remove a stain from the carpet, but at present they don't know what they need to do this. The seed has, however, been planted in their mind.

The next stage is that of the "Information Search", which is when the individual starts to research the products that are available for them to purchase. This initial research will form the foundation of any future actions that they take on the specific products that they read about.

After this comes the "Evaluation of Alternatives", which essentially means that they now turn their attention to looking at the different types of product out there and work out which one best suits their individual needs. This leads to a decision and therefore to the "Purchase" stage, where they buy the product that they have decided is the best for them.

The final stage is the "Post-Purchase Evaluation" stage, which is the stage where the buyer looks at the product they have bought. They now consider whether it was good value for money, whether it fulfilled their needs and, most importantly, whether they would make the same purchase again. They also consider whether they need additional products to go with the one they have just bought, such as cloths to go with cleaning products or game controllers to go with a new video game.

I am sure that you will almost certainly relate to this process as you read it through. It can be applied to absolutely every purchase, from massive purchases like a new car through to a simple decision such as where to place an online bet for the 3.30 at Kempton, even if the process is more elongated for the former of the two. Different people will spend a different amount of time on the different aspects of the CBDM model, but they will always be there, even if they only take a second or two.

## *At What Stage Does Your Site Enter?*

This is perhaps the most important question that you can ask yourself and the answer that you come up with could be at absolutely any point in the process, depending on the type of site that you have. Other factors that will influence your position include where your traffic comes from, what keywords they use (are they "buy" or "review" keywords?), whether your site is actually selling a product and a number of other factors as well. So you must look at your website and decipher exactly where visitors are in the CBDM process when they visit your site. Granted, you will probably be getting traffic from all the stages, but one section will dominate, and this is the section that you need to identify.

Your primary source for understanding exactly where the visitors to your site are in the CBDM process are the keywords that they use. Let's take the subject of home renovation for this example, and more specifically how to put up a new door. The first thing they do is type a phrase such as "how to put up door" or "installing new door" into their search engine – meaning that they have identified a need and are at the "Need Recognition" stage of the process. If your traffic comes from this sort of search term, you are coming in right at the beginning of the process.

Once they have completed their initial queries, they will most likely move onto looking for specific products that they will need, such as a pair of hinges – which is the "Information Search" stage. At this stage they might type in queries such as "best hinges" or "gold coloured hinges" into the search engine, as they try to find information on the best choice that they could make for their needs.

Moving on, once they have researched information about the different options open to them, they start to form opinions and begin settling on their preferred choice. At this stage they will decide that they should see if there are any alternatives to the product that they have found – alternatives that could be cheaper or more effective, or indeed both. So they could type in "hinges comparisons" or "alternatives to hinges" to find the info that they need, and if they come to your site with these, you are at the "Evaluation of Alternatives" stage.

Once they have looked at all the possible options and compared the different products on offer to them, they will come to a decision and make a purchase – meaning that they are at the "Purchase" stage of the model. They type in something like "buy hinges", "cheap hinges" or simply just "hinges" into the search engine and, from there, go onto a site and make the purchase. If you have people coming to your site at this stage, then you are possibly at the most lucrative point of the CBDM model!

The final stage is the "Post-Purchase Evaluation", and this is the stage where people will come back online after they have bought the product and look for additional items to go with it. It is possible at this stage for people to go all the way back to the beginning of the process and start looking for their accessories from scratch, or they could simply go back to the same site they were on and buy the extra items that they need.

The previous few paragraphs show you how to use keywords to evaluate where your visitors are in the CBDM process. This means that you can look at what the majority of people are searching for when they navigate onto your site and determine where you are in the process as a whole.

### The Need Recognition Stage

When you go through the above process, you will find that the vast majority of people are at the "Need Recognition" stage. For keywords, you will probably find the greatest traffic available at this stage. If you think about it logically, those at the need recognition stage will have a massive number of different paths they can go down. For example, one person could start looking at hinges, while another might look at tools and another could look for actual doors themselves. For each of these specific paths, they will head to the "Information Search" section of the model, where they will narrow down their search even more. This will continue until they reach the final aspect of the CBDM process, where the search will have narrowed to a fraction of that at the "Need Recognition" stage.

This means that the process is essentially a funnel that points downwards. When you factor in competition and search volumes, you can see that "Need Recognition" is the stage that has the largest search volume, but also the greatest competition. As you head down the funnel, the number of searches decreases, but so does the competition. Therefore, the bottom of the funnel has a small amount of competition, but also only a fraction of the search volume associated with the Need Recognition stage.

So let's put what you have just learnt into an easy to understand example. I am sure you are getting bored with the exciting world of hinges, so let's charge it up and imagine that a visitor is exploring the possibility of going to the theatre. At the Need Recognition stage, there will be loads of people searching for a term like "theatre" or "theatre tickets". If, however, you want people to buy specifically *Les Miserables* tickets for London theatres, you will find that only a small percentage of those searching will follow the funnel to your specific niche – the vast majority will be in different locations or want to see different shows. It is, therefore, imperative to target your content, as well as the traffic that you want to attract.

If you are getting lots of people entering your site at the Need Recognition stage, you need to ensure that you provide them with not just the information for this stage, but also enough information to fulfil their needs within the Information Search stage, the Evaluation of Alternatives stage and then finally lead them to a stage where they can purchase the item. You could even try to entice them back by including attractive options for the Post-Purchase Evaluation stage as well.

Everything above is basically a detailed way of saying you should target the content of your website. Many online affiliates understand about targeting the traffic they generate, but only a handful ever considers targeting the pages that this traffic lands on. If you do this, you can ensure that people at different stages of the CBDM process land at different parts of the site, meaning that they will find the information that they need and your site can cater for the needs of everyone searching.

## *How Your CBDM Model Will Affect Conversions*

If you don't understand where your visitors are in the CBDM process, you will not be able to provide them with the information that they need in order to go through to the purchase stage – the stage at which you will earn your money. If you are getting a significant amount of traffic from the Need Recognition stage, for example, make sure that you spend most of your time catering for their needs, so that they have the best chance possible of progressing through the CBDM purchase and ending up purchasing something.

This is not about taking your site as a whole and working out the strategy, however – you should be looking at every single page and understanding where the traffic is coming from, as different pages could be at different levels of the CBDM process. Your pages are essentially visual representations of the funnel, so one could be a page with information for Need Recognition, which then links to a page for those at the Information Search stage, and so on. Therefore, you should evaluate your pages and make sure that they serve the purpose they are needed for, or at least provide the chance for someone to move onto another page.

We saw above that the higher you are in the CBDM process, the more searches there will be, as well as the more competition, while lower down the funnel there will be fewer searches and less competition. This is true but you must also remember that the bottom of the funnel will much more targeted, and therefore you will need to think carefully about your strategy, based on factors such as your site style, niche and conversion goals. There is no correct or incorrect way of doing this – you just have to make sure that you cater to what the visitors need and what will make you the most money!

### CBDM Model Summary

Before moving onto the next section, let us look at the main points of the CBDM model.

- Knowing exactly where your traffic is in the CBDM process is vital, as this will allow you to tailor your site to the visitors' needs and ensure that they move down the sales funnel towards their purchase.
- Either an individual page or an entire site can take someone from the Need Recognition stage through to the Purchase stage – it is all about the way the information is presented and how easy it is for the visitor to access and understand.
- Look at the keywords people use to get to your site and ensure that you provide information that is relevant to the keywords that they use. When you have done this, you can begin to send them down the sales funnel, via other pages or through the same page.

## Understanding The AIDA Model

If you have ever moved in marketing circles, you will undoubtedly be aware of the AIDA model. For those that are not familiar with it, this section goes over what it means and why it is vital to your strategy when looking to optimize your conversion rate. By this stage in the book you should have created a solid base for the creation of content for your website. It might not be the most interesting aspect of affiliate marketing, but it is essential, much as how the foundations of a house are unglamorous yet integral to the overall operation. By the end of this book you will know how to get people to spend their money on your site on a regular basis, so keep reading – remember the skills you are learning are only the start of something that will change the way that you work online forever!

## What Is The AIDA Model?

AIDA is an acronym that stands for:

- **A**ttention:
- **I**nterest
- **D**esire
- **A**ction

Generally speaking your website will need to fulfil all four in order to make sales; that is, it must grab visitors' attention, before making them interested and peaking their desire, which will all in turn lead to the visitor taking action. The action could be the purchase of a product, the inputting of an email address or one of many other possible outcomes.

So how can all these areas be catered for? Giving the visitor something that catches their eye – a catchy headline, a pertinent point or even an effective image, creates **attention**. Once they have had their attention brought to the subject, you will then need to create **interest** by giving them information that is relevant and targeted towards their specific need – always ensuring that the information is delivered in a way to which they are susceptible (think back to the four types of visitor). When they are interested, you must make them actually want to make a purchase or input their details – essentially create a **desire** – which can be done by advertising the benefits and providing reassurance. The final stage – **action** – is a culmination of the efforts put into the first three stages and is where you hope that they earn you the commission that you have set out to earn!

### *Why The AIDA Model Is So Important*

Regardless of the conversion goal that you have – whether this is a lead, a sale or even just a click-through to a different site – the AIDA model is completely relevant to the way in which you work. This is due to the simple fact that gaining a conversion means that you absolutely must catch someone's attention, provide them with information, and make them want the product or service that you are offering and then provide them with the means to act on the desire that you have instilled in them. Just like the CBDM model and the four visitor types that you should now know about, you must understand this critical piece of marketing information.

The AIDA model isn't just something that you need to implement in general over the entirety of your website, however – it is a technique that you must use for every single page individually, particularly your sales landing page. Let's just consider why this is, using the landing page as an example. If people are going to see this page first, they must have their attention grabbed straight away, as otherwise they won't continue reading. Once their attention has been gained, they need to get information quickly and easily – and it must interest them, so that they don't move away to other pages and links in their search. The same goes for desire, as you are now on a roll and don't want them to get bored as they search your site for reasons to want what you offer! Then you should always have an option to make a purchase or complete an action clearly visible to them – without this all the previous work will have been wasted! This means that you control how people see your site and the emotions that they feel. We will look at the techniques you can use to do this as we progress through this chapter.

Although I said that the AIDA model should be used on every single page individually, it must also be in place across the website as a whole. Combining the two is usually the most effective method to use – just look at some of the most successful affiliate websites out there to see exactly how they do it!

## AIDA Model - Attention

As it is the first in the series of events, the logical place to start is with Attention. It is generally accepted in the internet world that a site has just seven seconds to grab the attention of a visitor, so it is important to create content and an overall site that instantly appeals to them. Obviously visitors differ – some will click away after two to three seconds, others will be more patient – but seven seconds is the average that you should work on.

So let's jump straight into the practical side of how you can grab a visitor's attention. There are five common tactics that you can use, which are listed below…

- *Page Load Time.* The seven-second rule encompasses the page load time, so if your site takes two seconds to load up, you then only have five seconds to grab the attention with your content! This means that making your page load quickly is vital, especially since it will also have a massive effect on your SEO operations, so it should be high on your list of priorities.

- *Animated Graphics.* Moving images automatically catch the attention of a visitor, meaning that they don't have to scan the page in order to find the vital section that will get their attention in the first place. Perhaps this could be a banner that scrolls through the benefits that a product has, or it could even just be a simple animation that shows one main feature. On the whole you should avoid flash graphics as some of your users will be unable to view them including of course the millions of

Apple Ipad users. Opt for simple animated gif graphics, which you can of course have designed by running a contest on Digital Point.

- **Use Text Intelligently.** Although most of a website is made up of text, it can still be used extremely well to create attention. This is most often seen in the main title of the page, which should be placed in a larger font than the rest of the text and also in a colour that stands out from both the background and the rest of the content. Remember that what you like might not always be the most effective – contrasting colours aren't always pretty, but they certainly catch the eye!

- **Make Your Copy Easy to Read.** People generally love copy (copy is the word used for any written or verbal set of words used to sell something) that they can skim over quickly to gain all they need to know, which is why many sites use bullet points to get visitors' attention. Also, the information should be at the top of the page – or "above the fold", as many in online marketing prefer to say. By this I mean that it should be visible without visitors having to scroll down to find it. Set your monitor to the smallest resolution commonly used – 800x600 – to see if your site is complying with this. If it isn't, perhaps try reducing the size of the header or removing any unnecessary clutter, as this will give you more space for the all-important content.

- **Create Great Copy.** Even if your website employs all of the above tactics, having poor copy or copy that doesn't make the visitor want to read it will cause them to leave as quickly as they came. To do this you need to use powerful language – language that grabs their attention because of the things that it says. At the same time however, the content must be believable, as otherwise their attention will be caught for entirely the wrong reasons.

Essentially your remit within the first seven seconds of a person's visit to your site is to make them want to spend their next few minutes further investigating what you have to offer. Most people value their time highly and therefore they are loath to commit to spending it unless they are sure that it will benefit them. If you manage to convince them that your site is worth a few minutes of their life, you have successfully managed to pass the attention section of the AIDA model.

## AIDA Model - Generating Interest

For this section, let's start with a quick question. Which of the following sentences is more interesting?

*"We sell apples and they taste really nice. See why our customers say our apples are the best in the world and why we are so good."*

OR

*"We can provide you with some of the highest quality apples in the country. With the finest taste and the perfect crunch, it's no coincidence our customers always come back for more, and you will too!"*

I hope that you agree that the second one is far more interesting than the first. They both say pretty much the same thing, but the second is written in such a way that it creates more interest within the reader. Why is this?

- *It's Believable.* People know when they are being lied to. Having "some of the highest quality apples in the country" is something people will believe; whereas saying that "our apples are the best in the world" is not. Have you seriously tried every single apple the world has to offer? Lying destroys trust and makes people lose interest in any other claims that you make, regardless of whether they are true.

- *It Uses Focused Language.* The best example of this is the fact that the second statement uses the word "you" twice, while the first doesn't use it at all. This means that the quote appeals directly to the reader and is therefore likely to get their interest quickly.

- *It's Specific.* Instead of just saying the apples are "nice", it says that they have a "perfect crunch". General statements don't inspire interest; specific statements about different aspects do.

Another thing to consider is the amount that you talk about yourself, as customers really do not care about the business side of your site. All they want to know is information that is relevant to them, such as the product that they will get and how much it will cost. Talking too much about yourself will push the customers away, because they won't feel valued by your site and will go somewhere where their slightly selfish needs are met. This shouldn't be a problem for a good writer though – there is always a way to make a point about you into a point about the customer. It's just a matter of thinking about how you say something, and not just about what you say.

So, here's a brief list of the things to do to create interest on your site:

- Use the word "you" as much as possible.
- Don't make outlandish claims – stick to the truth.
- Don't be vague. Tell the visitor about the exact benefits.
- Keep the copy relevant.
- Keep paragraphs short and snappy.
- Use interesting and relevant sub-headings.
- Use the top of the page to inform the reader exactly what the rest of the site is going to tell them, thereby giving them an incentive to keep reading.

## AIDA Model – Generating Desire

If you have managed to encompass all the teachings from the last section into your site, then you will almost certainly have given people the push they need to move onto the stage where they start to desire the service or product that you are promoting.

Much in the same vein as the last section, let's take a look at two different quotes. Which do you think sounds best?

*"The computer is fast and it has a good graphics card for gaming."*

OR

*"This computer takes you from 0-60 in a matter of seconds, making it the Ferrari of the desktop world. When this is combined with the powerful and advanced graphics card, there is no better computer for your gaming needs."*

I hope you've chosen the second quote again, for a large number of different reasons. It is more specific to the needs of the visitor, the language is exciting and it allows the reader to imagine just what the computer could do for them.

As in the previous section, "you" is used in the quote, as this once again makes the quote personal to the person reading it, therefore prompting the visitor's mind to imagine actually using it and the benefits it will give. No longer is it a computer that happens to be good for games. It's now a specific gaming computer that YOU can use to make your gaming experience infinitely better than before.

By making the readers think about themselves in relation to the product or service, you are instilling a sense of desire within them. The basic point is that the more creative you are in the way that you write on your site, the more you can connect with the reader on an emotional level. Connecting emotionally is the absolute key to making someone want something, so really think about the way that you word everything on your site.

So, here is a list of ways that you can create desire in those visiting your site.

- Use "you" so as to focus the attention on the readers and make them feel that the benefits are specifically targeted towards them.
- Use sensory language to engage with their emotions and make them feel that they really want what you are offering.
- Make them think they are missing out on something big. This is achieved by telling them about all the massive benefits they would gain from whatever you are promoting.
- Make sure it stays believable; otherwise they will know that you are lying to them.
- Testimonials are also great tools to use, as they provide proof to the reader that the service or product really does work and makes them think "I want to be as successful as those guys". Being part of a successful group is something that everyone aspires to, so by including testimonials you are effectively providing them with the chance to become a member of an exclusive circle.

The desire stage is very important, mainly because you have already committed so much hard work in getting the visitors to get this far in the first place. If you don't get this stage exactly right, your previous hard work will be wasted. So, follow the instructions above and make people want what you are promoting!

### AIDA Model - Time For Action!
So how do we get people to take action on the desire that we have created? Well, first and foremost you are going to need a link to the page where they can complete the action that you want them to. There are two types of links that you can use – text and pictures – but which one is better?

Really this question is a bit of a trick because the honest answer is that they are both as good as each other. Everyone is different; some people prefer a text link, while others like to click on a picture instead. Instead of putting all of your eggs in one basket, you must appeal to both types of people, and this means including a number of text links and image links (banners) within your site. In this way a visitor always has the chance to click on the link that they prefer to use.

There are a number of different ways in which you can encourage the visitor to your site to go through with the final action, with the first of these being a technique that creates urgency in the mind of the reader. This is a technique that is commonly used throughout the internet – even by some of the world's biggest sites – and makes the visitors think that they have to take action as soon as possible, as otherwise they might miss out. Ways of doing this include offering discount codes only valid for a day, warnings that stock is low and saying that the product will be discontinued soon. Amazon frequently lists stock levels, especially products with low stock levels, to create urgency. Always ensure that the statements you make are believable, as otherwise people will see through them and lose trust in your site, resulting in you losing a sale.

The next method to use is that of reassurance, because even when the visitor has clicked the "buy now" button and been navigated to the payment page, they will more than likely still have lingering doubts in their mind. Until they have clicked on the button that finalizes their order, there is always the possibility that they might change their minds, so you need to make sure that there are reminders of how good the purchase is, as well as reassurances about the safety of the purchase, all the way to that final click. Even if you are an affiliate website that takes people to a completely different site to process the order, you will need to provide reassurance up until they click off your page – then the other site has the responsibility of getting them to continue with the process. Customer testimonials are a great way to reassure potential buyers and get them to click your links that lead to merchant sites.

Another area that ties in with reassurance is that of recommendations, as people need a clear guide as to what product they should be buying above all others. This is especially true when it comes to products that offer many different options. If you are not pushing people towards one distinct option, you are not optimizing your conversions. Be careful however; don't be too pushy. Instead, perhaps make a list of the pros and cons of the different options, or tell the visitor which one you think is the best value for money. Doing it this way means that you can subtly place the emphasis on the option that you want them to choose, without looking as though you are not working in their best interests.

Once again with the above point, realism is the primary consideration. Don't always recommend the most expensive, as generally people won't need a year-long subscription to something or every single accessory added to their new laptop. Instead, it often works best to recommend a middle of the road product – one that doesn't cost huge amounts but still does the job. By doing this you will create trust – trust that is transferred into sales.

Finally, you should go back to the angle of creating urgency again, just in case the visitor has forgotten about this and is thinking about taking some more time to think about the purchase. Having these messages of urgency next to the pay button will prompt them to continue, especially as they have already come so far in the process. The fear of missing out due to indecisiveness can be a strong emotion and you can use this to get people to complete their order. A link to a merchant product with the anchor text "One Day Special Offer", "Buy Now Limited Stock" or "Buy Today Exclusive Discount" creates urgency and is far better than using simply "Buy Now".

This stage of the process is without doubt the most critical, as you need people to make purchases if you are going to make any money whatsoever. This means that you must make the action part of the AIDA process as easy as possible for people to complete. If you place barriers in front of them and don't provide the necessary impetus for them to complete their order, they will probably leave before spending their money. The Cautious Buyers mentioned earlier won't like the fact that there is no reassurance, while the Busy Buyers will be put off because they can't complete the order quickly because of the barriers. Make sure that you get this part of the process perfectly right, as if you do, most people will continue ordering instead of dropping out.

### *AIDA Model Summary*

Regardless of the goals you have set yourself, the AIDA model is relevant to you. Every single page should follow this model, as should the site as a whole. You should aim to move people through Attention, Interest, Desire and Action, all the way until they click on the "Buy" button and earn you commission.

Remember, you are the one who controls this process  - not the visitors. You can provide as much attention and information as you want, and create as much desire as needed, as well as an easy way to complete the action. Conversely, your decisions can cause your website to have a small amount of info, or a poor layout that doesn't inspire a reader to continue reading. Taking some time to think about the different sections of your website and work out where they fit in the AIDA model is very important – a little time doing this could save a huge number of missed opportunities in the future.

# Chapter 9 - Copywriting Techniques

Anybody can write an article, but writing an article that gets the reader to click the "buy now" button is another skill, which you as an online affiliate will have to learn. In this chapter we will take a look at:

- How to use the benefits of a product, not just its features, to make a sale.
- How to engage people's emotions when writing copy for the web.
- What kinds of feeling your choice of words can elicit from someone.
- 15 different questions that you can ask yourself as you are writing, and after you have finished writing, all with the aim of increasing the amount of conversions you get to their optimum level.
- How to use the hook, line and sinker approach to get conversions.

You simply need to learn tried and trusted techniques that will enable you to write copy that is powerful and gains high conversion rates, regardless of the niche in which your website is working. To start, let me guide you through the basics of features and benefits.

## Understanding Features vs. Benefits

### *Understanding the Difference*
Before we look at anything else, we need to ensure that we know the difference between a feature and a benefit. It would be a massive mistake to think that they are the same thing, but unfortunately many online affiliates writing copy for their sites make this very mistake all too often. We shall go over all this in more detail later, but at the moment you need to remember this:

**People convert based on the benefits, not the features.**

When you first look at why people make a purchase, you might assume that it is due to a certain feature, but this is not the case. They are buying because the feature gives them a certain benefit, whether this is a conscious or subconscious decision.

Obviously, when we are writing copy, we want to mention the features of a product, but you must remember to take every opportunity to stress the benefits that the features will

122

have for the visitor. Remember, whenever you mention a feature, the first thing that the visitor is going to ask is, "Okay, but what impact will that feature have on me?" Whether they do it consciously or subconsciously, they want to know the benefits of the feature. This means that it is up to the person writing the copy to let the potential customers know exactly what the product or service will do for them, as otherwise they might remain confused and decide not to buy.

## *Features and Their Benefits*

The best way to look at features and benefits is to use a few examples. So, below are a few products together with one of their features and the benefit the feature brings.

- **Plasma Television**. The feature here could be that the screen is 40" wide, but the benefit would be that this 40" screen allows you to see the screen in more detail and really immerse yourself in the film or football game that you are watching.

- **Desktop Computer**. The feature could be the fact that the computer has a huge hard drive, but the benefit that this would bring to the possible buyer is that they can store thousands of their favourite songs and films on it, without having to buy an external hard drive.

You might be thinking to yourself that you don't sell products that are as interesting as televisions or computers, so how can you possibly extol the benefits of your more mundane products? Well, everything has benefits, regardless of what it is. Let's take a look at some products that people might describe as boring.

- **Bath Mat**. A feature of a bath mat could be that it has extra sticky suckers on the bottom, and the benefit here would be that they provide extra safety when in the bath, as the user won't risk slipping.

- **Ink Cartridge**. The ink cartridge could have more ink in it than regular cartridges, so the user would receive the benefit of not having to buy a new one every week.

As you can see, even the most boring of items have benefits that their features can bring to any potential customers on your site!

### *Why You Must Create Benefit-Driven Copy*

When writing copy for your website, you must make sure that it is benefit-driven copy. To accomplish this you must remember that one feature could well have multiple benefits or different benefits for different people. You should ensure that you cover all bases by remarking on the individual benefits – not the individual features – of a product. Obviously there will be some products that have so many benefits that it would be completely unproductive to list all of them. In this case it is your job as the copywriter to ascertain which benefits will appeal the most to your target audience, and make sure that they are included.

One of the best ways to ensure that you get the benefits down on your copy is always to ask yourself what a specific feature actually does. This is the same process for determining whether something is a feature or a benefit; if you aren't sure if something is a benefit or not, ask yourself whether there is a benefit arising from it. It is fine to mention your features – in fact, you should certainly do so – but never only mention them, as the benefits are the more important information. It is often easier to think of the features as an introduction to the benefits section of your site. You should also remember to make the benefits obvious to all readers. I mentioned earlier that you should assume that people visiting your site are stupid – this still applies!

### *Understanding The Difference Between Features and Benefits*

If you can learn to tell the difference between the two, then you will be well on your way to writing effective copy that converts. You must also ensure that you fully understand your product, so that you can write knowledgably about the different benefits it has – I say "benefits" because every product will have more than one! Keep it simple as well, as many visiting your site are unlikely to be as intelligent as you are.

## Why You Must Evoke Emotions

Now we are going to look at how you can use the emotions that the visitors to your site have in order to increase the conversions on your site. This is done through creating a vivid image in visitors' minds regarding how they can benefit from your product, which will then inspire them to make a purchase. If you can stir feelings inside someone, then you are edging ever closer to creating that perfect piece of copy!

### *Persuasion Needs Emotion*

To write effective copy, you need to connect with the visitor to your site on an emotional level. Just think back for a moment to Chapter Eleven, where we discussed the AIDA model – Attention, Interest, Desire and Action. When we are engaging in emotions, we are attempting to influence the Desire part of the AIDA process through effective use of the correct words and phrases. Using emotions ensures that the visitor visualizes, imagines and feels the product – something that we look at in more detail below.

## *Visualize*

So let's start with the concept of "visualize". This basically means that we have to provide the material necessary for the visitors to paint a picture in their minds of the product. To do this, we must utilize both descriptive copy and specific copy, but there is one other thing to remember too – always ensure that the image the visitors get in their minds is a realistic one. Top authors have used descriptive and specific language in some of the greatest novels ever written – which is a large part of the reason why they are so great! Let's take this sentence, for example, from one of my favourite authors, F. Scott Fitzgerald:

*"The tapestry brick of the road was smooth to the tread of the great tires as they rounded a still, moonlit lake."*

This sentence at first glance doesn't seem that important, as it tells the reader absolutely nothing about the actual storyline. What it does brilliantly, however, is allow the reader to visualize the exact scene. We know exactly what the road looks like, what the lake looks like and even how the road feels against the tires of the vehicle. By using evocative words and ensuring that even the smallest details are included, the writer has painted a picture in your mind – the exact picture that he would have wanted to paint when he was writing the book many years ago. This teaches us that we should be specific and use descriptive words in our own copy, so that we can control exactly how the readers see the product when they start visualizing it.

## *Imagine*

When you have managed to get visitors to your site to start visualizing, you can then move them onto the "Imagine" part of the process. In this part, they will move from the visualization of the product through to actually imagining themselves in the picture as well. This means that you can then start to get the emotions going and make them imagine how they would feel when they were using the product that you are trying to sell to them.

The best way to get people to imagine themselves with the product is also probably the simplest, and that is to use the word "you" liberally throughout the copy. To add further to this, you should use sensory language; language that conveys emotion in a way that is appropriate to the product. Just make sure that you keep the copy realistic – with some sensitive subjects it can be hard to persuade people, for example, to imagine themselves being more confident when they actually currently suffer from a lack of confidence.

125

How do we ensure that the copy is realistic and that the customer will therefore move into the "imagine" stage? Well, the best thing is to use small steps, which will help you to persuade the customers to include themselves in the visualization of the product. You need to think about your copy in this situation as a kind of movie script, where you are directing but the customer is the main star. As the director you can tell the lead actor/actress exactly what they see, feel, think or touch and exactly the emotions they are supposed to feel when they carry out one of these actions. If you can make them do this, then you can move onto the last stage – Experience.

## *Experience*

You have managed to get the visitors to visualize the product and then imagine themselves with it, so what is the final goal of the process? Well, it is to get the readers to feel what it is like to own and use the product before they have even clicked on the purchase button! So how do you do this? It is achieved by making their imagination run wild, which will make them want to satisfy the emotions that you have instilled in them. You should also aim to rid them of any negative thoughts that they might have regarding the product that you are offering them.

Negative thoughts can be got rid of using their imagination, because if you can get them to the stage where they want to satisfy their emotions, they will be so preoccupied that they will forget all about the negative aspects of the product. When those negative thoughts are gone, they will be in the perfect position once again to satisfy your number one criteria – a conversion!

Perhaps the masters of using the Visualize, Imagine, and Experience formula are those from the car industry, who manage to get feelings and emotions running in virtually everyone watching their adverts or even seeing one of their cars driving down the road. I don't know about you, but I've never been inside an Aston Martin, let alone driven one, but when I see one, I immediately think of style, luxury and speed. In fact, I already feel that I know what it is like to drive one, even although I have never been in one! This is what you are trying to gain with your copy; you want the visitors to think they already know what it is like to own the product before they buy it.

## *Using Sensory Words*

We have mentioned sensory words already in this chapter, and they are incredibly important when trying to write excellent copy that engages people's emotions. To make full use of them, they should appeal to all five of the human senses;  touch, taste, smell, hearing and sight. We want to make sure our copy is focused around each of these senses, so as to enhance the feeling of realism among readers and to make sure that the picture they paint is exactly the one we want them to.

Let's look at some examples of how you can engage each of the senses...

- **Touch.** Try to describe what the product actually feels like. To do this you could use words like soft, velvety, sticky or spongy.

- **Taste.** Obviously some products can't use taste – after all, not many people are found tasting cars or laptops. However, if you are going to use it for products, you should use words like sweet, sour, spicy or bitter.

- **Smell.** Smell is a much under-utilised sense among copywriters, as it is an extremely powerful way to trigger people's emotions. Some examples of words you could use are perfumed, scented and minty.

- **Hearing.** Hearing really helps to get the descriptive part of your copy across well. Some examples of effective words are thud, crash, bang and whir.

- **Sight.** Sight is an extremely broad sense to talk about. Try mentioning the size, shape and appearance of the product you are trying to sell.

Regardless of the product we are selling, we must use these different senses to get the correct picture in the mind of the person reading the copy. Let them know what the product feels like in their hands, how it sounds when it is switched on, what smells come from it and any other sensations that they will experience through their five senses.

### Create Positive Feelings

Positive feelings are obvious, as you want people to think positively about the product you are trying to sell them, as otherwise they will never buy it! The different positive feelings that people need to experience obviously differ from one product to another, but you must make sure that you make them feel what you want them to feel.

Accomplishing this goal is actually very easy. Just think of what you want them to feel – perhaps this is confidence – and then use the word "confidence" throughout your copy. Phrases such as "you can be confident that..." and "you can have the confidence to..." will reinforce the confidence that readers have in the product.

## *Summary of Using Emotions*

There are a few different things that we need to summarize here:

- You must manage to evoke emotions in those visitors to your site. This goes hand in hand with the desire stage in the AIDA model. To elicit these emotions, you must use descriptive, specific and sensory language.

- You should place the readers in a situation where they can imagine themselves actually using the product. Use the word "you" frequently to achieve this.

- Make sure that all the copy you produce is both relevant and realistic, since if you start to go off on an abstract tangent, you run the risk of boring your customers or confusing them.

Never, ever underestimate how powerful emotions are when engaged in the business of selling. Getting copy to evoke these emotions is one of the keys to unlocking the maximum amount of conversions that your site can generate. Next, we shall look at some of the best copywriting tips and also go over some questions you can answer to ensure that your site is converting as well as it should.

## Basic Copywriting Tips

Your actual copy is possibly the single most important aspect of your site, so you need to ensure that it is nigh on perfect before you can be satisfied with it. You may feel a little overwhelmed with this chapter, and it may take time to absorb all the techniques this chapter contains. Remember, however, that Rome was not built in a day. A good affiliate will refine his copy over a period of time, as should you.

Although I have just stated that copywriting is incredibly important, it is not the only thing that you should be concerned with when it comes to ensuring that your copy converts at the highest possible rate. If you do not have the structure and format of your site laid out properly, such as sales funnels in place and the other techniques we have discussed, your copywriting will ultimately be worthless. So, make sure that previous aspects mentioned in this book are correct before you move on to the copywriting side of your site.

### *Essentials You Need to Know*

Before you even start to create content, there are a few things that you must consider first. You need to know certain things about your product, information about the types of visitor you expect your site to generate, information about your own business and even certain things about yourself. When you know all of these things, you can create a pitch that is perfectly optimized to selling.

After you have understood the above, you need to move to understanding your competition as, after all, they are the ones whom you are essentially going to have to overcome for your site to be a success. To get a good comparison between your business and that of your competitors, there are three questions you must ask yourself:

- Why should a visitor buy from my site instead of another site?
- Is my product superior to that sold elsewhere, and why?
- Is the service I provide better than elsewhere, and why?


Ask yourself these questions and try to understand  exactly what it is that makes you different from the rest. More importantly, think about how you can communicate this difference to those visiting your website when they are wondering where to buy.

After this, you must think about the problem that you are helping the buyer to solve. You might well have a business that is more reliable – and a product that is better – than the competition, but if you don't solve a problem for the visitor, they will never buy. Every single product solves some kind of problem, even if that problem is simply boredom, so make sure you know how your product is going to solve a problem for a visitor.

So now we need to move on and look at who your customer actually is. This is easy to do once you know your product well, as certain people will be in the market for certain products and therefore this should not take long to figure out at all. Once you have done this, think about their gender, how much money they have, their location and how aspirational they might be. All of these factors, plus many more that you will be able to think of, help you form a good picture in your mind of the exact type of person you are selling to, and not just a vague entity.

Finally, you must understand any concerns that your customers could have when it comes to both your site and your product. For example, they could be worried about how much the product costs, or perhaps they don't believe that the product works as well as you say it does. You certainly do not want to disregard these problems – you want to face them straight on and give the customers reassurance that their concerns are unfounded. Therefore, you must understand the areas that people will be concerned about, even before they access your site.

## Basic Copywriting Formula

When you have answered all these questions, you can move on to putting your copy together. To do this, you can follow a basic formula, which I outline for you below.

It is important before we begin to emphasize that this formula is not a rigid one, and you can – and should – adapt it to suit your own exact needs. The formula is, however, a really solid foundation for you to use to begin your copywriting. You might need to write a few different pieces of copy for your site, just so that you can split test them and see which is the best in terms of conversions.

The first thing that you need to address is the "what's in it for me?" question that visitors will ask when they visit your site. You should use this initial part of the copy to address why the readers should spend the next five minutes of their lives – which is a long time for webpage viewing when you remember that people's attention on a website is usually about seven seconds – reading the copy that you have written. You should also address this question regularly throughout the rest of your copy, to keep them interested and ensure that they don't stop halfway through. This first section of your copy links back very well to the AIDA model, because you are using it to capture their attention and encourage them to read on to become more interested in your product.

Now that you have gained their attention, you need to introduce the problem that your product or service will help them to solve. This is basically the literary equivalent of hanging a carrot in front of their nose and saying, "Keep reading, because we can help you solve this problem forever!" A good way to start this is by saying "Are you sick and tired of...?"

Next you are going to justify why the product is able to solve the aforementioned problem, which you first do by introducing yourself and your product properly. You can then move on to telling the customers why they absolutely need your product – something that is different from telling them why the product solves a problem. This appeals to their emotional and social senses, rather than simply pointing out a practical application for the product.

The next stage is simply to continue with the previous one, but to change tack slightly and let the reader know exactly why your product is better than that offered by competitors.

You want to leave the reader thinking that there is nothing better for their problem than your product, as this will mean that they are more likely to turn into a conversion without going away and checking out other products first.

The final thing to do – and one of the most important – is to reassure the visitor regarding any problems that they have. Even if you have the best product in the world, they absolutely will have reservations, so it is your job to get them through these reservations and tell them once again why your product is the best, why the price is perfect, what the benefits are and why they need it in their lives. You can use things like money-back guarantees here, or testimonials from other happy customers, to help placate any fears that they might have.

Nearly every single type of product or service can be sold using the basic formula that I have just laid out for you. As already mentioned, you might have to adapt the formula slightly depending on the product or service you are selling. Don't think that just sticking to this formula is a sure fire route to success, however – this is the groundwork, but you also have to make sure that the correct format and language is used to make the whole page effective.

### *Additional Copywriting Considerations*
Below are several points that you will need to think about, both as you are writing your copy and after you have finished it.

- Have you made sure that the visitor knows exactly what you are trying to sell to him? Remember the seven-second rule from the AIDA model I detailed earlier? If the visitor cannot tell straight away what is being sold to him, the chances are that he will click off your site rather quickly, therefore scuppering your chances of a conversion. Even if you are a review site, you must be able to tell the visitor what you are reviewing straight away.

- Make sure that you are focusing on the customer throughout much of the copy, and not on yourself. We have already mentioned that you should use "you" throughout your copy, as this makes the readers feel that they are closer than ever to actually using the product. They really don't want to know about you – it is good practice to assume that all customers are selfish and that all they care about are the benefits they can gain. So, let them know how you can help them.

- You should ensure that you are writing at the correct level for your visitors, as more often than not you will write at a level that is comfortable for you, i.e. a level that is far too intelligent for your average reader of web content. You might see that you use too many long words and complicated sentences, which are two things that the average reader won't get on very well with at all. Don't try to make your writing perfect and elegant – you're not writing a novel, you're writing web copy. The most important aspect of good web copy is that it is simple and straight to the point.

- Jargon can be a massive turn-off for people when they land on a website, as people don't like either having to research the meaning of a word, or guess what it means. This means that you should avoid using jargon as much as possible, and if you have to, you should include explanations wherever possible. Keep it simple, but don't come across as patronizing.

- The style of writing that you have is extremely important, as people react well when they are being spoken to in a conversational tone. A more formal tone is boring and will not leave the reader wanting to read more – in fact, it will more than certainly have them clicking off the page extremely quickly! Write exactly how you speak and you won't go far wrong with the copy that you create for your website.

- Do you have a penchant for exclamation marks?!!!!!!! Well, if you do, this is something that you should drop as soon as possible. People have come to associate exclamation marks with dishonest statements, and when you are trying to build a relationship with a reader, this is certainly not a good thing. Obviously there are times when you can drop in the occasional exclamation mark, but there really is no need to use them in every paragraph. Whatever you do, however, never use more than one at the end of a sentence – firstly it looks incredibly amateur, and secondly it makes you look as if you are lying.

- Capital letters can also be horribly overused in bad copy, even although most of us have been taught at school to use them in headings and subheadings. The fact is, however, that using capital letters in subheadings makes them harder to read, which obviously takes away from the page being scannable. The basic rule is to use capital letters properly – such as the initial letter at the beginning of sentences and in people's names – but not to use them for every word in a subheading or header.

- Clichés are something that you should definitely avoid for the most part when you are writing, as people see them as being completely unoriginal, as well as a device used by people trying to bend the truth at least a little. The odd one here and there doesn't hurt, but one in every paragraph is a definite no-no.

- Ensuring that the copy on your page is of the correct length is very important, as you should include enough information to get people's interest, but not so much that they get bored reading through all of it. There is no rule for deciding how much copy is the perfect amount – you just have to make sure that you get all of your salient points across without waffling on too much. It is extremely easy to write a long sales page that has all the information in it; it is far more difficult to write a condensed version that keeps the reader interested, but this is exactly what you have to do.

- You must ensure that the copy you have written is easy to understand, as there will be people of all different intellects visiting your site; you need to cater to the lowest common denominator. A good way to gauge whether you have achieved this is by evaluating whether a child could read what you have just written – if a child could read it, it will be suitable for almost every adult out there.

- When you read a book, you will notice that both the left and right hand sides of the text are justified – i.e. they run in a completely vertical line down the page, as in the rest of this book. This is all well and good for books, but is entirely the wrong approach when writing website copy. Justified text makes the sections of text look larger than they actually are, thereby putting the readers off before they even start to read. By having the text left-aligned, as in this bullet point, it will look much more manageable and therefore encourage people to read more. The more people that read through the site, the more conversions you are likely to generate.

- Make sure that you are not disrupting the flow of information that your visitors are receiving by using content that contains too many full stops. This is because full stops basically instruct the reader to finish reading – something that you certainly don't want them to do. Obviously you need to use full stops sometimes, especially as you want to keep sentences short, but don't use them every three or four words, as this will simply break up the flow of the copy and leave readers exasperated.

- You should ensure that the font size you use, and the type of font and the format, is easy to read when a visitor is skim reading your page. You should stick to the tried and tested fonts, such as Calibri and Arial, when writing content and avoid using less friendly fonts like Comics Sans. In fact, Comic Sans is probably the most disliked font in the world, and many people will refuse to read the information on your site simply because that font is used. You should also split test whether serif or sans serif fonts work better on your site, although I have had good success with both.

When it comes to the size of your font, there is no hard and fast rule: you must simply ensure that it is easy to read, even when someone has a very small screen resolution. Similarly, you don't want it to be too large either. To check this you should change your monitor settings to the lowest setting (usually 800x600) and then to the highest setting, and make sure that the copy reads well on both of them. I find that a font size of 12 is usually more than adequate. Finally, think about the format, which includes such things as images, the length of paragraphs, bullet points and the use of subheadings – all of which are subjects we have mentioned previously.

- You should make sure that you have addressed all the potential problems that a customer might have with the product you are promoting, which we have spoken about earlier in this chapter. Never ignore the potential objections that people might have; instead, tackle them and provide visitors with the reassurance that they need in order to prevent them becoming over concerned.

- Perhaps most importantly of all, you should ensure that you provide good justification to the visitors as to why they should buy your product, by first outlining the problem and then telling them how your product can solve this problem for them, including the benefits that the main features of the product have. If you cannot justify why a product should be bought, then you may complete everything else on this list, but you will never get a single sale.

The list above is in no way a comprehensive one, as there are various other methods that you can use to improve your copywriting as well. It is, however, a list that will get you on the right track to creating the best copy possible. You can then build on your new-found skills as you become more and more proficient. Just make sure that you get the basics right before you try to make your writing more and more elaborate.

# Hook, Line and Sinker

As you can guess by the title, this section uses the fishing metaphor of "hook, line and sinker" to show you how to land your fish, or in this case your customer and the conversion. Our hook, line and sinker strategy basically relies on the way in which you lay out the copy on the site, in addition to how you have laid out the whole webpage.

## *Hook, Line and Sinker Goals*

To work out what we are looking to achieve, we need to go back to our old friend the AIDA model: Attention, Interest, Desire, and Action. All the pages on your site should take a visitor on a journey through all of the aspects of the AIDA model, regardless of whether the page is a sales page, or a page simply designed to move the visitor further along the funnel and therefore closer to a conversion. Their attention needs to be gained, their interest fed, their desire stoked and then they must be encouraged to take action, whether this action is to make a purchase or just to click-through to a different page on your site.

Creating these types of page is not easy, but with some guidance and practice you can create them. They are like an art and a science combined, as they need certain action to be completed by you that are non-negotiable and exact, but they also need a creative element that you will provide. You need to get both of these right for your audience in order to gain the maximum number of conversions possible.

To ensure that each page on the website is as effective as possible, each one should have the hook, line and sinker approach.

As you might imagine, there are three stages to this technique.

- **Hook.** This is usually the header of the page and is designed to grab the readers' attention and encourage them to read on.

- **Line.** This is everything between the header and the final conversion, and provides all the information needed to interest the readers and make them desire the product.

- **Sinker.** This is the final call to action, which you hope will lead to a conversion.

If you think of the process as though you are fishing, the hook catches them, the line reels them in and the sinker finally lands them. If you can get the vast majority of people to follow this path that you have laid down for them, your copy will be well and truly on the right track.

### The Hook

As already stated, the hook is usually the header that you include on your webpage, so you must ensure that this header both grabs the reader's attention straight away and also creates some interest, so that they read on. You need to write a headline that quickly summarises what the product is and, most importantly, the main benefit that the product will bring to the visitor. To get them to read on, the hook must be clear, concise, positive and believable – if all of these are adhered to, you should have no problems getting the reader to keep on reading.

### Creating a Good Hook

Something that we have already mentioned is that you should not capitalize the first letter of every word in your headline, as this will make the copy much more difficult to read. Remember, you only have seven seconds to engage a visitor, so make it as easy as possible to learn about the product in that time. You should also refrain from using a full stop at the end of the headline, because this subconsciously tells the reader to finish reading.

The headline should be in the top centre of the page and should only cover a maximum of two to three lines, with one or two lines usually being the optimum length. You could also throw in some contrasting colours to draw attention to the headline. Basically, you need to do everything in your power to get the visitor to read the headline and then be interested enough to keep on reading. If they don't keep reading, you have a poorly written hook.

### Good and Bad Hooks

Below are two examples, with the first being a bad hook and the second being a hook that is far better and much more effective.

> "The Best Computer On The Market That Has Made Gamers Improve Their Skills – Reviewed"

This first hook is, quite frankly, terrible. Firstly, it uses capital letters to start every word, which makes it very difficult to read. In addition to this, there are no contrasting colours in the hook, which means that the key points aren't highlighted. There is no mention of "quick and easy" in the sentence and, perhaps most importantly, there is no benefit given. Sure, it says that gamers have improved their skills, but it doesn't mention the benefits that this improvement brings. Below is a much better way of writing this hook:

"Discover the computer that makes it quick and easy to overcome most of your opponents online and removes the frustration associated with lag"

This hook might be slightly longer than the first, but it is still well within the realms of acceptability. It does not have capital letters at the beginning of every single word and it uses contrasting colours to make a key aspect stand out. It emphasizes the benefit(s) and it also uses the words "quick and easy", as they are relevant to this product.

As you can see, this second hook gets across everything that we want it to. On top of this, it is both specific and believable as well. A good hook really makes a massive difference to the number of people that will actually read through your website, so you should make absolutely sure that every page on your site is completely optimized with the best hook you can think of. They might only be one, two or three lines, but you should spend as much time as needed ensuring that they are 100% perfect!

## The "line"

By now you should have caught the readers' attention with a great hook, so you need to move on and deliver the line. This means that we need to start engaging their emotions and really talking about the benefits that the product you are promoting brings, which, as you should remember, are not the same as the features that the product has. While keeping our writing focused on these two aforementioned points, we must also make sure that the formatting is perfect so that the reader can pick up the key points, even when they are skim reading.

The line will be the largest part of the copy on your page and will encompass the vast majority of the copywriting tips that we have spoken about in this chapter already. It is where you have the chance to really get the customer imagining and visualizing the product, and is also where you should bring those all-important benefits to the forefront of their minds.

## Creating a Good Line

Creating a good line is not difficult if you follow a few basic tips.

- Make the first sentence after the headline in bold type, so that the reader is immediately drawn to it when they have looked over the headline. This is even more effective if you have taken my advice and not used a full stop at the end of your headline, as it means that the copy flows perfectly from one section to the next. Even if readers are not consciously aware that they are doing it, they will be encouraged by this to keep reading.

- We have already mentioned bullet points and how useful they can be, so make sure that you get a bulleted list as high up the page as possible (above the fold). This will allow you to get your most important points across to the readers in a format that they find easy to understand. Placing them high on the page means that they will see these key points as quickly as possible, without the need to scroll, which is exactly what you want to happen.

- A good line doesn't have to be only text, as many great lines use interactive elements as well, such as quizzes, videos and games. Interactive elements are great at breaking up the text and giving the reader something else to do, so that they do not get bored. They also increase the excitement that they have regarding the product you are selling and, if these features are used correctly, they can also be a very effective way of increasing desire for your product. One great idea for an affiliate website is to have a quiz that recommends the product that they would be best suited to.

- Above all else, make sure that you play on the emotions of the visitors to your site and that you constantly outline the benefits that they will experience when they purchase your product.

If you include all the above points, you will have created a line that is incredibly effective at getting readers through to the final stage, where you can use the sinker to get them to complete the desired action.

### The Sinker

The main purpose of the sinker is to get the visitor to your site to complete the action that you want them to perform, whether this is signing up to a mailing list, purchasing a product or clicking through to another site, or even just clicking through to another page on your website.

Although we are effectively pushing them towards making a decision, we also need to take a soft approach at times and reassure them that they are making the correct decision as they are edging closer to the action that you want them to complete. We must also ensure that they do not leave the site to think about it, as the chances are that they will never come back. We need as many visitors as possible to take action now, not later.

## *Creating a Good Sinker*

There are two basic ways that you can create a call to action link: graphical and textual links. Depending on the type of customer that you get, they will prefer one to the other, so it is always a good idea to use them both on your site, so that both types of customer are catered for. It is also very important that visitors know exactly where a link will take them. One of the biggest reasons for customers leaving a site is because they click a link and find that it takes them somewhere that they don't expect it to, which is a sure fire way to erode any trust that's been built up.

To counter this problem of people not knowing where links will take them, make the target page abundantly obvious, even if it is a page away from your own site. In this situation, don't be afraid to tell them that they will be going to a different site, because this will take away any of the surprise or trepidation that visitors might feel.

Benefit-driven wording is also a powerful tool to use in your action links, as a call to action should stress the massive benefits of completing the action. Think of what the visitors are going to gain by clicking the link. Will they be able to buy something? Will they learn something new? Will they have the chance to eradicate the problem that they are suffering from straight away?

We have spoken briefly about urgency before and it is important that you use this within your sinker as well. The two main tactics to use for this are the "I want to be just like them" tactic, and the "I have to act quickly, or I might miss out" tactic. Both of these play on people's innate emotions and create the feeling within visitors that they have to act straight away. Some tactics that we can use to create urgency include limited discounts and a lack of stock availability, which will make the visitors believe that they have to act as quickly as possible, as otherwise it might be too late. After all, we do not want them to go away and think about it, remember?

Even if people have that sense of urgency, their concerns and fears about completing the action might still get in the way of them converting, so we must now assure them that the action is in their best interests, and that they can feel secure in progressing to the next stage. You need to pre-empt any concerns that they might have – such as about the quality of the product or the price being charged – and answer them directly, so that they are calmed and believe they are making the correct decision.

To further reassure people that the product is a great purchase, you can mention things like money back guarantees, as well as reassuring them that the product will work exactly as you have previously stated in the line section of the article. Basically, you always want

139

to be telling them, "You are making the correct decision and the time and money you spend will be more than worth it".

### *Hook, Line & Sinker Summary*

There is not a single page on your website that shouldn't have the hook, line and sinker approach applied to it, as it is this approach that allows you to navigate your reader through the AIDA model in a quick and effective way. Regardless of whether the page is a purchasing page, a review page or any other type of page, there will be a way in which you can implement this approach. The sections work in the following way:

- The **hook** is a headline that gets the attention of the readers, provides them with information as to what the copy is about and tells them of at least one of the benefits they will be able to find.
- The **line** is the main content of your page and must be formatted in the correct way, while also containing the language needed to engage with the emotions of readers and increase the interest and desire that they have in the product or service you are offering.
- Finally, the sinker is there to provide a call to action that people can take to move onto the next stage of your funnel, whether this is navigating to a page on your site, a page on another site or completing a conversion. It should have elements of urgency in it, but it should also offer reassurance to those who are still concerned about the action you want them to complete. You should make clear exactly what the customer will experience when they click on the link, so that they are not surprised and click off the site.

If you can include all of this in your site, you will have a hook, line and sinker approach that will work on virtually any affiliate site. When this is combined with all the other teachings in this chapter, you will have almost perfect copy for your site!

## Essentials of Great Copy

Before looking at the different types of content that you have on your website, let us just briefly review what we have learnt about writing the content.

- You need to make sure that every feature of the product or service you offer is justified with a benefit that this will give to the potential customer. To do this, write down all the features that your product has that you can think of and then write each feature's benefits next to them. When you have established your benefits, go through the copy you have written and make sure that you have included all of these benefits in the correct places, ensuring that the benefits really stand out in the copy. If you have not written your copy yet, use the list you've made as a guideline when you do come to write it.

- Make sure that you use emotion to draw the visitors into wanting the product or service that you offer. Write a few small pieces of copy – no more than two to three paragraphs – that create a picture in the mind of the visitors of them using the product themselves. You should be able to place this copy straight into your already existing content, although sometimes you will need to do some light editing to make it fit properly.

- Now go over the long list of questions and requirements that were covered earlier in this chapter, all of which are designed to ensure that your copy is of a high standard. Look at the basic formula we went through and ensure that the copy you have written adheres to this as much as is possible. Make any changes needed if you find yourself not complying with the points made or veering away from the formula.

- Make sure that you follow the hook, line and sinker approach that we have discussed in this chapter. If you follow this, you will find that you have copy that is solid and converts well, even with visitors who are sceptical to start off with.

## Creating Quality Review Sales Pages

The most important pages of your site will of course be your review sales pages. All the other pages of your site should act as a funnel to push visitors to your review pages. Yet the standard of affiliate review pages, across a wide range of niches, is on the whole extremely poor.

Referring back to the treadmill niche that we used earlier, let's use Google to search for "nordictrack commercial 1750 review". Take a good look at the first 20 or 30 results and mark each review good, bad or ugly. How did you rate the review pages viewed? Were they great quality or did you find them to be poor?

I'm amazed that so few affiliates use video in their reviews in spite of the rise of video websites over recent years, including the likes of Youtube and Vimeo. Merchants actually make this task a breeze for affiliates as most have their own channel on Youtube, crammed with quality professional reviews of their products. Go to www.youtube.com and search for "NordicTrack Commercial 1750".

nordictrack commercial 1750 | Search

## Search results for **nordictrack commercial 1750**

About 8 results

☒ Search options

### Summer Abs

BV Fitness Abs Workout -
Reality Fitness

by BVFITNESS **140,325 views**

Promoted Videos

### NordicTrack Commercial 1750

bit.ly Built for the gym, this treadmill features everything from a powerful 3.5 CHP DuraDrive motor to a spacious 20" x 60" treadbelt. The ...

by NordicTrackLive | 1 year ago | **10,308 views**

### Assembly 34588 **Nordictrack Commercial 1750** Treadmill

How to assemble the **Nordictrack Commercial 1750** Treadmill model # 34588

by IconCustomerCare | 2 months ago | **676 views**

HD

Once you have found a related video, it is so easy to add the actual video to your review site as most product videos have an embed option which allows you to copy and paste code directly to your review page. All you need to do to copy the code is to click the SHARE button, then the EMBED button, and next simply copy the code as below.

See how easy that was!

Now go to Google and search for NordicTrack Commercial 1750 Review once again. Do you notice how few of the review pages actually include the video? Seeking out videos that relate to your product, or better still creating your own videos, will give you a great edge over other affiliate sites.

## Creating Content That Converts

### *The Content Funnel*

To create review pages and other content that will lead to a conversion, the first thing that we need to look at is the content funnel. If you've read all the previous chapters in this book, which I sincerely hope you have, you will have learnt about the AIDA model, about CBDM process and about the all-important conversion funnel. If we use what we have learnt from these three different topics, we can easily put together a three-step content funnel. The content on our site must:

- Ensure that the visitors decide on a specific product that they want to buy, based on the content that you have placed on the site. The only exception to this is if you have a website that is product-specific, as there is obviously only one product on this site. For all other sites, however, the first task would be to ensure that this step is taken.

143

- Next the content should provide reassurance to the visitor that the decision he or she has made is the correct one. Basically, you need to be constantly letting the visitor know that he has made the right choice and holding his hand all the way until he has completed the conversion.

- Make them complete a conversion. This is the ultimate goal and this is the stage at which you will earn the money that you have worked so hard for.

I shall be the first to admit that the funnel above is a hugely simplistic one. What we are now going to do, however, is expand on each step by taking a look at the different types of content you can use in each of the three stages. We shall begin with a quick run-down and then look at each in more detail.

- **Stage One.** In the first stage of the funnel you can employ such devices as product selection quizzes and comparison tables. These will assist the visitors in making the decision of what the best product would be for them.
- **Stage Two.** In Stage Two, you can move on to using product reviews and personal stories. By the time they reach this stage, they should have already picked out a product that they are very interested in, so we need to use these two tactics in order to reassure them that the decision they have made is the correct one.
- **Stage Three.** Stage Three is the purchase, so to encourage them here we can include content discount codes and vouchers. Both of these will encourage them to move on with their purchase. These kinds of gesture will also make them like the site more, so that they are more likely to return and become repeat customers.

Now that we have looked at what content can be used where, let's take a look at those specific types of content in more detail.

### *Stage One: Comparison Tables*
A great tactic you can employ in your copy in the first stage of the funnel is the use of comparison tables. Such tables are used to compare different products to one another, creating content which is highly scannable. In some niches there can be hundreds of different products to choose from, however, so it is obviously not possible to include them all in the comparison table. In this instance, you would say something along the lines of, "These are the five best products, and you can see how they fare against each other in the

table below." You would then have a table that shows the five products, although depending on your needs you can have more or less than this number. There are a huge number of different things on which you can compare products, but the most popular are price, features and, most importantly, benefits.

When using comparison tables ensure that your table has a clear recommendation that is obvious to anybody who even simply quickly scans the table. I know that you are presenting the information so that people can ultimately make their own decisions about which product is the best, but sometimes your visitors will need some help. To show them the product that you recommend, you could consider using a star rating for each of the products being compared. When using a star rating system, you want to ensure that you have a top choice, a backup choice, a third choice, etc. People will then be clear as to which of the products are the best.

Even although you are looking to educate the visitor on the different merits of each product, you should always keep in mind that the table needs to be simple and easy to understand. I can't count the number of times that I've gone onto a site and seen a table that's absolutely stuffed with information about tens of different products. While the intention is obviously to provide the maximum value to customers, its actual effect is to confuse them and in many instances make them click away and go elsewhere.

So how do you ensure that the comparison table is easy to use? Well, you should firstly only compare the aspects of the product that people care about – leave out all the unimportant elements as they will only take attention away from the important ones. Also, you should make sure that you answer questions as quickly as possible using as few words as possible. For example, getting back to the treadmill niche, the comparison table could have an option as to whether the model can be folded after use. You can answer this with a simple "yes" or "no", which saves on space and makes the table look less cluttered. You can even ditch the yes/no answers and use ticks and crosses, which look great and are even easier to read! Make the table as easy as possible to scan, so that visitors don't get bored.

Using ratings for the different aspects of a product is also a good way to keep the table looking clean, and provides an extra push to those who are still not sure about the product that is the best for them. You can use numbers or stars; it really doesn't matter. What does matter, however, is that you ensure that your primary product comes out as the clear winner in the majority of categories. In terms of the way in which the table reads, however, look at it when it is finished and ask yourself, "Can someone quickly and easily understand the information presented here?" If your answer is that they can, you have created a good table.

There is one final aspect that every good table must have, and that is the important call to action. Ensure that all tables you use have a clear link close by that allows the user to get more information on the specific product. You could even have two links – one that goes through to a more detailed review of the product, and one that goes straight to the sales page. This is because some people will need further reassurance before buying, whereas others will be ready to purchase straight away. By having two links you are catering for them both.

## *Product Selection Quizzes*

Still at stage one we are now going to move onto product selection quizzes, which are not as common as comparison tables but just as effective. The most difficult part about a product selection quiz is their creation, as you need to have some kind of programming skills in order to create them. If you don't know how to do this, you can easily hire someone from a freelance site such as Elance. The main use of these product selection quizzes is to help readers to work out what product they actually want through a series of questions that they are asked. This obviously means that you have to work out what answers people could give and then work out the best products for them based on these answers. The quiz then filters them through to the matching products and delivers targeted traffic to that specific product's page.

When creating one of these quizzes it is important to ensure that the results are accurate, by which I mean that the results must meet different people's different requirements. Don't think that you can trick your visitors and simply point them all to the product that gives you the highest commission, as this of course would be a major mistake. Your personal opinion and indeed product preference should also be ignored in this instance, as just because a product might be better for you, it doesn't mean it will be the product of choice for your visitors. Just remember, if you make a good recommendation that caters to your visitor's needs, you are much more likely to generate a sale, and you are also more likely to see repeat custom, thanks to the trust you've gained due to the good advice that you have imparted.

When the visitor has finished the quiz, you must ensure that you provide a link to a review page for the selected product, and also of course, a link to the page where the visitor can turn into a conversion and buy the product. After all, some people will need that little bit of extra reassurance that a product review will provide them with, whereas others will be prepared to accept your recommendation and purchase the product straight away. Make sure that you cater for the needs of both types of visitor.

Product selection quizzes and comparison tables do not have to exclude one another, as they can be used in conjunction with each other very successfully. For example, you could have a comparison table and then provide a quiz underneath for people who are still unsure about which product they want. This will make it more likely that they will stay in the funnel and remain interested in the subject for longer.

If you manage to employ both of these tactics to a high degree, you will move them through stage one and can progress onto the content needed for stage two.

### *Stage Two: Quality Product Reviews*

Stage two of the funnel allows you to bring in tactics such as product reviews. In a nutshell, there are three different types of product review that you can create for your affiliate site.

- A multi-user review, where you write one review that takes into account the opinions of a number of different people.

- Multiple reviews from different users in a comment section on each page.

- A review that has been created by just one person or organization, such as a personal experience website might have.

Ratings can be used very effectively in product reviews as well, just as they can in comparison tables. It doesn't matter whether you use star ratings or numerical ones, provided that the ratings are easy for people to absorb when they are skimming through the content. To make this even easier, try to pick out just a few of the key points from the product and present your ratings near the top of the page. As we have already mentioned a couple of times, make sure that the recommendation is a clear one, meaning that you should refrain from giving each product a top rating. This means that you come out with a clear winner for visitors to see, which will prevent confusion. You can then rank products underneath this winner and can even have a product that you label as the worst.

In the pursuit of honesty – and therefore trust – you should also mention the negative points about a specific product when you are writing a review. Customers will notice that you are being honest and will really appreciate it, and they will also think that you are providing an independent review that is not trying to push a particular product onto them.

Therefore, if your product does not quite deliver in some areas, point this out to the customer. By doing this you look less biased and it will actually lead to more conversions, not fewer. Obviously you do not want to overstress the negative points – just drop them in occasionally and move on.

If you do use a banner, make sure that it is to a well-known brand and not to a site that the visitor has never heard of. Most people do not understand the concept of affiliate sites and won't realize that the banner is part of your money-making strategy. Instead, they will think that your site is important enough to merit companies such as Amazon and eBay paying to have their site advertised on yours, which will add credibility to your site.

### Using Personal Stories

The other tactic that can be used in stage two of the funnel is the personal story. Personal stories are designed to let people know about the experiences you have had with specified products and therefore they should always be written in the first person, as this will add that personal touch to the story. We have discussed in a previous chapter that language focused on "you" is the way to go, but in this instance the exact opposite is true; you want to use as much "me" language as possible! Despite this, however, you should still make sure that your personal experiences help to answer the questions that readers have, specifically about how the product can help them and most importantly of course, the benefits that it has.

If you are going to use a personal story, then you must make sure that your site is an amateur looking site, as a professional site won't carry the same trust in this instance. All you need to do with a personal story is write about how the product has worked for you, including how it has helped you overcome any problems and the results that you have experienced. Don't be afraid to mention some negative points, as this will create a sense of trust. Remember, your site is supposed to be independent and unbiased, so putting some negative points into the text will help to reinforce this perception among your visitors. You should try to be a little clever, however, and turn the negatives into positives, as opposed to simply saying "Product A was terrible at ….., and this is why…. ."

Personal story articles should not use professional looking images because people want to know that you actually own the product, so using professional pictures will plant a seed of doubt in their minds. On the other hand, using an amateur picture that you have taken, perhaps even featuring yourself, will prove to them that you own the product. For most people a simple photograph provides the proof that you are simply an owner of the product who is happy to talk about it because of the benefits it has brought you.

So that is the second stage of the funnel completed. Let's move on to look at stage three and see how you can encourage that final conversion.

## *Stage Three: Special Discounts, Bonuses & Vouchers*

You have helped the visitors choose their product and you have reassured them that their decision is the correct one. What you need to do now is seal the deal and get them to make the purchase. Without doubt the best way to do this is to direct them to a page that has special offers and vouchers for the product that they are interested in purchasing.

The idea of presenting vouchers and special offers to your visitors is not to sell to them. Instead, we want to make it look as though we are doing them a favour and ensuring that they get a very special deal through the extra value that they are receiving. The easiest way to do this is to approach the merchants themselves and obtain discount codes from them if they are available. Not all merchants are receptive to this, however, so in this situation you should use the generic discount  codes found on the site (if available) or, failing this, use things like free bonuses. Free bonuses can simply be some extra things that the product offers to people, so you can mention these and explain why these make the product even better value.

It is also possible to offer free bonuses that you have created personally. You might have an ebook or a report that you have created, which you can supply for free to everyone making a purchase of the specified product. This will obviously mean that you have to do some extra work in the creation of the "freebie", although doing so will give you the edge over other affiliates.

Before offering these free bonuses, however, it is important that you check the terms and conditions that your affiliate program has laid down. This is because some affiliate programs forbid affiliate sites from offering free gifts as an incentive, and if they find you doing this, they might stop you from promoting their products. I cannot stress enough how vital it is to check. With a bit of research you can find the affiliate programs that do allow you to offer freebies and work with them exclusively.

One incredibly important aspect of vouchers and the like is that you must be honest with people regarding what the vouchers etc. actually do. For example, if you advertise a voucher that promises 50% off to customers purchasing through your link and they then find out that to get this discount they have to spend over $1000, they are likely to be very annoyed and not continue with the purchase. Honesty will also add to the credibility and trust that your website has, therefore leading to more repeat business and more people being referred to your site by friends and family.

As with nearly everything else in the world of affiliate marketing, the one thing that you absolutely must do when providing vouchers and bonuses is provide an extremely clear call to action, so that people know exactly what they need to do. Use both text and graphics to get this point across and make sure that it is extremely visible. Just make sure that they cannot miss it and that they have no excuse for being confused!

### *Essentials of Creating Content That Converts*

In summary, creating content than converts means that you should take a look at the type of website you own and then look at where your customers will enter in the content funnel. After you have established this, you should then be able to decide on the best content to use in order to provide conversions for each of these stages.

Quizzes and comparison tables are a great idea if you want to help people choose a specific product to buy. You can then provide the reassurance that the visitor needs about their decision by using the tactics associated with the second stage, which are product reviews and personal experience stories. If you get both of these correct, you will simply need to seal the deal – something that you can do with vouchers and bonuses.

If you complete these three stages correctly, you will have gone a long way towards ensuring that your site is one that converts to its maximum potential.

## Creating Quality Product Reviews

It goes without saying that product reviews are one of the most effective ways to gain conversions. The good news for you is that regardless of your type of site, there is an approach that will work for you when it comes to product reviews. For example, amateur websites can use personal experience reviews, whereas authority websites can use a review that has the style of an authority testing one, which essentially means that you have tested the product for all the outlined features. Finally, you could use multi-user reviews, where visitors are able to leave their own opinions on your site regarding the product. Let's look at these three in a little bit more detail.

- **Personal experience reviews.** This sort of review should always be based on the experience you have with the product. You should not only mention the product's main features but of course the essential benefits.

- **Authority testing reviews.** These should be much more fact based and centred on information, rather than personal opinion. The objective with this type of review is to build up trust with your visitors by giving them useful and truthful facts about the product that will help them to solve their problems.

- **Multi-User Reviews.** These reviews allow visitors to the site to give their opinions on the product. This gives the impression that the site is providing a broad range of opinions and is therefore giving the best review possible. Be careful, however, that the comments left do not contradict your own.

Regardless of the type of review you choose, you should be prepared to research the product fully, as well as researching the marketplace. You should evaluate the competitors that you find in the marketplace and decide what the unique selling points are for your product.

## *Understanding The Rough Review Formula*

You might be very happy to hear that there is a rough formula that you can follow when you are creating reviews. Please note, however, that much of the time this only provides a basis for your reviews, as for some products this formula alone will not be enough to do the job. If you use it as a starting point, however, you will have a huge advantage over the competition. I have tested this formula countless times and it does work, bringing in great conversion rates on a whole range of different products and services. Below is a brief summary of each of the steps. Don't worry, however, as we won't be leaving it there – we'll go over each step in more detail later on.

The initial thing that you should do is go over the key benefits and features that the product has. This brief summary is for those people that we talked about earlier in the book; the people who want to see a brief piece of information and then go straight to the purchase page. So make sure that you include a link under or next to this part of the review!

Next you move on to accommodate the people who require more information on the product, so you talk about the problem that they might have and also about what the product actually does. You then tell them how the product will help them to solve the issue that they have. This means that you have told them what it is, how it works and whether it works well.

Next up comes a section devoted to the negative aspects of the product, as we have already established that including the negatives helps to build trust with the reader, as well as enhancing your credibility as an independent source. By the time the customers are at this stage, they should already have started to be convinced that the product is the right one for them.

151

You can then try to close the sale, mainly through looking at the value for money that the product in question offers to the consumer. We then quickly repeat the summary, just for those people who need reminding of the key points.

Let's look at each of the aforementioned sections in a little more detail now.

## The Product Summary

The summary should be kept short and should quickly outline the key benefits of the product, without boring the reader. It should also of course include a link to buy the product.

The way to ensure that the summary is done correctly is to split it into two sections. Firstly you want to have a very short paragraph at the beginning of the review that introduces the product that is going to be reviewed – two to three lines should be more than enough for this. You then move straight to a table below, which summarizes the key features that the product has and also the benefits that these features provide. A table is an excellent choice because it is incredibly easy to scan read, meaning that those with limited time or patience will find this appealing. It allows them to get a good feel for whether the product is good for them, before they are quickly ushered to the "buy now" button below. For those looking for a more in-depth review, it helps to set the scene and provides them with some early information that we can expand upon.

## The Problem and the Solution

Next we move on to the part of the review where we discuss the problem that the readers might be facing, as well as the solution that this product can provide. The first task that we have is to remind the readers what the problem is exactly, using a line such as "Do you need to solve the problem of..?" Try to connect with the readers by making it clear that you not only know the problem they are looking to solve, but that you can also empathize with the their feelings about this problem.

A good example of this would be on a website about weight loss. You can confide with the visitor that you are all too aware of how hard weight loss can be to achieve and that it can really be a mental strain as you battle through the daily grind of trying to drop a few pounds. Show them that you understand the position that they have found themselves in.

Now you have defined the problem to the reader, you can move on to letting them know exactly how your product can help them to overcome the problem. If we continue with the example of weight loss, you could say "This product can help with the problem because it does A, B and C, and this provides these benefits…" You can then look at the features that the product has, which you will be able to intertwine with extra benefits that it has, or with features that you have already mentioned, in order to emphasize them.

You have now told them what the problem is, and how you can help them to solve it with your product. Many people will wonder why your product is better than the others on the market, so this is the next thing that you need to tackle. A good way to do this is to provide another comparison table that lists the advantages your product has over competitors, or you could write a simple list of bullet points instead.

The length that you make this section is entirely dependent on how complex the problem is that you are trying to overcome, as well as how much you can actually find to say about the product. Ideally, you will be able to provide enough information to allow the users to feel that they have received an education on the product, but also keep the review short enough not to lose their interest. More important than the length, however, is the layout of the content. The layout should make the content easy to scan and read, because, regardless of the amount of content that you have, this will make the experience a pleasurable one for the reader.

If you are still concerned about the length of your copy, read it over and consider this question – are you providing all the relevant information needed to your readers, while also making sure that you are not filling half the content with fluff and filler? If the answer to this is "yes", your copy is the correct length!

## The Effectiveness

Now you can move to the section that tells the reader how well the product actually performs – which is entirely different from how the product works. The best way you can do this is to look at evidence that points towards the effectiveness of the product, such as studies conducted on the product, testimonials or personal experiences. Regardless of the type of evidence that you use, it should have one goal in mind – to back up the fact that the product works as well as you say it does. It is even possible to go through the claims on the product's own website and talk about them individually, using evidence (user reviews) to back each one up.

You should also mention how reliable the product is when it comes to solving the reader's problem by telling the reader of the benefits. You should have already started to do this in the previous section, but you can really ramp it up now and relate everything to the benefits that a product has.

153

## *Negatives*

Discussing the negatives, as opposed to ignoring them and trying to hide them from the reader, is an important way to build trust and credibility, as we have already mentioned numerous times in this chapter. Of course, there are some products that are so good that they have no negatives, which means that you don't need to have a negatives section at all. This is the exception rather than the rule, however – 99% of products will have some small flaw to them that you can discuss here.

It is important when discussing negatives that you are able to flip them around to being benefits. For example, if your product costs $100 more than the next competitor, you can say that this is because you have to pay extra for the quality that this product delivers. This will appeal to those looking to spend more on a product to obtain the best results – those who don't want to spend the extra will probably not have found their way to the page in the first place.

Turning negatives into positives is not always the easiest job, but with a little bit of thought it can nearly always be accomplished. When you finish talking about the negative aspects of the product, try to end on a positive note, as ideally you want the visitors to have a positive thought as the last thing that they remember from the section. So you could say that a new smart phone is mainly constructed from plastic but this actually makes the phone light and easy to carry around in a shirt pocket. Here you have mentioned a negative but finished on a positive note.

You might remember that one of the techniques we used in copywriting was bolding points, but it is important not to use this technique when you are talking about negatives that the product has. Although you want to mention the negatives, you do not want them to stand out to those who are skim reading the review. If you think that the negative section looks slightly bare without some bold text, put the positives within it in bold type instead.

## *The Call to Action*

When it comes to the call to action, the first thing that you want to do is ensure that the readers get a sense of urgency – a sense that they have to purchase the product before it is too late. By this stage you have already talked about the benefits, features, effectiveness and negatives of the product, and you hope that people will now be seriously considering making a purchase. The problem here is that some people might be concerned with the price, while others might be inclined to postpone the purchase while they investigate the product further on other websites.

So we need to give them a call to action that is both clear and attractive. Basically you have to tell them that they have read the review and know all that there is to know about the product, so now it is time for them to take action and make the purchase. Firstly we tell them about the price. If you are concerned about the price because your product is a higher value one, you can make it more appealing by breaking the cost down, For example, you could say that $60 is only $2 per day over the course of a month. Of course you would word it better than that, by saying something like "We can't believe that this product is available for just $2 per day!"

You can then add even more encouragement for people to buy by talking about the bonuses that are on offer, which we can compare to the cost of the actual product. For example, you could say that the cost is high, but the number of features and benefits that you get from the product more than justifies the expense.

It is incredibly important to concentrate on the language that you are using in this section and on how the copy sounds overall, as you want people to feel that you are trying to help them. They need to think that you are educating them and not pushing them towards purchasing a product from you, even if this is the actual truth of the matter. They need to decide naturally to buy the product and to think that they have made the decision 100% themselves. In reality, you have guided them most of the way through your use of the various techniques I have outlined.

During this final stage you also want to mention any discounts or voucher codes that you can offer them. They are now at the third stage of the funnel, which means that your job is to encourage them to spend their money on the product, earning you money in the process. By letting the customer know about the vouchers and discounts, you want them again to think that you are doing them a favour. This is a great time to introduce some urgency into the proceedings, as you can say that these offers are only available for a limited time, meaning that the customer has to act now. Don't rely exclusively on limited time offers, however, as you want them to buy the product because they actually want it, not because they have seen the discounts. Think of the vouchers as the final little push they need to buy, rather than a massive shove.

So now you have reached the end of the review and there is one final thing to include, which is your primary call to action, as well as a final summary. This final summary will ensure that the reader is reminded of all the most important and exciting benefits that the specified product has, meaning that they are more likely to click on the buy button, which you have placed very close by.

## *Dos & Don'ts*

Now that we have gone through the whole review formula, let's quickly look at a few dos and don'ts that you should bear in mind when you are writing your reviews.

- **Do** make sure that you use language centred on "you" (i.e. the customer) much of the time.

- **Do** make sure that you emphasize to your readers the benefits more than the features of the product.

- **Do** make sure that your review is easy for people to scan when they first land on your site's page.

- **Do** make use of all the information that you have learnt in this copywriting chapter to ensure that the text you create is perfect for the job at hand. It should seamlessly take them through the AIDA model, resulting in them taking that final action.

- **Don't** add what I call traffic-leaks by having banners on your review pages that promote other products. You must remember that your reviews are an incredibly important part of your conversion funnels, so you don't want people jumping ship halfway through as a banner advert distracts them and they click on it.

- **Don't** advertise the product that you are reviewing on the same page as the review – in fact, try not to advertise it anywhere on your site at all. Advertising will result in the credibility of your site taking a massive hit, as people will think that the company who sells the reviewed product are sponsoring you. The only sorts of banner that you should have are banners that are completely unrelated to your product, and they should ideally be banners advertising household names, so that your site looks more important than it is. Banners, just like AdSense banners, are still traffic leaks, however, so remember that you could lose customers through them. If you do use them, make sure that the links open in new windows and not in the same one as your own page.

- **Don't** assert that each product on your site is as good as all the others, as this will simply confuse those visiting your site and also damage your reputation with them. Your reputation will be damaged because it will be blatantly obvious that you are trying to make your visitors buy something — after all, why else say that all the products are good? Unless you have a product-specific site, then you must include multiple reviews,  and they should be ranked in order of how highly you recommend them. Regardless of whether you review 10 or 10,000 products, you should still have one product that stands out from the rest. Then list the alternatives to this product, as this makes you look trustworthy and as though you are not promoting only one specific product to readers.

## *Summary of Product Reviews*

The most important thing that you can take away from this section is that you should use the review formula that I have set out in order to take people through the review and ultimately to a conversion. You will often need to adapt it slightly to fit the type of product you are reviewing, but this formula provides the basic groundwork to write a great review. There are three very important things to remember when creating a review:

- Your content should be as easy to read as possible, so that people can skim through it and find the points that are of most interest to them.
- You must be honest about the product, as otherwise you will lose the trust and credibility that you need in order to have a successful affiliate site.
- You need multiple calls to action throughout the review, so that people at different stages in their decision-making process can easily buy the product and earn you commission.

If you bear in mind all the points that we have mentioned in this section, you can be confident in creating a review that is optimized to gain the best conversions possible for your site.

## Review Page Templates

Another good tip I can offer you is that if you have a number of related products, it is always great practice to use a standard template structure so that your readers can easily compare different models. For example, for the treadmill niche we could use for each review the following quick review index table:

- Motor
- Running surface area
- Folding
- Speed
- Incline gradient
- One-touch speed and incline control:  Yes / No
- Deck
- Max. User Weight
- Transport wheels: Yes/ No
- Operating Noise
- Warranty
- UK  Shipping
- US Shipping
- Canadian Shipping
- Euro Shipping
- Other Shipping
- Your Overall Star Rating

Having the main features above the fold, including of course a "Buy Now" button, gives your readers a good insight to each product at a glance, enabling them to jump from one product to another, comparing features. Also, laying out your review pages in this manner makes your review pages look professional and encourages your readers to view more pages.

Under the above feature table we can then review the treadmill in far more detail, again, however, using a set template with the same subheadings for all treadmills. You should ensure that you take the time to include all relevant information required. Don't leave the reader seeking more information as they will simply head back to Google search again, leaving you without a sale. I am far too busy even to contemplate setting up a site targeting the treadmill niche, but to aid you in your quest to create quality review pages I have set up a dummy treadmill review page to aid you, which you will find at www.onlinecashcow.com. What do you think of it? How does it compare to the existing reviews in the niche?

## Final Thoughts

Creating good quality copy is a skill that takes time to master. I realize that many of you will find this chapter a tough read, but the simple truth is that if you learn to employ the techniques discussed, you will make more money. If you take the trouble to study affiliate websites, and I urge you to do so, you will find that a large proportion of affiliate webmasters lack good copy creation techniques. In reality affiliate websites with poor copy are simply throwing money away!

It is virtually impossible for those new to affiliate marketing to get their copy 100% correct at the first attempt. Tweaking your copy over a period of time and monitoring the results of the changes is a tactic employed by all good online affiliates.

# Chapter 10 – Email Marketing

## Email Marketing Overview

In Chapter One I stressed why you must ensure you build a list. By building a list, I am of course referring to collecting email addresses from your users. Email Marketing, or List Building as it is commonly known, is yet another technique you will have to master. The different aspects of Email Marketing include:

- What the reasons are for building an email list and why it is so important that you do so.

- How you can design opt-in forms that are incredibly powerful and boost your subscriptions to a high degree.

- Getting your subscribers to trust you, as this is the perhaps one of the most important aspects of email marketing.

- How to ensure that your emails are delivered, and delivered at the right time to ensure maximum open rates.

- How to make your subject line as compelling as possible, because this one line holds the key as to whether your email will be opened or simply condemned to the receiver's email junk folder.

- What you should include within the main body of your email.

- The frequency with which you should contact your subscribers.

The main goal of email marketing is of course to build a targeted contact list of those who have a high degree of interest in the products you are promoting. I have found that such lists are indeed highly profitable. Let's tackle in greater detail exactly why you should build a list.

## Why You Should Build A List

The main reason for creating a list is probably not the reason that you first thought of. The main reason is that it helps you to spread your risk. But what do I mean by that exactly? Well, if you are like most affiliate webmasters, most of your traffic will come from Google, as Google has by far the largest proportion of search engine market share. The chances are high, or in reality extremely high, that at some time in your affiliate career you will receive a penalty from Google that will result in you losing some of your "free" traffic, for at least a short period of time. If, or should I say when, this happens, you need another way to attract traffic, and this is where an email list proves vital.

So, if you consistently collect the email addresses of a percentage of your daily visitors, you will always have targeted potential customers that you can contact and market to. Obviously the bigger your list, the more profitable it should prove to be. From my experience I now actually generate more revenue from my list than through earnings from affiliate links on my websites. But why is this? Well, many of those who visit my websites may only do so once. Once they have found what they are looking for, even if they have indeed signed up to one of the gambling sites I promote, they may never return. In reality I have no way to know who they are or anything about them so that I could contact them and sell to them again. If, however, they subscribe to my list, perhaps tempted by a special or exclusive bonus, then I can contact them over and over again. From time to time I can send them more special offers which of course means that in the long term they make me more money, compared to those "invisible" visitors who simply click my affiliate links. So the first thing that you should understand is that an email list is like insurance for your website traffic, plus of course a great method to boost revenue in the long term.

Email lists are incredibly important because they encourage people to become repeat visitors to your site. Even if a subscriber decides not to take up an offer from your newsletter, you could prompt him to revisit your website, which in turn could lead to a sale. Email marketing helps you to create a relationship with your website visitors and to connect with them in a personal way. This means that you have a second, third, fourth etc. chance to make a repeat sale on your site. Even if visitors have subscribed to your list but not actually purchased anything initially, they have still given you the chance to persuade them to change their minds and buy a product from your website at a later date. I have had subscribers that have not initially been tempted to buy, but at a later date have done so, weeks, months or even years later.

One-off special offers, exclusive offers or even new products are also a good way to utilize email lists. Every so often a merchant that you are affiliated with will roll out a new product or special promotion that you can simply send to your list. As your list should be crammed with those with a high interest in your chosen niche, you will find that the conversion rates from a targeted list can be very high, so highly profitable.

In respect to the actual value of a targeted list, many so-called gurus tout an amount that equates to $1 per subscriber. This of course means that if you have an email list of 1,000, then you should be able to generate $1,000 in revenue per each email blast. I personally do not think you can put a set value on a list as there are simply too many variables. For example, the value and indeed commission of the promoted products, the quality of the newsletter copy, the quality and popularity of the product promoted plus many other variables.

In reality the actual revenue generated from a list will be determined by many factors, although if you target your subscribers in the correct manner, your list should indeed outperform sales generated from affiliate links in the long term. What you should be able to see now, however, is that there are many advantages to creating a list.

## How To Build A List

It is possible to build and run a list entirely by yourself, but the time and effort that this would take is something that is beyond most who are new to the world of online affiliation. Your best option is to use an established service that offers you a complete solution. There are many online companies that offer email marketing services, which you can find by typing something like "auto responder service" or "email marketing software" into Google or any search engine.

I have tried most of the leading providers and to be 100% honest have not found any company that even comes close to matching the service offered by Aweber.com. The bad news for those building their affiliate websites on a tight budget is that Aweber is not free. You can try Aweber for as little as $1 for a trial month, which then increases to $19 for up to 500 subscribers after the trial period has expired. The more successful you become at attracting subscribers, the more Aweber will charge you simply because you will be using more of Aweber's resources. Check Aweber's website for full pricing details - http://www.aweber.com/pricing.htm

When creating an email list, I strongly recommend the use of a double opt-in. A double opt-in simply means that after the person subscribes to your email list, they will receive an email that asks them to confirm their subscription. The double opt-in serves two purposes. Firstly it ensures that those who subscribe are 100% happy to do so and secondly it helps to stop those using false emails, or spammers, from trashing your list. Remember the main aim of list building is to build a highly targeted list of potential repeat customers. Those who prefer not to go the route of using a double opt-in in general create lesser quality lists.

When you get to the stage of creating double opt-in forms, you want to ensure that you add a personal touch. This means that where possible you should tailor all forms, validation requests and indeed newsletters to each individual, using at least their name in the "Dear…" part of the email. This will help build a relationship with your subscribers, plus, as I have experienced, boost the number of emails that are actually opened and read (open rate). Personalising forms and newsletters is a breeze with Aweber as you simply insert fields. Aweber is renowned for its knowledge base, which includes many "how to" videos and webinars. Aweber also has great customer support so help is only a phone call or email away.

So how do you get your visitors to subscribe to your list? Well, the most obvious thing that you must do is to provide a reason for them to do so. A good email form will have some form of "hook" that should entice the reader to subscribe. In real terms this means that you should offer potential subscribers some kind of free gift, such as an ebook, special offer, exclusive offer or some form of valuable information. Make sure that you make the "free gift" something that will actually be of value to your readers; use something unique that you know will appeal to those interested in your chosen niche. For example, yet again relating back to the treadmill niche, you could offer a free treadmill training plan, special discount codes or even a guide on essential treadmill maintenance. Make the effort with your "hook" and this will pay dividends in the long term with a steady stream of subscribers. If you find your hook is not appealing to your readers, simply try another.

There are a number of different ways that you can find something to entice readers to become subscribers. You could:

- Offer discounts by listing merchant discount codes
- Write your own ebook about an important topics of the niche
- Create a unique product review video
- Write a report on the top products

Regardless of what you do, just remember:

**Anything that you give away must provide good value to the subscriber, even though it is free.**

163

Perhaps the most important thing that you should remember in respect to list building is that it is a slow process. You cannot simply bombard your list with sales pitch after sales pitch – you have to gain their trust first. If they get to know you as someone who provides interesting and informative information, then when you do make a recommendation, people will trust it and be tempted to buy on your recommendation alone. In fact, a lot of the time you won't have to send a sales pitch to them – the quality of the information you provide will cause them to visit your website automatically when they require products in your niche.

The relationship that you have with your subscribers is the most important aspect to any list, not how big the actual list is. I have heard of numerous examples of people actually buying huge lists from other affiliates, but then getting barely any responses to the emails that they sent, simply because there is no relationship between them and the subscribers. Even if you have the budget to do so, don't buy a list; in fact NEVER buy a list! You can, however, pay someone in a similar niche to send out an email on your behalf to their subscribers. Before doing so, sign up to their list first so that you can gauge the actual quality of the newsletters being sent to subscribers.

## *The Opt-In Form: In-Line*

So let's take a look at subscriber opt-in forms in more detail. The first area that we are going to cover is the in-line form, which is a form that is displayed on your website, in most cases in the sidebar. It could be displayed on the home page or, as employed by many affiliate webmasters, on every page in a set position on the sidebar above the fold. If you have opted to use Aweber, you will find dozens of email form templates that you can easily and quickly add to your site, which will save you the expense of hiring a designer. Some forms will work better than others, so don't "fall in love" with a form. Take the time to change your email form from time to time and monitor the number of daily subscriptions. Changing the image of the form or even the text can boost conversions, which will mean more subscribers joining your list.

Don't expect a form with text such as "Sign Up To Our Newsletter" to drive a large percentage of your readers to become subscribers. Be creative with the actual text you use on your form. For example, if you are offering a free Ebook on the top products in your niche, you could use text such as "Top Ten Widgets Revealed!" or "Don't Buy Widget Before You Have Read Our Essential Buyers Report!" Simply be creative! Again, test different forms of copy to increase conversions!

The in-line opt-in form is the most common type of form used by affiliates and there is a reason for this: it is very easy to load and has been used by affiliates to great effect for years. In fact, I would go so far as to say that I would recommend this type of form to be used on your sites, although not exclusively, as it can be used in conjunction with the other types of email form – a topic that I will discuss a little later in this chapter. Regardless of the type of form that you use, however, you can always have the in-line form there as a back-up option.

### The Opt-In Form: Pop-Up

Another type of opt-in form, which was often found on affiliate websites just a few years ago, is that of the traditional pop-up. The basic concept of this type of form is that it would "pop up" in a window, when someone accessed a website. Pop-ups used to be an extremely popular tool. Most pop-up type form scripts have settings so that you can vary the actual time before the pop-up form appears and on which pages the pop-up form appears.

The fact that this type of pop-up form can be set to be extremely intrusive has meant that they are loathed by surfers and have become incredibly unpopular. Most surfers exit the site instantly when this type of pop-up appears, as it is simply seen as an attempt to bully them into making a purchase or subscribing. It is also the case that many internet browsers, such as Internet Explorer, Chrome and Firefox, now block pop-up windows, meaning that they are no longer effective.

Perhaps the only endearing feature of the pop-up form is that you can adjust their settings, so they don't necessarily pop-up as soon as someone comes onto the site. Additionally, they are compatible with cookies. This means that once someone has seen a pop-up form, they won't see it every time they log onto the site, at least for a while anyway. This takes away some of the risk of them being too intrusive on people's browsing experience on your site.

My advice however is this: do not use pop-up forms for your website. There are other options out there that are much better and I always steer clear of this option altogether.

### The Lightbox Opt-In Form

Instead of the above option, I would thoroughly recommend the pop-over or Lightbox type of opt-in form. Like the previous option, this type of form still pops up, or rather pops-over and does not open in a new window. Instead it darkens the website area, and then places a lightbox over the content on the page. People can then either close the box or, you hope, use it to subscribe to your email list.

165

I will be honest and say that this type of opt-in form is still an intrusive way to collect emails, but it is a lot less intrusive than the old style pop-up opt-in form. Additionally, it can be timed to appear after each visitor has viewed your content for a set amount of seconds, and can be set to appear only on predetermined pages. It also works with cookies, so each user only has to experience the pop-over form once.

In my experience a lightbox opt-in form, when used correctly, can be extremely effective, vastly increasing subscriber conversions. Obviously you have to use it in the correct way, by setting the options in a non-aggressive manner, but if you do so, then you should reap the rewards of increased subscribers. Let's look at an example to show you just how effective it can be.

## *The Power Of A Lightbox Form*

Typical subscriber conversion rates using optimized traditional in-line email forms general range from 0.5% to 2%. For one of my major sites, with daily traffic of around 3,500, I was only managing a subscription rate of 1% generating around 35 new subscribers each day. To be honest, as this site was targeting an online gambling niche, which I believe is one of the hardest to attack as an affiliate, I was quite pleased with the existing sign-up rate because in real terms I was generating just under 13,000 subscribers a year.

Early in 2011, I started to notice a buzz amongst fellow affiliate webmasters about a new pop-over lightbox Wordpress plug-in. The plug-in in question was Pop-up Domination. After just a few days of testing and tweaking the plug-in's settings, I was amazed that my actual subscriber conversion rate increased to a stonking 3.5%. In real terms this meant that my daily subscribers increased from 35 per day to a just over 122 per day, which I would never have believed possible!

Talking to other affiliates it was clear many were experiencing the same sort of results. Over the course of the following year, conversions fell a little, which I suggest was simply down to the form appearing on more and more affiliate sites, surfers getting used to the plug-in and learning to close the pop-over down to view content. As I write, I still have Pop-up Domination running on my sites with an average conversion rate of just over 2.5%. Pop-up Domination cost me around $40, which I'm pretty sure I earned back in less than an hour or so, so well worth the initial outlay in my opinion.

I will say, however, that I do not use Pop-up Domination on all my pages, instead preferring to use a combination of in-line forms on home pages and the pop-over plug-in only on selected non-sales pages.

### *Tips For Implementing A Lightbox*

Testing the effectiveness of a Lightbox on your site is absolutely imperative. Just because it worked on my site does not mean that it will have the same effect on yours. Here are a few pointers on how you can test a pop-over lightbox on your site:

- **Have it appear only once per visitor.** If your Lightbox pops up more than once every seven days per visitor, it will simply start to annoy them and make them think your sole motive is to collect their email address.

- **Have it appear after about four to five seconds.** Remember that seven seconds corresponds with the amount of time that you have to catch someone's attention while they are on your site. You don't want to go beyond seven seconds, because by that time readers will have engaged with your site, and you will interrupt them in what they are reading. You want to make sure that it is no sooner than three seconds, however, as this gives the site time to load properly and the visitor time to get a very brief understanding of what your site is all about.

- **Monitor your Lightbox's performance constantly.** This goes for both the number of subscribers that you generate and the time that people spend on your site (the bounce rate). I will discuss bounce rate in the Google Analytics chapter later in this book. Ultimately you want your subscriber rates to increase, but you also want to ensure that the Lightbox is not having an adverse effect on your bounce rate, (visitors quickly leaving your site), as this could lead to fewer conversions. Remember, the primary purpose of your website is to generate as many conversions as possible.

### *Opt-In Tips*

- **Only request essential information.** The more information that you request from your readers, the more suspicious they will be. You really only need to ask for two fields; their email address and their first name. Anything else is unnecessary and will result in a decrease in your conversion rate.

- **Be creative with your submit button text.** Replace the standard "Submit Now", button text with something more imaginative such as "Send me my free ebook now!" or "Send me my free discount codes now". Doing so will help a little with your conversion rate as it reaffirms to the user why they are subscribing.

- **Reassure potential subscribers that they won't be spammed.** People are very protective of their email addresses as they are becoming used to companies passing on their details to third parties. Make sure that you emphasize that you will not do this by saying something like "We hate spam, so we promise not to send your details to anyone else."

- **Make sure your list complies with CAN-SPAM regulations.** CAN-SPAM is a US law that aims to protect people from receiving spam emails. Services such as Aweber will help you to comply with this law and stick to the guidelines laid down – we will look at these guidelines in more detail later in this chapter. You might be thinking that you don't live in the US, however, so there is no need to observe this law. Well, legally there isn't, but not to do so would be a very bad business decision. Observing the law helps your trust with subscribers to increase and therefore means that your emails are opened more frequently and that you get better conversion rates. It also must be noted that many affiliate programs insist that you comply with Can-Spam regulations or you risk losing your account.

- **Make the double opt-in very clear.** The problem with double opt-in forms is that some people don't realize that they have to confirm their subscription by email. Make sure that you tell them during the actual sign-up process exactly what they must do to confirm their subscription.

## Trust & Deliverability

As I have already mentioned in this chapter the key to building a great and indeed profitable list is to build trust with your subscribers. Well that's all well and good, but how do you actually do that?

### *Gaining Trust From Your Subscribers*

Ensuring that you have a good relationship with your subscribers is the only way that you will be able to make money from your email list. Simply put, people who don't trust you won't take heed of any recommendations that you make, and this will mean that they won't buy any products from your site. Perhaps it is easier to think of it like this: if a complete stranger recommended something to you, you probably wouldn't pay much attention, but if your best friend recommended the same product, you would be tempted to buy it.

So when does the process of building trust start? Well, it starts from the moment that they land on your website – not from the moment that they sign up to your list. You must create a good impression from the first second that they begin interacting with you – which is why I didn't recommend using standard pop-up opt-in forms that most people who browse the internet have come to despise. Even if you did manage to get someone to subscribe while having a site that did not inspire trust, you would have a lot more work to do with your emails to gain the trust needed. So, make sure that everything is perfect from the start.

You should ensure that you keep building up trust throughout your relationship with your subscribers – there will, or should, never be a point where you can simply say, "They trust me enough; now I will simply sell them any crap so I can cash in." Just like a friendship in real life, you can't break the trust or the friendship will be over.

Every single aspect of this chapter is an integral part of using emails to gain more conversions. I will be the first to admit that it is not the most exciting chapter in the book, but it is incredibly important, so please stick with it and heed the advice given.

### *Ways To Destroy Trust*

We are going to start by looking at how you can destroy the trust of your subscribers. You might be thinking that this is an odd place to start, but think of it like this: if you know the things that you should avoid doing, it makes it easy to work out what you should be doing instead. So, in order to gain trust, you should positively avoid:

- **Sending spam or selling subscribers' details.** If you sell on your subscriber details, which in turn leads to someone sending your subscribers spam, they will eventually realize who is at fault, YOU! This will lead to your subscribers unsubscribing from your list and to your brand starting to gain a bad reputation.

- **Harassing people constantly.** People will expect you to try occasionally to sell them something, but they won't stand for it if you do it every day. Put yourself in their shoes: would you trust someone who was constantly badgering you to buy their product? It makes you sound desperate for the sale, which is never a good tactic.

- **Emailing people when you have nothing to say.** What's the point in talking to people just for the sake of it? Usually it is better to space your emails out and ensure that each one offers value to the subscriber, instead of sending one every day that offers nothing.

- **Making it tough for people to unsubscribe.** Although you want to build up a large list, you also want to make it easy for people to unsubscribe. After all, if someone wants to opt out, they are not very likely to purchase from you anyway, so there is no point in having them on your list. Letting those who want to leave your list do so, with as little effort as possible, will leave you with a highly targeted subscriber base.

- **Hiding behind your emails.** Don't worry about letting people know where the emails are coming from – be open and transparent in everything. You should also make sure that there is a way for them to contact you in the email, to create even more trust.

## How To Build Trust With Subscribers

So, now you know what you should not do, let's look at what you should do! You must always:

- **Make your information correct**. Ensure that all the information you send to subscribers is both correct and that it is relevant to the overall niche that you are working in. For example, if someone signs up for a guitar-playing course, then you should only send them information about guitars, songs and other guitar-related subjects. You should not send them offers to learn Spanish or to trade shares. By keeping the emails relevant, your subscribers will know that you are not trying simply to exploit them.

- **Make the information useful**. All the information you send to your subscribers should be of use to them. You will remember that people only care about something if it helps them to solve a problem, so make sure that each email fulfils this role.

- **Make it easy for people to unsubscribe.**

- **Be clear about who you are** – don't hide behind the emails.

- **Comply with CAN-SPAM law**, even if you don't reside in the US. This is purely a business consideration, as your emails will always be delivered to their desired targets and you will also gain trust with your audience. In fact, the CAN-SPAM Law is very important, so let's look at it in some more detail…

## *Understanding The CAN-SPAM Law*

There are a number of different facets to the CAN-SPAM Law, so let's look at some of the most important when it comes to your email list. The first thing to take from the law is that you should not use misleading "to" and "from" information. In other words, the emails should not seem as coming from someone other than their actual source. This is a common technique used by most spammers. Let's suppose they are trying to sell fake Dell computers: they might send out emails to people with a "sender" address that looks almost identical to an address used by Dell. This practice obviously only has one purpose – to trick people into believing that they are the real deal. You should never do this, firstly because it is incredibly dishonest, and secondly because it will massively affect the trust that you have built up with your list over time.

Misleading subject lines are also a big no when it comes to complying with the CAN-SPAM Law. These types of subject line are designed specifically to get people to open the email, using subjects like "Congratulations, You've Won A Prize!" but when the email is opened, there is no relevance to the subject line– you have not won a prize. This misleading subject line will mark you out as a dishonest person straight away and lead to a surge of unsubscriptions.

While it is fine to send out advertisements about your products and services, CAN-SPAM insists that you make it abundantly clear that they are adverts and not informative pieces. This is so that people cannot use official sounding documents to back up their product, when in reality it is something that they have simply written themselves. Just putting "THIS IS AN ADVERTISEMENT" at the top of the email does the trick.

One thing that we have already mentioned is that you should not try to hide behind your emails – always include a way in which people can contact you. In fact, it is a requirement under CAN-SPAM Law that you have an address included within the email. If you don't want to go this far, at least include an email and phone number. Alternatively – and probably a much better idea – you could get a PO Box.

This will be the third time that I have mentioned this point, but it bears repeating as it is in the CAN-SPAM Law – you must make it easy for people to unsubscribe from your emails! Also, when they unsubscribe, you should make sure that you accept this and don't bother them anymore. This will be no problem if you are using one of the major email services like

Aweber, as the opt-outs are carried out automatically. If you haven't invested in the services of one of these companies, this is another reason why you should!

That is really all there is to say regarding the CAN-SPAM Law. One thing that I should add as a caveat to the end of this: if you employ someone, make sure that they are aware of all of these rules and regulations too. After all, they might be the ones doing the work, but it is your hard earned reputation that is on the line.

## Email Deliverability

Email deliverability is extremely important for one reason and one reason only – if your email is never delivered, you have no chance of using it to make a sale! You are not even giving someone the chance to decide whether to open it – it is simply confined to the pile of lost emails sitting somewhere in cyberspace. Deliverability is the absolute key when looking to get good conversion rates.

Spam filters on even the least advanced systems are becoming more advanced and much cleverer at filtering out emails, meaning that even if you aren't spamming – which you won't be – you will often find it tough to get an email delivered. Non-delivered emails obviously include those that are sent to incorrect email addresses, but the most common type are those that end up in trash folders, as most people don't check this folder and simply delete it every once in a while. It is your goal to get your emails delivered to the inbox, not to the trash, junk or spam box of your subscribers.

Some email providers are stricter than others when it comes to filtering out what they consider to be spam emails, so you will have to deal with them as well. In fact, it is sometimes the case that they won't even let an email get through to the spam box of a specific email address if they deem it to be spam. This means that sometimes even honest emails – such as the ones you will be sending out – can go undelivered, which is another challenge for you to overcome.

## How To Increase Email Deliverability

There are a number of ways to increase the chances of your emails being delivered to their intended targets, the first of which is to encourage your subscribers to provide you with the email address that they use the most. Many people have two or even three different email accounts; when they sign up for ebooks and the like, they will put in their secondary email, so that they can get the free gift and then never have to check the emails again. Sometimes it is worth being very specific with your request – "Please provide your primary email address" is a good way to ask for it.

We have already spoken about double opt-ins as using this method will help with the deliverability of your emails. With double opt-in only people who really want to receive the emails will get them, which means that they won't delete them so often that they start to get classed as spam.

The address books that are found within different email providers' set-ups are also important, because if you can get subscribers to add you to their address book, it will mean that they have marked you as trusted and therefore the email provider will deliver your emails without problems. Even some of the biggest companies in the world request that you add them to your address book; if they do it, why shouldn't you? In fact, it is worth adding this request onto the bottom of every single email that you send, just to remind people constantly to do it.

Link shorteners, such as TinyURL should be avoided, as should linking to any URLs that have been blacklisted by ISPs. It might be the case that shortened URLs look better, but many email providers have started to become suspicious of them as they redirect a request. This means that if you use them, you always run the risk of your emails being automatically condemned to spam folders. It's not worth the risk just for the sake of a slightly prettier URL.

There are two different types of email that you can send out – HTML and text. There are many companies that only send out HTML versions of an email but the problem is that not every email service has the ability to read HTML, which means that you run the risk of not allowing a portion of your subscribers to ever read what you are sending. By sending out both types of email, you allow your readers to make their own choice as to which one they want to read.

One of the ways that spam filters decide which emails are spam and which aren't is through looking at the words that are used in both the subject line and the body of the text. Examples of the sorts of word that will class an email as spam include "porn", "make money", "pharmaceutical", "enhancement" and "sex". For this reason, you should avoid using words that could have been blacklisted by the spam filters. If you do have to use them, don't try to hide them. Some people will write things such as "p0rn" or "s3x" to try to fool the filters, but this doesn't work – filters are much cleverer than we give them credit for! Also, an email containing this type of language is not trustworthy at all, so nobody will ever act on them.

Images within an email can also lead to the email not being delivered, especially if you have excessive numbers of images or oversized images. This is because spam filters have become wise to one of the newer tricks that spammers have been using, which is to paste all the text into an image and then simply send one large image within the email, instead of plain text. This means that images are often being blocked now, even if they are honest and harmless.

The final thing to consider – and one of the most important – is to use a reputable email service like Aweber. The reputable services will have agreements with ISPs that mean their emails are not automatically placed into the spam folder. If you have a spare few dollars a month, then a service like this could in the long term be worth its weight in gold to you.

### *Basic Email Marketing Summary*

By now you should have a good understanding of exactly how to gain trust with your subscribers. Let's take a little time to recap.

- Trust is incredibly important when it comes to getting conversions through emails. To gain trust with your subscribers, make sure that your emails are always informative and offer good value to the reader. The more trust your subscribers have in you, the greater the chance they will purchase from you.

- The CAN-SPAM Law is important, even if you are not from the US. Complying with it will increase the trust that people have in you and it will also ensure that your chances of getting an email delivered are vastly increased.

- You should always use double opt-in forms. This will make sure that all the email addresses you have are real and that only people who want to receive your emails will get them.

- Send plain and HTML versions of each email to your subscribers, so that you don't alienate those unable to open HTML emails.

- Try to avoid words that will trigger the spam filter.

## Understanding Open Rates

Getting email marketing right is not as easy as you may at first have thought. Firstly you need a "hook" to entice visitors to subscribe. Once they have subscribed you then need further "hooks" to keep your subscribers opening your emails, plus of course, slowly but surely you must also build trust with your subscribers. You may be surprised to learn that the actual number of your visitors that open your emails, will only be a fraction of your total subscribers. The graph on the following page displays average open rates for many popular niches.

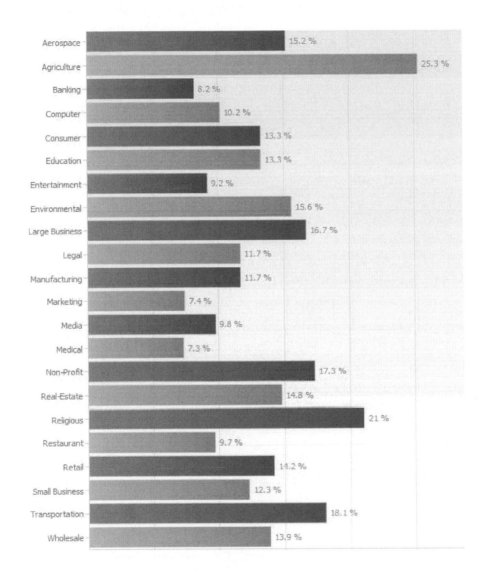

As you can see from the above graph, average open rates are disappointing. In many cases 90% or more of your emails will not even be opened! The email that you send to your subscribers that will have the greatest open rate, in most cases surpassing the 95% mark, will be the very first email you send to new subscribers. This of course will be the email sent to subscribers who were enticed from your initial hook. From experience, although I don't want to "spook" new subscribers with a hard sell, especially in the very first email I send them, I include at least a couple of juicy offers in the very first email. I will cherry pick the very best offers I have and include them with the hook that I used to tempt them to subscribe in the first place. I will also ensure that they receive the hook and the "juicy" offers as soon as they have verified their email address. Aweber lets you set up automatic emails so that the first email is delivered to the new subscriber's inbox within a minute after the subscriber has verified his subscription. From my experience this is always the most profitable email I send to subscribers, simply because the open rate is so high.

## How To Improve Open Rates

The likelihood of someone opening an email from you has much to do with the relationship that you have with the recipient, as well as with the degree of trust that they have in you. Those with a good relationship and high trust levels will find that they automatically get more people opening their emails, even if your subject lines are woeful to say the very least. Remember, however, an open rate of 20% in the long term is above average, excluding of course the very first email you send to new subscribers.

To help improve your email open rates you should not underestimate the power of a well-composed subject line. Think of it this way: your reputation and trust might get 20% of your subscribers to open the email, but having a good subject line can tempt many more of your subscribers to doing the same. As well as the subject line, there are also a number of other factors that you must consider. You should look at the type of traffic you get, the niche that you operate in, whether you use double opt-in forms – in fact, there are so many factors that it's impossible to list them all.

When trying to put a figure on what you should be aiming at in terms of an open rate, it is best to start with a target of around 10% to 20%. If you reach this target, then in all honesty you have done a great job.

## The Importance of Email Subject Lines

Subject lines, as I already said, are important when trying to tempt subscribers to open your emails. They are basically the email equivalent of the headline on a webpage, or even in a newspaper. They are there to fulfil the first two aspects of the AIDA model – attention and interest – by standing out from the rest of the emails in the inbox and gaining the reader's interest regarding what the email is about. Take a moment to think about which emails in your inbox you choose to open and which ones you simply push to your junk folder.

Email subject lines are very similar to website headlines, particularly in the prolific use of "you" language. In addition, they should have the same urgency attached to them and adopt the same principles as we discussed in the copywriting chapter. Don't think that a good subject line will always lead to the highest open rate, however – they are there as a way to build trust as well as to get conversions, so sometimes it's better to get more trust and a few less opened emails in the long run.

Let's look at that last point in a bit more detail. Imagine you run a store that sells fridges, and you decide to send out an email to your subscribers. If you put the headline as "Congratulations, You've Won $5,000!" you are likely to get a high open rate. Once they see that this is untrue, however, they will lose trust in you. It is better to have a subject line that says something true, such as "10% Off All Fridge Orders Today", which won't get as many people opening the email, but will build up trust when they see that the content is truthful and there to attempt to help them if they are looking for a new fridge. So, remember that when it comes to who opens your emails, it is quality over quantity. 20 people opening an email with a genuine interest in the offer that you have is better than 200 opening an email that is built on a lie.

So you want to make the subject line relevant and ensure that it doesn't mislead anyone. It doesn't have to be the greatest in the world – it just needs to be worded in a way that gains people's attention, and it needs to tell them what they will find in the email.

## Tips For Writing Good Subject Lines

Below are a few tips that will help you to create great subject lines for your emails:

- Don't use the subscriber's name too often. In the course of collecting emails, you will undoubtedly collect the first names of all of your subscribers. Many affiliates then use the acquired first name in the subject line of every single message that they send out. I, however, would really not recommend this at all. It used to be a powerful trick to boost open rates, although now many have realized that the internet isn't a particularly personal place, so this tactic is far less effective.

- Subject lines should always be short – nobody wants to read an essay in the subject line. Make sure that it is long enough to provide all the relevant information that you need to generate the reader's attention and interest, but don't make it so

177

long that it bores the reader. Also, certain email providers will only allow a certain amount of space for each subject line.

- Intrigue is good. People like to be intrigued; therefore subject lines that create this will do well. In the next section of this chapter we will look at some examples of how to employ intriguing email subject lines.

- Ellipses (…) can increase email open rate, as they add the sense that there is more to read in the body of the email text. Remember that we said full stops make people think that they can stop reading? Well, ellipses work in exactly the opposite way.

- Create some kind of urgency in your subject line, but only do so if you are confident that you can get it right. Urgency in every single email you send is not recommended, however, so use this tactic sparingly.

- I have already said that trigger words should be avoided, but you should also make sure that you don't use capital letters. This is partly to do with deliverability, but mainly because, in many people's minds, capital letters = spam, so they won't open the email.

- People will not always read the entire subject line, so make sure that the vital information is right at the beginning. That way, everyone will see what the message is about, regardless of how lazy or busy they are!

- Make sure that the subject line is relevant. I have mentioned this before, but it is extremely important. If people know that you always tell the truth in your subject line, they will have no reason to distrust you and not open the email.

- Never leave the subject line blank, as you are simply wasting the opportunity to catch people's attention. Without a subject line, how can people possibly tell whether they want to see the contents of your email?

- Always make sure that you offer something to those opening the email. Remember, you are the one trying to help them, so just saying, "Please visit our site" is not going to have much effect. If you say, "Please visit our site and receive a free ebook", however, more people will take up the offer.

## *Good Subject Line Examples*

Below are some good examples of subject lines that really do work. I know this as they have all been tested, which you should also do with your email subject lines. Please feel free to use these as templates, but test them first – what works for me might not work for you!

- **Five Amazing [topic] Predictions For This Year!** – This subject line creates intrigue, because people want to know what these amazing predictions are. The topic is also included in the title, so they will know what the email is about. You could go one step further and place ellipses at the end for extra effect.

- **Improve Your [insert skill] In Just 24 Hours** – With this subject line, you are letting the reader know that you are going to teach them something that could be valuable to them. Intrigue is also created as they will want to know how you are going to do this and the line also uses "you" language to engage the reader.

- **Find Out The Quickest Way To [insert goal]. (Limited Time Only)** – "Limited time only" obviously increases the urgency that people will feel when reading the email, and it also uses "you" language.

- **Fantastic News About Your [insert service]** – Once again, it uses "you" language and there is also intrigue, as readers will want to know what the great news is that could benefit them. If they think that they are getting good news, they'll open the email straight away!

As I mentioned above, the most important thing regarding email subject lines is to test them a few times, and then test them some more! Your list will be different to everyone else's list, so the people on it will have their own likes and dislikes when it comes to emails.

The one thing that you should remember above all others in respect to open rates is that the number of people opening the emails you send is directly related to the amount of trust that they have in you. The other massively important aspect is the subject line, and when trust and a good subject line are used together, you will get very good results. Remember that a good subject line isn't always the one that gets the most opened emails, however – you want people to open your emails who are likely to convert, not people opening them because they have been attracted by a lie.

Subject lines that are short usually work best. These subject lines should always be relevant and they should focus on the recipient by using "you" language. Make the subject line and the actual content relevant to each other as well, so that the two flow together seamlessly.

Spam triggers do prove to be a real problem and, although they are not your fault, they could well stop your emails reaching the intended mailbox. Make sure that you word your emails correctly to avoid these triggers. Above all, however, test your subject lines – one type of subject line will work better than others in every single niche.

## Content & Frequency

Last but not least you must give considerable thought to the actual content you send to your subscribers. There is no point in getting everything else right, which would result in a great open rate, only to confuse your subscribers with your actual copy.

### *The Email Content*

What is content? The content is the main body of text that is found when people open up an email. It provides a way to take subscribers through the rest of the AIDA process – Desire and Action – and, you hope, end up with a conversion. This is usually the same, regardless of the type of email you are sending out. If you send a sales pitch, you want to make people desire the product and then take action by clicking on the link to buy it, while if you are sending out a purely informational email, you simply want to create desire so that the readers visit your site.

There are times when you are not trying to create Desire and Action, however, although this is the exception rather than the rule. This happens when you are deliberately trying to ensure that people don't feel compelled to visit your site, so that you can assure them that you aren't constantly trying to sell them something. Remember, it is important to mix up the types of email that you send so that people keep their trust in you.

The main focus of all email sending activities should be to get a relationship going with readers, even if you are sending out a sales pitch to them. In fact, if you are looking to send a sales pitch, you should ask yourself whether it is contributing to this on-going relationship. If the answer is no, you should not be sending it at all.

When you sit down to write these emails, the most effective strategy is usually to make them personalized. Firstly we need to look at commonly used types of email.

## Understanding Different Types of Emails

There are a few different types of email that you should become familiar with. These are:

- Informational emails. These are used to create trust in your subscribers and usually contain non-sales oriented material that is designed to help them out, such as tips and useful hints.

- Relationship building emails. These are obviously there to build up a relationship with the readers of your emails. One of the most effective ways to do this is to ask them for feedback and other comments about your site or even products that you feature on your site. Just remember, however, people don't do things for free – make sure that you give them something free if they do send a comment!

- Update and pre-sale emails. These are designed to give advance warning to readers of the emails of a product launch that may well be of interest to them. Readers will find this helpful, and at the same time it will increase the chances that they will buy the product from you.

- Sales emails. These are obviously targeted to sell products.

- Follow up emails. When someone has made a purchase, you can send him or her an email to ask certain things, such as their satisfaction with the product or whether they would like to buy additional items for the product itself.

When you send out these types of email, they will usually be classified as either informal or formal emails.

## Informal Emails

As the name suggests, these emails have quite a relaxed approach to them, and you come across as though you are talking to a close friend. The following example shows the tone that could be used in these.

*"Hi John,*

*Just wanted to pick your brains for a sec… Have you ever looked at Google Analytics and wondered why you aren't getting more traffic? I used always to be in this position, but wanted to let you into a little secret that I found out…"*

Obviously your email would then go on and provide more details, but the above example shows the type of attitude you want to portray. It needs to be friendly but still have an element of a sales pitch too, although make sure that it isn't too noticeable. The most vital aspect of these emails, however, is that they help to strengthen the relationship between the subscriber and you.

Writing informally should involve a few of the things that we talked about in the copywriting module. For example, you could use:

- Short, sharp and snappy paragraphs
- "You" language
- Bold text, sub headers and easy to read bullet points
- Call to action links that are incredibly easy for the reader to find

You might be wondering why we don't change our copywriting approach when we write emails instead of web content. Well, you have to remember that regardless of the medium, people are still sitting in front of their computer reading it, so the same rules apply. Make sure that your copy is easy to read and also fun for the reader as well if you want good results!

It is always good if you can provide an independent resource to back up any claims that you make in an email. The best way to do this is to look through recent news stories and see if there have been any developments in the world that relate to your product. For example, if you run a site about muscle growth supplements, you could quote a news article about a new plant or herb that has been proved to assist in this regard, and then direct the person reading to a site that sells this product. Whether you include a link to the article or not is your choice, but remember that you might leak traffic through the link so think carefully before including it.

### *Formal Emails*

So let's move on to formal emails, which are not actually dissimilar to informal ones. The one key aspect in which they differ is in the tone that they have, as formal emails are not as friendly as the informal ones. The same rules about how to write the copy and how pushy to be with a sales pitch still apply.

The main use for formal emails comes when you are trying to come across as an authority on a specific subject, as when doing this you must sound professional and like a business, not an individual. Don't go overly formal, however, as this will simply end up coming across as boring – make sure that you add a slight bit of personalization into the emails and at least use the reader's first name in the email. This will make the readers feel that you are addressing them individually and not as though you are simply sending a blanket email out to everyone.

Links can be a great way to increase the amount of authority that you have, as you can link to other sites that have authority in the niche and therefore essentially piggy back their reputation. Employing this tactic can also have the effect that your readers trust your content more as you provide sources for your information. This can mean that you retain a formal approach while also providing interest and value to the reader.

### *Email Content Tips*
There are a number of things that you should consider when sending out any type of email.

- You should always have at least one link to your site, as this will help to drive visitors from your emails to your site. After all, the more visitors to your site, the more chances you have of making a successful sale, regardless of the niche that you are in.

- It is important to give people a reason to visit your site, such as giving them half an article and then telling them that the rest can be read by clicking on the link that you have provided. You must ensure, however, that the article is of good quality, and that it actually entices the reader to visit your site to read the remainder of the article. In this case you will not only gain more traffic, but you will also gain trust.

- Always remember what the ultimate goal is for everything that you are doing in relation to your site – to get conversions and therefore make more money. Therefore, your emails must include all the components needed to push people through the sales funnel and lead to them converting on your site or from links to merchant websites included in emails. Even if the emails are part of a pre-written series, you need to ensure that they all build up to one final aim. For example, if you run an online course, you might want to send out previews of different modules to readers. This will not only give them value and improve the trust that they have in you, but will also lead up to them wanting to sign up for the course once the emails stop.

- Finally – and perhaps most importantly – you must ensure that every single email you send out gives some kind of value to your customers. This is even more true than usual when you send out an email promoting a product, because promoting one that simply doesn't work or is of no value to them will see your trust decline incredibly quickly. Even if you think that a certain email could make you some short-term money, don't send it if you think it will damage your relationship with your readers – it's not worth it in the long run!

## *Email Frequency*

So, how often should you send emails out to your subscribers? Well, the answer is not a clear-cut one, as it varies from list to list. There are many different things to think about, such as the niche you work in, how your list has been collected, the types of subscriber you have and the information that you send out to them. The more astute of you will have realized that this means one thing and one thing only – that you must test the frequency of your list!

One very good way to ensure that you get the number of emails you send correct is to tell readers what to expect when they sign up. For example, on the sign up page you could say "signing up to these emails will mean that I send you three emails per week, all containing information that is useful to you when it comes to [insert topic]". This will mean that people know what to expect and that your emails will get a much better open rate – leading to better conversion rates.

Open rates can be a really good way to test how often you should send emails. If you are sending out two emails per week and see that the open rates on a particular day seem poor, then target a different day. I have found that sending emails between 6.30pm and 7.00pm produces by far the best open rates. This is of course the time when most people have returned from work, had dinner and perhaps sat down to check their inbox, so my email should be right at the top of the subscriber's inbox. This is common sense, but you would be amazed by how many affiliates send emails at crazy times such as midnight, so that the email is perhaps 18 hours old and sitting at the bottom of the user's inbox when the subscriber actually gets the time to check their email.

If you find that open rates are falling or that you have had a recent glut of cancelled subscriptions, check for any feedback unhappy subscribers may have left for you, which you can do if you are using Aweber. I cannot stress strongly enough how important it is to act on feedback from your subscribers no matter whether the actual feedback is positive or negative. An unhappy subscriber may well have left you angry feedback to attack you, but in reality if you understand why the writer is so annoyed and act on the underlying problem, in the long term he may have done you a favour.

You must always bear in mind that, as well as your regular emails, you will also want to send occasional broadcasts. Broadcasts are basically emails that you decide to send in between the normal emails, so are an additional email to factor into your equation. These could be something urgent that you need to tell the subscribers such as a new product launch, or something special that you want to offer them that has become available at the very last minute.

Perhaps the most useful piece of information that I can give you is this: the less you sell, the more you can email. Basically this means that the more good information you give to people, the happier they will be to receive regular emails. If you are only really sending out sales emails, they won't want to get them every day, as they provide no value to them. You need to strike a balance between sending too many emails and not enough, as either can affect the number of conversions that you generate.

For the actual content of your emails you should ensure that you take notice and act upon the following points:

- Every single email should aim to build up the relationship that you have with the subscriber. This relationship is the most important factor when it comes to getting conversions through the practice of sending emails to your subscribers.

- Informal emails are by far the more popular type of email to send, especially among affiliates. They allow you to come across as informal and to interact on a personal level, which will increase the trust that people have in you. In fact, even the most formal of emails should have some personal element to them if they are going to be effective.

- Regardless of whether you are constructing emails or web copy, you should still write in exactly the same way. People read both on their computer screen, so are still attracted by the same things. Remember great copy generates sales!

185

- Make sure that you have at least one link to your site on EVERY email you send to your subscribers.

- Monitor the open rates of the emails you send so in time you can find the optimum day and time to send emails to your subscribers.

Now you should have a decent understanding of exactly what you need to do to build a highly profitable list. Affiliates who take the time to work on their list building techniques will of course be the ones who profit the most.

# Chapter 11 – On-Site SEO

Up until this chapter most of the content of this book has been geared to your potential website visitors. For example, you have learnt how to design your site in such a way that even "stupid" visitors can find the articles they require quickly. You have learnt about different types of visitor and how to create specific copy to cater for their exact needs. You have even learnt how to entice your visitors to perform specific actions which in turn leads to a conversion that boosts the balance of your bank account. What I have not yet discussed is exactly how you are going to get visitors to find your website. In reality you could create a stunning website with perfect copy catering to all your potential visitors' needs, but if potential visitors don't know about your site, or indeed can't find your site, then all your hard work will be in vain.

On-site SEO (search engine optimization) is simply the process of making the content of your site search engine friendly. Good on-site SEO makes it easy for search engines to classify each page of your content for key phrase searches made by search engine users, who are of course your potential visitors. To be honest, many so-called SEO experts try to make the process of SEO sound far more technical than it actually is. In reality you don't need to be a SEO genius to get pages of your site ranking highly in Google search results. You simply need to make sure that your content follows set rules, which I will cover in this chapter.

Most of the online affiliates I know and talk to on a regular basis would not class themselves in anyway as SEO experts. I would say, however, that most earn far more than many self-proclaimed SEO experts.

As the name suggests, on-site SEO is search engine optimization that takes place within the confines of your own website. There are a huge number of different aspects that can be optimized – many more than you would probably initially imagine – and they should all be combined to create a site that is completely optimized.

Some of the major areas of on-site SEO include:

- The text on the site
- The source code of the site
- The site's URL
- Pictures and videos on the site

- How the different pages on the site are linked together
- The load time of a site

While there are undoubtedly many more than these six areas, these are the ones that you need to focus on – the ones that all new affiliates should understand and implement on their site. As you continue your SEO education, you will find more and more ways to enhance your on-site SEO as you develop as an affiliate.

So, basically, on-site SEO can be defined as:

*The way you organise and label specified elements of your content to enhance rankings for specified key phrases within search engine results.*

## Why is On-Site SEO Important?

If the actual on-site SEO of your site is poor, then no matter how good your content, you will struggle to attract visitors from search engines. SEO is the process of using various techniques to increase your presence in search engine rankings – with particular emphasis on the rankings that Google supplies. For example, if you have a great review page, which details the features and benefits of the XTZ Folding Treadmill, then you want those searching for key phrases such as "XTZ Folding Treadmill", "XTZ Folding Treadmill Review" and "Buy XTZ Folding Treadmill" to find your review page through search engine queries.

The actual process of ranking pages for specified key phrases in search engines is done in a number of different ways, but can be broken down into two distinct camps – on-site SEO and off-site SEO. Both of these are extremely important because without the visibility that SEO gives you, you will not generate any traffic from search engine queries (organic traffic).

## What are the Different Aspects of On-Site SEO?

As you might imagine, there are many different tactics you can employ to boost your on-site and indeed on-page SEO, so let's take a look at the some of the most important elements.

### *Keywords*

The first thing that you should do is check that your content is optimized for the keywords that you are targeting by making sure that they are prevalent in your copy text. You must understand that keywords are the absolute cornerstone of any good SEO campaign and therefore you should take the time to research key phrases that relate to your niche and are actively used by those searching for products and information in that niche. The keywords that you use both on-site and off-site should work together so that you get maximum "SEO power" for your efforts.

When using targeted keywords in copy, one mistake that those new to online marketing make is to overuse the key phrases by including them in their articles too many times. The repetition of key phrases in articles is commonly known as keyword density. The actual phrase "keyword density" may sound a little complicated although in reality it is not. Keyword density is simply the percentage of occurrences of a single keyword or even keyword phrase in your copy. Let's say that you have an article where the main key phrase is "blue widget". Your article is 500 words long and you have used the keyword phrase "blue widget" 20 times in your article. To calculate the actual keyword density for a specified keyword phrase you simply use the following formula:

Number of times the keyword phrase is used / total number of words of the article * 100

So to calculate the keyword density of the blue widget example article, we start with the number of times the keyword phrase has been used (20), divide by the total number of words in the article (500) and multiply by 100. The formula: (20 / 500) * 100 gives us a key word density of 4%.

If maths is not your strongest point, you can simply use online tools to check your articles to find the keyword density quickly for a number of keyword phrases for a specific article. To find such tools simply type "free keyword density tool" into your favourite search engine.

Years ago, when search engine algorithms were less sophisticated, a common tactic employed by online affiliates was to "stuff" keyword phrases into their articles to a high degree, which resulted in their articles containing a very high keyword density for targeted key phrases, in many cases over 20% or indeed in some cases much higher. Years ago, (although it must be noted this tactic no longer works) using a high keyword density of targeted keyword phrases in articles tricked search engines to rank the content highly. Nowadays employing such a tactic will result in such content being "flagged" by search engines, with the effect that the article will not rank at all.

The question I can virtually hear you asking me is, "What is the optimum keyword density I should aspire to?" This question, together with perhaps hundreds of other SEO questions, is subject to a high degree of debate. There is actually no definitive answer, although many people will tell you to create articles with a keyword density of between 2% and 4%. I would say that you should not worry too much about keyword density but simply concentrate on producing good quality articles. My own approach is simply to produce a quality article, and then run the article through a free keyword density tool. If my article has a keyword density of less than 1%, I simply make a few adjustments to the text to push up the keyword density to 1%. If the article I have produced naturally had a keyword density of over 2%, I would simply leave it as it was, although you will find that if you are concentrating on creating quality copy, this will rarely occur. I can probably say that in my time as an affiliate I have never naturally produced articles with a keyword density of over 2%. Remember the name of the game is to produce quality articles that inform your readers and entice them to click affiliate links. Stuffing copy with key phrases will make your articles unnatural to read and in many cases will drive your readers to click the back button on their browsers.

You will find that articles with a high keyword density for targeted key phrases are on the whole poor quality articles that do not read in a good manner.

As a general rule ensure that your articles never surpass a key phrase density of 3%, which equates to a thousand word article containing a targeted key phrase 30 times. Most of the time, an article like this would look unnatural. Again I will stress that you should concentrate on producing quality copy and then simply ensure that the keyword density is at least 1% and, preferably, in most cases does not surpass 2%.

## *Title Tags*
The title tag of each of your pages is another extremely important element in respect to on-site SEO. The title tag is simply the main text that describes your article's content to search engines. After the overall content of your article, the title text is perhaps the next most important on-page SEO element. If you take a moment to Google "folding treadmills" and take the time to look at the search results that are displayed, you will see the importance of title tags, as they are displayed in a bold blue coloured font for each search result.

You should ensure that each title tag you use starts with your main key phrase and gives a clear and concise description of the actual page content. Also note that title tags can be a maximum of 70 characters. If your title tags exceed 70 characters in length, they will be truncated, so ensure you give considerable thought to the title tags you use.

Also of great importance is that the actual content of your title tags can affect the number of clicks you generate from search engine results. Remember, people scan internet content, including search engine results. From experience I can tell you that cleverly composed title tags can generate more clicks than higher ranked search engine search results. For example, let's say you were using Google search because you wanted to buy "blue widgets". Which one of the search results below do you think you would click first?

**Blue Widgets Review**

www.widgetsreview.com/blue-widgets-review/

Blue widgets are now more popular than ever before.

**Smith & Co Blue Widgets**

www.smithco.com/blue-widgets/

Smith & Co stock a great range of Blue Widgets

191

**Blue Widgets Sale – EXCLUSIVE DISCOUNTS – FREE Delivery**

www.widgetworld.com/blue-widgets-review

Top Quality Blue Widgets At Rock Bottom Prices, Save up to 50%!

From the above examples of search engine results listing, I would guess you would be drawn to the third listing and I would also suggest that this listing would generate more clicks than the two listings above it. From experience I can tell you that clever use of the title tag can vastly increase click-through rate (CTR) from search engine results. I'm amazed that many affiliate webmasters spend time on ensuring that they include the correct key phrases in their title tags but give little thought to optimizing their title tags for increased clicks for search results.

A word of warning, however! Although there is nothing wrong with being creative with title tags in effect to steal clicks from webmasters with better rankings, you must ensure that your title tags do not mislead those who read them. As already mentioned, part of the Google algorithm actually monitors users who click search results and their later actions. If users click-through to your site from Google search results, and then quickly return to the search results (SERP Bounce) because they do not find what they are looking for on your site, either because they have been misled or because your content is poor, then this action in effect counts as a negative vote for your site. There is now strong evidence that sites that accumulate a set number of negative votes are deemed to be classed as poor quality sites by the Google algorithm, which results in the entire site being dealt a penalty, with the result of the loss of all rankings.

## URL Structure

The URL (uniform resource locator) you give to each page of your website is another vital aspect of on-site SEO. By default Wordpress uses a horrible URL structure which produces URLs such as www.yourwebsite.com/?p=123. Using such a poor URL structure would of course mean that a great article you may have produced entitled "Blue Widget Review" would be given a default URL by Wordpress such as www.yoursite.com/?p=1, whereas to rank well in search engines you would need an URL such as www.yourwebsite.com/blue-widget-review/. Of course using the default Wordpress URL structure, which in effect produces such naff URLs, is going to seriously damage your chances of gaining good search engine rankings. The good news, however, is that you can change the appearance of Wordpress URLs with little effort.

To change your Wordpress URLs to search engine friendly URLs, simply login to your Wordpress backend, which you would do by going to www.yoursite.com/wp-admin and entering your username and password. Then click Settings and then Permalinks, which you will find on the left hand side of the screen. You will then see the screen below:

All you need to do now is click the "custom structure" radio button and enter */%postname%* just as displayed above. Ensure you do this BEFORE even loading your first article!

To optimize your URLs for search engines you must ensure that each and every URL at least starts with your article's targeted key phrase. For example if you had an article such as "Blue Widget Review" then you could name your URL www.yoursite.com/blue-widget-review/, www.yoursite.com/blue-widget-review-buyers-guide/, or even www.yoursite.com/blue-widget-review-with-discount/. It is essential for good on-site SEO that your article's main key phrase is used at the start of the URL, which is the section of the URL that always follows the domain name.

When you enter a new article into Wordpress, the actual URL, provided that you have changed the custom URL structure, is simply automatically generated from the article title.

In many cases you may not want the exact title of your article as the article URL. When adding or editing posts to Wordpress, you will see the following at the top of the edit post or add post input screens:

To change the actual URL of any article simply click the edit button and type in the URL you require. Always check you are 100% happy with the URL BEFORE you post articles. Also, note that Wordpress sometime truncates URLs depending on how long it actually takes you to type in each article title, which is another reason you should double check your article URL before posting your article.

### *Meta Description Tags*

Meta Descriptions Tags do not really play a role in search engine rankings but for boosting click-through rate from search results are vital. Unique meta descriptions should be entered for EVERY single article you post on your affiliate site. Meta descriptions comprise of HTML code in the format as shown below:

*<head> <meta name="description" content="This is where you would give a description of your article. This text will usually be displayed in search results under the title tag.*
*</head>*

For those who have no coding experience there is no need to panic as you will simply be entering your meta description tags, without the need for any coding, using the All in One SEO Wordpress Plug-in. Every time you add or update a post using Wordpress, providing of course you have loaded the All In One SEO Plug-in, you will see the following SEO input fields.

All in One SEO Pack

Upgrade to All in One SEO Pack Pro Version

Title:     0     characters. Most search engines use a maximum of 60 chars for the title.

Description:     0     characters. Most search engines use a maximum of 160 chars for the description.

Keywords (comma separated):

Disable on this page/post: ☐

For every article you post you should enter all three of the fields listed above: title, description and keywords. The data you enter into the field will not be displayed on your actual article's webpage but will be displayed in search engine results. Your article may have a main title of "Blue Widget Review" but by entering a more creative title in the All in One SEO Pack title field, such as "Blue Widgets Sale – EXCLUSIVE DISCOUNTS – FREE Delivery", you can feed a more creative and indeed more clickable title to search engines.

Getting back to meta descriptions, let's again take a look at the Google search result page for the query "folding treadmills".

**Folding Treadmills** | Fold Away Treadmills | Compact Folding ...
www.fitness-superstore.co.uk › Treadmills
Products 1 - 24 – **Folding Treadmills**, fold away treadmills for easy storage. Buy
compact & portable **folding treadmills** With Fast Free UK Delivery.
↳ Folding Treadmills | Fold Away ...   - NordicTrack T9 Si Folding ...   - Treo Fitness

| Page: | PA: 33 | mR: 4.25 | mT: n/a | 89 links from PRO ONLY Root Domains | Root Domain: | DA: 53 |

**Results for FOLDING TREADMILLS**   McAfee SECURE
www.argos.co.uk/static/Search/.../FOLDING+TREADMILS.htm
Items 1 - 9 of 9 – Shop for **FOLDING TREADMILLS** at Argos.co.uk. Check stock online
& reserve for in-store collection and payment, or arrange home delivery for ...

| Page: | PA: 1 | mR: 0.00 | mT: n/a | 0 links from PRO ONLY Root Domains | Root Domain: | DA: 79 |

Best **Folding Treadmills**
walking.about.com/od/treadmillreviews/tp/treadmillfold.htm
by Wendy Bumgardner
28 Aug 2011 – Top picks for best **folding treadmills** for walkers and runners,
chosen from treadmill reviews.

| Page: | PA: 59 | mR: 3.96 | mT: n/a | 50 links from PRO ONLY Root Domains | Root Domain: | DA: 93 |

If you take a good look at the above search result listing, you should now know that the first line of each listing is the article title, or, if you are using the All In One SEO plug-in, the title you entered in the title field. The next line of the listing is the URL of the page, with the following two lines being the meta description. The meta description is simply a short paragraph of up to 160 characters that you should use to give a brief summary of your article. The meta description is in reality used by webmasters as another option to entice readers to click-through to their site, just like the title tag for those in the know, but in a little more detail.

Again be creative with your meta descriptions by using the 160 characters to sell the benefits of your article.

## *Meta Keyword Tag*

Due to the meta keyword tag being exploited over the years, Google no longer uses the meta keyword tag as detailed on the Google Webmasters blog - http://googlewebmastercentral.blogspot.com/2009/09/google-does-not-use-keywords-meta-tag.html. This does not mean, however, that you should leave the keyword meta tag field empty each time you post a new article.

Google may well now disregard the meta keyword tag but other search engines certainly do not. Although a large proportion of your organic traffic will come from the Google search engine, I have found that on some of my sites up to 30% of my organic traffic actually comes from other search engines. Remember your goal is to drive as much targeted traffic as possible to your site. Also of note is that many of the web's directories, including some of the leading directories, actually use meta keyword data for categorizing listing. I have noticed many free backlinks in my backlink profile from leading directories that have certainly used meta keyword data to define the correct category for my listing.

For each article ensure that you enter meta keyword data, although don't simply cram dozens of different keywords into the All in One SEO Pack Meta Keyword field. Simply enter three or four keywords that are highly relevant to your article, with each keyword separated by a comma. For example for a Blue Widgets Review article you could include the following keywords:

blue widgets, blue widgets review, buy blue widgets

## *Robots.txt*

The basic premise of the robots.txt file in relation to Wordpress, is that there are two different tags that you can place within your main source code – one that allows search engines to index your site, and another that in effect blocks them. As you can imagine, you want your site to be "readable" by search engines which will lead to your pages being listed in search results – if it isn't, that is SEO suicide!

You can easily view your robots.txt by simply visiting the following URL: www.yoursitename.com/robots.txt

To check whether your site is open to search engines, your site's robot.txt should include the following:

User-agent: *

Disallow:

The above contents of a robots.txt file would result in all search engines being able to read all the pages of your site.

Now compare the above to a robot.txt file that is blocking search engines:

```
User-agent: *

Disallow: /
```

As you can see from these two examples above, the only difference is the use of the forward slash " / ".

To understand how the robots.txt actually functions, let me explain the above commands. The "User-agent: *" simply means that the action applies to all robots. The "Disallow: /" tells the robot that it should not visit any pages on the site.

Using Wordpress, once again you don't have to worry about coding. Wordpress has a privacy option, which in effect gives you two options. You can either allow search engines to index your website or block search engines from indexing your website.

When you first install Wordpress, you should initially block search engines from indexing your site because your "blank" website is going to undergo many changes as you set it up ready for your content. To block search engines simply log in to your Wordpress backend, go to settings and select the privacy option. You will then be presented with the following screen:

 Privacy Settings

Site Visibility          ○ Allow search engines to index this site.

                               ● Ask search engines not to index this site.

Simply click the radio button "Ask search engines not to index this site" and then click the "Save Changes" button.

Once your site is ready to be accessed by search engines, and you are 100% sure that no further major changes are going to be made to the structure of your site, you can then open up your site to search engines.

## Privacy Settings

Site Visibility            ⦿ Allow search engines to index this site.

                           ○ Ask search engines not to index this site.

The actual privacy option settings of your Wordpress installs must be checked from time to time. I can remember talking to a newbie affiliate only a few months ago who was complaining that even although his site contained over 300 quality articles, not a single one was indexed in Google. He spent a good 20 minutes telling me how his site had been wrongly penalized by Google only for me to discover that his robots.txt file was actually set to block! Never overlook the obvious.

### *Optimizing Images*

Every website should contain at least some images as images are not only used for information purposes but can also aid conversions. Although most webmasters do take the time to ensure basic on-page SEO is carried out to a high degree, for some reason many forget, or simply do not bother, to SEO their website images.

There are three basic stages to optimizing an image:

- Optimizing image file names
- Optimizing image alt tags, titles & captions
- Optimizing image file sizes

The first stage is to make sure that the image file name includes the main key phrases for the page on which it is going to be displayed. For example, for our now world famous Blue Widget article, if we are going to display a picture of a blue widget, the image file should of course be something like blue-widget.jpg and not something like image1.jpg. If your article is going to include multiple images, don't over optimize by giving all your articles very similar names such as blue-widget1.jpg, blue-widget2.jpg and blue-widget3.jpg. Instead keep using the main key phrases at the start of the image file name but be more descriptive, using more key phrases that actually describe the images such as blue-widget-portable, blue-widget-turbo-model and blue-widget-extreme-model. If you are using image buttons on your article page, for instance a buy now button, again don't use a file name such as buy-button.jpg, but opt for a file name such as buy-blue-widget.jpg.

The second stage in optimizing images for search engines is to make sure that the image ALT tags also include your page's main key phrase, which should be at the very start of the alt tag. The ALT tag is the little box that pops up when you hover your cursor over an image on a webpage. If you take the time to visit a dozen or so affiliate sites, you will find that many webmasters have not bothered to include ALT tags or have failed to include their main key phrases in ALT tags. Again with ALT tags, if your article contains multiple images, DON'T use exactly the same text for each image. Make each ALT tag on each page different, but ensure you start each ALT tag with your main key phrase.

As you may have guessed, Wordpress makes things easy for you for adding ALT tags and indeed descriptions to your images. When you import an image into Wordpress you will see the following window:

| Title | * | folding_treadmills |
|---|---|---|
| Alternate Text | | |
| | | *Alt text for the image, e.g. "The Mona Lisa"* |
| Caption | | |
| Description | | |

You will also notice that there are extra fields waiting for your input. The title of the image is very important. By default Wordpress automatically uses the file name. For the title text, use the same text in this field that you are going to use for your ALT tag. If you enter text in the "Caption" field, you will find the entered text displayed below the image when you view your article. Using caption text is another good way to give your on-page SEO a further little boost, so whenever possible include captions, which of course should include your key phrases.

To give you an even better understanding of how to optimize images for on-page SEO let me show you the exact text I would use to optimize an image for the "NordicTrack T14 Folding Treadmill"

| | | |
|---|---|---|
| Title | * | NordicTrack-T14-Folding-Treadmill |
| Alternate Text | | Nordic Track T14 Folding Treadmill |
| | | *Alt text for the image, e.g. "The Mona Lisa"* |
| Caption | | Nordic Track T14 Folding Treadmill Our Number 1 Seller |
| Description | | Nordic Track T14 Folding Treadmill Main 500 x 500 Image |

The description text is of no use for SEO but is a great aid to identifying images at a later date in your Wordpress media library. With the above input for the Nordic Track image, Wordpress would generate and insert the following code into your webpage.

```
<div id="attachment_63" class="wp-caption alignleft" style="width: 538px"><a href="http://www.onlinecashcow.co.uk/nordictrack-t14-folding-treadmill/" rel="attachment wp-att-63"><img src="http://www.onlinecashcow.co.uk/images/NordicTrack-T14-Folding-Treadmill.jpg" alt="Nordic Track T14 Folding Treadmill" title="NordicTrack-T14-Folding-Treadmill" width="500" height="500" class="size-full wp-image-63" /></a><p class="wp-caption-text">Nordic Track T14 Folding Treadmill Our Number 1 Seller </p></div>
```

Let's compare this code with code from an image that has not been optimized with the image text fields left blank.

```
<p><a href="http://www.onlinecashcow.co.uk/nordictrack-t14-folding-treadmill/" rel="attachment wp-att-63"><img src="http://www.onlinecashcow.co.uk/images/image1.jpg" alt="" title="NordicTrack" width="500" height="500" class="alignleft size-full wp-image-63" /></a></p>
```

Can you see the difference? I can't stress enough how important it is, for on-page SEO to optimize your images.

## *Optimizing Image File Size*

Although the actual size of your image files is not really a true element of on-page SEO, it is simply common sense that if you have large graphic files, or a large number of images on any page, then the loading speed of your page is going to suffer. Remember the seven-second rule? Your goal should be to make every page of your site load as quickly as possible, because most who browse the web simply do not have the patience to wait for slow loading pages. Wordpress does auto compress images and there are many free image compression tools available online as well as professional graphic packages such as Photoshop and Paintshop. Test the pages that contain images on your computer and ask friends and family to do the same on their computers. If anyone reports that pages that contain images are loading slowly, either compress the images further or consider removing the offending images from your articles.

## *H1 and H2 Headers Tags*

Header tags are another important aspect of on-page SEO. H1 and H2 headers, if used in the right manner, can play a vital role in how search engines perceive the content of your pages. Headers are, as you might expect, text on a website that denotes the title of a webpage or the start of a new section, just as used in this book. As you might well imagine, the headers are important for the way that search engines analyze a site, as they provide quick information regarding the general content of a webpage– something that they then use to position webpages in their search engine results.

The phrases H1 and H2 and indeed H3 and H4, simply refer to the prominence of text on a page, with H1, with a larger font, being deemed the most important. By default Wordpress will automatically wrap H1 tags around your article titles. I only use H1 and H2 tags, using H1 tags for article titles and H2 tags for subheadings, which produces a format that readers can easily scan.

Although search engines give more weight to H1 tags, there is no evidence that creating content that solely uses H1 tags can in effect "cheat" search engines. I have seen many affiliates try to manipulate the power of H1 tags but to be honest articles using this tactic simply don't look right. Simply stick to using H1 header tags for your article titles and H2 tags for subheadings and you will be on the right track as regards your on-page SEO.

## *In-Site Links*

In-site links are another important aspect of on-site SEO for numerous reasons. The first reason is obvious and is nothing to do with SEO, as it is simply the fact that people visiting the site need to find it easy and intuitive to use. If your users can't find what they are looking for, they will simply look elsewhere. The second reason has everything to do with SEO, however, as it involves the way that Google crawls through all websites and indexes the content it finds. No page of your site should ever be isolated – by which I mean that EVERY page of your site should be able to be found by clicking links on other pages from your site. In theory, if you loaded your homepage, and then clicked every link and every subsequent link on all pages loaded, in time you should have opened every single page of your site.

Your most important pages, your money-making pages, which should of course include your sales pages, should be clickable from any other page of your site. The way to make this possible is simply to add links to these pages on your site's sidebar, either on the left or right. As these important pages are linked to all pages, including of course your homepage, in time authority and PageRank will be passed to the pages linked in your sidebar, which will result in increased PageRank and increased rankings. To give you a better understanding of this technique, let's say you have an article – yep, you have guessed it – entitled "Blue Widget Review". This page should be linked to all other pages by placing a link in your sidebar using the link text (anchor text) such as "Blue Widget Review". This would produce a link that looked something like this – **<u>Blue Widget Review</u>**. In time, as you add content daily, which in turn has the effect of adding new internal links pointing to your sidebar, you will find that you actually increase your search engine ranking for the phrase "Blue Widget Review" and for other phrases, depending on the number of links in your sidebar and the anchor text used. Of course, this takes time: great rankings do not appear overnight.

Take the time to look at affiliate sites and take note of the links and anchor text they have used in their sidebars. Also take the time to check the rankings for the anchor text used. Of course affiliates with thousand page plus sites will gain more SEO power from sidebar links than those affiliates with thin type affiliate sites comprising less than a hundred pages.

### *Site Speed*
Although many believe that site speed is an important aspect of on-site SEO, in reality site speed is not a major element of the Google algorithm. There are many aged authority sites that still rank extremely well even although their pages take longer than average to load.

Site speed, however, is important because, as I have said elsewhere, those who browse the web will not wait more than a few seconds for your website to load. Ensure that you check the load time of your site at least once a week. Pingdom Tools have a great little online script - http://tools.pingdom.com/fpt/ that allows you to check your site's load time easily. You can also use Google to find other such free tools.

There are a number of ways that you can increase the speed of your site, but the most important is to ensure that there are no oversized images or videos on the site that take an eternity to load. It is also important to make sure any banners on your site load quickly and that the server hosting them isn't a slow one – if the banners are slow loading, consider replacing them with adverts from a different source.

## How Should I Implement On-Site SEO?

As you should know by now, on-site SEO is not rocket science. The implementation of on-site SEO is something that many new affiliates worry about, usually to the detriment of actually just getting on and getting it done. Make sure that each article you post on your site, including all images used, conform to every element discussed in this chapter. Take your time; don't skip some elements because you don't have time or you can't be bothered. A good analogy is to think of on-site SEO as a tasty cake recipe; you can of course skip the odd ingredient or two from a recipe, but if you do, the final result will simply not taste as good as it should.

# Chapter 12 – Off-Site SEO

## Google's New Algorithm

Before actually dealing with off-site SEO techniques, I feel that you should know of the mammoth changes that webmasters have had to endure over the 18 months or so prior to publication of this book. Arming you with this knowledge will give you a good understanding of the benefits and pitfalls of certain techniques.

On February 24th 2011 Google rolled out a new algorithm that literally wiped out tens of thousands of webmasters overnight. The new algorithm, now known as PANDA by most affiliate webmasters, in my opinion ripped up, or should I say shredded, the rules of SEO overnight. Webmasters who had "owned" top positioned, highly profitable search engine rankings for years, awoke to find that their sites had been penalized with their rankings destroyed. Webmaster forums were buzzing with threads full of horror stories as many started to realise that the days of "gaming" Google were well and truly over!

To understand why the Google PANDA update hit many webmasters so hard, you need to understand the SEO landscape pre Google PANDA. Google has always stated that the content it indexes and ranks, quality of content is always the key factor. Most experienced webmasters will tell you that pre Google PANDA this was simply not true.

Until the dreaded PANDA roll-out, there had not been a major Google algorithm update in real terms for over five years. Of course there had been thousands of minor algorithm tweaks, although most were easily "sidestepped" by experienced webmasters. Until PANDA, the Google search engine algorithm had been flawed because you could easily "buy" great rankings by building links. In my opinion Google is directly responsible for most of the spammers that frequent the web. It had become a well-known fact that even "spammy" links pointing to "crappy" content pages could prove effective for ranking in Google search results.

Many webmasters "milked" the flaws in the Google algorithm by simply building sites on which they could sell links. The flaws in the Google algorithm actually helped sustain a link-selling market in which billions of dollars of links were bought and sold each year. Up to February 24th 2011 many top Google search engine ranking pages (SERPs), were to an extent "owned" by webmasters who had simply copied others' articles, re-spun the content and then simply built thousands of links that pointed to their pages. Google SERPs were a mess!

With the introduction of the Google PANDA update, Google killed off sites that simply copied content or re-spun content. Further updates during 2011 and 2012 devalued spam links and also, I believe, actually damaged sites that had such links in their profile.

More and more types of link are being devalued each month with more and more affiliate sites losing their rankings. Most webmasters have not caught on yet to the fact that many types of link can now actually damage a website's rankings. When an affiliate site suffers a drop in rankings, most webmasters blindly build more links, which simply makes matters worse. I said some time ago that I was taking the opposite approach and was starting to remove suspect links pointing to my pages; I have been amazed by how many of my rankings have increased by doing so.

Actual site structure and on-site SEO is now far more important than link building post PANDA, although I know that many will disagree. I have actually removed large sections of link-building techniques from this book and boosted the on-site SEO sections, which in real terms means that those who follow my advice will be safeguarded against Google penalties as they will be building 100% white hat type sites. Good SEO white hat techniques have, of course, been around for years although until recent times such sites have been outranked by webmasters with good link building skills.

There is no doubt that the Google algorithm now relies less on the incoming links to a site than perhaps ever before. Although many links do still have a value, many webmasters have noticed that big brand type affiliate sites, ranking extremely well, in many cases are utilising mostly their own internal links. It seems clear that a site's internal link structure is now of prime importance.

Many suggest that Google is now switching to other metrics to rank webpages, including SERP bounce rates and click-through rates. It seems that gone are the days when even a poor quality webpage with crappy "spun" content could be ranked highly because it had quality links. In respect to content, it now seems clear that quality content is now of prime importance in order to rank in Google.

## What Is Google PANDA?

Firstly Panda is NOT a live algorithm. Panda is actually a machine-learning background job that runs firstly on what many are calling a training dataset, with results exported, normally monthly, to the actual Google search results. We already know that Panda targets duplicate content, and indeed pages with a high percentage of ads above the fold, but in reality Panda does far more. Looking at sites that have been hit, it is clear to see that many Pandalized sites did not contain duplicate content, a high degree of ads or even poor content. So why were these sites targeted by Panda?

If we are honest, many affiliate sales pages may indeed be well written, but are of little use to readers. For example, if we take a look at typical Pokerstars review pages, many contain exactly the same information. If you read 100 such review pages from 100 different webmasters, most are basically the same and offer nothing new. The same can be said for virtually every niche!

The key, of course, is to try to understand how PANDA classifies good and poor content. I for one have been saying for some time that bounce rate from Google search pages must be a key factor or at least a starting point. I suggest you should read the article by Peter van der Graaf entitled "PANDA In Detail". One section of the article states:

*"This means that while bounce-rate (in this case: visitors returning to search results quickly) isn't used as a direct ranking factor, it is used to teach the Panda new tricks. Signals like bounce rate are fed as bamboo to the Panda background system with the instruction to find out what patterns can be derived from characteristics that form thin content, unnatural text and excessive on-page advertising. The system picks various combinations of attributes combined to get a high degree of certainty for someone's spammy activities"*

Digging a little deeper I also found a research paper by the man responsible for Google Panda algorithm, Biswanath Panda himself. The document gives an insight to Massively Parallel Learning of Tree Ensembles including examples. I found the following section detailing an experiment for computational advertising very interesting.

*"We measure the performance of PLANET on the bounce rate prediction problem. A click on a sponsored search advertisement is called a bounce if the click is immediately followed by the user returning to the search engine.*

*Ads with high bounce rates are indicative of poor user experience and provide a strong signal of advertisement quality.*

*The training dataset (AdCorpus) for predicting bounce rates is derived from all clicks on search ads from the data size for various numbers of machines.*

*Each record represents a click labeled with whether it was bounce. A wide variety of features are considered for each click. These include the search query for the click, advertiser chosen keyword, advertisement text, estimated click-through rate of the ad clicked, a numeric similarity score between the ad and the landing page, and whether the advertiser keyword precisely matched the query."*

From the above we can deduce that an ad clicked with the user quickly returning to the search engine is classed as a negative signal. We can also deduce that an ad receiving more than expected clicks, with the user not returning to the search can be classed as a positive signal. It is also interesting to note that there are other considerations taken into account, which I have been testing.

Some webmasters who had sites hit hard by the Google PANDA update have managed to regain ranking by carrying out the following:

- Removing duplicate content
- Removing poor quality content
- Lowering their sites' Google bounce rate

If you are confused by the term "bounce rate", let me tell you that it simply represents the percentage of a page's visitors who leave a site without visiting any other pages of the site. In this instance I am referring to visitors from Google search results. Could Google really be using this data for part of its algorithm? Well it seems highly likely to me.

Let's think about this concept for a moment. If a page ranks on the first results page of Google search results, for, let's say, the phrase "blue widgets", and users click the search listing, visit the page, quickly "bounce" back to the Google search results and then click on another URL for the same search phrase, does this basically tell Google that the initial page is not a good result for the search phrase? Well this seems to make sense to me. As a matter of fact, I have seen many of my pages on multiple sites jump in the rankings, with most of the said pages having a low bounce rate. Guess what I have also noted for some of my pages with high bounce rates? Yes you are correct. Some of my pages with high bounce rates have fallen in Google's search results.

I for one have always favoured building big brand type affiliate sites, which indeed seems to be paying dividends, even more so since the PANDA roll-out. This is why I urge you to aim to create one "mega" affiliate site adding at least a thousand pages a year rather than taking the easy option of creating several thin affiliate sites.

## What Is a Backlink?

A backlink is basically clickable text that links to another webpage. Think of each backlink on other sites that link to your site as a positive vote. As I said in the previous chapter, on-site SEO and off-site SEO work together. Let's imagine you have a great review page for blue widgets, and you have taken the time to optimize the review page for the key phrases "blue widget" and "blue widget review". To enhance your rankings in Google search results you would need links on other websites with the clickable text (anchor text) of "blue widget" and of course "blue widget review", ensuring of course that the link URL used was the exact URL of your blue widget review page. The more links you acquired (as above) on different websites, the more you would in time boost your ranking in Google Search Results depending of course on the quality of the links.

## Understanding Link & Content Relevance

There is no doubt that the anchor text of links is one of the metrics used by Google, but it is far from being the only one. In recent times many suggest links are actually being devalued. Search engines have the ability to look much more deeply into the context surrounding a page. Other signals regarding the page relevance are also taken into consideration.

Are the other links on the located page very close to the niche and quality of your own high quality and niche related sites? If so, this can be taken as a positive signal. Your site may gain trust by association with other quality related sites. This is why you may see links to such sites as Wikipedia in articles that have obviously been created to boost search engine rankings. On the flip side of things, if the links closest to your own are for other niches such as Viagra or adult material, this may appear as a low quality link. It looks as if the link is coming from a link farm, and that is a bad signal.

Where on the page does your link appear? Is your link located in the body of the page content, in a sidebar, or buried at the bottom of the page? Better page placement can indicate higher quality links. This is referred to as "link prominence" and also can be applied to on-page SEO in terms of keyword placement.

Does your link's anchor text fit within the context of the writing surrounding it? Does that content logically relate to the content of the page your link is pointed at? This is another positive signal that your page is of high quality. This is often referred to as "proximity".

Modern search engines are highly intelligent and look at more than just the raw textual content. They can actually look deeper into the structure of a page and the section on which your link is located. In doing so they can determine the section's topic by way of header tags, or the nearest bold highlighted text, which often act as titles or headers to the nearby content. As you can imagine, a close relation between your page and these headers is another positive signal.

So let us suppose that the nearby content links and headers are all related to your page's content. This is excellent, but to take it a step further, it is even better if the overall topic of the page on which your inbound link is located is closely related to your own page's topic.

You should be able to see where I am going with things at this point. You want relevant inbound links, and if the general topic covered by the entire site that is linking you is of similar nature to your own, this is another very positive signal. It tells the search engines that this site is dedicated to the topic, and in linking to your related page, they consider your content of value.

## Understanding PageRank

Even those new to the world of SEO will have in most cases stumbled across the term "PageRank", but the chances are you won't be too sure of what it is or whether it is really something that you need to be concerned about. In fact, even those who have been in the online affiliate business for a long time are still at loggerheads when it comes to deciding whether the PageRank of a site, or indeed page, is really that important at all. I can tell you that many webmasters put too much emphasis on PageRank as they use it as their main metric for link building and incorrectly think that PageRank plays a vital role in how their pages rank in Google.

### *What is PageRank?*

PageRank was developed by Google during the very early stages of the search engine's development and is in fact named after one of the founders of the company, Larry Page. Page noticed that most of the search engines of the day seemed to have a very unfair way of ranking the importance of the different pages displayed and therefore he set out to make the results more useful to the users of their service.

To determine the popularity of the different pages, Page deemed that the best method would be to look at how many other webpages linked to a particular page, as people would only link to a page if they thought it helpful or worthwhile. The result was PageRank – a system that takes the amount of links pointing to a site and converts them into a rating, with a value ranging from 0 to 10. I must stress now that pages with a rating of, let's say,

PageRank 5 do not rank higher in Google search results than pages with a lesser PageRank value.

A new website is assigned an initial PR0 rating and in time, as more and more links start pointing to the new site's pages, the actual PageRank of the site's pages will increase. There are of course major problems with PageRank because it is so easy to "game". In reality you could start a new website tomorrow and simply buy links that point to your pages, guaranteeing that when the PageRank toolbar data is exported, which generally occurs every three to six months, the PageRank of your pages would increase. I for one wish that Google would admit defeat and drop PageRank, because this would overnight kill the crazy link selling industry and, better still, make webmasters concentrate on their content rather than the PageRank value of their pages.

Of course over the years there have been a number of tweaks to the way that PageRank works and nowadays the formula used to calculate wouldn't be out of place on a mathematics paper for a Masters Degree student. The basic premise still remains however – the more links, the higher the PageRank.

### How is PageRank Calculated?

As I said, the formula used to calculate PageRank is a highly complex one and has been since its inception. To prove this, just take a look at the formula many suggest Google uses...

$$PR(A) = (1-d) + d(PR(t1)/C(t1) + ... + PR(tn)/C(tn))$$

Now I'm not even going to go through this formula and analyze it, as it goes over the heads of 99.99% of the world's population – including mine! Instead, we'll break down the components and see what Google actually takes into account when determining PageRank.

Okay, so we know that PageRank's main component is links, but surely all links aren't equal in the value that they give, are they? Well, the answer to this is a resounding, "No". Pages that have a high PageRank will automatically give a better boost to the PageRank of the site to which they are linking. All links are weighted and therefore lots of links from pages with a PageRank of 0 will not give the boost that a handful of links with a PageRank of 5 will give.

## Is PageRank Important?

There are conflicting views within the SEO community about the importance of PageRank, although it is generally agreed that PageRank is nowhere near as important as it used to be. At the same time it would be complete folly to ignore it altogether. For this reason, webmasters still to some degree pay attention to the PageRank of their pages and do actually work on increasing PageRank for their sites – even although there are other factors that are far more important. It must also be noted that the number of links pointing to a website does affect the number of pages Google indexes, plus how quickly Google indexes them. For this reason alone you should ensure that your link structure passes PageRank to your important pages.

Another reason that PageRank is important – for better or for worse – is that people will trust your site a lot more, especially webmasters, if you have a higher PageRank. Granted, the average member of the public won't ever look at your PR and will go on to factors like the presentation of the site, and of course your content, but the more technically savvy could well take a peek. Boosting your site's PageRank will make link exchanges with other webmasters in your niche much easier, simply because most still believe PageRank is far more valuable than it really is.

## How to Check PageRank

There are a number of different ways to check a site's PageRank. Remember that each page of a website can have a different PageRank value so it is very important not to check just your homepage but all your important pages.

SEO Quake is a free tool that can be downloaded for either the Google Chrome web browser or for Firefox, and provides you with a number of different details about a site – one of these being the site's PageRank. There are also many other browser plug-ins you can use, but I prefer SEO Quake, which can be download free from www.seoquake.com.

## How to Increase PageRank

The main way to increase the PageRank of your pages is quite an obvious one, and that is to "acquire" links to your pages from other sites in your niche with already established PR levels. This can be easier said than done, however, as sites with higher PR are often loath to give their links away for free to other sites, especially not to those in a similar niche that can't return the favour with a link back of the same PageRank value. One way to get round this problem is to ensure that all the content posted on your site is of the highest quality. This means that better sites will think that the content on your site is worth sharing with their – hopefully thousands – of visitors. Alas, however, even if your site contains great content, many webmasters will not be interested in giving a link away for free, or in most cases not even interested in exchanging links with your site due to your low PageRank value.

So, as you should now be aware, initially acquiring quality links to your pages is going to be a tough task. Most webmasters at this stage make the decision of breaking the terms and conditions set out by Google and get their cheque book out. You will find that although most webmasters will refuse a polite email asking for a link exchange or in most cases simply ignore your email, when a payment is mentioned, this does generate a response.

I would suggest that rather than buying links, you simply write a dozen or so quality articles, although I must stress that the articles you write must be of the very highest quality, and offer the articles to webmasters in exchange for a link. Again most webmasters will not be receptive to your request but in time you will find webmasters who will be happy to accept a quality article in exchange for a link.

## How to Find Quality Pages for Your Links

If you are building a quality site, complete with quality content, then little by little you will naturally acquire natural links on other websites, although at first this can be a painfully slow process. Although Google has devalued many types of links, it is fair to say that you still can game Google rankings with some types of links. So how do you determine which pages are best for your links?

As I have already stated, many affiliates simply use the metric of Google PageRank, although this is a big mistake. There are many sites with high PageRank that have virtually no ranking value at all. So how can a novice affiliate gauge what pages do have a value and are great pages to obtain links?

Well, firstly, PageRank is a metric you can use, but only with other metrics. The process of determining which sites would be ideal for links can prove to be a nightmare for inexperienced webmasters. Don't simply go all out to get links on pages with high PageRank as there are other important aspects you should consider.

A good page for possible link placement should have the following, all of which we are about to discuss:

- PageRank – PR2 or better
- A good backlink profile
- A decent Alexa score

- Low number of outbound links
- Relevant content

## *Existing PageRank*

Start by seeking out websites in your chosen niche that have a homepage PageRank value of at least PR2. Beware of established websites that have a PageRank value of PR0 as Google has penalized many such websites for illegal practices such as selling links. Many affiliates, myself included, believe that links on such sites pointing to your pages can have a negative effect on rankings.

## *Existing Backlink Profile*

Another good technique to assess the quality of a webpage is to take a look at the links it has gained. Many times you may find a great page that is relevant to your niche with a high PageRank value, but in reality the PageRank of the page has been "gamed" with non-relevant spammy links. Such sites may be days away from being dealt a penalty by Google. To check the backlinks of any webpage simply use a backlink tool such as www.backlinkwatch.com or use Google to search for other tools by entering the key phrase, "free backlink checker". Check the quality of the inbound links. Are the links relevant or are they from various untrustworthy sites from many different niches?

## *Estimating Existing Traffic Using Alexa*

If a website in your chosen niche has healthy traffic, it should be an ideal target for a link. The trouble is, however, that determining if a website has a steady stream of traffic is not as easy as you would think. You could of course simply ask the owner of the website but many webmasters do not want to part with this information or could simply lie to you. If you visit Alexa.com and type in the full URL of the website you will then get a free report, which you can compare with leading websites in your niche to determine the site's traffic levels. As a very rough guide if a site has an Alexa Traffic Rank of over 10 million, then it generates very little traffic whereas a website with an Alexa Traffic Rank of fewer than 2 million does indeed have a steady flow of daily traffic.

## *Outbound Links*

Many webmasters build a network of sites simply so that they can sell links to other webmasters. Ideally, you want links on pages that have no other links. If you are offered a link on a webpage that contains an article that already has several external links, then of course this will not be ideal, as the page could be classed as a spam by many search engines. Try to obtain links on pages where your link is the only link if possible.

## *Relevant Content*

The name of the game when acquiring links is to try to get links that look natural. You may find a great blog about someone who is delighted with his or her new treadmill purchase, which of course would be a great page for a link to your treadmill affiliate site. As your link would fit in nicely with the existing content, and there are, ideally, no other links on the page, your link would look completely natural. There would of course be no use in acquiring a link on a cake recipe website, even if the page had a high PageRank value, because a link to a treadmill site would look extremely unnatural.

## Link Exchange Requests

Every day I receive dozens of requests for link exchanges. Many of the requests are generated from software apps which seek out relevant sites and then, in real terms, "spam the crap" out of webmasters such as myself and of course you. Some of the requests are of course genuine manual requests from webmasters, although the simple truth is that 99.99% of the requests for link exchanges will offer you no value.

Many webmasters will simply build crappy sites with decent PageRank hoping to entice you to exchange three-way links, which means you get a link on their crappy high PageRank site and they then ask for a link for their main site on your site. Some webmasters will even purchase dropped domains with healthy PageRank values although the actual domain is not relevant to your niche, hoping that you will be enticed by the healthy PageRank value. The link they want on your site will of course be to their main site and not to the crappy sites they are offering to place your link on.

Below are a couple examples of the barrage of link requests I receive on a daily basis.

*Hi,*

*My name is xxxxxx xxxxxxx, Web Marketing Consultant. Ive greatly enjoyed looking through your site xxxxxxxx.com and I was wondering if you'd be interested in exchanging links with my websites, which has a related subject. I can offer you a home page link back from my related websites all in Google cache with backlinks which are:*

> *fit-fuers-abi(dot)com PR5*
> *online-casino-games.mypoker4u(dot)com*
> *scarborough-casino(dot)com*

*If you are interested, please send me the following details of your site:*

*TITLE:*

*URL:*

*I'll add your link as soon as possible, in the next 24 hours. As soon as it's ready, I'll send you a confirmation email along with the information (TITLE and URL) regarding my site to be placed at yours.*

*I hope you have a nice day and thank you for your time.*

*Kindest regards,*

******

*Hi,*

*As an on-going process to increase the link popularity of our casino site, we are looking for some good quality sites to exchange links with our website. I recently came across your site through Google Search and found it beneficial and informative for our site's visitors.*

*For our mutual benefit, I would like to Exchange Links with your website, in return I will post your link at same value page without any delay.*

*If you find the whole concept interesting, then i request you to send your site details to be added ASAP. Also send me the exact page where you will place my link. I'll be happy to add your link first.*

*If you'd like to discuss this further, please feel free to contact us at (email address removed)*

*Expecting an earlier Reply!*

*Kind Regards,*

Basically what I am telling you is not to waste your time with this sort of link exchange. As your site gains popularity with search engines you will see the floodgates open with link exchange requests. Simply condemn most of them to your junk folder.

## Google Penalties

Google clearly state that links should not be acquired to boost either rankings or PageRank, as in their statement below:

*Your site's ranking in Google search results is partly based on analysis of those sites that link to you. The quantity, quality and relevance of links count towards your rating. The sites that link to you can provide context about the subject matter of your site and can indicate its quality and popularity. However, some webmasters engage in link exchange schemes and build partner pages exclusively for the sake of cross-linking; disregarding the quality of the links, the sources and the long-term impact it will have on their sites. This is in violation of Google's Webmaster Guidelines and can negatively impact your site's ranking in search results. Examples of link schemes can include:*

- *Links intended to manipulate PageRank*

- *Links to web spammers or bad neighborhoods on the web*

- *Excessive reciprocal links or excessive link exchanging ("Link to me and I'll link to you.")*

- *Buying or selling links that pass PageRank*

So what happens if Google detects that you are either buying or selling links? Well from experience, although from a good few years ago when I indeed did venture into the dark side, I can tell you that if you are detected selling links, you will lose any PageRank gained. Worse still, you run a fair chance of losing any Google search engine rankings you may have worked extremely hard to obtain. Even worse still Google actively encourages webmasters to report other webmasters who engage in buying or selling links so you have to be extremely careful if you do decide to bend the terms and conditions set out by Google.

Just a few years ago there was a very profitable market in directory links. Many webmasters set up directories and then built up the PageRank of their directories simply so that they could sell thousands of links. Many directory webmasters were making five-figure monthly sums or even much more, simply by selling links on their directory sites. For some time there was no doubt that acquiring directory links with high PageRank values did indeed boost a site's rankings, so as you can imagine the demand for directory links was indeed great. Google soon caught on and took action against thousands of directories. Many directory webmasters saw the PageRank of their sites removed overnight, which of course wiped out their income. Not only did they lose their PageRank, but most also lost their rankings as did those who had built their rankings using high PageRank directory links.

Most of the directories that were penalized by Google never regained their PageRank or rankings. Those that did had to make major changes to their sites and had to endure many months of being penalized by Google. From that day building links with bulk high PageRank directory links for better rankings was in reality ended.

Webmasters, however, were still not beaten by Google and quickly sourced other links to boost their rankings. Many gained superb rankings by acquiring mass links in article directories, although once again Google took action and devalued such links. Many still use automated software apps to spam forums, gaining links in profiles and forum posts. Others use automated blog comment posting apps to automatically post comments in Wordpress blog posts. The truth is that these "shady" techniques only work temporarily until another webmaster reports you or the links are flagged by Google, which of course results in a penalty. Those sites that gain rankings from cheap spam backlinks have only a short life span and soon vanish from Google's results pages, never to return.

## Reporting Paid & Spam Links To Google

Accepting that their results pages could easily be open to cheating, Google perhaps surprised many webmasters by giving them the option to report paid and spam links. Would you report a fellow webmaster if you found a site had overtaken your site in the search results with the use of either paid or spam links? Well, if you would, then you had better ensure that your backlink profile is squeaky clean, because drawing attention to your niche, for sure, will lead to Google checking other sites chasing the same search results, your website included.

**Help us maintain the quality of Google search results.**

We work hard to return the most relevant results for every search we conduct. To that end, we encourage site managers to make their content straightforward and easily understood by users and search engines alike. Unfortunately, not all websites have users' best interests at heart. Some site owners attempt to "buy PageRank" in the form of paid links to their sites.

Google uses a number of methods to detect paid links, including algorithmic techniques. We also welcome information from our users. If you know of a site that buys or sells links, please tell us by filling out the fields below. We'll investigate your submissions, and we'll use your data to improve our algorithmic detection of paid links.

**Report paid links**

Website selling links:

[                    ]

Website buying links:

[                    ]

Additional details:

[                    ]

[Submit]

In recent months Google has adopted a new ploy, of which many webmasters are highly dubious, to detect artificial or "unnatural" links. Many webmasters have reported receiving the message below through Google Webmaster Tools.

### *Google Webmaster Tools notice of detected unnatural links*

*We've detected that some of your site's pages may be using techniques that are outside Google's Webmaster Guidelines.*

*Specifically, look for possibly artificial or unnatural links pointing to your site that could be intended to manipulate PageRank. Examples of unnatural linking could include buying links to pass PageRank or participating in link schemes.*

*We encourage you to make changes to your site so that it meets our quality guidelines. Once you've made these changes, please submit your site for reconsideration in Google's search results.*

*If you find unnatural links to your site that you are unable to control or remove, please provide the details in your reconsideration request.*

*If you have any questions about how to resolve this issue, please see our Webmaster Help Forum for support.*

*Sincerely,*

*Google Search Quality Team*

It must be noted that the above message appears to have been sent to webmasters just a few weeks after Google had penalized many large blog networks, which many webmasters utilized to gain high PageRank links to boost their rankings. It seems clear, however, that some of the webmasters who received the above message were not guilty of using the blog networks.

Some suggest that Google is simply "fishing" in order to panic webmasters into revealing other link networks so that Google can in effect shut them down too. More worrying is the fact that many who received the message reported that a few weeks later their sites were penalized, in many cases losing all of their search engine rankings.

It seems clear that Google has stepped up a gear in the fight to stop webmasters from "gaming" the Google algorithm by simply buying links.

## The Google Sandbox

Years ago, there used to be a lot of debate on most webmaster forums about the "Google Sandbox". Many believed there was no such thing. From my own personal experience I can tell you that the Google Sandbox definitely does exist and, as you are going to be building a new site, you stand a high chance of experiencing the Google Sandbox effect.

So what is the Google Sandbox? Well, consider the Google Sandbox as a restrictive throttle on new sites that limits rankings. It is not uncommon for a new website to be launched and to rank as expected initially, only for all rankings to be degraded four to eight weeks later. Many webmasters have suggested that this has been due to a Google algorithm filter that monitors how quickly new websites gain links, with websites that gain links too quickly being pushed into the Sandbox and losing ranking for a short period, usually of up to eight weeks.

I have experienced the Google Sandbox effect many times with new websites, and the chances are high that you will too. If you do, simply keep on adding fresh quality content daily and you will find that in most cases within a month or so your site will regain its ranking.

# Link Building Techniques

## *Understanding Link Bait Techniques*

You should now be starting to understand that buying links on others' sites is not a good long-term strategy because sooner or later Google is going to catch you. I have already discussed how you could trade quality content for links but what other methods could you employ to build links to your site? Many webmasters have already started to think "out of the box" in respect to link building, with many adapting a policy of creating articles, not to generate sales but to generate links. The term "Link Bait" is used by many to refer to the idea of creating content with the specific purpose of the said content going viral on the internet. The general concept is that those who view the content will freely link to it and pass it on to their friends who will also link to it. Good link bait articles, images or even videos can generate thousands of links in weeks, especially if they become popular on social network sites. Creating such content in hopes of attracting naturally occurring backlinks can be done in a variety of different ways, and your link bait can develop in many forms. Actually getting your link bait to go viral, however, is no easy task.

Good link bait content relies upon your exploitation of human emotion. You need to pull the reader's strings so to speak in order to create an emotional reaction. This can be done by posting content that is controversial, funny, touching, cute, or which draws on any other natural emotions. Depending on what market space you are working within, there are many types of hot topics that can be addressed. An opinionated article addressing one of these topics can incite discussion regarding your opinion on other sites, often with a link to your original writing as a result.

## *Link Bait Examples*

In the UK perhaps one of the best known examples is Compare The MeerKat  which cleverly used the Compare The Meerkat website to generate links and traffic for their insurance affiliate site. Many of their prime time TV commercials simply promoted Compare The Meerkat.

Smashing Magazine simply used reviews on top of free Wordpress themes to generate links and traffic. Check the backlinks of the actual page to see how successful this was.

Matt Cutts proves how effective link bait can be with his "how to report paid links" article.

### *Creating Link Bait Content*

It really isn't all that hard to develop content which your readers will want to link to, but it does take a little effort on your part to brainstorm and come up with new ideas that will work in your favour.

Let your mind roam free and write down anything that comes to mind that may work. Do not bother censoring yourself during this phase of the process. Don't worry, as you won't be using everything you write down. What seems like a stupid idea may in time lead you to a perfect idea. No matter how strange, far off, or simple the ideas may seem, write them down!

After spending some time putting together a large collection of notes and having completely tapped your flow of creative juices, filter through the ideas. Break everything down into its own content and concept components. Consider what the delivery format of the idea will be for the link bait. This is your concept component. Is it going to be a blog post, a newsletter mailing, widget, top ten lists or even a video? Then review the subject matter. This is your content component. What are you going to write about? Separate all these details into two lists.

Now move forward with your content list and evaluate the subjects critically. Are any of the ideas time sensitive? Can they wait for a relevant news story to come around which would complement them? Do you have ideas in the list that you really want to write about immediately? Is there anything in the list that is not of immediate importance, yet can be saved for a dry spell where fresh content and ideas may be hard to come by?

Once your content and subject matter have been prioritized, you can begin a virtual jigsaw puzzle of mixing and matching your ideas against your concept list. Is your content something that potentially will make it onto social bookmarking or tagging sites? Take the time to study bookmarking and tagging sites and make notes of what type of content is successful. Does your content have the potential to be interactive? Maybe a poll or other interactive concept can be brought into play.

By attaching your priority content to the right concept, you can accelerate the effectiveness of your link bait by playing to the novelty of your intended audience. By sticking to this process, you will find that matching content and concept to one another may become second nature, and that you can create link bait quickly from any little ideas that you have.

Don't be afraid of failure. If at first you don't succeed, then try and try again!

### *Free Blog Hosting*

Another great free way to build links is to create blogs on free blog sites. The key to this, however, is to create blogs that actually look like real blogs. Many of the free blog hosts will delete blogs that appear to be created for the sole aim of link building. The way to get around this is simply to set up a free blog as a personal blog. Make at least a couple of posts about your daily life or one of your hobbies, ensuring of course that the content fits in with the niche of your affiliate website. Simply keep adding one or two posts a week, and after a month or so add a couple of links to your site. Repeat this process over and over again and in time you will have a network of blogs and dozens of links.

## Free Blog Hosting List

Below is a list of the main free Wordpress hosts

- www.wordpress.com

- www.blogetery.com

- www.blogates.com

- www.blogger.com

- www.blogsome.com

- www.tumblr.com

Most of the above allow you to create multiple blogs although in some cases you will have to use a different email address during the sign-up process. You will find many others if you type "free Wordpress blog hosting" into Google.

### *Tagging and Social News Sites*

Sites like Digg, StumbleUpon, Delicious, and Reddit can be highly effective properties on which to build links to your pages. Building a link campaign centred around social media sites such as these can work wonders for you, and becoming popular in these communities can unleash a flood of traffic and backlinks to you.

Although these sites can bring in a large amount of traffic, it is generally low revenue traffic for the publisher. The real strategy here is to rake in the additional backlinks that result from the popular interest in what you have posted. As an example, look at any story which has made the Digg homepage. A front-page placement on Digg can result in tens of thousands of viewers, and hundreds of additional backlinks. While the viewers may come and go, those links are left behind feeding your site's strength within search engines.

While acting out your social media strategies, you may want to keep these "best practices" in mind.

- Work with the community. The key to social media sites is the "social" nature of their traffic. Offending or irritating the site's community can quickly lead to being called out, or exposed and ridiculed by the readers. Your success depends on the response of those readers, so work with them in your postings, give them what they want and be a positive contributor to the community as a whole. Work towards building a solid reputation among your peers on the site.

- While writing articles for social news sites like Reddit, Digg or Propeller, stick to the topics that relate to your business. You may find that your articles catch on and rise in rank quite quickly for your targeted keywords. The relevance of your inbound links will be higher than those made in an unrelated post. Be sure to use your competitive keywords in both the title of the article itself and the title of the submission on the social site. These are generally the most common elements used as anchor text when people link into your posts and articles.

- Delicious and StumbleUpon are structured in a way quite different from other social news sites. Delicious is a social bookmarking service, in which users "tag" pages on the web to which they wish to return easily at a later date. StumbleUpon is similar with some added content discovery options. Both sites have an option for viewing popular pages in the system, leading users to content on hot trending topics.

Users coming to your site via a tagging or bookmarking site tend to hold a general interest in your topic. So as opposed to someone who may have found your page via a catchy headline on a social news site, these users are generally more targeted towards your business market. Therefore the traffic might not be as big, but the quality is much better, which also leads to lots of opportunities for users to link back to your content. These sites are best used in an attempt to reach major influences in your market space, and can lead to some high quality backlinks of significant power.

## *Link Building on Wikipedia*

Due to its strict No Follow policy on outbound links, you might not at first consider Wikipedia to be an ideal property for link building. Wikipedia, however, is seen as an authority site in the eyes of many users so links found in Wikipedia articles are given significant trust and often lead to links from other publishers writing on the topic. Some of these publishers have a significant influence in your market. Therefore building trust and respect within the Wikipedia community can bring in significant rewards for your time. This will require a time investment on your part as building trust in the community does not come overnight. The following are some of my best tips for proceeding with a Wikipedia campaign:

- Be patient as you build up your credibility. Develop an extended history of contributions, get a user profile page with Barnstar awards and do your part towards appearing as a virtuous member of the fold before doing anything that may be viewed as self-serving. Having a visible track record of contribution is a must within this community. Combat spam and contribute as often as possible. Avoid doing these things anonymously.

- Before editing any articles, be sure to negotiate any terms of the edit with the main editor in charge of policing the article. If you are going to edit an article, get the main editor's blessing beforehand.

- Make use of the "watch" function at Wikipedia to keep an eye on articles of significance or importance to you. There are a few great tools out there that will actually email you to notify you of any changes that occur. Check out TrackEngine, URLyWarning or ChangeDetect for more options.

- The flow of link juice can be directed within Wikipedia. Make good use of this!

- Play the popularity contest and make friends within the community. As in life, friends will stand up for you when you're in a pinch. If an article that is significant to you were to get an "Article for Deletion" nomination, this would be a good time to have friends who can stand up for you.

- Do not edit anonymously from your own computers. Wikipedia has tracking tools that can easily detect anonymous editors and this may damage your reputation. WikiScanner, for instance, is a public domain tool, which can take anonymous wiki posts and identify the organization that has made them. Keep this in mind, and do not take the risk. People in the community take Wikipedia quite seriously.

## Donations to Charity / Sponsor Websites

Another way to acquire links, perhaps less known by many webmasters, is by charitable donations. Sometimes these links don't cost much money at all and can come with much authority if placed on the right domain. This, however, is another of those tactics that Google frowns upon. You may be able to add legitimacy to your link by supporting projects relevant to your own content, but there is no guarantee that this will be accepted in Google's eyes.

Finding these types of site requires a lot of time and effort. You can however utilise search engines, by searching for phrases such as sports sponsorships or phrases related to your niche. Of course I cannot list specific URLS as that would damage the actual sites and pages. Think "out of the box" a little, seeking out, for example, teams that play popular sports but in lower divisions or perhaps young sportsmen and women. I was recently talking to a webmaster who had sponsored a charity bike ride, which is another good example. The actual homepage of the charity bike ride event was PR7 with extremely high page and domain authority!

## Paid Directory Submissions

Quality online directories can be a great source for quality backlinks. The bad news is that quality directories often charge a fee for inclusion, which many new affiliates simply cannot afford. When your finances allow, the following directories are thoroughly recommended:

- Yahoo! Directory
- DMOZ
- Business.com
- Best of the Web

## Blog Commenting

There must be millions of blogs online nowadays with perhaps the most popular being Wordpress blogs. A great way of building links is to post comments on blogs and include a link to your site. Don't spam blogs, however! Take the time to post a relevant reply to the initial blog post as this should keep your comment on the site. Ensure that any blog commenting you undertake is of course on blogs in a similar niche to your own. Make sure your comments actually add value to the initial blog post and that you are not simply adding a comment for a free link. Most blog owners remove comments that are clearly just spam.

# Bad Link Building Techniques

## *Bad Links Kill Sites!*

By now you should realise that you need links from other websites to your site. The trouble is that acquiring the wrong types of link will unfortunately lead to your site's demise. As you make your way in the world of online affiliation, you will, and of course must, seek out others in your niche. This will lead you to forums, of which most will have some kind of marketplace. During the first four months of your site's life, don't worry too much about link building. Don't be tempted to buy link packages offered by sellers who promise you an instant ranking boost. If you do, the chances are extremely high that Google will penalize your site, condemning it to the depths of search results, perhaps never to return. Never, repeat, never buy any of the link packages listed below:

- Bulk Directory Listings
- Social Network Links
- Link Wheel Links
- Forum Profile Links
- Wordpress Comments Links
- Side Wide Links

A good tip is never to buy links you can't remove yourself. If you pay somebody for bulk links, you really don't know on which sites your links will be placed and you have in most cases zero chance of getting them removed. Most of those who sell bulk links will sell to anybody who is willing to pay the price, no matter if the site niche is gambling, treadmills, Viagra or even porn. After a month or even less, your links will be nestled with a wide variety of other links on sites that have become spam sites. Don't buy bulk link packages!

## *Don't Sponsor Blog Themes!*

Just a few years ago a great way of building thousands of links was to sponsor Wordpress themes. The basic Wordpress theme is, as you should know by now, to say the least plain and ugly. Most people who use Wordpress load a theme to make their site more appealing, exactly as you will do. A tactic employed in the past by some webmasters was to contact Wordpress theme designers and get them to design a theme for their targeted niche. Once the theme was coded, targeted encrypted links were added to the footer of the theme, which were extremely difficult to remove for those who used the theme. The themes were given away free which resulted in many of the themes being downloaded thousands of times which in turn generated thousands of links.

Many webmasters gained great rankings using this tactic, even for ultra-competitive key phrases. Alas, after about a year Google started to clamp down on Wordpress footer links, with many webmasters that employed the tactic reporting that their rankings had been hit hard. What goes around comes around, so when offered such links, avoid them!

### *Beware of Xrumer!*

XRumer is a Windows program that posts forum spam with the aim of boosting search engine rankings. It has been claimed that the program is able to bypass techniques commonly used by many websites to deter automated spam, such as account registration, CAPTCHAs, and e-mail activation before posting. The program makes heavy use of a database of known open proxies in an attempt to make it more difficult for administrators to block posts. In the short term you can gain good ranking with Xrumer although the ranking will not last as your website will be banned from Google and other search engines.

## Take Your Time!

You must remember that building an online cash cow takes time! Those that take shortcuts with their off-page SEO, such as buying link packages, spamming and acquiring links on sites without first carrying out research, I guarantee, will find their sites penalized by Google in the long term. You will hear other webmasters gloating about how they have in effect beat Google although you can be sure they will not tell you when their site has been penalized.

In my time as an online affiliate I have seen many affiliates gain great ranking with black hat tactics, in some cases pushing my rankings down. Such affiliates come and go and will never have a long-term future as affiliates, because they never learn to build affiliates sites that are capable of sustaining rankings for the long term.

# Chapter 13 - Buying Affiliate Websites

This chapter, Buying Affiliate Websites, is a chapter I did not want initially to include in this book because many new affiliates will simply end up buying a website that in most cases will never make them a penny. Worse still, those who do take the shortcut of buying an existing site rather than building their very own from scratch, will miss out on many basic techniques that all affiliates have to learn during the stages of initial research and site creation. Many will say that they can still learn these techniques by reading the early chapters of this book, but actually it is from the real physical "doing" of these techniques that new affiliates learn.

In reality, if you are looking to take shortcuts at such an early stage of your affiliate career, then it is highly probable that you will be looking to take further shortcuts with future elements of building your site. But hey, the decision is yours.

Ignoring my comments above, I will say that buying an existing affiliate website can of course be a great way to give yourself a head start. Buying an aged affiliate website, complete with a half decent backlink profile, quality content and better still existing revenue is a route some new online affiliates do take although most end up buying "potential" rather than obtaining value. Online market places such as Flippa.com, Digitalpoint.com plus marketplace sections on popular online webmaster forums such as affiliates4u.com are crammed with affiliate websites offered for sale. Before you open your browser to search the latest "website for sale" listings, I must warn you of the high risk involved in buying existing affiliate websites and equip you with a little knowledge so that you don't become the latest newbie buyer to be scammed.

## Webmasters Overvalue Their Websites

In general, most affiliate websites offered for sale are overpriced and in many cases overhyped. Virtually all webmasters overvalue their websites because they factor in all the time they have spent on development, even though the bottom line for a website's actual value is a multiple of the site's average monthly profit. In real terms, most of the time webmasters try to cash in on a website's possible potential, or try to justify a high price tag by referring to what established websites in the same niche are earning, which in many cases is complete nonsense.

229

Websites offered for sale at what seems like bargain prices are, in 99.99% of cases, not what they seem. I have witnessed many new to the world of affiliate marketing being damn right scammed by experienced webmasters that simply prey on those with little knowledge. I have heard many horror stories over the years, which include websites that are sold with existing revenue mysteriously "drying up" once they have been sold, plus in some cases websites losing links, resulting in the website losing existing ranking. The sad truth is that a high percentage of affiliate websites offered for sale are indeed a bad investment, especially for new online affiliates.

## Tricks, Lies & Damn Right Scams

I'm going to climb back onto my soapbox again and tell you that I would strongly advise any new online affiliate first to build their own site from scratch before even contemplating purchasing a website. The knowledge you gain from building your own site will help you no end when you try to evaluate websites that are offered for sale at a later date. For those who simply will not listen to me I'm going to do my utmost to inform you so you don't get scammed. Let's look at common tricks, or should I say damn right scams, that some webmasters employ to entice you to buy their sites.

### *Duplicate Content*

Never buy a website that has content that has simply been copied from other websites. Websites offered for sale with listings such as "fully automated" basically just scrape, or should I say steal, content from other sites. Most offered for sale are just days or weeks old and may actually rank to some degree. The sad truth is that Google and other search engines will penalize all such sites in the very near future. A good test is to copy a sentence from a content page and paste it into Google (enclosed in quotes) to see if you can find any pages with exactly the same content. For example, I took the text below from a website offered for sale at flippa.com, added quotes to the start and end of the sentence and pasted it in to the Google search box.

*"The Venetian Resort Hotel Las Vegas is located on the Strip and close to the famous attractions which draw millions to this city every year. This five-diamond purveyor of Las Vegas accommodation is close to many casinos and shopping options. The McCarran International Airport is roughly 5 miles from the Venetian Resort Hotel Las Vegas."*

A quick search revealed dozens of websites with exactly the same content! I checked over a dozen pages from the website with exactly the same results. The website only consisted of copied content so of course offered no value at all. Such websites, you may be surprised to hear, do actually sell, mostly however to inexperienced webmasters. Don't ever contemplate buying a website that contains duplicate content!

### Poor Quality Content

For any website you may be thinking of buying, it is of great importance that you take the time to actually read a large proportion of the content. Some webmasters will build sites using copied content from other sites that is simply run through an article spinner, so that the content appears unique. Spun articles are very poor quality articles that don't read at all well. Take a look at the content below which has been run through an article spinner:

*"Given that a player can succeed or misplace their whole load in a lone hand at a no boundary money game, you will require a superior bankroll than at a maximum game. No boundary bankrolls are deliberate in buy-ins the similar method that contests are calculated."*

*"Several poker players shells out for every session of poker as it appears, plus those duties are frequently taken from the "entertainment" part of their daily or weekly finances. As playing fun poker is a completely excellent manner to spend time, but if you are captivating your pastime more gravely you should utilize some types of bankroll management."*

As you can see the above content is basically "Gobbledygook" and of no use at all! A site may be offered for sale with the seller claiming the site has 200 quality articles, and you may indeed find that the articles on the homepage are indeed good quality. In many cases if you dig deeper into the site's content, you will find that much of the content is simply spun garbage.

## Faked Earnings

Anybody with even basic Photoshop skills can fake a screenshot that seems to show genuine earnings. As a general rule, a website will sell for 10 to 24 times its actual monthly profit. I prefer to buy at no more than 12 times monthly profit, although I will go up to 18 months for an extremely good quality established site. It is extremely difficult to verify actual earnings of a website offered for sale. For example a webmaster could have two or more websites in a similar niche with one actually generating no monthly sales. The webmaster could claim the site is generating a healthy monthly income but in reality the actual sales are being generated from another site. The webmaster may even offer you the login of his affiliate program backend, so that you can check the monthly earnings, which are of course genuine, but not actually from the site he is selling. I am sad to say that I have seen many webmasters employ this tactic over the years.

## Fake PageRank

A website offered for sale may seem to have a good PageRank score, let's say PR5, but in reality the PageRank is fake. Many webmasters will simply set up a 301 redirect on an aged domain with a decent amount of PageRank, which results in the PageRank being passed temporarily to the website offered for sale. Once the website has been sold, the 301 redirect is removed, which results in the sold domain losing its healthy PageRank after the next PageRank Toolbar Update. To check if a website's PageRank is actually genuine, you can use the free online tool – http://www.checkPageRank.net/, although clever webmasters can make fake PageRank appear genuine.

## Removed Backlinks

Another tactic employed by some webmasters is to remove backlinks once a website has been sold. This of course results in the website losing rankings and later PageRank. The webmaster offering the site for sale may have a large network of sites and simply uses his network to link to the site offered for sale. Also of course the webmaster could have simply purchased links on a short-term basis prior to listing his site for sale. Before buying any site take the time to check the full backlink profile and ask about how the links were acquired and if they are permanent. You can of course check the backlinks of any sites using free backlink checkers such as http://backlinkwatch.com/. You should always take the time to examine the backlinks of a site you are thinking of buying, before you commit to purchase. Are the backlinks of good quality and from other websites in a relevant niche? Do any of the backlinks have PageRank? Have the backlinks been gained by spamming, with most of the backlinks appearing to be low quality blog comments or forum posts?

Remember, you can gain good rankings in the short term with low quality link building techniques, but such rankings never last. Some dishonest webmasters will build literally tens of thousands of low quality backlinks, simply to gain temporary good search engine rankings. They will then try to sell the site as quickly as possible before the site is hit with a penalty.

### *Warning – Always Use Escrow!*

Another tactic employed by some webmasters is to offer a quality site for sale, take payment but never actually pass on the website to the buyer. Again I have seen this occur time and time again over the years. If you ever do purchase a website, then ensure you use some form of ESCROW service. ESCROW is simply a method of payment where a third party holds the actual payment, which is not passed on to the seller until the buyer has received the goods.

## Penalized Sites

Sometimes you may stumble upon an affiliate website offered for sale that indeed looks like a quality site and even seems offered at a rock bottom price. Remember that in recent times many webmasters have been hit hard by changes to the Google algorithm, which has resulted in many websites losing their rankings. Many such websites of course are quickly put up for sale. Such websites may well look like an attractive proposition, especially those with a history of good earnings, but in reality if the website has been hit by a dreaded Google PANDA penalty, the website's earning potential may have gone forever.

Take the time to check if the website still ranks for any profitable key phrase. Examine the website using Alexa.com and actually search for the key phrases listed in the Alexa "Search Analysis" tab as below.

**Search Traffic**

The percentage of site visits from search engines.

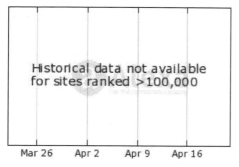

| Period | Percent of Site Traffic |
|---|---|
| Last 30 days | - |
| Last 7 days | - |
| Yesterday | - |

**Top Queries from Search Traffic**

The top queries driving traffic to anewbody.co.uk from search engines. Updated monthly.

| | Query | Percent of Search Traffic |
|---|---|---|
| 1 | treadmill | 17.29% |
| 2 | tradmill bremshi | 4.10% |
| 3 | treadmill reviews | 3.91% |
| 4 | treadmill commercial | 3.53% |
| 5 | bremshey treadmills | 3.20% |
| 6 | momentum treadmills | 2.45% |
| 7 | reebok t4.2 | 1.73% |
| 8 | second hand treadmills | 1.68% |
| 9 | bremshey scout manual | 1.66% |
| 10 | running machines | 1.57% |

If you find that the website no longer ranks highly for any of the queries listed in the "Top Queries From Search Traffic", then you know that the website has recently picked up a penalty.

I read many webmaster forums and have a keen interest in forum threads that relate to websites hit with a Google PANDA penalty. The bad news is that only a small percentage of PANDA penalized sites have recovered. Buying such sites you are basically paying for the site's previous earning power, which in most cases will never return.

As you can see from the above points mentioned, buying a website offered for sale is a potential minefield. As a new online affiliate you are exactly the type of customer many dishonest webmasters are looking for. Building your own site, although a slow process, will give you the knowledge you require to evaluate websites offered for sale.

## Ranking Key Phrase Types

If the site is indeed generating traffic from search engines, then take a look at the actual types of key phrase that are generating the traffic. Are the key phrases that are generating the traffic key phrases that will also generate sales? I would rather buy a website that generated 50 uniques a day for decent "buying" key phrases, than a website with 1000 daily visitors generated from poor quality key phrases that simply don't convert into sales.

### *Low Ranking Key Phrases*

Many webmasters are clueless in respect to ranking key phrases highly in search engines. Great sites to buy are those with a number of key phrases that "nearly rank". By "nearly rank" I am referring to "buying" key phrases that rank on page two or even three of Google search results. If a site has such key phrases, I will check the quality and indeed existing backlinks for each of the key phrases, and then of course check the backlinks of the pages that rank in the top five spots in Google for each of the key phrases. If the sites that rank top five for each of the key phrases do not have an impressive backlink profile, or are thin type affiliate websites, then I know that with some work building good backlinks, plus adding quality content, I can vastly increase the site's rankings and in doing so increase traffic and increase sales.

## Buying Websites from Flippa.com

Flippa.com is by far the leading website for buying and selling websites. If you visit Flippa, you will find thousands of websites and domains in hundreds of different niches offered for sale. Each site offered for sale has its very own sales page, which gives a great deal of information. Each sales page has an option for you to make a bid (or in some cases a buy now option) plus a message section where you can ask the seller a public question. Most sites on Flippa are sold in an online auction format, although some sellers also include a "buy now" price. Most auctions on Flippa run for between one and four weeks with most of the bidding activity occurring during the final day of the auction. Unlike Ebay auctions, there is no manic bidding frenzy in the final few hours of each auction, because after each new top bid, the auction is extended for four hours. This can prove highly frustrating because popular website auctions can in effect go on for days.

If you look at the very top of a Flippa sales page (example overleaf), you will find that the top section of the page has:

- the website's main sales title
- a screenshot of the actual website
- the URL of the website
- how much time of the website's auction remains
- the current bid
- an option where you can make a bid

Flippa requires all sellers and buyers to register before they can either buy or sell websites and registration must be verified with a telephone number.

The next section of the sales page deals with the website's actual visibility, such as PageRank, Alexa Rank, Google links, inbound links and domain registration. This section also includes complete.com data. Although I am not really a fan of complete.com, I will say to you that if the complete.com data is available, do take a look. I prefer to do my own research, as detailed earlier in this chapter, rather than rely on the data supplied, because, as I have already stated, much of the data can be manipulated.

Next you find a description of the website that has been input by the seller. To the right you will find traffic and financial data, although this should be taken at face value. All those who sell sites on Flippa have the option to upload files, such as verified Google Analytics and financial data, which of course proves that the information they are giving is true. If the seller has chosen not to upload such files, then in my opinion the traffic and financial data should not be trusted. At the bottom of the sales page you will find a section where you can post public questions to the website owner. Take the time to read all the questions and answers if you are interested in purchasing the site.

Also important is that Flippa has a great feedback system, which can be accessed for all members by simply clicking their user names, revealing all their transactions.

## Flippa

Buy and sell websites.
2,904 buyers and sellers online right now

Search listings [Search]
Advanced Search

| Featured | New Listings | Most Active | Ending Soon | Just Sold | Price Range | Browse | Deals | Sell Your Website |

### Top Affiliate for new SEO Software, Huge Growth & Marketing Potential.

SEODemon.org

Public Auction has not yet reached the reserve price
Listing closes in 6 days, 15 hours

☆ Watch This Auction    [f Like]    [8+1 0]

**$3,000**    14 bids

$ [_____]    [Place Bid]
(Enter $3,050 or more.)

**$12,500**    [Buy It Now]

Seller accepts payment using Escrow    ?

| Site Visibility | | Domain | | SEMRush Stats | |
|---|---|---|---|---|---|
| Google PageRank | 3 | Registration Date | 29th Dec, 2011 | SEMRush Rank | - |
| Alexa Rank | 660,716 | Compete Stats | | Keywords in Google | - |
| Links in Google | 0 | Compete Ranking | - | Site Content | |
| Inbound Links | 2,803 | Compete Uniques | - | Possible Copies Found | - |

*View extended due diligence data for this listing*

## Description

### Quick Website Overview

SEODemon.org is an affiliate website promoting the Ultimate Demon SEO Software and offering a $40 off coupon for the one-time fee license + bonus site lists. Read more about coupon/bonus lists further below.

Ultimate Demon software was released a little over 3 months ago by one of the industry's most respected SEO Software companies, Edwin Soft, the creators of Bookmarking Demon and Article Demon (2 very well known SEO Softwares on the market).

The website runs on WordPress with Thesis Theme installed (paid license).

### Ultimate Demon Prices & Affiliate Commission:

**$397 One Time Fee** - YOUR COMMISSION: **$144.59 per Sale**
* $357 from seodemon.org

**$47 Monthly Fee** - YOUR COMMISSION: **$19.04 Recurring Revenue**
* no coupon for monthly

### Running the Website:

It's on complete auto-pilot, the only thing you would have to do is send the bonuses to the buyers who requests them, after you check the RegNow order ID provided by the buyer matches the one shown in your RegNow account.

### All Natural Traffic, Never Paid for Advertising:

That's right, I have never paid for any type of advertising anywhere, the only work done off-site was obviously seo work.
Marketing it and advertising it would definitely improve sales and gain more exposure for the website.

**SEODemon is without doubt the #1 affiliate website dedicated to promote the Ultimate Demon software, why?**

- **Great Search Engine Rankings**
Valid Page Rank 3
Ranking keywords:
#3 - ultimate demon
#1 - ultimate demon coupons
#2 - ultimate demon discount
#4 - ultimate demon review
#7 - ultimate demon vs senuke
#20- social bookmarking (very high competition)
+ many others.

### Claimed Site Age

| Site Established | 30th Dec, 2011 |
|---|---|

### Claimed Traffic

| Page Views Per Month | 743 |
|---|---|
| Uniques Per Month | 452 |

### Reported Revenue

■ Profit  ■ Revenue

$900
$800
$700
$600
$500
$400
$300
$200
$100
$0
Jan    Feb    Mar

### Claimed Financials

| Gross Revenue *(avg per month)* | $809 |
|---|---|
| Net Profit *(avg per month)* | $809 |

### Monetization Methods

| Advertising Sales | No |
|---|---|
| Product or Service Sales | No |
| Affiliate Income | Yes |

### Site Uniqueness

Content is claimed to be unique
Design is not claimed to be unique

### Seller

**capitanu** 100% $23K
Add Seller to Watchlist    ☆
Communicate with Seller
Ownership verified by file upload
Hide this Listing    ⊘

## *Why You Should Buy From Flippa*

As I have already said, you can buy websites from other sources, including many affiliate or webmaster forums, although for peace of mind I strongly urge you to buy from Flippa. Over the years, time and time again, I have witnessed many inexperienced investors paying way over the odds for established affiliate websites, especially when purchased from affiliate and webmaster forums. A good analogy would be someone swimming out into shark-infested waters and then emptying buckets full of blood and guts around them. This scenario I would compare to an inexperienced affiliate posting on an affiliate webmasters' forum that he had a big budget for quality sites. Sorry, but the honest truth is that if you don't have the experience and knowledge, then you are going to be ripped apart!

In general you will pay more for sites, links and even content if you buy from niche affiliate forums. There are many quality webmasters who make a good living from flipping affiliate websites, especially to inexperienced affiliates just like you. I'm not saying you can't buy great sites from affiliates' forums at the right price but I am saying that if you don't have the required knowledge, you are odds on to pay over the odds. Sorry, but that is simply a fact!

Your best approach would be to buy from Flippa, taking the time of course to carry out detailed research. Although I have tried to do my best to dissuade you from starting with a purchased site, I will admit that if you do indeed find a bargain, it could kick-start your affiliate career. Remember most affiliates fail as they simply do not acquire the skills to convert traffic to actual sales. Many new affiliates will spend a good few months building up a half decent site only to lose interest when the money does not come rolling in after a few months, resulting of course in them listing their site for sale on Flippa.com. Also many affiliates simply do not optimize their sites for conversions. An unoptimized site earning, let's say, £50 per month can easily be optimized with just a few hours' work to double or even triple monthly income. Also there are many neglected affiliate sites, ranking perhaps on page two or three for their main key phrases, which could easily be pushed to a much higher ranking with a little work.

## Understanding Traffic Types

A website may be listed for sale with healthy monthly traffic but you must realize there are different types of traffic. What you are looking for is traffic from leading search engines, especially Google of course, which is generated from search results (organic traffic). Never buy a website, trusting the claims of decent traffic, before taking a good look at the site's Google Analytics statistics. Low quality traffic can be purchased for a few dollars but such traffic is in reality useless. Most social media traffic is low value with traffic from StumbleUpon, which can easily generate thousands of visitors in just a few days, ultra-low value.

Many webmasters do, however, harness paid traffic methods such as Google Adwords for profit. Remember however, that to determine the actual profit such sites generate, you need to find out exactly how much is being spent on Google Adwords each month. Last Autumn I was offered a site with a monthly turnover of £2,000. The site was offered to me for just £10,000 when normally sites sell for at least 12 times their monthly profit. On closer inspection the webmaster was actually buying traffic from Google Adwords at a cost of £1,600 per month, so in real terms the site was only making a profit of £400 a month.

## Buying An Affiliate Website: Your First Purchase

If you are determined to dive into the shark-infested waters of website sales, then for your initial purchase follow this very important advice. Treat your first purchase as a high-risk speculative gamble and only use money you can afford to lose. I have seen inexperienced webmasters buy affiliate websites for five-figure sums when in reality the actual websites were worth less than four figures. If you visit Flippa.com you will find that websites sell for as little as $20 to as much as six-figure sums, so stick within your budget!

### How To Value Websites

As a general rule, websites sell based on 12 to 24 times their monthly profit using an average of the website's earning for at least the previous six months. You do not of course simply take the website's last month's profit, because this could have been higher than normal due to many factors, hence why you take an average based on six months' profit. If a website has only been generating revenue for a couple of months, it is much harder to value and more of a speculative gamble. You will have to take a good look at how the website is actually generating income and try to determine if the monthly profit is sustainable.

But what about a website that has no earnings? If a website has no monthly earnings, other factors come into play. The seller is bound to mention the hundreds of hours he has devoted to his site, but in reality the value is just a matter of valuing the content and design. After all, we know that we can buy content from the likes of Elance and we can get good Wordpress themes from Theme Forest. Early last year I noticed a website for sale that had a pleasing design and 120 pages of decent quality content. I knew for a fact I could buy such content for around $15 an article, if not cheaper, and I had noticed a very similar theme for sale at Theme Forest for $50. I put a maximum value on the content of

$1,800 (120 x $15) and generously, well in my opinion, added other $200 for the design as it was unique. My $2,000 offer was rejected as the seller was looking for at least $10,000. I of course instantly lost interest, not only in the website but also in the seller. The website went unsold for over a year and was later sold for just $1,500. As I have already said, most webmasters overvalue their websites!

## Buying Existing Websites For Content Stripping

From time to time I will buy websites, not because I want to develop them, but simply for their content. As an online affiliate you will always be literally crying out for content. You need daily fresh content to post on your site, plus of course you need weekly fresh content for external blogs that you utilize for link building and even more content for link exchanges. In all my years as an affiliate, very rarely have I had a backlog of content.

Sometimes, if you are extremely lucky, you may stumble upon on a website for sale that relates to your niche. If the content meets your quality standards and the price is right, you could simply purchase the website, take it offline, and then use the content for your requirements.

## Don't Say I Didn't Tell You So!

By now you should realize some of the major risks in buying existing websites. You should also now have a good idea of what exactly you should be looking for. Remember that just because a website made £1000 last month, or even £1000 a month for the last six months, there is no guarantee that it will make a penny next month. Many affiliate websites are in reality just one penalty, or one hack away from doom. Be careful out there!

# Chapter 14 – Mass Traffic from Images

As I edited this chapter, I was also taking note of the many new posts that appeared on the webmaster forums that I read. April 2012 was what can only be described as a horrible month for thousands of affiliate webmasters. Not only did Google roll out PANDA 3.5, but also an anti-SEO algorithm update that basically wiped out many affiliate webmasters. To get an understanding of the chaos the latest Google algorithm updates caused, take a look at this forum thread from a well-respected webmasters' forum:

http://www.webmasterworld.com/google/4435785.htm.

Although I understand the frustration of webmasters who witnessed the demise of their Google rankings, I must say that they were extremely foolhardy to rely so much on Google for their traffic.

As someone new venturing into the world of online affiliate marketing, take heed of the mistakes made by those hit hard by the latest algorithm changes. Although Google dominates search engine traffic market share, in today's world search engines only account for a fraction of user searches. Many users no longer use search engines at all for search, instead opting to use apps, social networking sites or other methods.

This chapter and the next will help you generate traffic from multiple sources, which you must implement to safeguard your business for the long term.

## Target Google Image Search!

You may be surprised to find that after these opening comments I am still focusing on the Google search engine; after all I strongly stated that you should diversify your traffic sources. Google Image Search, however, is a different entity to the main Google Search and surprisingly much less targeted. Although Google applies strong filters to the content it in effect "lets" rank highly in the main search, the same cannot be said for Google Image Search. Even a website heavily penalized in the main Google search can rank highly in Google Image Search, although many affiliates have not realized this fact.

# Never Underestimate a Woman!

One of the great aspects of working online is that you can learn something new every day. The internet is evolving, as are search engines and social networks. He who thinks he knows it all in effect knows nothing!

One day I noticed my wife searching for a new outfit in a most peculiar way. Instead of using Google search, typing in a phrase such as "summer dresses" or "dress store" she had instead clicked on Google Image Search and typed a more specific query such as "white sleeveless dress with bolero". This resulted in hundreds of pictures of the exact dress type she was looking for.

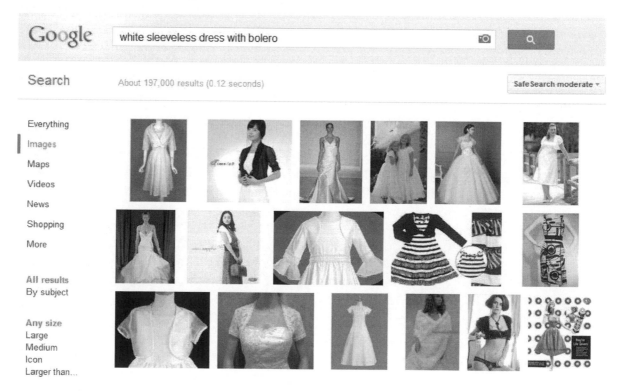

In turn, she clicked on the dresses she liked, which took her to an online store, where she checked out further details of the dresses that had taken her fancy before clicking the "buy now" button, reducing the balance of our bank account. On closer inspection, the actual online store where she had made her purchases was not even ranked on the first two Google search results pages, but the store did rank extremely highly in Google Image Search for literally hundreds of dress-type key phrases. It seemed clear to me that the online store had sidestepped the ultra-competitive normal Google search results and simply targeted images, because they understood exactly how their potential customers searched and just how profitable image searches could be. With years of experience under my belt why had I not thought of using Google Image Search for generating sales?

Now, of course, for many products targeting image search is simply not going to generate sales, although for many others, especially dresses, shoes, boots, or indeed all types of clothing, image search would be ideal. Targeting image search is ideal for any niche where visually comparing products is undertaken before making a purchase. I am pretty sure that this method would also work for celebrity gossip type sites, as many people seem fascinated by what celebs are wearing and who they are out with. I am sure that other niches such as greeting cards, paintings, art forms and hundreds more could target image search for sales. You just need to think a little "out of the box" of ways to exploit Google Image Search for profit.

To understand the potential of targeting image search, let's use the Google Adwords External Tool to examine the searches for "wedding shoes".

| | Keyword | Competition | Global Monthly Searches | Local Monthly Searches |
|---|---|---|---|---|
| ☐ | [wedding shoes] ▾ | High | 135,000 | 135,000 |

| | ✓ Save all  **Keyword ideas (100)** | | 1 - 50 of 100 ▾ | ‹ › |
|---|---|---|---|---|
| | Keyword | Competition ▾ | Global Monthly Searches | Local Monthly Searches |
| ☐ | [wedding shoes] ▾ | High | 135,000 | 135,000 |
| ☐ | [blue wedding shoes] ▾ | High | 6,600 | 6,600 |
| ☐ | [wedding shoes uk] ▾ | High | 5,400 | 5,400 |
| ☐ | [ivory wedding shoes] ▾ | High | 5,400 | 5,400 |
| ☐ | [designer wedding shoes] ▾ | High | 5,400 | 5,400 |
| ☐ | [manolo blahnik wedding shoes] ▾ | High | 5,400 | 5,400 |
| ☐ | [cheap wedding shoes] ▾ | High | 4,400 | 4,400 |
| ☐ | [flat wedding shoes] ▾ | High | 3,600 | 3,600 |
| ☐ | [white wedding shoes] ▾ | High | 3,600 | 3,600 |
| ☐ | [purple wedding shoes] ▾ | High | 3,600 | 3,600 |
| ☐ | [dyeable wedding shoes] ▾ | High | 3,600 | 3,600 |
| ☐ | [pink wedding shoes] ▾ | High | 3,600 | 3,600 |

As you can see from the above, the exact search volume for "wedding shoes" is a mighty 135,000, in addition to hundreds of other long-tail search phrases. For normal Google search, the competition for all these search queries is very high. The good news is that you will be amazed how even the biggest online brands don't optimize their images, so getting your images into the first few image search results is in most cases a breeze.

I have taken the time to experiment with targeting image search and have had great results. The main benefit, of course, is that you can generate highly targeted traffic with little effort, even for highly competitive search queries. Better still, you can do so WITHOUT the need for quality articles. I managed to rank hundreds of images targeting specific products with pages that only consisted of an image and a title. These pages, of course, did not rank in the main Google search but did rank in Google Image Search extremely highly.

I am sure many affiliates have not even considered targeting Google Image Search as they are so wrapped up in avoiding the barrage of penalties with which Google has hit affiliate webmasters in recent times. Sometimes, however, things can be overlooked because they are so simple!

Before I explain exactly how you start the process of targeting Google Image Search, I want you to take note of a couple of very important points. Firstly, I am not for one moment suggesting that the bulk of your content should be images alone. I found that my test image site was actually penalized in the main Google search, with, after a month, none of the image pages anywhere to be seen in the top 100 or so main search page results. Targeting image search should not be your main emphasis as your main goal is, of course, to create a quality authority type site with at least a thousand quality articles in your first year. Secondly, you must ensure that if you decide to target image search, you do so from a dedicated section of your website. You will find that your image section, as I have already stated, will get penalized in the main Google search index. If you have quality articles in your image section, the chances are high those articles will get penalized too. Keep your images in their very own section!

## Keyword Research

Anyone with even a basic knowledge of SEO will know that picking the correct keywords is perhaps the most vital step you can take in regards to SEO, and this is very much the case when trying to rank in Google Image Search. You must make sure that you are looking for keywords that are related to how people actually use images to help them in the buying process. If a bride-to-be was searching for "wedding shoes", she would, of course, start with this search phrase. After browsing images relating to her initial search, the chances are high that she would refine her search to match her exact requirements. So she would start searching for "wedding shoes" but end up searching for a more specific phrase such as "White Manolo Blahnik Wedding Shoes". You will find that such long-tail key phrases are extremely easy to rank in Google Image Search and of course easier to rank in the main Google search index. I would rather rank for specific long-tail key phrases than more general key phrases, simply because the long-tail key phrases are those closest to the end of the search funnel and so are the ones that lead to the searchers finding exactly what they want, resulting in them clicking the "buy now" button. You will be simply amazed by how many leading online stores don't optimize their images, which in real terms opens up the possibility for you to rank for their brand product keywords using their images.

## Image Usage

Most merchants will be happy for you to use their images and will in many cases provide direct links to their images for you to use. The problem is that most of their images are not optimized so in their current state are no use to you. Remember, however, that by using your browser, and I recommend Firefox for this process, you can in effect copy any image from an online webpage by simply right-clicking on it and then clicking "save image as". Doing so will enable you to save the image directly to your computer, giving the image a more SEO friendly file name. For example, you might want to save an image of White Manolo Blahnik Wedding Shoes that the online store has given the file name of 138563692.jpg. When you save the image, simply enter the filename:

white_manolo_blahnik_wedding_shoes.jpg.

Although most merchants will not have any problem with you using their images, a small percentage may not allow you do to so. It is always a good idea to read the merchant's affiliate terms and conditions in detail. If you are unsure about the usage of images, simply contact the merchant and ask them. Remember that merchants set up affiliate programs because they want to increase their sales, so most will help you. Many of the merchants I have contacted about using their images have actually supplied me with more images, in some cases actually better than those they were available online. Don't be afraid to ask merchants for images!

## Long-tail Keyword Research

Selecting keywords is not a complex process, but one that you should take your time with. The basic rule with the process of optimizing for Google Images is that you should target long-tail key phrases that where possible include the colour, the brand name and a precise product description, such as "White Manolo Blahnik Wedding Shoes" and "Jen & Kim Darling Creme Wedding Shoes". For most niches it should be easy to find hundreds of such key phrases.

### *Build Your Product Image Keyword List*

Firstly take the time to examine the top few hundred products in your chosen niche and create a list of specific product long-tail key phrases. If you are struggling to create your list, simply jot down a few of your general keywords. For example, for shoes your main keywords could be:

- Wedding Shoes
- Designer Shoes
- Dress Shoes
- Prom Shoes
- Woman's Shoes

Simply enter the first of your main keywords into the Google Adwords Keyword Tool, ensuring that you have set the "Match Type" (on the right hand side menu bar) to "exact". Also make sure you select the location you are targeting. Once the results appear, simply sort the results by clicking on either "Global Monthly Searches" or "Local Monthly Searches" depending on your target demographic. For each of your main keywords simply cherry pick the best long-tail keywords. This process should help you create a great list of long-tail key phrase.

## Image Section Setup

Again I will stress that if you decide to target image search, you must do so from a new section of your site. Simply buy or use a free Wordpress photo gallery theme, of which you will find thousands using Google search or in Themeforest.net. Before installing your theme take the time to plan your categories. I also strongly suggest that you should use an image sitemap (http://wordpress.org/extend/plug-ins/google-image-sitemap/) alongside a normal sitemap .

## Choosing the Right Image

Let's look quickly at how important choosing the right image is. The basic rule is this – the image is incredibly important to the person searching, but Google couldn't care less about it at all. Basically, Google will rely wholly on you and the different visitors to tell it whether the image is relevant to a specific keyword. This means that your image must appeal to visitors, matching exactly their search query. The main function of every image you use for targeting image search is to get the users to click on the image and land on your website. To understand exactly what I mean, go to Google Image Search and enter "White Manolo Blahnik Wedding Shoes".

Take a good look at the images below. As you can see, many of the images simply do not match the search query. Also for those images that actually do, some are far better than others.

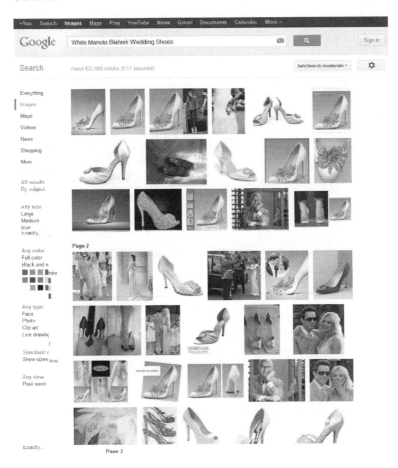

I can't stress how essential the choice of each image used actually is. I would opt for an image that really did showcase the product as below:

You could actually "think out of the box" a little to boost your click-through rate. For example you could add a sales label in a contrasting colour (red) or even a discount offer if available. Doing so will boost the click-through rate of your image because everybody loves a bargain buy!

### *Optimizing Images for Google Image Search*

If you want to get the best possible results for each of your images, then you need to ensure that each image is optimized to the highest possible standard. In order to do this you are going to have to take great care with your image optimization.

Before you upload an image to your website, you must ensure that the long-tail keyword is the actual file name of your image. The file name should always contain the keywords that you are targeting, such as white_manolo_blahnik_wedding_shoes.jpg. If you don't include the keywords in your image file names, your images will simply not rank in Google Image Search. You can tweak the image details much further to optimize the image BEFORE you upload it to your website. Go to your PC folder that contains your images, find the image you are about to upload, hover your mouse icon over the image name and click properties. A new window will pop-up; when it does, just click the details tab.

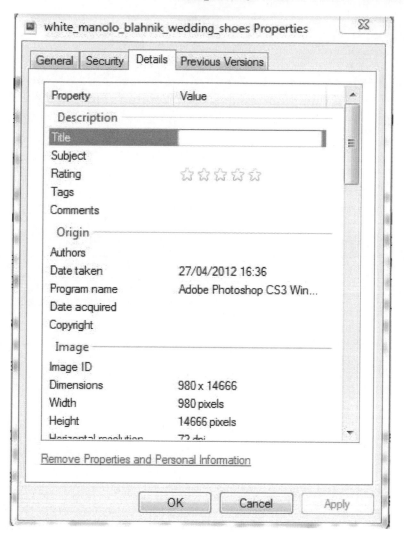

For the White Manolo Blahnik Wedding Shoes image I would enter the following details:

**Title:** White Manolo Blahnik Wedding Shoes

**Subject:** White Manolo Blahnik Wedding Shoes

**Rating:** 5 Stars

**Tags**: Wedding Shoes, White Shoes, Manolo Blahnik Shoes, Best Wedding Shoes

**Comments**: White Manolo Blahnik Wedding Shoes

# Chapter 14 – Mass Traffic from Images

The overall goal is to make sure that your keywords are well represented in the image's details.

Now you have optimized the image as much as possible — more so than a large percentage of images that you find online — it is time to head over to Wordpress and upload it, where you can also add on a number of other aspects of on-page SEO. In fact, the SEO done here is absolutely vital to the overall success of your images ranking highly in Google Image Search.

The first thing that you need to do is make a new post – a post that has the image keywords as its main title. So your post name should have a title that matches your optimized image file name such as "White Manolo Blahnik Wedding Shoes".

After you have completed adding the post title, you will then need to add a little content to the page. This doesn't need to be much – 100 words are fine. I have actually managed to rank images without any content text. although I suggest that you add it. For the content ensure that:

- The main keywords are included at the very start of the content.

- The image keyword is used as a link at least once to another page on your site.

For example, you could finish your text with a link to a merchant where the reader can actually buy the product. For the anchor text of the link use something like:

"Buy White Manolo Blahnik Wedding Shoes".

After you have completed the content – which shouldn't take very long – you are ready to upload the Image. Go back to the on-site SEO page and read again the section that details SEO for images. To recap:

- **Title:** Make it interesting, but include the keywords.

- **Alternate Text:** This is a vital part. Make the alternate text as long as possible and make sure that both your main and image keywords are used within it at least once.

- **Caption:** Use this to enter a detailed, yet informal, caption about the image.

- **Description:** Write 50 words or so about the image and include the keywords.

251

- **Link URL:** The link to the image.

- **Alignment:** Make sure that the image is aligned to the text.

- **Size:** Not really important. Choose what is appropriate to your site.

- **Tags:** Add relevant tags

Now you have inserted the image into the Wordpress post, you still need to make a couple of small changes before you publish your post. First, hover over the image and click the icon that appears. Then change the horizontal and vertical spacing to 10 pixels, as this will ensure that it isn't tightly bunched against the text.

Now that you have the image formatted correctly within your post, you can increase the optimization a little further:

Make a new category and add the post to the category. The category should also match the image keyword, so in the case of White Manolo Blahnik Wedding Shoes, the category could be wedding shoes or even Manolo Blahnik Shoes. If you categorise your posts, this makes it far easier for your visitors to find what they are looking for. For example, a visitor may have found your site by searching images with a key phrase such as "White Manolo Blahnik Wedding Shoes". She may decide she does not like the Manolo Bahnik Wedding Shoes but may go on to find shoes she likes in the same category of your site. Categorising your post is of prime importance!

## Build Up Your Image Gallery Section

Your goal should be to build up your image gallery section over time so that it contains hundreds of product and, of course, each image page should link directly to the product. You will find that gallery pages can be added in minutes, as they only comprise an image and a little text, so simply get into the habit of adding a few each day.

# Chapter 15 – Additional Traffic Generation Techniques

With the good SEO techniques you have learnt in earlier chapters, in time you will start to generate traffic from Google Search and search engines such as Bing, Yahoo, Ask and many other lesser known search engines. You will also generate traffic from image search from the major search engines and little by little you should also be building a quality list. Although this is a great start, you must diversify your traffic generation further to safeguard the long-term future of your affiliate website. No matter how successful your website becomes in attracting visitors from search engines, you simply must devote quality time to build traffic from other sources.

## Building a Brand

You may be surprised to find a section on building a brand in this chapter, but the fact is that if you are successful in creating a brand for your affiliate website, then a healthy stream of daily traffic will follow. So what is branding? Well, it is simply creating awareness about your business, making your business instantly recognisable, making your business stand out from the crowd, so that people know exactly what your business is and what it stands for. Don't underestimate just how powerful online branding actually is. For many of the things you buy, the actual brand of the product plays a vital role in the final purchase. From fizzy drinks to beer, from coffee to t-shirts, the brand of the product is just as important as the product. Think about the brands of fizzy drinks you buy, think about the brands of clothes you buy and you should start to understand just how important the brand is to you.

### Build a Brand – "The Way to Rise above the Cesspool"

Building a brand online is just as important as building a brand for a brick and mortar business, if not more so. There is no doubt that in recent times Google and other search engines have started to favour brands, with many suggesting that online brands gain increased rankings from their actual brand strength. The Google CEO, Eric Schmidt, recently stated that the internet was a cesspool, with brands, he said, the way to rise above the cesspool. If you want to create an online affiliate business that will survive in the long term, then from day one you have to plan how to rise above the cesspool, as Eric Schmidt said, and create a quality, trusted brand. But how do you build a brand and what metrics do search engines use to determine brands? Well for sure you cannot build a brand by simply getting a shiny new logo designed and adding it to all your web presence, as some web designers would make you believe.

253

## *Choosing a Name for Your Brand*

Choosing a name for a new affiliate website is a process that I and many other online affiliates struggle with. I usually spend days before I stumble onto a name that seems just right. A great tip I can give you is, "Don't be a bland, be a brand." There is good reason why leading search engines have opted for names such as Google, Bing and Yahoo, and why leading merchant sites use names such as Amazon, Ebay and Argos. Do you think Google would have created the same brand identity with a brand domain such as searchengine.com? Many affiliates, in my opinion, put too much emphasis on including key phrases in their domain name, often creating sites using domains such as best-widget-bonus.com, with little thought of creating a brand. I am not, of course, saying that the domain name is the "be all and end all" of building a brand online, because it sure is not, but it definitely plays a vital role.

Take your time choosing the name of your website and remember not just to describe, but also to distinguish, as you want your brand to set you apart from your competition. Let's imagine that you are going to launch a treadmill affiliate website. Which one of the domains below would you imagine was the best to build as a brand?

- best-treadmills-online.org
- bargain-treadmills-online.net
- treadmilltoday.com
- cheaptreadmills.info

From the domains listed above, I would opt for treadmilltoday.com or something along the same lines, rather than using keyword rich domains, especially those with hyphens. Try to use a domain name that is easy to remember, preferably comprising no more than two words. You could of course opt for a name not even using any of your main niche keywords, just as Google, Yahoo and Bing have chosen to do.

Also, the domain I have chosen above uses a .com domain which is the most recognised domain extension. As a general rule, once you decide upon a name, also buy the .org, .net and .co.uk or the domain for your country, because this will stop other affiliates "stealing" your brand traffic in the future. Imagine that in a year's time you have built treadmilltoday.com into a thousand page authority site and have worked extremely hard building your brand, generating hundreds of search queries each day for "treadmill today". Imagine your horror if one day you found new sites launched such as treadmilltoday.org, treadmilltoday.net and treadmilltoday.co.uk. Simply protect your brand by buying other domain extensions.

## *Your Brand Logo*

In respect to your brand's logo, the best advice I can give you is to keep it simple. Many affiliates go OTT with their logos, creating logos that are intricate and hard to reproduce on other mediums. If you take a look at the logos of the internet's biggest brands such as Google, Yahoo, Amazon and Ebay you should note, in respect to design, just how basic these logos actually are. Concentrate on the actual words of your brand, rather than images that relate to your brand. Ensure your logo looks crisp and sharp on all mediums such as on the web, on images, on videos, on business cards, on letters and even on merchandise such as t-shirts. Once you start telling the world about your brand, perhaps by posting great advice on forums and blogs, then you should also use your logo as your profile image. Ensure you "stamp" your logo on every piece of content you load online, including images and videos. Also note that on many occasions profile and gravator images are very small, sometime as small as 100 pixels x 100 pixels. If your logo is too complex, then when displayed at such a small size it will be unreadable, so make sure your logo is easy to read even when displayed at a very small size.

## *Brand Strategy*

Your actual brand strategy will depend on a few very important factors:

- Who you are targeting.

- Which products you are targeting.

- How you can build confidence and trust.

### *Your Brand's Target Audience*

Defining your target customers should be the first research you carry out for your brand. If you do not understand who your potential customers actually are, then how can you sell your brand to them? For example, in the online bingo niche a large proportion of players, over 75%, are women. In the online poker niche over 90% of the players are men. In the console gaming niche it is fair to say that a high proportion of players are under 25, while in the life insurance niche, most potential customers would be considerably older.

### *Brand Product Considerations*

Once you have established who your potential customers are, you need to think about the products you are targeting them with, because this will play a vital role in how you want to be perceived. For an affiliate site selling fashion for those aged under 25, let's say aged 16 to 25, your brand will have to adopt a cool, hip or perhaps even edgy feel. If your brand is targeting the same age range but selling educational books, it should have a completely different feel. Building your brand will in effect play a large role in how you design your website and even the style you use to write your content. There is, of course, no point in creating content for gamers which reads as if it their dads wrote it, nor any point in creating content for fashion for over the 50s which reads as if teenagers wrote it.

### Where Do Your Potential Customers "Hang Out" Online?

Every niche, even micro niches, has communities online. Such communities come in the form of forums, blogs, chat rooms, Facebook groups and many other guises. Infiltrating communities in your chosen niche is a tactic you must employ. Simply seek out as many as possible by creating new accounts, using your brand name for your username, your website URL and your logo for your profile image. Spend time each week reading through each community, taking the time to "give away" your knowledge to help others. Don't spam! In fact don't even mention your website at all in most cases. Just concentrate on giving good advice to those who seek assistance and in time you will find traffic coming from the niche communities. It does, however, take time. Over the course of a year your brand should be established with those who are active in the communities, as you should have left a steady stream of quality informative posts, all of which display your logo and your brand name which links to your website.

Ensure that the posts you make are of the very highest quality so little by little you build your authority with the communities. Never get involved in community disputes, which from experience I can tell you flare up from time to time. Doing so could destroy your credibility overnight.

### Building Confidence & Trust

I actually agree with the comment made by the Google CEO, that the internet is a cesspool in regards to affiliate sites. I am sick and tired of reading online product reviews where every product is given a glowing review. I am also sick of reading reviews that have clearly been written by someone with no knowledge of the product or service. I am also sick to the back teeth of reading reviews that have simply been copied or rewritten from merchant sites. A great way to build confidence and trust, which, alas, many affiliates seem to have overlooked, is simply to be honest. In my lifetime I have purchased many great products but very few, if indeed any, have been 100% perfect. Most products or services have at least a couple of flaws, which we all understand because no product or service can be perfect for everybody. Being 100% honest in your copy, forum and blog posts is such an easy ploy to adopt, and yet is undertaken by few affiliates. Actually seeking out minor product flaws to include in your sales pages and mentioning those flaws to those who ask for advice on "which to buy" will make other readers sit up and notice your brand. Helping potential buyers to choose the product or service that is actually right for them, rather than making you the highest commission, will build trust with your readers, resulting in them returning to your site and buying again, plus recommending your brand to their family and friends.

## *Monitoring Brand Growth*

So you have done all of the above and how do you now measure your success? How do you know when you actually have created a brand? Well a great way is to take a look at your Google Analytics data. Firstly, is the number of searches for your brand name increasing? If so, especially if your brand name does not comprise key phrases alone, you can class this as a sign of success. Another great metric is seeing search engine users using your brand name alongside products or services they are searching. For example, returning to our treadmills, you might see "(your brand) folding treadmill reviews" or even "(your brand) York 218 Treadmill". Finding such key phrases in your analytic reports is a clear indication of people classing your affiliate site as a brand. Another good indication of brand awareness is an increase in direct traffic, users who simply go directly to your site because they are either existing customers or have been recommended to visit your site.

Natural links to your website are also, to some degree, another good metric of brand awareness. If you find natural links posted by people who recommend your site, especially with your brand name as the anchor text, then this is another great sign that your brand is growing. Take the time to Google your own brand name to see how your brand is being discussed on linc. In time you should find hundreds of references to your brand on forums, blogs, Facebook, Twitter and dozens of other social media websites.

## Video Marketing

You sure don't need the film-making skills of Steven Spielberg to create videos to drive traffic to your website. Many popular YouTube videos are actually recorded with smartphones or even cheap hand-held video cameras. You can easily edit videos by simply using free software such as Windows Movie Maker, which you will find on your Windows computer or by using IPhone and Android apps which enable you to edit videos directly on your phone. I am not going to discuss how to make videos as there are hundreds if not thousands of tutorials online. Simply use Google to find the tutorials and practise making videos, as it is a very simple process!

## Use Video Sharing Sites to Drive Traffic to Your Website

The starting point for your video marketing efforts should, of course, be YouTube. Let's take a quick look at some of YouTube's statistics.

- 60 hours of video are uploaded every minute, or one hour of video is uploaded to YouTube every second.
- Over 4 billion videos are viewed a day.
- Over 800 million unique users visit YouTube each month.
- Over 3 billion hours of video are watched each month on YouTube.
- More video is uploaded to YouTube in one month than the three major US networks created in 60 years.
- 70% of YouTube traffic comes from outside the US.
- YouTube is localized in 39 countries and across 54 languages.
- In 2011, YouTube had more than 1 trillion views or almost 140 views for every person on Earth.

One of the great aspects of YouTube and indeed all video sharing sites is that those who upload their videos are given the option to allow their videos to be shared. A user may well post an amusing video on YouTube, but if the video becomes very popular (goes viral) and the share option is enabled, the video could be posted on thousands of other sites. Your goal should not only be to get good numbers of views from YouTube visitors, but to get these users posting your videos on as many other sites as possible. A video initially posted on YouTube that succeeds in being posted on Facebook or Twitter can generate hundreds of thousands of views, which in turn could send thousands of visitors to your website.

### YouTube Social Statistics

- 500 years of YouTube video are watched every day on Facebook, and over 700 YouTube videos are shared on Twitter each minute.
- 100 million people make a social action on YouTube (likes, shares, comments, etc.) every week.
- An auto-shared tweet results in six new YouTube.com sessions on average, and we see more than 500 tweets per minute containing a YouTube link.
- Millions of subscriptions happen each day. Subscriptions allow you to connect with someone you're interested in — whether it's a friend or the NBA — and keep up with their activity on the site.
- More than 50% of videos on YouTube have been rated or include comments from the community.

- Millions of videos are added to "favourites" every day.

You simply cannot overlook the video market as a great additional source of driving targeted traffic to your website!

## *SEO Techniques for Videos*

Just like your content pages and indeed images, for greater search visibility you should ensure that you use good SEO techniques for every video you upload, no matter on what site you upload it. If you use good SEO techniques for your videos, you will find that in the long term your videos outrank others using similar key phrases.

SEO techniques for videos are very similar to those for images. For every video you upload simply ensure that you take note of the following:

- Key phrase(s) MUST be included in the video file name.

- Key phrase(s) MUST be included in the video title.

- Key phrase(s) must be included in the video description.

- Key phrase(s) must be included in the video tags.

- As many relevant key phrases as possible must be used in the tags.

It is also a good idea to include your site URL in the first part of the description, such as http://www.yoursitenow.com and next to use the main title. For example if you create an informational video about the benefits of the Blue Widget, the file name should be:

blue_widgets_review.mpeg

and the video title should be:

Blue Widget Review

The video description could be:

http://www.yoursite.com/blue-widget-review/ Blue Widget review showing the latest new model with even more superb benefits.

The title tags should be: blue widget, blue widget review, new blue widget, best blue widget.

### *Video Marketing Research*

Take the time to see how your competitors are using YouTube to drive traffic to their affiliate websites. Search for the main products you are promoting on YouTube, taking note of how they are being promoted by others. Make a mental note of the views each video has received so that you have some idea of which videos are most popular. For example take a look at this treadmill review video produced by the manufacturer:

http://www.youtube.com/watch?v=OCtOYcYXTlQ

Now take a look at how an affiliate has also used the video:

http://www.youtube.com/watch?v=cH7ILYJf9kl

It seems clear that the affiliate has simply asked the merchant for a copy of the video or used an online app such as catchvideo.net to copy the video. If you are going to use a video from a merchant, take the time to add value to the video to make it even better than the original. For instance you could add your very own brief review to the start of the video using Windows Movie Maker, or simply add a couple of text screens at the start of the video that show the basic facts and benefits of the treadmill. You could even hire someone from Fiver.com to record you a small section to add to the product video for just $5 if you are not happy doing it yourself. Always, however, add value!

### *Build Your YouTube Channel*

Taking the time to upload just two videos a week will over a year give your YouTube channel over 100 videos. After a year, even if your videos were only generating 10 visits a day, this would equate to 1000 views a day, 30,000 views a month and 360,000 views per year. At first you may find that the number of views your videos receive will be disappointing, but in time you will find that you understand exactly what viewers interested in your niche want to see. You will find that some of your videos simply don't take off while you will be amazed at the views others generate. Simply keep at it, taking note of what others in your niche are doing in video marketing, especially taking a good look at their video views totals, and learn from their successes as well as, more importantly, from your own efforts. Ensure you make all your videos "sharable" and even add videos to your very own review pages. Simply Google "add videos to Wordpress" to learn how to do this, which is really just a simple process of copy and paste.

## *Video Sharing Sites*

Most readers of this book will at some time have viewed videos on YouTube but perhaps do not know that there are literally dozens of other free video sharing websites. A popular YouTube video which contains a link in its description can send hundreds if not thousands of visitors a day to your website. A video that you create to promote your website should not be just loaded onto YouTube but onto all these quality video sites:

- *YouTube*

  URL: http://www.youtube.com/

  YouTube is by far the "big daddy" as regards online videos. Owned now by Google, thousands of new videos are loaded onto YouTube every day. Popular YouTube videos can attract millions of view from across the globe. Many smartphones and indeed cameras now have software that automates the process of uploading videos to YouTube, so your actual video can be live within minutes of you ending filming. There are, however, many more video sharing sites so ensure that when you upload videos to YouTube you also at least update your videos to the other video sharing sites listed below.

- **Dailymotion**
  URL: http://www.dailymotion.com/us
- **Metacafe**
  URL: http://www.metacafe.com/
- **Break**
  URL: http://www.break.com/
- **LiveLeak**
  URL: http://www.liveleak.com/
- **MegaVideo**
  URL: http://www.megavideo.com/
- **VideoSift**
  URL: http://www.videosift.com/
- **Vimeo**
  URL: http://vimeo.com/
- **Veoh**
  URL: http://www.veoh.com/
- **Yahoo Video**
  URL: http://video.yahoo.com/

### *Buying Links on YouTube Videos*

Another good ploy to generate targeted traffic through videos, which I'm surprised many affiliates don't seem to have thought of, is simply to buy links on existing videos that are generating healthy daily views in your niche. You can find out how many daily views a video is generating by checking the number of views over a few days. Most YouTube users create videos for fun, so they don't understand that their videos' views actually have a value. Remember popular videos can attract thousands of unique visitors a day! Before making an offer to buy a link on a video, you need to ensure that the video is getting decent daily traffic. In many cases you may find a video that relates to your niche with a great number of views, which may seem ideal. The views, however, could have been generated in the past and for all you know the video may no longer be generating daily views.

The simplest way to ensure the video is still getting daily views is to make a note of the numbers of views at a set time each day. Doing this for a week should give a good understanding of the daily views the video attracts. Another way of tracking the video traffic in more detail is to use a service such as www.trendrr.com. Trendrr is free and is a "must use" site for tracking YouTube views. Simply create an account, enter the URL of the YouTube video you want to track and copy and paste all the tags of the video. That's all you need to do! Easy as 123!

### *Calculate How Much a YouTube Link Is Worth*

So you find a good YouTube video that you know generates views for your target niche. Let's say you have been tracking the views of a Galaxy S2 smartphone video, both manually and by using Trendrr. What next? How do you calculate a value for a monthly link on the video description? Let's say the tracked video generates 10,000 views per month, as our tracking has shown that the video generates 2500 visitors per week. Most viewers of the video WILL NOT click a link in the video's description. I always prefer to work on a modest click rate of 1% (1 click in a 100 views). For 10,000 monthly views working on our projected click rate of 1%, I would estimate 100 clicks per month. Remember that it is always best to underestimate the number of projected clicks; hence why I'm using the misery figure of 1%. To get some idea of how much each click is worth; let's say that we are dealing with a video that details someone unboxing a brand new Galaxy S2 smartphone. For some reason "unboxing" videos seem to be very popular, which I guess is down to the fact that potential buyers want to see exactly what they will get for their money. For example look at the views for a video that shows the unboxing of a Galaxy S2 phone –

http://www.youtube.com/watch?v=CKOP8u9Cy7w, or this video that shows the unboxing of an Asus tablet http://www.youtube.com/watch?v=Jaeg116kePI.

## *Estimating the Value of Video Clicks*

You can quickly estimate the number of clicks a video will generate but now you have to find a way to value each click. The market leader by far for buying clicks is of course Google, so let's use Google data to estimate the value of clicks.

- Firstly go to this site:
  https://adwords.google.com/select/TrafficEstimatorSandbox

- In the "Enter Keywords" box enter the main key phrase of the video. For example: Galaxy S2.

- In the "Max CPC $" box enter 1000 and in the "Daily Budget $" box simply enter 100.

- In the "Available Countries and Territories" enter your specified country e.g. "United States" or even "All Locations".

- Then select your preferred target language.

- Next select "Exact Match"

- Now click "Estimate" which should load a new screen as below:

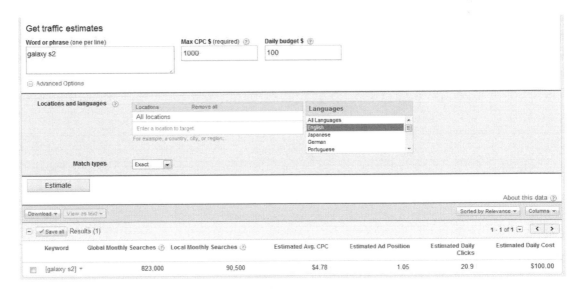

The information of interest is right at the bottom of the screen so let's look at this in more detail.

| Keyword | Global Monthly Searches ⑦ | Local Monthly Searches ⑦ | Estimated Avg. CPC | Estimated Ad Position | Estimated Daily Clicks | Estimated Daily Cost |
|---------|---------------------------|--------------------------|--------------------|-----------------------|------------------------|----------------------|
| ☐ [galaxy s2] ▾ | 823,000 | 90,500 | $4.78 | 1.05 | 20.9 | $100.00 |

From the above we can see that for the search phrase "Galaxy S2" you would have to pay $4.78 per click using Google Adwords. So for 100 clicks we would expect to pay around $478 if we ran a Google Adwords campaign. Of course, we don't want to pay such a high amount and we have a great advantage over the YouTube video owner as he / she will in most cases not know how to value their video traffic. Also of great importance is your actual conversion rate. If you were buying clicks at the rate above, and for every $478 spent (100 clicks) you generated just 2 sales that earned you in total $60 in commission, then you would find yourself losing $417! Paying $20 for such a link, however, would of course be highly profitable!

## *Making an Offer to Purchase a Video Link*

To contact the video owner simply click on their YouTube account name, which you will find displayed under the video. This will take you to their profile page. Search the profile page for contact details, such as Twitter, Facebook or even an email address. Your goal is to get their email address so that you can make them an offer. If you have to contact them by Twitter or Facebook, then simply do so, stating that you have a proposal for them. Don't go OTT with your proposal, nor make an offer in public. When the time comes to make an actual offer, use something like the example below.

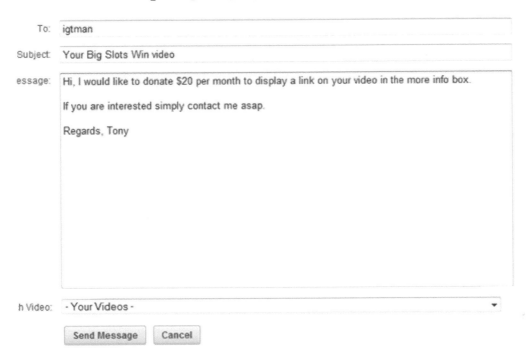

If the video owner accepts, you will have secured quality, targeted traffic at a fraction of the cost of a Google Adwords campaign. Starting with a low donation figure gives you plenty of scope to barter if the video owner wants a bigger monthly "donation". Remember, however, you are in business to make a profit!

If the owner agrees, don't commit for the long term until you have actually witnessed the number of clicks the video generates and, of course, how the clicks convert.

## Article Marketing

Article Marketing is the process of writing informative articles relevant to your specific niche and posting the articles onto quality article directory websites. The main goal of each article you post is to drive traffic to your affiliate website from links added to the bio section of each article. I must state that in recent times many article directories have been hit extremely hard by algorithm changes. Just a couple of years ago articles posted on ezinearticles.com, articlebase.com and many other article directories dominated Google's search results pages. Many marketers exploited article marketing, producing poor quality spun articles just to gain good rankings. It came as no surprise when Google started to hit article directories hard, in effect banishing most articles to the depth of search listing results. However, other search engines, especially Bing.com, still rank quality articles highly, so article marketing should be another technique you employ.

There are thousands of article directory sites, although the ones listed below are the ones you should concentrate on:

- knol.google.com

- ehow.com

- squidoo.com

- hubpages.com

- ezinearticles.com

- examiner.com

- articlesbase.com

- seekingalpha.com

- technorati.com

- buzzle.com

- goarticles.com

- gather.com

- suite101.com

- brighthub.com

- ezinemark.com

- ideamarketers.com

- infobarrel.com

- selfgrowth.com

- helium.com

- articlesnatch.com

A good article posted on an article directory can generate a steady stream of targeted traffic to your affiliate website. A good article can generate thousands of page views a month or in many cases many more. Most articles only generate a few hundred page views each year, or even less, as most of those who tackle article marketing do not possess the techniques required to create articles that push readers to click the article links.

Let's imagine that one of the products your affiliate site promotes is a book that gives advice on many different aspects of detoxification. Most affiliates would simply target the book title, resulting in dozens, if not hundreds, of affiliates targeting exactly the same key phrases. A better option would be to think "out of the box" creating an article that concentrates on one of the most popular aspects of the book. For instance, you could create an article on how to make your own detox drink, such as "How to Make the Lemon Detox Diet Drink." Let's actually search for this long-tail key phrase in Bing.com.

As you can see from the above, articles from article directories actually do still rank well in Bing.com, with articles from Ehow and Ezines in the top five results. If you go to the Ezines article and scroll down to the bottom of the page you will see the article's general statistics.

Submitted On July 10, 2009. Viewed 31,043 times. Word count: 528.

As you can see, the article has had over 31,000 views. Now let's enter the same key phrase into Google.

Again, you can see articles on the first page of Google search results, which shows that you must not underestimate the power of article marketing. Simply follow the techniques below and you should find that you get much more traffic and generate more sales from every article you write!

## Article Title and Keywords

Most article writers simply "think up" a catchy title for their article and that is their entire technique for naming their article. This is a big mistake! Working this way you will get some traffic when your article goes live, which simply comes from the regular readers of the article directory site you have submitted to. Creating titles in this way, however, will in most cases guarantee that in less than a week the traffic will dry up! For your article to generate traffic for weeks, months or even years to come you are going to have to rank well not only in article directories but also in search engines. The way to do this is to have good long-tail keywords as your article title. Let me show you how you can do this.

Before writing any articles for article marketing, carry out keyword research to find long-tail key phrases for your article titles. For example, if you have an affiliate site that promotes computer tablets, seek out which keywords generate exact match queries of 3,000 or more and have low competition. To do this, simply go to the online keyword external tool and type in your main keyword. I will stress again that you MUST have the "Match Types" set to "exact" as show below.

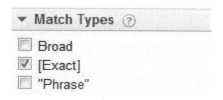

When the results appear, click on the "Competition" header option twice, so that the results are sorted in competition order with those with the lowest competition levels listed first. Now look for keywords with global monthly searches of more than 3000.

Using the main key phrase "tablet computing" I quickly identified some quality low competition key phrases for articles:

"What is Bluetooth" – 9,900 global monthly searches

"What is Android" – 40,00 global monthly searches

270

There were of course many more and I could have found hundreds more by using many different main key phrases. From using the two key phrases found you could create the following articles:

- What Is Bluetooth? Top 10 Bluetooth Tips & Tricks

- What is Android? Are You Ready for Ice Cream Sandwich?

(For those of you not familiar with the Android operating system, Ice Cream Sandwich is the very latest version.)

### Writing Your Article

Many article directories accept articles with as few as 250 words. I strongly advise that your articles should be at least 400 words and pack a punch, as you should have learnt in previous chapters.

For the articles you create for article directories always ensure that your article starts with your main keywords, beginning, for example: *"What is Android is a question that is commonly asked due to….."*

Make sure that you add impact to the first sentence so that you capture the reader's attention and then simply give about three to five important facts about the article's topic. Use a keyword density of no more than 2%.

You will notice that when you post an article to an article directory, there are other input boxes. Let's take a look at these.

**Article Summary Box:** Most article writers simply pluck a paragraph from their article and use this in the Article Summary Box. Again this is a mistake! Make sure the text you enter in Article Summary Box starts with your article title. This is essential! I prefer to use at least the first sentence of my article as this includes the article title and the killer leading line that contains the punch to read the remainder of the article.

**Article Keywords Box:** In this box you simply enter keywords that relate to the article. Make sure you enter your main keywords.

**Author Resource Box:** The main aim of writing an article is to get the article readers to visit your site. Most article writers do not utilise the resource box in the correct manner and have something like this:

*"Dave Jones is the owner of **Smartphones Now**."*

Do you think the above would entice the reader to visit his site? I think not. Remember we are trying to get a high click-through rate (CTR) so we need to really think about the resource box. How about this content for the resource box?

*"Is Your **Android Phone** Malware Free? For The Very Latest Android News, Android App Reviews, new Android Smartphones releases, visit **Smartphones Now**."*

Obviously you would have links to the anchor text above (in bold), which are of course backlinks to your site. Do you think the above resource box would entice readers to click the links? It still amazes me how many article writers simply type a basic bio in the resource box and let potential traffic go down the drain!

**YOU MUST USE THE RESOURCE BOX TO ENTICE READERS TO CLICK THE LINKS!**

### How Many Articles Should You Write?

The more good quality articles with good titles, keywords and good calls to action in the Author Resource Box you write, the more traffic and sales you will generate from your articles. It is as simple as that! Every week on affiliate forums I read posts from marketers who are moaning that they have had no sales. I look at their article directory profiles and find that they have written perhaps a dozen poor quality articles in six months. If you want to make money from article marketing, then you are going to have to work at it! You should be writing several articles each week and not just one or two when you feel like it. Those who make money from article marketing work extremely hard at it.

## Spread the Word – Blog and Forum Posting

Another great way to drive traffic to your website is to give away some of your expertise for free. Simply seek out forums and blogs in your niche. For example, if you are running a smartphone affiliate site you could build your online credibility by helping out users who are having problems with their smartphones. Use your brand name when you register to blogs and forums in your niche and of course add the URL of your site. I must stress that you must not simply spam blogs. Ensure that everything you post is of the highest possible standard and is highly informative. Do your utmost to help others find solutions to their problems, which in turn will result in others reading your posts and visiting your website.

## Build a Presence on Facebook

These days it seems there's a Facebook page for every business, no matter how small. Even my local dry cleaner has a "Follow us on Facebook" sign in their window. Getting a business page up and running is another important task you simply must undertake.

So why should you think about creating a Facebook page for your affiliate marketing business? Well for starters, it's free! It's also a great way to start engaging with the people you want do business with, and better still it is easy to undertake. Here are just a few reasons why it's a great idea to have a Facebook page for your affiliate marketing website:

- Instant communication with your followers
- Another platform for your business
- Help in building your brand
- You can match up all your different products, services, and affiliates on Facebook
- You can keep in touch with your less tech-savvy followers.

Creating a "branded" Facebook page for your affiliate marketing site is quick and easy, and you can have it all up and running within 10 minutes by following these simple steps.

### *Getting Started on Facebook*

We're going to look at how to create a Facebook page for your affiliate marketing business in just a few simple steps.

Firstly, you'll need a personal Facebook account. You need this in order to create and administer the business page. If you already have a personal Facebook page, you can skip ahead to the next step. If you don't have a Facebook page of your own, you'll need to create one. Don't worry, you won't have to become a regular user of Facebook or share personal information about yourself if you don't want to. The only information you have to supply is your name, an email address, and your date of birth, and all that information (with the exception of the email address) can be made up if you don't want to share your personal details.

So to create your own personal page, go to Facebook and enter your details in the sign up area.

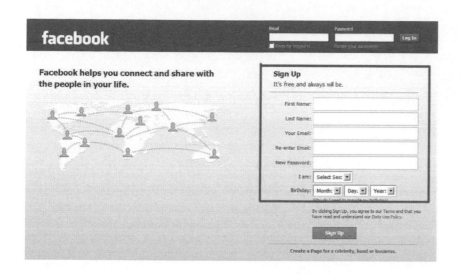

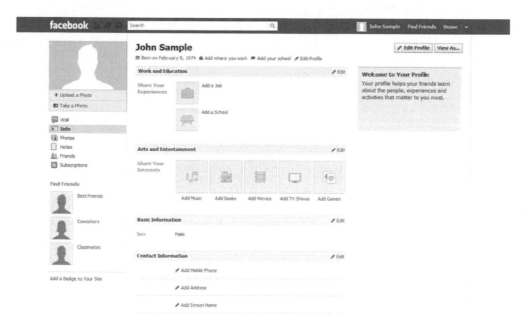

Once you are on your own personal page, there are several ways you can begin to create your business page. The first way is to go to the search box at the top of the screen and type "create". As soon as you start typing, Facebook should start suggesting options below the box, and one of the first options should be "Create New Facebook Page."

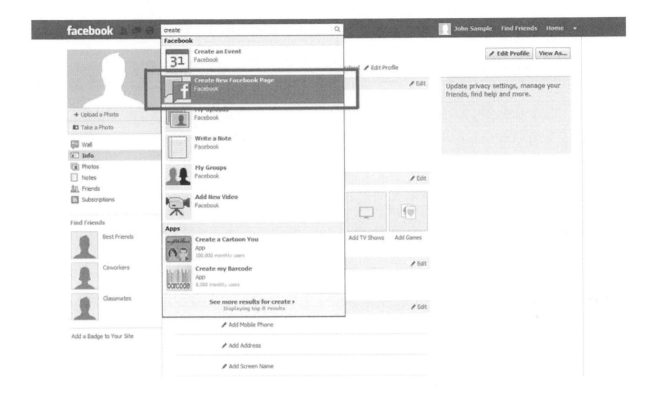

Another way is to find the link at the bottom of the page, but if you already have a personal Facebook page of your own, it can take a lot of scrolling to get to the bottom of the page because of all the status updates in your timeline.

Once you are at the new page creation screen, you will be prompted to choose what type of page you want to create. Now this could differ depending on what type of affiliate marketing you are into. But for the purposes of this "tutorial" we'll choose the "Brand or Product" option, and from the dropdown box we'll choose "Website". Don't get too hung up on this step, as you can change this later from your page settings.

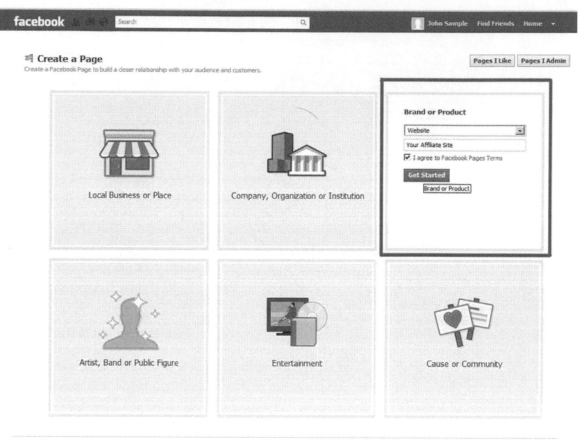

The next step is to upload a profile picture. This is optional, but it's a good idea to add a picture to your affiliate Facebook page, as otherwise your followers will just see a question mark next to your updates where the profile picture would normally be.

The picture should be square and will be displayed at 160 x 160 pixels, so the best options are a logo or picture that represents your brand. This is the image that your followers will see, both when they visit your page and also when you post an update.

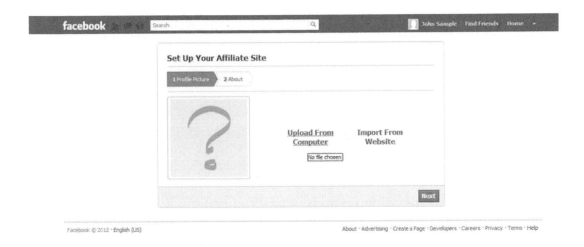

Next you will be prompted to enter your business details. Here you should write a few sentences about your business. Be as specific as possible, as this is what people will see when they visit your page. There is also the opportunity to add as many external links as you like here. You can add one for your website, your Twitter, some of your "recommended" partners and whatever else you can think of.

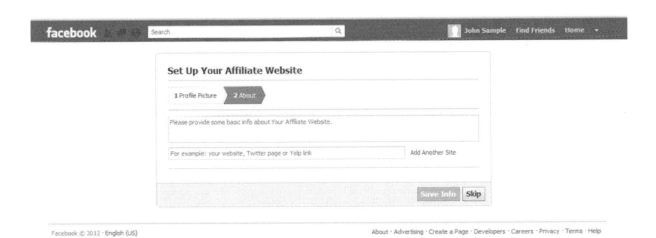

That's it! Technically you have now done all you need to do to create your affiliate Facebook page. If you've had enough you can leave it there for now and come back later to add the bells and whistles. But if you're still raring to go, you can move on to the next few optional steps.

## Finding Followers

You should now be on your affiliate page and you will be prompted to "Like" your own page. It's not compulsory, but unless you have a good reason not to, you should "Like" your page.

Next you will have the option of inviting friends. You can choose as many friends as you want from your personal Facebook page and invite them to "like" your business page. Go ahead and do this now, or you can wait until later if you want to take some time to think about whom to invite.

You will now also have the chance to invite your email contacts to "like" your page. Facebook will scan your email records, if you allow it, and will send email invites to people you choose from the list.

## Your First Status Update

Facebook will ask you if you want to make your first status update. Again, this is optional, and if you want to come back and do this later you can. A good example of a first update might be something like, "Welcome to our new Facebook page! We're looking forward to sharing lots of great information with you all about our niche. Check out our website to learn more." Obviously in the place of "our niche" you'd put something specific about whatever niche you are choosing to affiliate market.

## Blast Off

Your page is now fully operational, but there a couple more things you can do to get it looking great. First, click on the section where it says "About" below your profile picture (logo). This will take you to the profile page where you can edit the information to add lots more details. Be as descriptive as possible so that people visiting your page will see everything you have to offer.

There is an option on this page to change your business type using the drop-down box at the top of the page. There are some other options here that were not offered at the page creation stage, including choosing the "Websites and Blogs" category and then selecting a sub-category from the drop down list. You should do this if your affiliate business type is available from the list.

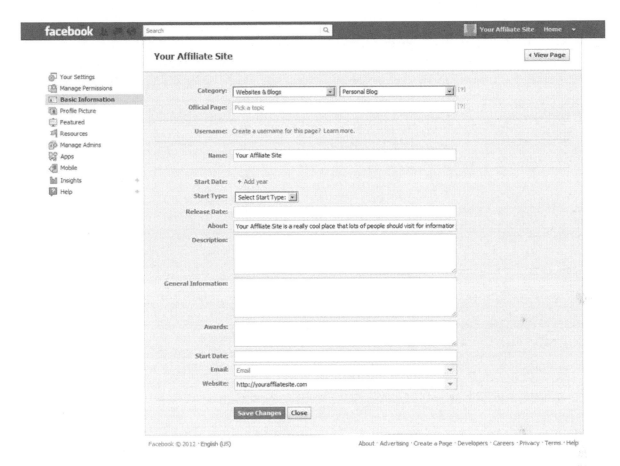

## Adding a Cover Image

With the new timeline system Facebook implemented early in 2012, there is now an option to add a cover photo to your page. The dimensions of this photo are 851 x 315 pixels, so you should either make your picture this size (you can use free image editing software like Gimp) or bear in mind that your image will be cropped to this size and try to choose something that has roughly the same proportions.

Facebook has some requirements about what can and can't be displayed as your cover image. You **cannot** have any kind of advertising text or calls to action like "Buy Now" or similar, and you cannot display specials like "20% off" or anything like that. In general it's better to have an image that captures the essence of your affiliate business. It might be a collage of other images associated with your brand, which for an affiliate marketer might be logos of some of your affiliates' products. Alternatively, you could create a variation or

279

an extension on your logo that fits these proportions. This could be a great opportunity to get creative and design yourself a variation on your existing logo.

Here are some amazing cover image examples to get your creative juices flowing:

If you're handy with graphics editing software like Adobe Illustrator or Photoshop (or the free option mentioned earlier, Gimp), you can create a good cover image for your page. If you have the money and the inclination, it is also possible to hire a graphic designer to make you a killer cover image. Most graphic designers will be au fait with Facebook's size and content requirements and will be able to create one fairly quickly and inexpensively, depending on your needs.

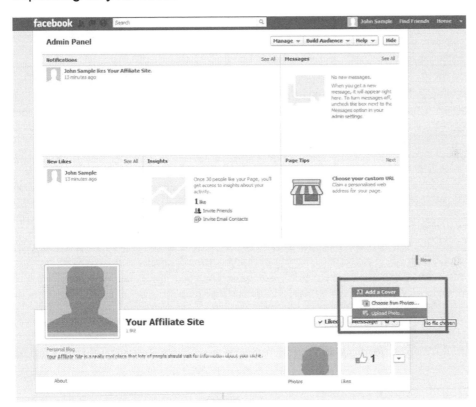

Once you have added a cover image, you are pretty much set, and now all you need to do is start adding useful content and figuring out ways to get more people involved with your affiliate marketing page.

### So You've Created Your Page, Now What?

The famous adage from *Field of Dreams*, "Build it and they will come," should be your guiding principle when it comes to social media. Even if you have zero followers on a particular platform, you should still be trying to find things to post that are relevant to the people that you *want* to be following you. Remember, people will check out your page before they decide whether to follow you or not and if they see lots of interesting updates, they will be more inclined to "like" your page.

Make sure your Facebook updates are interesting and give them catchy attention-grabbing titles. Also be sure to include a thumbnail picture with all your posts.

### Create Interest

Here are a few more tips for things you can do to increase interest in your page:

- **Link the Page to Your Website:** Add a "Like me on Facebook" section to your website or blog. There are numerous free widgets for doing this on platforms like Wordpress and Joomla, and you or your web designer should be able to integrate this very quickly and easily to your existing website. This creates a great channel between your affiliate marketing website or blog and your Facebook page.

- **Generate discussion:** There is the option on Facebook to create a poll. Start polls and encourage people to share their opinions about various topics related to your brand. Getting people talking and giving opinions is a good way to get people excited, and when they are excited, they are much more likely to buy things!

- **Create photo albums and post videos:** Your Facebook page updates are not limited to text; you can also upload video and photos. Create albums of pictures related to your niche and link video clips that your followers will find useful. It might be a YouTube clip of someone giving a tutorial about products related to your brand. Remember, it doesn't all have to be original material; you can be valuable as a curator of other people's content.

- **Add an opt in box:** Many affiliate marketers depend on their subscription list to drive sales, and you can add a subscription option to your Facebook page in order to gain more subscribers. Facebook has a few apps that deal with this, and between Facebook and a Google search you should be able to find a free, user-friendly widget to integrate your Facebook page with your preferred mail out service.

- **Add some apps:** There are countless free Facebook apps that you can add to

282

your page using Facebook's search feature. Some examples are a big Twitter button on your affiliate page and an RSS feed of your blog. A little digging will yield lots of great ideas for which apps to add to your page. For example, check out this list of Top 10 Facebook apps for social engagement by InfoTrust.

- **Talk it up:** Facebook was created to make communication easier, so use it in the way it was intended. If someone responds to one of your posts with a comment, acknowledge what they've said and encourage them to comment in the future. The same thing goes if somebody comments on your page. Remember, every time somebody comments, all their friends see that comment, as well as your responses, so it's in your best interests to encourage discussion about your page and get people checking you out. This all adds up to higher brand awareness and reaching more people.

## Pitfalls

As well as all the things you should be doing, there are a couple of things that you should try to avoid doing with your affiliate marketing Facebook page.

- **Avoid doing the "hard sell."** People know when you're trying to shove a product down their throat, and Facebook really isn't the place to do that. You'll get much better results if you focus instead on becoming a person of value to your followers. Use your page to let people know about cool stuff that's going to be useful to them. By doing this, you'll soon find that it flows on to you being able to market your products and affiliates in indirect ways. In fact, you might even find that your brand ends up marketing itself, and all you need to do is sit back and reap the rewards. And that's the holy grail of affiliate marketing, right?

- **Don't let the page become a "Ghost Town."** A lot of businesses start a Facebook page with the best intentions, but for one reason or another it soon becomes dormant. It's a bit of a chicken and egg thing, but you shouldn't be discouraged if you only have a handful of followers for the first few weeks, or even months. Just because you only have five followers, and they're all members of your family, there's no reason why you shouldn't be posting useful and interesting content regularly.

If someone stops in to check out your page and sees that there's been no activity for weeks, there's not a whole lot of incentive for them to follow you. On the other hand, if you're adding fresh content on a daily or weekly basis, people will be much more inclined to hop aboard when they visit your page and see all the cool stuff you can offer them. You know that feeling when you find a blog or a website that has just what you've been looking for, all in the one place, and you find yourself going for the bookmark button or subscription form before you've even finished reading the first couple of sentences? Your page can be that for other people if you just put in a little thought and effort.

## Using Twitter

When Twitter started to become popular I simply did not get it! Why oh why would I want to know what people were eating for breakfast or where they had been last night. I will be completely honest and say I was not at all impressed by Twitter in its early form, as you may have already guessed. To understand the benefits of Twitter you have to dig beyond the mundane dross that is posted by many Tweeple, because when you do, you will find that Twitter is actually another great tool that you can harness to send targeted traffic to your website.

### So How Does Twitter Work?

Of all the many guises of social media, Twitter is by far the most basic. Those who "tweet" have just 140 characters to ask a question, answer a question, tell the world what they are doing or tell the world what is happening around them. Twitter has become a great source for breaking news as "tweets" can be made from all types of computers and smartphones. During disasters in recent years, of which there have been far too many for my liking, people who were actually there covered them all on Twitter. Twitter is a great source for finding out what is happening in the world from those to whom it is happening.

### How to Make Twitter Work for You

There are many Twitter Wordpress plug-ins available although many of are no value. Most, although not all, automatically post your Wordpress posts to your Twitter account. Don't use Twitter simply to mimic your Wordpress website, but instead use it as a communication tool in the same way as we discussed for blog and forum posts. Seek out potential customers in your niche and help them with their problems to build your online credibility. By all means use Tweets to create links to important articles of your website such as industry news or even the launch of new products. Don't, however, go overboard! Think of your Twitter account as a mini-website with your Tweets being the articles. Your goal should be to create a quality account over time full of informative and helpful Tweets.

### *How to Create an Authoritative Twitter Account*

In time, if people like what you have to say on Twitter, they will follow you. Building up a large following on Twitter, together with building up the number of people you follow, will build your credibility, influence and contacts. Ensure that the Twitter account you use for business is only used for business. If you need to post personal Tweets, then create another Twitter account. Take note of the tips below to build a Twitter account that oozes authority.

- Complete your Twitter bio including uploading your logo.
- Add a link to your Twitter Feed to your affiliate website.
- Follow those that work in your chosen niche.
- Reply to the Tweets of those who work in your niche, especially those who are not following you.

Take your time building your Twitter account. Don't go crazy following hundreds in one day, but simply seek a few to follow each day.

# Chapter 16 – Pandas, Penguins & Other Google Monsters

For years Google has been preaching to webmasters that in the eyes of Google, content is king. In reality from my experience of Google search results this simply has not been true. Up until Google rolled out the PANDA algorithm in February 2011 any crappy page of content could be ranked highly with links alone. When Google rolled out Panda version 1.0 back in February 2011, in effect the game had changed. For years Google had been stating that quality content was the way to rank highly in Google, although experienced webmasters knew, and actually achieved, quality rankings of even poor quality pages, simply with the acquisition of links. Let's be honest and say that Google has been flawed for years and many, myself included, have profited.

## Understanding Google Penalties

If you are going to become a successful affiliate for the long term, you must learn how to identify Google penalties and more importantly how to combat them. Although Google started to "change the game" back in February 2011, most webmasters still don't understand exactly what is happening. I'm amazed by how many webmasters blindly try to combat penalties by simply acquiring new links, which, in my opinion, in most cases makes matters worse. To help you, I am going to detail the main Google algorithm changes that have occurred in the last year, starting with the very first roll out of the Google PANDA algorithm.

## Google PANDA

I have already mentioned Google PANDA in previous chapters of this book so you should already have a good understanding of why the Google algorithm had to change. When Google rolled out PANDA on February 23rd 2011, webmaster forums were besieged by thousands of webmasters reporting that their websites had been hit. Literally overnight, thousands upon thousands of webmasters were wiped out, with their websites stripped of their high rankings leading to, in most cases, a severe drop in revenue. Most of the websites that were hit by the very first roll-out of PANDA and indeed subsequent PANDA roll-outs have not recovered to this day, which has resulted in thousands of affiliates leaving the industry. Take the time to read this forum thread from the Webmaster's World forum (http://www.webmasterworld.com/google/4261944.htm) to understand the effect the introduction of PANDA actually had on webmasters.

Google had actually been targeting webmasters who were "gaming" their search results for some time, although it was clear that with the introduction of Google PANDA, Google really had shifted up a good few gears with their efforts. Google reported that the initial PANDA update affected up to 12% of search engine queries although it seemed like a much higher percentage, especially when PANDA was rolled out to Europe during April 2011. Being honest, although many webmasters are going to hate me for saying this, most websites that were hit were rightly targeted. Prior to the roll-out of Google PANDA, search results were crammed with copied content, spun content and pages simply full of adverts. Although there is no doubt that some quality websites were caught innocently in the crossfire, most websites that were hit deserved to be hit.

## Understanding Google PANDA

I read all the leading webmaster forums and SEO blogs so can tell you that nobody claims to have the definitive answer as to how Google PANDA actually functions. As mentioned earlier in this book, the Google PANDA algorithm is a highly complex artificial intelligence program that in effect learns to differentiate between good and bad content, although how it actually does this is not known. Prior to the introduction of PANDA it was reported that Google used human quality testers to rate thousands of webpages manually. The testers were given webpages to view and rate with Google, which then used the metrics of the reviewed webpages to determine good and bad content, demoting content deemed to be poor and promoting content deemed good.

What does seem clear is that PANDA does indeed "learn" to identify poor quality content. To test the Google PANDA algorithm I created a test site that targeted uncompetitive key phrases. The site comprised of 50 quality pages, with each page targeting one specific uncompetitive key phrase extremely well. It must also be noted that not one of the pages had any affiliate links as I wanted to determine the actual SERP bounce rate. By SERP bounce rate I am referring to the number of visitors who visit a page from Google search results and then return immediately to the search results without viewing another page of the website.

The SERP bounce rate I achieved was under 15% which in real terms meant that most of those who visited the website (85%) found the answer to the query they had typed into Google. I simply sat back and waited for the next Google PANDA roll-out, which occurred a few weeks later, resulting in an actual increase of rankings for the site. Straight after the Google PANDA update, I butchered the content of the test website, making drastic changes to 15 of the pages. For the pages I changed I simply spun the content so each of the pages read extremely poorly. This resulted in the SERP bounce rate increasing to over 82% for the pages changed. After making the changes I simply left the site and waited for the next PANDA roll-out. Over a month later the PANDA update arrived resulting in ALL pages losing their rankings. I must stress that not just the spun pages lost their rankings but all pages lost their rankings. Straight after the update I moved all the poor quality pages into new sub-directory of the website, and again waited for the next PANDA update. The next PANDA update arrived with no change in rankings for any page of the test website. I simply left the site and waited for the next PANDA roll-out which resulted in a return of rankings for the quality pages in the main directory but no change for the poor quality pages in the new sub-directory.

Now I know many will not take the results of my testing seriously as I have not included full results. I have actually taken my testing much further with all results recorded which I may use for another book dedicated to Google PANDA, that is, of course, once I have recovered from the ordeal of writing this book! If you do take the time to find PANDA recovery cases on internet webmaster forums, you will see that some have recovered from a Google PANDA penalty by either completely removing pages with a high Google SERP bounce rate or simply moving poor quality content to its own sub-directory, which is exactly what Hub Pages and other article directories have done. It seems clear to me that PANDA is not a site-wide penalty but a directory-wide penalty.

## Recovering from Panda

For those reading this book perhaps with websites that have been "Pandalized", the good news is that you can indeed escape the dreaded Panda penalty. To date I have managed to get two sites back from the dead, with a third site well on its way, or at least I hope so.

One of my websites was hit by Panda 1.0 and was hit extremely hard, losing most of its 100 daily unique visitors from Google as you can see below.

288

It took time, but I actually managed to lift the Panda penalty the site had clearly received. My tactics for recovering from Panda are as follows:

- Use Google Analytics to find pages with a high SERP bounce rate and either remove the pages or move them to their own sub directory.

- Remove any duplicate content you may have loaded on to your website.

- Search for other websites that may have copied your website content. Report any scrapper sites that may have been copying your site's content, using the official Google form. You can easily find the form by typing "Google report scrapper pages" into Google search.

- Add more quality pages to your site.

Also of great importance is the fact that many have also stated that once a site has been Pandalized, simply removing low quality pages has not been enough to get the site ranking again. If you look at the analytics above, you can see the site above did recover, although it was quickly Pandalized again. I believe it is simply not enough, in most cases, just to remove low quality content. You have to raise the overall quality of your website once you have been hit.

## Identifying Pandalized Websites

Google issues penalties for a number of reasons and also rolls out other algorithm changes that can dramatically decrease or increase website rankings, so how do webmasters know if they have been Pandalized? Well there is an easy way to establish if a drop in rankings is due to a Panda. Basically, Panda updates roll out each month. If a drop in traffic coincided with one or more of the Panda Iteration dates below , then the chances are extremely high that the website has been Pandalized.

**Google PANDA Iterations to April 27th 2012**

- February 24, 2011
- April 11, 2011
- May 9, 2011
- June 18, 2011
- July 22, 2011
- August 12, 2011

- September 28, 2011
- October 5, 2011
- October 13, 2011
- November 18, 2011
- January 18, 2012
- February 27, 2012
- March 23, 2012
- April 19, 2012
- April 27, 2012

In real terms, Panda is just in its infancy and will become far more "knowledgeable" in future years. It seems clear that although Panda can already detect many poor quality pages, it still has a long way to go before it can detect all. I believe that due to Panda's current flaws, Google has added other algorithm updates in its quest for quality. Major algorithm updates in the last year include:

- Freshness Update - November 3, 2011
- Ads Above The Fold - January 19, 2012
- Penguin - April 24, 2012

Let's take a quick look at the three major updates mentioned above.

## *Freshness Update*
This update was rolled out during November 2011 with Google's Amit Singhal stating that...

*"Given the incredibly fast pace at which information moves in today's world, the most recent information can be from the last week, day or even minute, and depending on the search terms, the algorithm needs to be able to figure out if a result from a week ago about a TV show is recent, or if a result from a week ago about breaking news is too old."*

I was surprised that this update seemed to go unnoticed by many affiliates with very little "noise" posted on webmaster forums. A great tip I can give you is to make sure you simply don't let your content become out of date, so take the time to update your content when it is a couple of months old, even if you just edit a couple of sentences.

## *Ads Above The Fold Update*

This algorithm update was rolled out early during 2012 and hit many webmasters extremely hard. Matt Cutts, head of Google's Web spam team posted on the Google blog:

*"In our on-going effort to help you find more high-quality websites in search results, today [19 January] we're launching an algorithmic change that looks at the layout of a web page and the amount of content you see on the page once you click on a result...*

*This algorithmic change noticeably affects less than 1% of searches globally. That means that in less than one in 100 searches, a typical user might notice a reordering of results on the search page."*

This algorithm caused quite a stir on webmaster forums with many reporting a loss of rankings. It must be pointed out that most of the websites targeted by this algorithm update did have ads above the fold that made up more than 30% of the total above the fold content.

## *Penguin Update*

The Penguin algorithm update has been by far the most devastating so far this year. As I write this chapter (May 2012) most webmaster forums are virtually buzzing with reports of websites being hit. So what is the Penguin update? Well according to the Google blog,

*"A few sites use techniques that don't benefit users, where the intent is to look for shortcuts or loopholes that would rank pages higher than they deserve to be ranked. We see all sorts of webspam techniques every day, from keyword stuffing to link schemes that attempt to propel sites higher in rankings."*

From reading the thousands of reports posted, it seems Google is now actively seeking out webmasters who have acquired links. Earlier this year, Google effectively closed down many blog networks known for selling links. In addition to this it seems that Google was examining the backlinks of websites extremely closely with thousands of webmasters receiving the "Google Webmaster Tools notice of detected unnatural links" message as shown in the previous chapter. Many webmasters simply came clean with Google reporting their own unnatural links that they had "acquired", which of course gave Google a great amount of data for unnatural links. Perhaps not surprisingly many of those who lost rankings during the Penguin update did have unnatural links profiles with many freely admitting on webmaster forums that they had purchased links to boost their Google rankings. Others hit have also reported that they do have pages that they have over-optimized, in ways such as high density of key phrases, and overuse of H1 tags.

## Google PANDA – The Future

Although many webmasters suggest that Google search results are deteriorating, in reality they are really viewing Google's search results through webmaster eyes. Slowly but surely, through the monthly Panda updates and of additional algorithm updates such as Penguin, Google is not only fighting back against spammers, but heavily penalizing pages that have been ranked by means of purchasing links or key word stuffing. The Google search engine is perhaps going through its biggest ever transition as Google attempt to really make content king.

## Final Thoughts

The days of simply buying Google rankings with links, or gaming the algorithm by keyword stuffing or other "black hat" methods, will, I believe, within the next year be gone forever. Google is now fighting a war with webmasters who have been, shall I say, bending the rules. I know of many webmasters who have been gaming Google for many years who have now been virtually wiped out overnight. I would imagine that more major updates will be rolled out during 2012, with more webmasters feeling the wrath of the Google anti-spam team.

The main reason I decided to add this chapter to this book, at the very last moment may I add, is so that you know the consequences of bending the rules. Last night I spoke to a webmaster who has had his monthly revenue cut from over £10,000 a month to just a few hundred pounds a month, simply because he took shortcuts. Now, as his site is so heavily penalized, with thousands of spammy backlinks he has no chance of getting removed, he will have to simply start all over again.

Remember you have been warned!

# Chapter 17 – A Beginner's Guide to Google Analytics

## Why Are Analytics Important?

If you are going to become a successful affiliate, you need to understand how your visitors find your website, how they use your website and how they leave it. For instance, you may have a steady stream of daily traffic, but if a large proportion of your visitors are leaving within seconds (high bounce rate), it should be clear to you that you have a major problem. Knowing how visitors find your site, be it from search engine queries, social media or other mediums can be a great aid in determining just how successful you have been in driving visitors to your site and a great aid to increasing your traffic further. Finding the main pages from which visitors leave your site can also be a great aid in finding holes in your content funnels. Understanding which of your sales pages generates the highest number of sales is a great aid in tweaking other sales pages to increase conversions.

Studying your website's analytics data is a task that should not be neglected, because if it is, then you are simply working blind.

## Introduction

Google Analytics is an extremely useful – and free – tool from Google that can be used to get a huge number of different statistics on how your website functions and is performing. In this chapter I am going to cover the basic metrics so that you have the knowledge to carry out a basic audit on your analytical data, which will help you refine your website to increase traffic and conversions.

### *Understand "Not Provided" Analytics*

From November 2011 Google announced that those using Google search who did so while logged into their Google account would be pushed by default to SSL. In real terms this means that search data for such users would be lost, hence the dreaded "not provided" text being displayed in analytical reports as shown below.

| Keyword ⌄ | None ⌄ | Visits ↓ | Pages/Visit | Avg. Time on Site | % New Visits | Bounce Rate |
|---|---|---|---|---|---|---|
| 1. | (not provided) | 241 | 3.38 | 00:05:34 | 56.85% | 44.40% |
| 2. | tragamonedas gratis | 110 | 4.36 | 00:08:06 | 53.64% | 30.91% |
| 3. | tragamonedas gratis sin descargar | 34 | 4.74 | 00:05:36 | 47.06% | 20.59% |
| 4. | tragamonedas cleopatra gratis | 33 | 6.52 | 00:11:17 | 60.61% | 24.24% |
| 5. | maquinas tragamonedas | 32 | 3.56 | 00:02:04 | 43.75% | 40.62% |

From my personal experience up to 10% of search query data is no longer available, which for most webmasters, including myself, is extremely frustrating. However, Google Analytics is free and you still have in most cases access to 90% of your website analytics, which you will find is of great benefit to you, so let me show you how to use it.

## Getting Started With Google Analytics

The first thing to mention before we even begin is that you are obviously going to need a Google Analytics account. Creating an account is a simple process that you can complete in a couple of minutes. To create an account simply go to http://www.google.com/analytics/ and click the "create an account" button. Then follow the onscreen instructions. Once you have created your account, you need to place the Google Analytics code on your website. As you are using Wordpress, you can simply use the Google Analytics Plug-in mentioned earlier in the Wordpress chapter. Simply ensure you are logged in to your shiny new Google Analytical account, ensure the plug-in is loaded on your Wordpress install, log in to your Wordpress backend, and go to Settings. Then select the Google Analytics option and simply click the "Authenticate with Google" button. You will find that the plug-in auto detects your Analytics account and it is then just a matter of selecting the correct profile, if you have more than one. For the option, "Where Should the Tracking Code Be Placed", keep things simple by selecting the default, which is in the header. Now you just need to click "Track outbound clicks & downloads" and click the update button.

On average, for new Google Analytics accounts you need to wait around 24 hours before your account is activated and data appears in your analytics reports. If for some reason after 24 hours no data seems available, check your Google Analytics Plug-in and click the button, "Re-authenticate with Google".

### Google Analytics Homepage

In time the Google Analytics homepage will become one of the most popular URLs you visit. The actual homepage URL is:

http://www.google.com/analytics/home/

A good tip would be to bookmark this URL so that it is easy to access. Also note that you will also need to input your login details to use Google analytics so keep these details in a safe place.

Once you have logged in to Google Analytics, you will see the following screen, although please note that where it says "SITE NAME" you will see your own site(s) name.

To access your site's analytics data simply click on your site's name.

### Visitors Overview

The Visitors Overview screen of Google Analytics contains a huge amount of information, which I am going to split it up into sections so that you are not overwhelmed. Most of the screen is taken up by the graph, however, which looks like this:

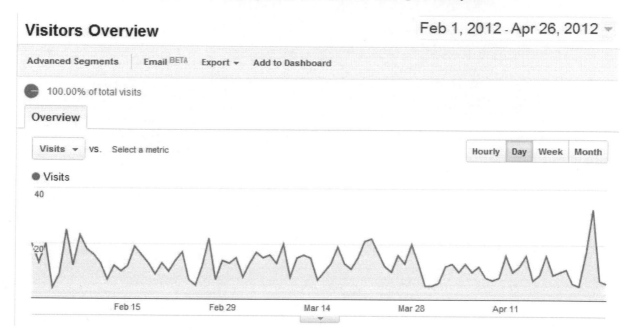

The graph shows you the number of visits that a site has had for a specific date range, usually a month although you can change the date range to any range of your choice. By "visits", I am of course referring to the number of people who have navigated to your website, regardless of the page on which they have landed. Every time someone visits your site, the number increases by one, even if the same person visits multiple times. We will come back and look at this graph in more detail later in this chapter. Just remember for now that it charts a specific range of dates, in this case Feb 1st 2012 to April 26th 2012, although you can customize the actual date range to your exact requirements.

Below the graph you will see text data and a pie chart containing details of new visitors and returning visitors as below.

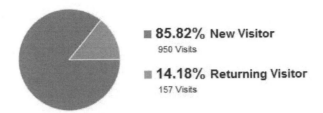

**968 people visited this site**

Visits: **1,107**

Unique Visitors: **968**

Pageviews: **1,631**

Pages/Visit: **1.47**

Avg. Visit Duration:
**00:00:41**

Bounce Rate: **75.61%**

% New Visits: **85.73%**

■ **85.82%** New Visitor
950 Visits

■ **14.18%** Returning Visitor
157 Visits

The data displayed in this section is very straightforward but vital to how your site is performing. The first data displayed, *Visits*, simply corresponds to the total number of visitors you have received for the specified period. This figure includes those who have visited your site more than once in the specified period, while the figure below is actual unique visitors.

The *Pageviews* data tells you how many total pages have been viewed by your visitors. One visitor might only look at one page, while another might look at ten pages.

Next we come to the *Pages/Visit* section, which is an extremely handy piece of data to take a look at on a regular basis. As the name suggests, it shows the average number of pages that a visitor has viewed on your site. Working out the average is simple: Analytics simply takes the number of Pageviews and divides it by the number of total visitors, giving the average.

The next piece of data, *Average Visit Duration*, tells you how long your visitors actually remained on your site, which in this case is again low. Looking at the data above the actual number of views per visitor is only 1.47 and the average visitor time on site is just 41 seconds. You might assume that this is an indication that the site is not performing, as visitors leave having on average viewed less than two pages in just over 40 seconds. On the other hand, this metric could actually be showing you that the site is performing extremely well, with most visitors quickly getting the information they require and then simply clicking an affiliate link that takes them to an external product page so they can make a purchase. Of course, you would have to take a good look at your site's page clicks, or lack of clicks, to determine if the low page/visits was an indication your site was performing well or poorly.

We have discussed the **Bounce Rate** in earlier chapters but it might still be something that some of you are unfamiliar with. It is basically a figure that shows the number of people who visit your site and then leave immediately, without navigating to a different page. Therefore, if you had a bounce rate of 100%, it would mean that every visitor had gone no further than reading one page of your site. In general the lower the bounce rate the better, although again, a high bounce rate could simply mean that your visitors were simply clicking affiliate links to buy products. You simply can't say a high bounce rate is an indication of a site performing poorly, as you have to investigate other metrics.

The next data displayed, **New Visits**, simply tells you the percentage of visitors who have visited your site for the first time.

Below the above data you will find even more information, which tells you more about your visitors.

| Demographics | | Language | Visits | % Visits |
|---|---|---|---|---|
| Language | ▸ | 1.  en-us | 742 | 67.03% |
| Country/Territory | | 2.  en-gb | 223 | 20.14% |
| City | | 3.  en | 56 | 5.06% |
| **System** | | 4.  bg | 18 | 1.63% |
| Browser | | 5.  es | 9 | 0.81% |
| Operating System | | 6.  en_gb | 8 | 0.72% |
| Service Provider | | 7.  pl | 6 | 0.54% |
| **Mobile** | | 8.  c | 4 | 0.36% |
| Operating System | | 9.  es-es | 4 | 0.36% |
| Service Provider | | 10. pt-br | 4 | 0.36% |
| Screen Resolution | | | | view full report |

This gives you information about the demographics of your visitors plus how they are accessing your site. Again this data can prove to be vital to your success. For example, if your site promoted products that were only shipped to the UK, but using the above data you found that a large proportion of your visitors were from outside the UK, then of course you would be going to lose sales. You would quickly have to find similar products that could be shipped to the countries of your visitors.

Also of great importance are the browsers that visitors are using to browse your site. Does your site display in the correct manner in all browsers listed? As for mobiles, how does your site view on the mobile operating systems listed?

Just on the opening screen alone of Google Analytics there is in effect so much data that you can use to great effect. Let's now take a look at the data in more detail.

### *Annotations*
A great new recent feature of Google Analytics is the function to add annotations to the graph. As you can see from the graph below, on Feb 10th the site suffered a big dip in traffic, due to the site being hacked. It is always good practice to add annotations to your website's graph for events such as substantial changes in daily traffic and even changes made to your website such as perhaps the creation of new sections or new marketing activities. By doing so you will create a complete timeline of your website's progress.

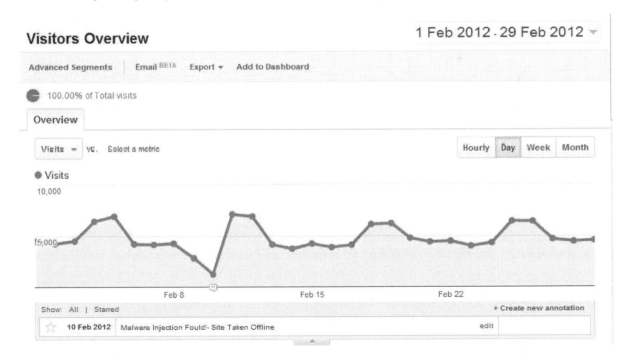

The next part of what we call the Dashboard looks even more interesting than the first and it also provides vital areas of information for us to look at. Here's what it looks like:

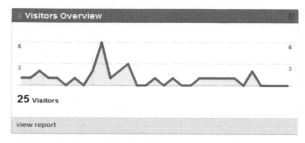

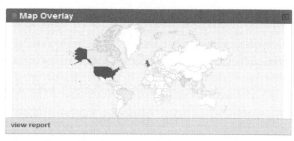

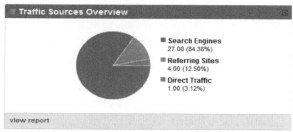

The sections here are easy to explain. The Visitors Overview shows the number of unique visitors in the time period (those visiting multiple times are counted just once in this). Map Overlay lets you see a visual representation of what countries people are visiting your site from. Traffic Sources Overview and Content Overview both show exactly where your traffic is coming from.

## *Working With Google Analytics Graphs*

When you run your mouse over the top of the graphs, you will see a little circle appear in different places. If you hover over these, the exact details for that day will appear in a little box. This is a handy way to see a day's stats without having to click further into the tool.

You'll also see that the dates can be changed by accessing the date section in the top right of the main graph. Simply click on the arrow to the right and you will see that the section expands and that you can make your selection. There are two ways to change the date: either enter the date manually, or use the calendar to select specific days quickly. The calendar is shown in the screenshot below, with the date range of December 1st 2011 to February 14th 2012 selected:

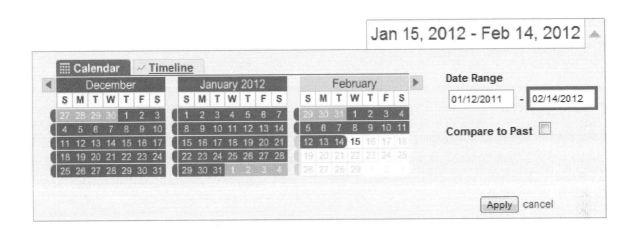

Now all you need to do is click on "Apply" to change the graph, or click on "Cancel" to revert to your original graph again.

You can also use the graph to display other stats as well – it doesn't need to display only the number of visitors. To do this, click on the tab to the top left of the graph and change it to one of the other options on the left side.

If you want to compare two different sets of figures, simply click on the "Compare Two Metrics" button and you will see two graphs overlaid on top of each other.

## *The Navigation Menu*

The navigation menu will always be on the left hand side of the page but it does not stay static; it changes as you move around the site. Whenever you want to return to the main page, however, simply click on the "Dashboard" link.

## More Advanced Google Analytics

We will now go over in more detail a number of important things that Google Analytics can be used for, such as how to look at the visitors to your site, what different things you should specifically look for and a few little hints and tips as well, which make life a lot easier when using this tool.

## *Visitors Overview Again*

First we are going to look again at the Visitors Overview. This is accessed by clicking on the Visitors tab on the navigation menu. You get a screen looking like this:

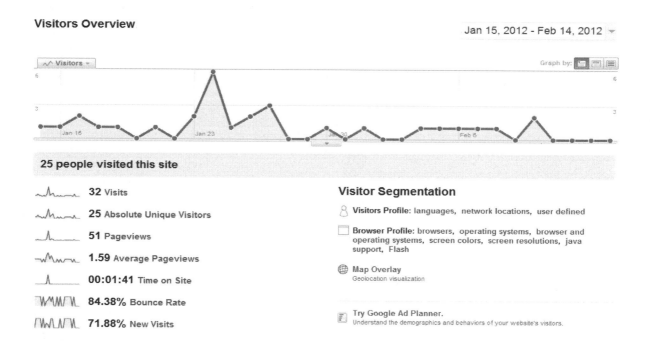

You will notice that the total unique visitors are shown twice on the information below the graph (once as "*25 people visited this site*" and again under Absolute Unique Visitors), because it is possibly the most important statistic. Both figures refer to exactly the same thing, however, so there is no need to get confused. The different figures shown here are essentially the same as the ones described in the last section, when we looked at the Dashboard.

There is something new here, however, which can be found underneath this graph and figures: the Technical Profile, as shown below. This will give you information on the different browsers that people have used to access your site, which can be useful when optimizing the way that your site looks for a certain browser.

## Technical Profile

| Browser | Visits | % visits |
|---|---|---|
| Firefox | 16 | 50.00% |
| Chrome | 10 | 31.25% |
| Safari | 3 | 9.38% |
| Internet Explorer | 3 | 9.38% |

view full report

### *Watching Out For Inconsistent Wording*

You will notice that the Dashboard and the Visitors Overview pages display a couple of pieces of inconsistent wording when you look over them, which can be confusing. For example, the Dashboard talks about "Pages/Visit" while the Visitors Overview talks of "Average Pageviews". These are exactly the same things. Similarly, "Average Time on Site" and "Time on Site" are the same as well.

## Links to Other Pages

Within Google Analytics you will see a number of different links to other pages. I am not going to cover all of these because once you understand the different terms and phrases, you will be able to click on most of the links and investigate them yourself. In fact, the best way to learn is to stumble around and see what you can find! You can always get back to the Dashboard by clicking the link on the left hand side of the page. We are, however, going to look at a few of the more interesting screens, starting with Time on Site.

## *Time On Site*

If you click on the "Time on Site" link when you are on the Visitors Overview page, you can see a detailed overview of the amount of time that each visitor, on average, has spent on your site, as shown in the screenshot below.

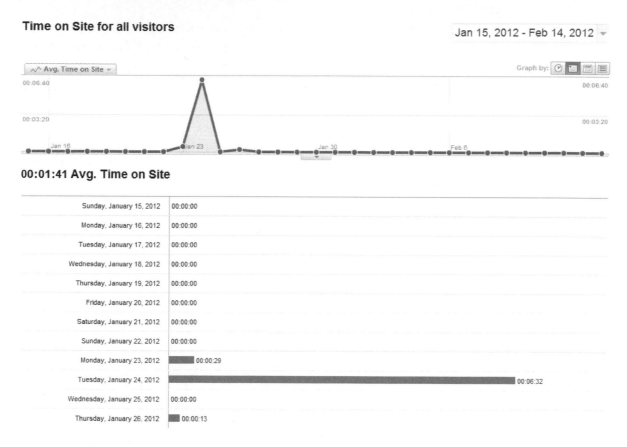

The top graph simply shows the amount of time that people have spent on your site over the last month, which gives you the perfect opportunity to see whether people are being engaged by your content or not. In the vast majority of cases, the higher the figures per day, the better it is for you and your site.

Simply looking at the average time can be useful, but it isn't the most reliable of figures. For example, the figure of 1 minute 41 seconds displayed above is enough time for people to skim through a couple of posts or perhaps sign up to a mailing list, but you cannot be sure that they are doing this. So, it is nice to see that figure going up, but there are more important metrics when it comes to analyzing your site.

For an easier view of how long people spent on your site on a specific day, use the bar chart underneath the graph. This is useful as you can work out when you added new content or indeed made changes and see if the changes resulted in better metrics.

## *"Today's" Stats Suddenly Disappearing*

You will notice from time to time that the details for the current day disappear, which is a common problem experienced by most. This is only temporary and I have learnt to work one day behind, generally ignoring the day's stats until the following day when they are complete. It is easy to change the graph so that it doesn't display "today's" results, but even easier simply to ignore it.

## *New vs. Returning*

The New vs. Returning screen is accessed through the "New vs. Returning" tab on the visitors' section of the left hand menu and can be extremely interesting. The screenshot below shows exactly what it looks like.

**32 visits from 2 visitor types**

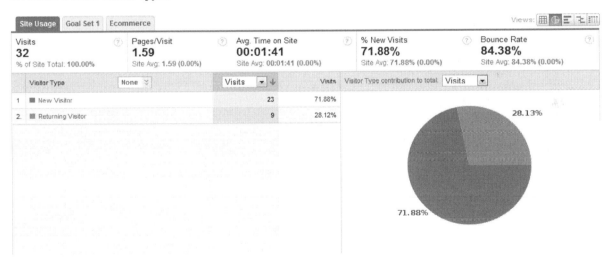

This screen will, as the name suggests, show you the number of new visitors – i.e. people who are visiting your site for the very first time – and the number of return visitors. The above screenshot shows that 28.13% of visitors are returning visitors, which can mean two things. It could mean that the majority of visitors don't like the site, so they aren't coming back after they have left. Alternatively, it could mean that lots of new people have found the site for the first time during the specified period. You will get the maximum amount of use from this chart when you extend the date range to cover a longer period, such as six months.

## Using the Stats to Your Advantage

I've known many affiliates – including myself – who have spent far too long worrying about minor issues that show up on Google Analytics, so it is important to know exactly where to draw the line in terms of the information that you use. This is a difficult question to answer however, as different sites will need to look at different stats in more detail than others.

Perhaps the best piece of advice is that you should make sure that you look at the stats over a long period of time. For example, if you see that you have fewer visitors than normal for a day, don't panic: simply check back a few days later and see if the trend has continued. Most of the time it will have normalized again and the lack of visitors was just a blip. If it hasn't returned to normal, however, you can start to investigate the reasons.

Don't be discouraged either if your number of visitors shoots up, only to drop again straight away. This is known as a "spike" and it will happen from time to time. In fact, as you get more experienced, you will work out how you can cause these spikes (hint: most of the time it is by writing a really good content).

The next section looks at how we can compare the different stats that you will find – something that is very important when looking to use Google Analytics to its full potential.

### Comparing Statistics

Comparing stats is extremely important, but it is also slightly tricky. This is mainly because you must do certain things in a certain order. The first thing to do is to go the Dashboard and expand the date tab by clicking the arrow to the right of it.

Now you need to check to see if the first set of dates are what you want. In this example, we are going to compare the stats from December 2011 to the stats from November 2011. So, first the correct range for December must be selected, as seen below:

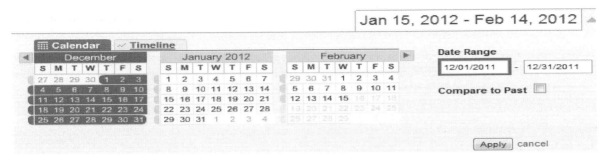

If you simply click on the date corresponding to the start of the specific period and then on the last day of the period, you will select the whole range of dates in between as well.

Next you need to click on the box beside "Compare to Past", which allows you to select a second range of dates. This might come up exactly right straight away, as Analytics tries to pre-empt what you want, but more often than not you will need to manually adjust it by selecting the dates in the same way as before.

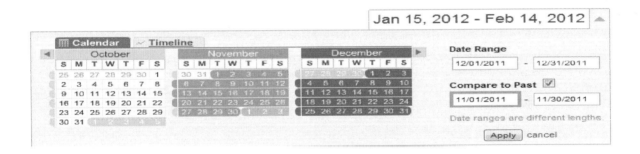

Now click the "Apply" button and you will see a graph similar to the one below.

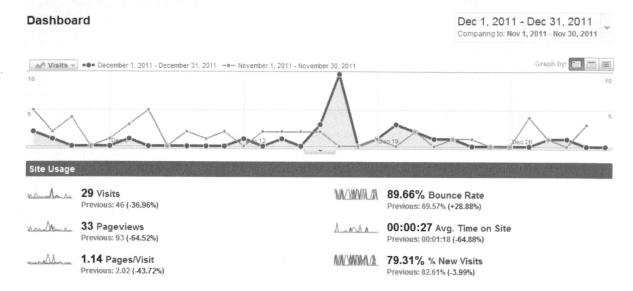

Above the graph you'll see a legend, which tells you which line corresponds with which selection. In the above example, November is the green line and December is the blue line.

You'll also notice the different sections under "Site Usage" underneath the main graph, all of which have percentages next to them. If the percentages are in red, it means that the figure has got worse, while a green one indicates a positive change. I have used a site for this example that has lain dormant for a while, so it's no surprise to see the figures dropping quickly! You can also compare the different graphs by hovering your mouse over one of the lines on the graphs.

## *Make Fair Comparisons*

To make comparisons fairer, it is best to compare stats on a week-to-week basis, or on a month-to-month one, because you will then weed out any unexplained spikes or drops and gain a good indication of how your site is performing. You should not simply look at the comparisons on their own, however, but instead try to remember what you did on your site during the different weeks. If in one week you only made one post, while the next week you posted loads of articles and new content, then the comparison is not really fair!

Now that we have looked at comparing the stats, we need to see how to use the different options available for evaluating traffic sources. This is not only the most interesting part of the whole tool to many people, but is also very important too.

## Traffic Sources

Traffic sources are essentially the different ways in which people navigate to your site. Four main categories are shown on Google Analytics.

- **Direct traffic.** These are the visitors who have typed your URL straight into their browser and visited your site. They might also have clicked on your link in their browser's bookmark folder or their favourite's folder.
- **Referring sites.** This refers to visitors who have clicked on a link to your site from another website, aside from search engines (see below).
- **Search engines.** When someone types in a query in a search engine, they might then click on the link to your site. This type of visit is classed within "search engines".
- **Other.** Traffic from any means other than the above three, such as your own custom campaigns.

You can see the different types of traffic that you are getting by clicking on the Traffic Sources tab and then on Overview. When you do, you can also see a list of the top traffic sources below the main chart, as on the screenshot below.

**All traffic sources sent a total of 32 visits**

3.12% Direct Traffic

12.50% Referring Sites

84.38% Search Engines

- Search Engines
  27.00 (84.38%)
- Referring Sites
  4.00 (12.50%)
- Direct Traffic
  1.00 (3.12%)

**Top Traffic Sources**

| Sources | Visits | % visits |
|---|---|---|
| google (organic) | 26 | 81.25% |
| thedigitalpost.co.uk (referral) | 4 | 12.50% |
| (direct) ((none)) | 1 | 3.12% |
| yahoo (organic) | 1 | 3.12% |
| view full report | | |

| Keywords | Visits | % visits |
|---|---|---|
| why use ppc | 8 | 29.63% |
| (not provided) | 5 | 18.52% |
| why to use ppc | 4 | 14.81% |
| site:.com blog -"comments are closed" + i... | 2 | 7.41% |
| top 5 twitter tools seo | 2 | 7.41% |
| view full report | | |

If you click on a link within the top traffic sources, you will get taken to another page with more info. This doesn't work with direct traffic, however, where you'll be taken to a page that shows some basic stats again.

## Referring Sites

When you click on the link that says "Referring Sites", you'll be shown a list of all the different sites that have sent traffic your way in the defined time period, as below:

**Referring sites sent 124 visits via 19 sources**

| | Visits | Pages/Visit | Avg. Time on Site | % New Visits | Bounce Rate |
|---|---|---|---|---|---|
| | **124** | **1.61** | **00:00:51** | **87.90%** | **73.39%** |
| | % of Site Total: 44.13% | Site Avg: 2.37 (-32.05%) | Site Avg: 00:03:02 (-71.74%) | Site Avg: 79.00% (11.26%) | Site Avg: 69.04% (6.30%) |

| | Source | None | Visits ↓ | Pages/Visit | Avg. Time on Site | % New Visits | Bounce Rate |
|---|---|---|---|---|---|---|---|
| 1. | myblogguest.com | | 38 | 1.84 | 00:01:47 | 78.95% | 71.05% |
| 2. | stumbleupon.com | | 29 | 1.45 | 00:00:18 | 100.00% | 55.17% |
| 3. | forex-ninjas.com | | 8 | 1.00 | 00:00:00 | 100.00% | 100.00% |
| 4. | ezinearticles.com | | 6 | 1.00 | 00:00:00 | 100.00% | 100.00% |
| 5. | www.slowfoodottawagatineau.org | | 6 | 1.00 | 00:00:00 | 100.00% | 100.00% |
| 6. | earningdiary.com | | 5 | 1.60 | 00:00:53 | 100.00% | 40.00% |
| 7. | slowfoodottawagatineau.org | | 5 | 1.00 | 00:00:00 | 100.00% | 100.00% |
| 8. | sn132w snt132.mail.live.com | | 5 | 3.20 | 00:03:44 | 0.00% | 40.00% |
| 9. | asktristramlodge.com | | 4 | 2.75 | 00:01:09 | 100.00% | 75.00% |
| 10. | thedigitalpost.co.uk | | 4 | 1.00 | 00:00:00 | 75.00% | 100.00% |

Filter Source: containing ▾ [        ] Go   Advanced Filter        Go to: 1   Show rows: 10 ▾   1 - 10 of 19 ◄ ►

These sites are ordered with the site that has sent most traffic placed at the top, but you can easily change this. Just click on a different column header and it will order the sites by this preference instead. For example, you could click on Bounce Rate and then determine which sites are sending you traffic that is truly interested in the pages on your site. To sort in reverse order, just click the same header a second time.

## Search Engines

This is exactly the same as the Referring Sites page, but instead of showing sites, it shows the different search engines people have used to locate your site.

## *Keywords*

The Keywords section can be found via the "Keywords" link on the Navigation Menu. This link will only show up, however, if you are already looking at one of the Traffic Sources pages.

As you know, keywords are the words or phrases that people type into their preferred search engine – usually Google – in order to find websites that provide the information that they are looking for. Google Analytics shows you a list of all the different keywords that people have used in order to arrive at your site via a search engine.

**Search sent 27 total visits via 11 keywords**

Show: non-paid | total | paid

Views: 

| | Site Usage | Goal Set 1 | Ecommerce | | | | |
|---|---|---|---|---|---|---|---|
| Visits | Pages/Visit | | Avg. Time on Site | | % New Visits | Bounce Rate | |
| **27** | **1.52** | | **00:01:06** | | **70.37%** | **85.19%** | |
| % of Site Total: 84.38% | Site Avg: 1.59 (-4.72%) | | Site Avg: 00:01:41 (-34.32%) | | Site Avg: 75.00% (-6.17%) | Site Avg: 84.38% (0.96%) | |

| | Keyword ⌄ | None ⌄ | Visits ↓ | Pages/Visit | Avg. Time on Site | % New Visits | Bounce Rate |
|---|---|---|---|---|---|---|---|
| 1. | why use ppc | | 7 | 2.14 | 00:01:51 | 71.43% | 85.71% |
| 2. | (not provided) | | 5 | 1.00 | 00:00:00 | 80.00% | 100.00% |
| 3. | why to use ppc | | 4 | 1.00 | 00:00:00 | 25.00% | 100.00% |
| 4. | site: com blog -"comments are closed" + internet marketing +"rece... | | 2 | 1.00 | 00:00:00 | 50.00% | 100.00% |
| 5. | top 5 twitter tools seo | | 2 | 2.00 | 00:07:43 | 50.00% | 50.00% |
| 6. | youtube marketing | | 2 | 1.00 | 00:00:00 | 100.00% | 100.00% |
| 7. | introduction to blogging | | 1 | 3.00 | 00:00:57 | 100.00% | 0.00% |
| 8. | jamie wright did i make a mistake | | 1 | 1.00 | 00:00:00 | 100.00% | 100.00% |
| 9. | jamie wright twitter wv | | 1 | 1.00 | 00:00:00 | 100.00% | 100.00% |
| 10. | microscope keyword | | 1 | 3.00 | 00:00:28 | 100.00% | 0.00% |

Filter Keyword: containing ▾ [          ] Go  Advanced Filter          Go to: 1  Show rows: 10 ▾  1 - 10 of 11 ◀ ▶

This is a great way to work out whether your SEO strategies are working. If the keywords that you have been targeting do not appear in the list, perhaps you need to concentrate on them more! Alternatively, you might also find some search terms that you had never even thought of but which are bringing you traffic!

You must remember when optimizing your site that the most important aspect by far is quality content. After all, there will be other affiliates out there probably vying for the same traffic that you are targeting. Simply blow them away by creating quality content always remembering that content is king!

## Content Overview

The Content Overview page is found by clicking on the "Content" link. It looks like this:

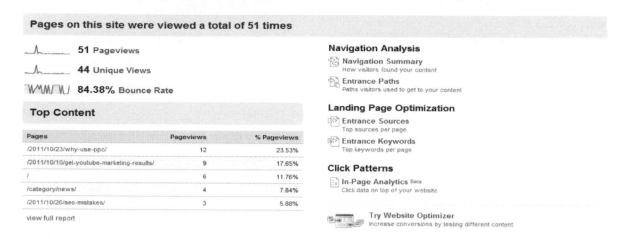

Perhaps the most useful piece of information that you'll find on this page is the list of the top five pages on your site, ranked in order of the number of visitors. If you click on "view full report", you'll see a much more detailed analysis of the pages on your site, which can be sorted just like the previous pages. One thing that you should remember is that a forward slash on its own refers to the site's homepage.

## Navigation Analysis

On the Content Overview page, you'll notice some other links, with one of these being "Navigation Summary". This can be found on the right-hand side. Click on this and you'll open up a new page looking like this:

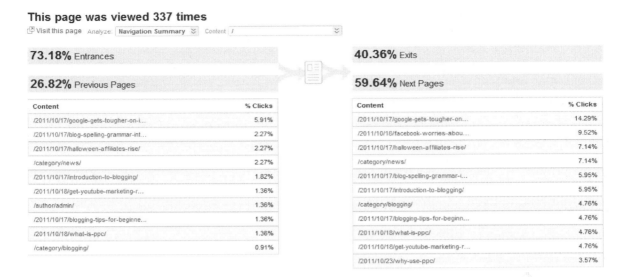

**This page was viewed 337 times**

Visit this page   Analyze: Navigation Summary ⌄   Content /

**73.18%** Entrances

**26.82%** Previous Pages

| Content | % Clicks |
|---|---|
| /2011/10/17/google-gets-tougher-on-i... | 5.91% |
| /2011/10/17/blog-spelling-grammar-int... | 2.27% |
| /2011/10/17/halloween-affiliates-rise/ | 2.27% |
| /category/news/ | 2.27% |
| /2011/10/17/introduction-to-blogging/ | 1.82% |
| /2011/10/18/get-youtube-marketing-r... | 1.36% |
| /author/admin/ | 1.36% |
| /2011/10/17/blogging-tips-for-beginne... | 1.36% |
| /2011/10/18/what-is-ppc/ | 1.36% |
| /category/blogging/ | 0.91% |

**40.36%** Exits

**59.64%** Next Pages

| Content | % Clicks |
|---|---|
| /2011/10/17/google-gets-tougher-on... | 14.29% |
| /2011/10/18/facebook-worries-abou... | 9.52% |
| /2011/10/17/halloween-affiliates-rise/ | 7.14% |
| /category/news/ | 7.14% |
| /2011/10/17/blog-spelling-grammar-i... | 5.95% |
| /2011/10/17/introduction-to-blogging/ | 5.95% |
| /category/blogging/ | 4.76% |
| /2011/10/17/blogging-tips-for-beginn... | 4.76% |
| /2011/10/18/what-is-ppc/ | 4.76% |
| /2011/10/18/get-youtube-marketing-r... | 4.76% |
| /2011/10/23/why-use-ppc/ | 3.57% |

Above this part of the screen, you will see a header named "Navigation Summary" and underneath it a single forward slash. This forward slash means that you are looking at information pertaining to your homepage. If you click on the drop down menu next to "Content" (it's around the middle of the screen), you can change the page to a different one.

You will also see some percentages on the page in bold letters. These signify how many people have landed on that page first (73.18% entrances) and how many got to that page from a different page on your site (26.82% previous pages). Obviously when the percentages are added together, they come to 100%.

On the right hand side there are some more percentages to look at. The first shows how many people left the site after they had looked at the page in question (40.36% exits) and how many people went onto another page on the site (59.64% next pages). Once again, the two percentages will add up to 100%.

Underneath the percentages you will see a more detailed breakdown of both Previous Pages and Next Pages. If you click on the link to one of these pages, you will be taken to another page, where you'll get a more thorough analysis of the data.

Obviously there are a lot of other ways to use this page – especially in the "Analyze" drop down menu. Why don't you play around for a bit and see what else you can find here? It should all be pretty self-explanatory but very useful at the same time!

This chapter only covers the basics of Google Analytics. Again there are many great resources online, the best by far being:

http://support.google.com/googleanalytics/?hl=en

Also of note is that as I write this chapter Google is actually running two versions of Google Analytics. I must admit I'm a little of a Luddite and I prefer the old version, which Google has craftily added to the footer of the main Google Analytics homepage.

# Chapter 18 - An Introduction to Google Webmasters Tools

Google Webmaster Tools is a very powerful suite of tools and statistics offered free by Google in order to help webmasters make their websites more visible to Google and to detect possible problems. No matter if you have a small hobby website or a gigantic e-commerce network, utilizing Google Webmaster Tools can help you improve many aspects of your business's online presence. Because of the breadth of its services, from Search Engine Optimization metrics to sitemaps, from audience data to general troubleshooting guidance, Google Webmaster Tools is the most popular suite of webmaster tools for the most popular search engine.

## Website Usability

If you want your website to become successful, then you need to know that it is functioning in the right manner, which is exactly why Google Webmaster Tools is so important. Not only does it show you valuable data, allowing you to test parts of your website and helping you to generate things like a robots.txt file and load sitemaps, but it also will generally warn you when something negative has occurred. The most typical alerts include crawl errors, which occur when Google has issues indexing pages of your website, malware infections, when your website has been targeted by hackers, slow loading pages and even when your website has suffered a large decrease in visitors.

On top of all the technical reasons why people choose to use Google Webmaster Tools, there is also the topic of usability. A lot of the tools are designed to help you improve the overall experience provided by your website. Regardless of how amazing the content is on your website, if people are having troubles accessing it in a quick and simple manner, you will lose visitors.

Google Webmaster Tools helps address usability concerns by providing information that relates directly to the end experience. One of the diagnostic tools allows you to analyze the page load times, something that, if too high, can cause users to hit the back button before even looking at your content. Additionally, you can run various preview tests to see what your website's results and pages look like through the virtual eyes of a Google's search engine spider.

# How to configure GWT for your website

### Creating a Google Account

In order to use Google Webmasters Tools, you will need two things: a Google account and, of course your own website. To create a Google account, you can simply navigate to http://www.google.com/ and click the "Sign In" button in the top right. This will direct you to the Google login page, where you will see a "Sign Up" button, located again in the top right. Click this, provide the necessary information, and create your Google account.

### Adding Your Website to Google Webmaster Tools

Next, go to the Google Webmasters Tools home page, which you can find at http://www.google.com/webmasters/tools/home. You will see a large red "Add A Site" button in the centre of the screen—click it. A prompt will display asking you for the URL of the website that you would like Google Webmaster Tools to manage. Enter the full URL of your website and then click the continue button.

### Verify Ownership

At this point, Google needs to verify that you are indeed the owner of the website that you just provided. Although there are multiple ways to prove this, the recommended option is by far the most simple. The screen that you are now looking at will have a list of instructions that you need to follow.

**Recommended:** Upload an HTML file to your server

You can use this option if you are able to upload new files to your site.

> **Instructions:**
> 1. **Download** this HTML verification file. [google921803fd6cfc9b51.html]
> 2. **Upload** the file to http://www.bingoscout.com/
> 3. **Confirm** successful upload by visiting http://www.bingoscout.com/google921803fd6cfc9b51.html in your browser.
> 4. **Click** Verify below.
> To stay verified, don't remove the HTML file, even after verification succeeds.

VERIFY    Not now

First, download the HTML verification file generated by Google to an easily accessible location on your computer. Then take that file and upload it, through an FTP client or otherwise, to the root directory of your website. For example, if your website was www.yourwebsite.com/, the file needs to be located at www.yourwebsite.com/google123.html. Ensure you upload the Google verification file to the correct location because if Google can't "see" the file, you will not be verified as the website's owner.

Once you have uploaded the HTML file to your root directory, simply visit the file in another window or tab through any web browser and then click "Verify" on the Google Webmasters Verification page. Congratulations, you are now recognized as the owner of the website you provided! If you have more than one website, then simply carry out the above process for each additional website.

## Google Webmaster Tools Dashboard

Whenever you click on a website's web property link found on the Google Webmaster Tools home screen, you are greeted by that website's dashboard display. This screen serves as a way to check up on your website by displaying data generated by various tools in the suite.

Information included on the dashboard includes your highest search queries, crawl errors, your site's keywords and your current sitemaps. The dashboard is intended to be used as nothing more than a reference. There is no way to manage anything directly through the dashboard.

## Google Webmaster Tools Message Centre

By clicking on the "Messages" button, you are directed to the message centre of Google Webmaster Tools. This message centre serves as a way for you to be alerted of important messages from Google regarding your website. It is a good idea to pay close attention to the messages you receive, because they should often be addressed as quickly as possible. You also receive messages when you perform certain actions like linking your Google Webmaster Tools account with Google Analytics or changing the settings of your site in Google Webmaster Tools.

I must stress that it is vital that you check messages that appear in the Google Webmaster Tools message centre. In most cases messages other than those that relating to changes of your settings will indeed need urgent action. Let's take a look at some of the messages you may receive.

### *Change in Traffic Messages*

A message with the title "*http:www.yourwebsite.com/: Big traffic change for top URL*" alerts you of either a vast decline or increase of daily visitors to your homepage. If your website's homepage traffic considerably increases, the message you will receive will simply be:

*Search results clicks for http://www.yourwebsite.com/ have increased significantly. Yay!*

If you have suffered a heavy decrease in daily visitors, the message will be:

*Search results clicks for http://www.yourwebsite.com/ have decreased significantly.*

Of course, Google is never going to tell you why there has been a vast change in your daily traffic, so you are going to have to find what has caused the change yourself. If you are lucky enough to have received the "increased significantly" message, the increase in traffic could be down to new content you have created that is ranking highly, an increase of rankings for your key phrases, an increased number of your pages indexed in Google or some other reason. For the "decreased significantly" message, in most cases this is the result of a drop in your search engine rankings or problems with the actual functioning of your website.

### Unnatural Links Message

It must also be noted that Google will contact you if you have been found to be "gaming" Google search results. As I write this chapter, Google is really starting to clamp down on webmasters "gaming" search results by acquiring links. As I have said previously in this book, there is a mammoth underground market in link sales. Hundreds of thousands of links are bought and sold every day. If you opt to take short cuts by simply purchasing links, then you could receive the following message from Google:

*Google Webmaster Tools notice of detected unnatural links*

*We've detected that some of your site's pages may be using techniques that are outside Google's Webmaster Guidelines.*

*Specifically, look for possibly artificial or unnatural links pointing to your site that could be intended to manipulate PageRank. Examples of unnatural linking could include buying links to pass PageRank or participating in link schemes.*

*We encourage you to make changes to your site so that it meets our quality guidelines. Once you've made these changes, please submit your site for reconsideration in Google's search results.*

*If you find unnatural links to your site that you are unable to control or remove, please provide the details in your reconsideration request.*

*If you have any questions about how to resolve this issue, please see our Webmaster Help Forum for support.*

*Sincerely,*

*Google Search Quality Team*

If you receive such a message, then you are in big trouble! Most webmasters who have received the above email have reported that a few weeks later their websites were penalized, resulting in a vast drop of daily visitors.

### *Malware Warning Message*

All websites are prone to some degree to malware attacks, especially Wordpress. You can minimize the risk by ensuring that you keep your Wordpress install & plug-ins up to date and that you secure your install by using the all techniques detailed earlier. It has to be said, however, that the chances are high that in the long term you will suffer some form of malware attack. The internet is simply riddled with thousands of websites infected with malware with the webmasters of the sites not even knowing their websites are infected. If Google detects your website is infected you will receive the following message:

*Dear site owner or webmaster of http://www.yourwebsite.com*

*We recently discovered that some of your pages can cause users to be infected with malicious software. We have begun showing a warning page to users who visit these pages by clicking a search result on Google.com.*

*Below are one or more example URLs on your site which can cause users to be infected:*

*http://www.yourwebsite.com*

*http://www.yourwebsite.com 2012/*

*http://www.yourwebsite.com /2012/05/*

*Here is a link to a sample warning page:*
*http://www.google.com/fgfrtfggfl?URL=yourwebssite.com/*

*We strongly encourage you to investigate this immediately to protect your visitors. Although some sites intentionally distribute malicious software, in many cases the webmaster is unaware because:*

*1) the site was compromised*

*2) the site doesn't monitor for malicious user-contributed content*

*3) the site displays content from an ad network that has a malicious advertiser*

*If your site was compromised, it's important not only to remove the malicious (and usually hidden) content from your pages, but also to identify and fix the vulnerability. We suggest contacting your hosting provider if you are unsure of how to proceed.*

*Sincerely,*

*Google Search Quality Team*

IF you receive the above message, then you must take swift action. Google will add a message to EVERY page you have listed in Google search results as shown below. This will of course result in a vast decrease in traffic as most "searches" will not click-through to your site. If your website is hosted with Hostgator then you should instantly contact Hostgator support and ask them to check your account for malware. You may be surprised to know that Hostgator actually do this for free! Once Hostgator have scanned your account and cleaned all files, reply to the malware notification you have received from Google, enclosing the email from Hostgator that details the cleaning process. After around six hours, provided of course that your website is indeed malware free, Google will remove the warning messages from SERPs.

Everything

Images

Maps

Videos

News

Shopping

More

Eugene, OR
Change location

Any time

**Illuminati News** Welcome Page
www.illuminati-news.com/
This site may harm your computer. ←
Oct 6, 2011 – All this chaos, genocide, ethnic cleansing and disaster we see in this
world have a genuine purpose. It is all very carefully planned by a few ...

| **Illuminati News** | The Secret Order of the Illuminati
illuminati-news.com/moriah.htm
This site may harm your computer. ←
Dec 9, 2011 – Bringing news to you since 1998 ... **Illuminati News** Presents: ... his
whole thing with the Illuminati and a Shadow Government may be unreal to ...

**Illuminati News**: News & Updates Index Page
illuminati-news.com/index3.htm
This site may harm your computer. ←
Oct 31, 2011 – CLICK ON THE PICTURE ABOVE AND CHECK OUT THIS DVD
SERIES! VERY HIGHLY RECOMMENDED! Wes Penre, **Illuminati News**. * * * ...

Over the years I have had websites cleaned by Hostgator only to find, the very next day, the malware returns. If you find yourself in this situation, I would strongly suggest you sign up to Securi.net. Securi is not a free service as it costs $89 per website, although in my opinion they offer a great service. Once signed up to Securi, you simply give them access to your site and they take care of the whole cleaning process, including detecting and fixing any vulnerability in your website code so that the malware does not return. They even contact Google for you once your website is clean. Better still, your $89 subscription with Securi is for a full year's protection and cleaning.

It is vitally important that the actual CMS of your website, in your case Wordpress, is always up to date. Wordpress does a great job regularly rolling out updates that include additional features but more importantly fix security issues that have been recently found. Running an out of date Wordpress install will leave your website at a high risk of being hacked. If Google notices your website is running an older version of Wordpress you will receive the following message:

*Dear site owner or webmaster of http://www.yourwebsite.com/,*

*Your site appears to be running an older version of Wordpress. Google recommends that you update to the latest release. Older or unpatched software may be vulnerable to hacking or malware that can hurt your users. To download the latest release, visit the Wordpress download page.*

*If you have any additional questions about why you are receiving this message, Google has provided more background information in a blog post about this subject.*

*Best wishes,*

*Google Search Quality Team*

If you receive the above message, don't panic, Google is simply trying to help you. Simply log in to your Wordpress install and select the "Update Wordpress" option.

If you rarely check your Google Webmaster Tools messages, but still want to be updated on anything that Google has to say about your website, you can forward the messages received in the message centre to a specified email address. Simply go to the Google Webmaster Tools home page and click the "Preferences" button found on the left. Then simply specify the email address and message language, and finally click "Save Preferences". I strongly suggest you do this!

## GWT - Site Configuration

The sitemaps section of the Site Configuration menu contains a wealth of information and tools to help you add and indeed monitor your website's sitemap. As stated in the Wordpress chapter, you will be installing a sitemap plug-in to generate your sitemap. Once your website is up and running and your sitemap is installed, you simply need to add the location of your sitemap to Google Webmaster Tools.

To add your sitemap simply click on the "Add/Test Sitemap" button in the top right corner.

Sitemaps                                                    ADD/TEST SITEMAP

By me (0)      All (0)

No sitemaps found for this site.

This will open up a small window asking you if you would like to test a sitemap, submit one, or cancel.

Sitemaps

ADD/TEST SITEMAP

By me (0)    All (0)

No sitemaps found for this site.

Add/Test Sitemap

http://www.roulettemachines.org/

Test Sitemap    Submit Sitemap    Cancel

In order to test your sitemap, in effect to see if Google can read it, enter the path of the sitemap in the box and click the "Test Sitemap". Google will take a moment to test the sitemap and then offer you a look at the test results. Clicking on the "View Test Result" link will allow you to evaluate the location and type of the sitemap, in addition to seeing any errors that were found. Using the Wordpress Sitemap plug-in you should not run into any problems, provided that you have installed the plug-in correctly.

If your sitemap passed the test with no errors, you can then proceed to submit it. Go back to the Sitemap section of Google Webmaster Tools and click the "Add/Test Sitemap" button again. Enter the path of the sitemap and this time click "Submit Sitemap". If it was successful, you will receive a message saying that your sitemap was submitted.

The actual number of URLs submitted in your sitemap in many cases will not match the actual number of URLs included in the Google index, although for a healthy website, there should only be a small disparity.

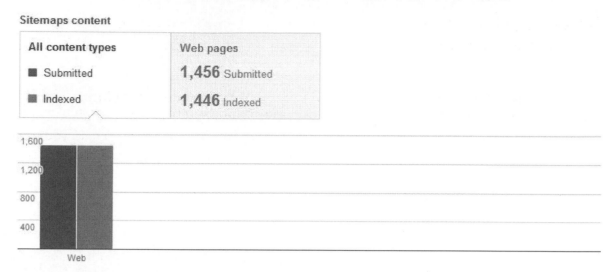

# Google Webmaster Tools

## *Crawler Access*

Clicking the "Crawler Access" button found in the site configuration tab will bring you to a screen that allows you to view, test, create and edit your robots.txt file. On the main screen you can view your current robots.txt file, its address, any blocked URLs, when Google initially downloaded it and the current status. Underneath this display is the test interface, which allows you to test a new robots.txt before uploading it to your website. In general, it is always a good idea to double check your robots.txt thoroughly before uploading—there are some popular websites out there that have at one time blocked Google from crawling huge portions of the website by accident!

Click the "Create Robots.Txt" in the middle of your screen to navigate to Google's robots.txt generator. Choose "allow all" and then pick out any files that you do not want crawled. After you have generated an ideal robots.txt, review it and click "Download". Upload this robots.txt to your website's root directory and you're done.

If you discover that there are some directories or URLs that you do not want displayed on Google's search engine result pages, but do not want to go through the trouble of remaking a robots.txt and waiting weeks for Google to remove the page, you can click the "Remove URLs" button found to the right of the "Create Robots.txt" tab. Click on "Create A

New Removal Request" and specify the directory or URL that you wish to block from the SERPs, and Google will remove it from their listings.

## Site links

On Google's search engine result pages, a website listing can occasionally feature several sections of that website listed underneath the listing in the form of indented links. These are called site links and are generated automatically at Google's discretion. While you may not have control over whether they display site links underneath your website's listing, you are given the power to remove individual ones. It must be noted that Google does not generate site links for all websites and that for new websites it may be many months before you find site links listed in Google SERPs.

If you want to remove any site links, simply click the "Sitelinks" button found in the site configuration section. Here, you will be able to specify particular search result URLs along with the site link URLs, effectively giving you full control over what ends up getting displayed under your website's Google listing.

## Change of Address

Google likes to know in advance if you plan to move your website to a new domain. In order for you to retain your listings on the search engine result pages, you will need to use this feature of Google Webmaster Tools. Clicking the "Change Of Address" button in site configuration brings up the change of address tool, which you can then use to read up on Google's guidelines for moving a website and the various steps you should take when moving.

## Settings

The "Settings" section of site configuration allows you to adjust three different things. First, you're allowed to "target" Google users in various geographical locations. This is useful if you own an e-commerce website or have an informative website aimed at a certain slice of the world. Secondly, you can set up a preferred domain URL, with or without the "www." The last option allows you to adjust the crawl rate, or the duration of time between Google crawl bot, or spider, visits. This should usually be set to the recommended option, unless you have a particular reason for limiting it. I strongly suggest that you do not change the crawl rate.

Settings

| Geographic target | ☐ Target users in: United States ▼ | Learn more |
| Preferred domain | Restricted to root level domains only | Learn more |
| Crawl rate | Restricted to root level domains and subdomains only | Learn more |

## URL Parameters

If you have a single page with multiple URLs, Google will generally combine them for search purposes and select whatever URL is detected as being the "best" to display. In most cases you should not need to change these setting and should see the screen below.

URL Parameters

Currently Googlebot isn't experiencing problems with coverage of your site, so you don't need to configure URL parameters. (Incorrectly configuring parameters can result in pages from your site being dropped from our index, so we don't recommend you use this tool unless necessary.)

 Use this feature only if you're sure how parameters work. Incorrectly excluding URLs could result in many pages disappearing from search.

Configure URL parameters »

However, sometimes Google gets this wrong. Click the "URL Parameters" button found in site configuration to modify the URL parameters to your taste. Inexperienced webmasters should simply steer well clear of this option!

## User Administration

The "User Administration" button under site configuration allows you to modify and manage the Google accounts associated with the particular website's Google Webmaster Tools profile. This is of course very useful if you want to give others access to your Google

Webmaster Tools data, such as a partner or perhaps somebody who is helping you to identify problems with your website.

### *Your Site on the Web*

The focal point for most Google Webmaster Tools users is the "Search Queries" section of Your Site on the Web. This incredibly useful page displays information including how many times your website was displayed on Google search engine result pages, or impressions, and how many people actually clicked those listings. In addition to that, it displays the individual search queries that people searched for that brought up your website.

At the top of the search queries page you will find a graph that shows impressions and clicks over a specific time range.

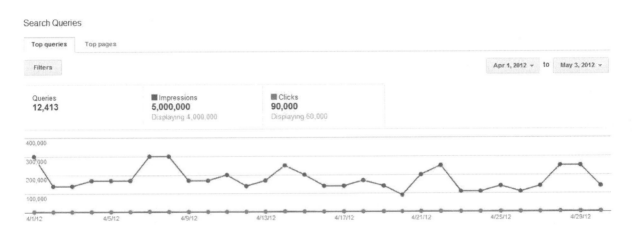

You can adjust the time range up to a 90 day period, and you can also set filters for the type of search queries, such as, all, mobile, image etc., the location of queries and queries with 10 or more impressions and clicks. Also there is another tab "Top Pages", which you can click to show the most viewed pages of your website.

In the middle of the page is a large horizontal graph that displays impressions, clicks, click-through rate and average position. This data is extremely useful because you can see how your site is actually performing in SERPs. For example, if you are ranked high in Google search results for the search phrase "blue widgets" but the actual number of clicks displayed is very low, then of course you need to work on your page title and meta description to entice more "searches" to click your listing in Google search results. Using this data is a great way to find out just how good your page titles and meta tags actually are at enticing people to click them. Surprisingly many affiliates don't use this data, which of course means they never prime their page titles and meta tags for higher click-through rates.

## Links to Your Site

The "Links To Your Site" button shows a list of URLs from other websites that link to your website. In addition to the URLs, you are also shown anchor text and any redirected links. This information is a great tool for finding out just how successful you have been in getting others to link to your website. Remember the art of getting others to link to your pages is of prime importance as Google classes natural links that you gain to your site as a positive vote. In time, provided you create quality content, you should find the number of links to your site increasing, although again, this takes time.

## Your Site on the Web Content Keywords

Clicking "Content Keywords" brings up a list of what Google considers the most significant keywords on your website, and any relevant variations of them. This data is typically used alongside search queries to educate webmasters on how people are finding their website through Google's search engine.

A keyword's significance is determined mostly by the rate at which it appears on your website. If you see a keyword near the top of this list that appears as though it is completely unrelated to the content of your website, there is a chance that your website has been compromised by hackers, so you should thoroughly check every part of your website for any signs of tampering. For example, if your website consists of content related to treadmills and you find keywords relating to other niches such as pharmaceuticals, gambling or even celebrity news, then your website has indeed been compromised. In most cases what will have happened is that links will have been injected into your website's code that you and your readers can't see, but search engine spiders, such as Googlebot, can see. Again I'm sorry to say that this is something I have experienced.

A couple of years ago I was horrified to find that one of my main websites lost all its rankings in Google overnight. I loaded up Google Webmaster Tools expecting to find a message detailing a penalty but found nothing. When I examined key phrases in Google Webmaster Tools and indeed Google Analytics, to my horror I found hundreds of key phrases relating to Viagra. Loading up many pages of my website I could not see these links, and it was not until I ran a few pages through the "Fetch As Googlebot" option that I could indeed see them.

### *Internal Links*

Clicking the "Internal Links" option brings up a somewhat detailed list of internal links, or links that navigate users from one page on your website to another. In this section the top internal links should be your main navigation links.

### *Subscriber Stats*

The "Subscribers Stats" section will show you how many Google users have subscribed to your website's feeds through any of the numerous Google products that allow you to subscribe to a website. Although this list excludes subscribers that aren't using a Google product, the actual number of subscribers is typically much higher, although this list is still a good reference point.

## Google Webmaster Tools +1 Metrics

### *Search impact*

The "Search Impact" button in the +1 Metrics section allows you to gauge the impact that +1s have on your website's search performance. The list displayed here contains impressions and +1 data, and shows the relation between +1s and click-through rates, or CTR, a useful metric for those who are actively building +1s.

You can further sort the list by choosing particular sets of data that you want to see. You can choose +1 annotated impressions, which is when someone sees your website on a search engine result page because of their personalized search settings, or +1 annotated clicks, which is the same but displays clicks instead of impressions. The last two sets of data are the same as the previous two, except without +1 related data.

### *Activity*

The "Activity" section of +1 Metrics allows you to review the number of times that people have +1'd your individual pages. Choose from "New +1s" or "All +1s" to see different sets of data, which you can further sort by specifying particular time parameters. Additional information provided includes the source of your website's +1s—either from the inside or from other websites.

## *Audience*

Clicking the "Audience" button will bring you to a page that gives you information and statistics about the different people who have +1'd your website. Google prioritizes privacy, so no personal information will be displayed, including age or specific location, unless your website has been deemed trustworthy by accruing a minimum amount of +1s

# Google Webmaster Tools - Diagnostics

## *Malware*

The "Malware" section of Diagnostics will display any malware Google may find on your website, as detected by Google. Normally Google will display the following message in this section.

> *Malware*

> *Google has not detected any malware on this site.*

As already stated in this chapter, if you receive a malware warning error, then you must take immediate action!

## *Crawl Errors*

Clicking "Crawl Errors" under Diagnostics will bring up a list of any problems Google has experienced when crawling your website. If you properly constructed a robots.txt file, you will probably have little to worry about. However, if your website is large and intricate, or you are having problems with your hosting, there are a number of different alerts that may show up in this section and you should be aware of them.

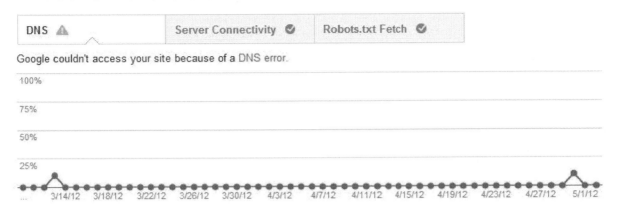

These particular alerts include server errors, URL errors, access denied errors, and soft 404 errors, all of which have to do with the Google crawl bot being unable to access the site. Other alerts are DNS errors, not followed alerts, robot failure, and site errors. These are just as important and harder to fix. DNS problems stem from your domain information, while not followed alerts are generated when a link is crawled but not indexed because of the no follow command. If you have problems with your hosting with frequent "down time", then of course Google will not be able to find your pages, which will result in crawl errors. You may find that you have problems with a specific section of your site that could be due to structural errors. Keep an eye on crawl errors to identify possible problems with your website.

### *Crawl Stats*

The "Crawl Stats" section shows you valuable Google bot behaviour data. This is very useful for determining the actual rate at which your website is crawled and aids in troubleshooting any crawl errors. The page displays three different graphs as shown below:

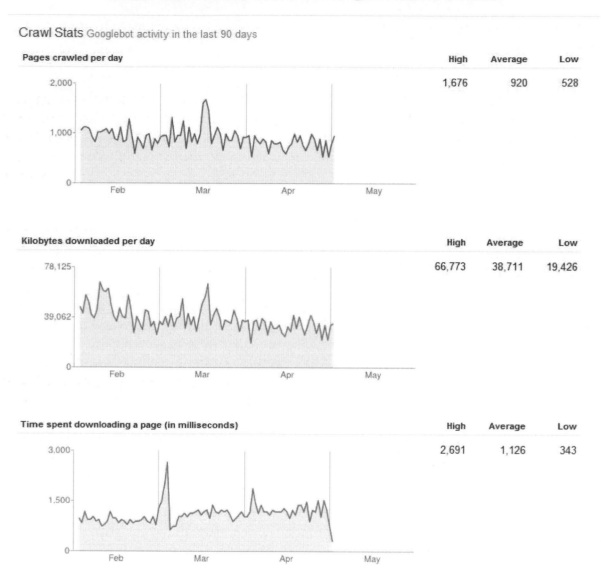

The first is "Pages crawled per day", which is fairly self-explanatory. This graph displays the number of pages on your website that the Google bots have crawled, per day. The second graph is "Kilobytes downloaded per day", which shows you information about how much data the Google bot salvages from your pages every time it crawls them. Lastly, the third graph shows the duration, in milliseconds, that the crawling process took on a page-by-page basis.

### Fetch as Googlebot

Clicking "Fetch As Googlebot" brings up a tool that shows how a particular page on your website looks to the Google crawl bots. You can only use this tool a limited number of times per month, but this number is fairly high. In order to use the tool, simply enter in the URL of the page you want to see through Google's eyes and click "Fetch". You can specify whether you want to pretend as though it was searched through the web or through a mobile format if desired.

This is a great tool to see how the Google Spider actually sees specific pages of your site. If you think your website may have been compromised, perhaps with malware, run a few pages through this tool. If you find links that are not visible when you view the page normally, then your site has indeed been infected.

### HTML suggestions

The "HTML Suggestions" section of Diagnostics displays possible issues detected when Google is crawling and indexing your website's various pages. I recommend that you view this page on a semi-regular basis in order to address any identified issues as quickly as possible.

Although the recommendations displayed in this interface are not detrimental to your website's success, handling them can improve your rank on the search engine result pages and therefore increase traffic. Typical alerts include problems with the title of your page, the meta description or keywords, and content that was unable to be indexed for one reason or another.

## Google Webmaster Tools - Labs

### Custom Search

The Labs section of Google Webmaster Tools allows you to test various parts of your website. The "Custom Search" button will bring up a tool that allows you to simulate a highly customized search of your own website to help you build it correctly.

Enter whatever search terms you want in the search box and then choose an edition. By choosing "Standard edition", you will see a traditional search engine result page that includes ads, while choosing "Site Search" will not display ads at all. After choosing the edition, clicking "search" will display a list of pages on your website that Google has associated with the search query you chose.

### Instant Previews

Visiting the "Instant Previews" section of Labs will allow you to compare a live page on your website with Google's instant preview of that page. Enter the URL of the page you want to compare and click "Compare". It may take a while to load, but after it does, you will be shown a comparison. This is a diagnostic tool that is helpful for popular websites, since they get a lot of traffic and are concerned with how Google's instant previews for the pages on their website are displayed.

### Site performance

The "Site Performance" button will navigate you to a tool that allows you to check the performance of your website. Currently, in order to get this data, you need to download a program called Page Speed. It displays information including the average load time of pages, any performance related trends over time and even suggestions that may help you optimize your pages with speed in mind. This is a great metric that can help you determine if people are turning away from your pages because they are taking too long to load.

## Google Webmaster Tools - Other Resources

As Google creates different products that aim to aid webmasters, they will list them in the "Other Resources" section of Google Webmaster Tools. Examples of tools you might find in this section include the Rich Snippets Testing Tool, which double checks how your website's Rich Snippets mark-up gets displayed on the search engine result pages. For details of Rich Snippets browse this url:

http://support.google.com/webmasters/bin/answer.py?hl=en&answer=99170

The Google Merchant Center can be found in this section, a tool used by e-commerce webmasters to integrate various Google products and services.

Google Places is also listed under "Other Resources", and is an invaluable tool for any webmaster that has a physical business location. This will allow you to integrate your website into Google Places, effectively making it easier for people to find the content, products or services you offer.

## Integration with Google Analytics

As you already know from the last chapter, Google Analytics is another official product that is similar to Google Webmaster Tools. We saw how Google Analytics allows you to review extremely in-depth information about the people that visit your site, including data such as when, from where, and their behaviour on your site. Because of the usefulness of Google Analytics in conjunction with Google Webmaster Tools, Google allows you to link both of these products together to provide synchronized data.

When you link your Analytics and Webmaster Tools accounts together, you will be able to see various statistics normally only provided by Webmaster Tools through the Google Analytics interface. In addition to that, you will be able to view different data reports generated by Analytics through Google Webmaster Tools. Because of this improved usability, it is to the benefit of almost all webmasters to link these accounts together as soon as possible.

In order to do that, you first need both types of accounts. Once you have both, you can navigate to Webmaster Tools and click "Manage Site" next to the website that you want to link with Analytics. Click on the "Google Analytics Property" link and then "Save".

If you have a problem associating the accounts together, there is probably a good explanation. If you are trying to manage a company website, try to find out if someone had previously created or attempted to link a Webmaster Tools account with an Analytics profile. If they have, you will have to obtain that account information to proceed, or delete their association all together and start from scratch.

# Chapter 19 - Affiliate Networks

## Amazon Affiliates

The Amazon Affiliate scheme is undoubtedly the most popular affiliate scheme online, used by huge numbers of people to sell all kinds of different products. The fact that it is so popular proves that it is a very worthwhile program to join, but what are the different things that you need to know about it?

### *About Amazon Affiliates*

Amazon is a company that is known to everyone with an internet connection, selling an enormous variety of different products in countries all around the world. Their affiliate program has been running since way back in 1996, which means that they have been in the industry almost since its inception. Affiliates were allowed to use banners on their websites that, when clicked on, benefited the advertiser whenever the visitor bought anything. Obviously the system has come on a long way since then, but the basic premise is still the same.

### *Merchants & Products*

It is virtually impossible to say exactly how many products Amazon offers within their affiliate program, simply because there are more added every single day. A conservative estimate would put the figure at tens of thousands, although obviously you will only want to use a small niche offered there.

Unlike other types of affiliate programs, there is only one program that can be joined within Amazon. This program gives you access to a wide range of different advertising resources – such as banners and widgets – as well as ways to keep track of your earnings. It is tough to pick out a list of the top Amazon merchants because there are simply so many, but suffice it to say that any merchant on the site has been thoroughly vetted and can be trusted to work with.

### *Amazon Payments*

Commission is earned whenever a visitor going to Amazon via your site purchases an item within 24 hours of your referral. Commission rates start at 4% and have caps for each category (if you are an affiliate of the Amazon US site). For example, consumer electronics have a 4% commission rate attached to them, with a maximum payment of $25. Commission rates rise as the number of sales you make rises, in the following manner:

- 1-6 sales receive 4% commission;
- 7-30 sales receive 6% commission;
- 31-110 sales receive 6.5% commission;
- 111-320 sales receive 7% commission.

Those making huge numbers of sales (over 3131 items per month) can get a commission rate of 8.5%, but only a handful of sites ever manage this.

For payment, you can choose to be paid by either cheque or through a bank transfer. You can also choose to be paid in Amazon gift vouchers with a higher value than the monetary payment. Payment is made approximately two months after the qualifying period and is not made until the affiliate is owed at least $100.

*Advantages*

- The massive variety of different products that they offer.
- They are a trusted name and people are willing to spend their money there without question.
- They provide great support to their affiliates in terms of assisting with advertising.
- Good rates of commission if you sell a lot of their products.
- 24-hour cookie system means that you can pick up sales that are completely    unrelated to the product that you are advertising on your affiliate site.

*Disadvantages*

Although there is no doubt that the Amazon Affiliate network is an excellent choice for both old and new affiliate marketers, there are a few small disadvantages:

- The cap on individual items means that selling high value items is often not as profitable as you would hope.
- Payments take a rather long time to process.
- Each Amazon site is country specific, so you will lose sales if referrals do not come from the correct country.

# Affiliate Window

Affiliate Window – unlike Clickbank and Commission Junction – is not a name that many people outside the world of affiliate marketing have heard of, but it is making a big name for itself with leading online merchants and online affiliates. As the United Kingdom's biggest affiliate marketing network, it is often the perfect choice for anyone from the UK, looking to start out in the world of affiliate marketing.

## *About Affiliate Window*

Affiliate Window is a British founded in 2000 by Kevin Brown – a former affiliate marketer himself – and now represents some of the biggest names of British commercial companies, such as Play.com and Boots. Its mission statement states that it wants to go about "enabling partnerships" in a way that is "accountable, transparent and ethical" – three important factors that every prospective affiliate marketer should be looking for.

## *Merchants & Products*

Affiliate Window works with over 1,500 merchants, many of whom are household names within the United Kingdom. These include companies offering holidays, pharmaceutical products, finance products, clothing and online services, such as dating and gambling. All the different merchants are allocated a unique AWIN number, which is between 0 and 100 and reflects how well each of the merchants is performing compared to the other merchants on the site. This index constantly changes, but some of the most successful include:

- British Airways
- Play.com
- Boots
- ASDA
- BHS
- John Lewis
- Opodo
- Match.com
- Ziinga.com
- HMV

## *Payments*

The payments system used by Affiliate Window is much loved, as it is regarded as being extremely easy to use, and has a low threshold for making withdrawals. This threshold is set at just £25 which is half what many other affiliate networks allow – meaning that you can get to your money a lot quicker!

The commissions you earn vary with the different merchants with which you choose to work. Most of them offer rates of around 3-10% of the sale value, which might not sound a lot but can really add up depending on the amount of sales you generate! Other merchants offer a flat rate for every sale, regardless of how much the sale is worth.

### Advantages

- A low threshold for withdrawing your earnings from the site.
- Excellent tools – the site provides you with everything you need to advertise your chosen product, as well as all you need to keep track of your earnings. It also provides a number of handy statistics for you to analyze and use to improve your sales efforts.
- Regular promotions that give away prizes such as holidays and electrical goods.

### Disadvantages

- They charge affiliates a £5 administration fee to join, although this is refunded with your first payment.

## ClickBank

ClickBank is the market leader when it comes to the affiliate marketing of informational products – i.e. products that can be both bought and delivered over the internet. Clickbank is one of the first names that you come across when looking for a suitable affiliate marketing network and is the preferred choice of thousands of affiliates across the world.

### About Clickbank

Clickbank was founded in 1998 and processes 26,000 transactions every single day, Clickbank is open to affiliates from all over the world and currently allows 150 different nationalities to work within the site. It is easy to sign up and even easier to start earning commissions!

### Merchants & Products

Clickbank has over 12,000 different merchants, all with at least one product to sell in a wide range of informational niches, such as dating, online business, online games and gambling. Regardless of your chosen niche, you will be able to find suitable Clickbank products to promote. Commissions are set by the retailer of the product but are generally upwards of the 50% mark – it is high because informational products are usually harder to sell than physical ones, plus cost little to duplicate, so you are well rewarded for your efforts.

There are a number of highly successful products on the site, although most products have a short life span of usually just a few months. As I write the ten most successful Clickbank products are:

- Fast Cash Commissions (Affiliate Marketing Product)
- Mobile Money Machines (Affiliate Marketing Product)
- The Magic of Making Up (Relationships Niche)
- Million Dollar Pips (Forex)
- Penny Stock Egghead (Penny Stocks)
- The Lotto Black Book (Gambling)
- Rocket Spanish/French/Russian/German/Arabic (languages)
- Mobile TV Elite (Mobile TV)
- Truth About Abs (Health)
- The Diet Solution Program (Weight Loss)

### Advantages
- They have a huge range of different informational products for sale.

- All the products are vetted by Clickbank to ensure that they meet strict standards – so the sales you make are less likely to be refunded to the customer.

- Commissions are usually very large, with the highest being around the 75% mark.

- Incredibly detailed tracking and reporting on sales.

### Disadvantages
- Informational products are usually harder to sell than physical products from established retailers.
- There is a lot of competition from other users for the more successful products, meaning you have to work hard to gain a foothold in the market.

## Commission Junction

Another popular affiliate network is Commission Junction, as it is also one of the largest, containing thousands of the world's leading merchants. It is a great choice for those new to the world of affiliate marketing, as it offers great support to affiliates, fast payments plus good reporting.

### *About Commission Junction*

Commission Junction was founded in 1998, but was bought by ValueClick in 2003 for a considerable sum. Due to the fact that it is so well established, it has a long list of clients (merchants), most of whom are household names with established reputations – which should increase your affiliate sales because of the trust these brands have.

Although the main element of Commission Junction is affiliate services, it has recently also branched out into the world of media and tracking, which is one of the reasons that merchants choose Commission Junction over other companies – it provides a fully comprehensive service. Out of the top 500 retailers that use affiliate marketing, over 60% use Commission Junction for this service.

### *Merchants & Products*

A huge number of different types of products are available at Commission Junction literally covering thousands of different niches. Unlike some other affiliate sites, however, all the companies advertising through Commission Junction are well-established names and the quality of the products is extremely high.

Instead of looking at the best affiliate programs to join, it is easier to look at the best types instead, as there are so many individual programs. Some of the most profitable niches are:

- Travel
- Banking
- Gambling
- Web hosting
- Software

All the above niches can earn you commissions of nearly $100 or more per sale, meaning that they are at the very top level when it comes to profitability. Pay particular attention to the "travel" niche, as this can be a really big earner – especially if a whole tour group books through your affiliate site!

*Payments*

When it comes to the specific commission earned per sale, again the amount differs with each merchant that you promote. Because the products are from well-known brands, they are generally easier to sell, but the downside is that the easier they are to sell, the more competitive the niche.

If you want to withdraw your money from the site, the threshold is set differently for cheque and direct deposit withdrawals. For the former the amount is $100, and for the latter the amount is $50. One good point, however, is that the money comes straight from Commission Junction and not from the advertisers, which means that you can combine lots of commissions together to reach the threshold amount.

*Advantages*
- It offers a massive range of different products and advertisers.
- There are a massive number of different advertising methods to use for free for every single affiliate program.
- The tracking system is very good, so you are paid your commissions on time and accurately.
- Commission comes straight from Commission Junction and not from the advertisers themselves.

*Disadvantages*
- The payment threshold for cheque payments is quite high.
- Commission is only protected for six months – if the threshold has not been reached by this time then it is deleted.
- Some merchants have to approve offers before a sale is made, which means that the merchant can decline some affiliates.

## TradeDoubler

TradeDoubler is an affiliate marketing network with a large number of advertisers, although it is not as well-known as some of the other networks such as Commission Junction. It offers a number of additional services to clients, such as online marketing campaigns and search management, meaning that it attracts a number of large clients reaching across most of Europe.

### About TradeDoubler

TradeDoubler was founded in Sweden in 1999 and over the years has developed into, among other things, one of Europe's biggest affiliate marketing networks. It now employs 561 people and has offices in 18 different countries, as well as generating 32 billion impressions (visible adverts) every month across the internet, leading to 14 million leads per month. These massive figures go to show that it is a network that everyone in the world of affiliate marketing needs to explore.

### Merchants & Products

TradeDoubler has many different merchants on the site, with the figure currently somewhere around the 2,000 mark. They also have 140,000 advertisers, all promoting at least one of the merchants on offer. These merchants cover a broad spectrum of different industries, from travel right the way through to online dating. It is entirely up to the advertiser what they choose to promote.

The large businesses that TradeDoubler works with across Europe include:

- Lastminute.com
- Tesco
- Jessops
- Expedia
- BT
- Singapore Airlines
- Apple Store
- The Body Shop
- Mothercare
- Thomas Cook

### Payments

All payments are delivered to you straight from TradeDoubler, so there is never any need to wait around for different merchants to send a cheque or make a bank transfer. This also means that you get one large sum instead of lots of smaller ones into your bank account – something that many people find very appealing.

Payments are scheduled each month, with a low threshold. This is particularly good for those looking to spend only a small amount of time on their affiliate marketing efforts, as the amounts that they earn are smaller.

The commission earned from a specific advertiser is set by the advertisers themselves, and not by TradeDoubler. This means that commissions can vary widely from one company to another, so you must choose carefully which companies to promote.

### Advantages

- A very large number of different advertisers to choose from.

- Most advertisers are well-established brands, meaning that their products are easier to sell to the public.

- Monthly payments of commission, regardless of the amount earned.

- Great customer support via email, phone and instant messenger.

### Disadvantages

- High competition from other affiliates when advertising the different merchants.
- A relatively small amount of advertising material when compared to other sites, although in recent times this is improving.

# E-Junkie

If you have an affiliate website, the chances are that you need various buttons and other tools in order to facilitate both a professional appearance and a simple sales process – something that E-Junkie specializes in. It also provides an affiliate program where you can link up with some large companies and promote their products – all completely for free! E-Junkie has a mixture of informational and physical products for you to promote, so everyone can find what they are looking for here!

### About E-Junkie

E-Junkie was founded in 2004 in Tucson, Arizona and was originally created as a vehicle to help the founder sell his software online. Since then it has expanded into a major affiliate marketing company offering products from thousands of different advertisers, as well as plenty of other services for both advertisers and affiliates. Although the website is slightly unprofessional when compared to other affiliate marketing companies, it is still a company that you can trust implicitly.

### Merchants & Products

E-Junkie works with a large number of different merchants and therefore gives you the opportunity to promote nearly 5,000 different products on your site. Included within this mix of products are those that can be sold 100% online (informational products) and those that are physical products, such as health remedies. All the products have a simple page of information, telling you how much the product costs, details of the product and, most importantly for affiliates, information about how to enrol in the affiliate program. It is impossible to tell which of the products on E-Junkie are the most successful, but below are some of those offering the best commission and the best chances of making a sale:

- The "No Sweat Parenting" series of audio recordings
- Mass Twitter Account Creator
- Products from fashion group "Fyberspates"
- The "Make Money Blogging" course
- TOP ROD Xtra Capsules
- Marketing Plan Template Kit
- Jump Start Your Credit
- How to Make Money Online for Newbies
- Easy Guide to Google Plus
- The "Teaching Money Skills" Workbook

### Payments

All the different affiliate programs set their own commission structures for the products that they sell, which means that you have to look through a number of different products to determine which one in your niche offers the best rates.

When it comes to receiving payment for your sales, the combined commission from all of your efforts is paid directly from E-Junkie and not from the individual merchants. The only withdrawal option is PayPal so you must ensure that you have an active Paypal account.. Payments are made at the end of each month, regardless of how much commission you have earned.

### Advantages

- They offer a huge range of products to promote.
- Payments are made monthly.
- The service is completely free to use.

- All payments come from E-Junkie in one sum, making your affiliate accounts easier to manage.

### Disadvantages

- The site looks out-dated and could do with some revitalization.
- Some of the products are not of the highest quality, which means that they are tough to sell to consumers.

# LinkShare

LinkShare is not one of the largest names in the world of affiliate marketing, but the clients that the company works with certainly are! Many predict that Linkshare, with its diverse portfolio and a commitment to customer service, will soon be a leader within the industry. It offers a huge array of tools and options for all publishers, which makes it a great choice for new affiliate marketers looking for some guidance in the world of online marketing.

### About LinkShare

LinkShare is a company owned by Rakuten Inc. and is a truly international organization, with offices in New York, London, Tokyo, San Francisco, Tampa and Chicago, as well as partners from all corners of the globe. It was founded in 1996 and in the last 16 years has built up a client base including many Fortune 500 companies, such as American Express and Avon. As well as affiliate marketing, it also offers services in Search Engine Marketing and lead generation, meaning that merchants see it as a "one stop shop" for all their online marketing needs.

### Merchants & Products

LinkShare has partnerships with over 1,000 major companies throughout the world, which means that the affiliate partnerships that they offer can both be trusted and be profitable – after all, selling items from already established companies is the easiest form of affiliate marketing. The commission rates are set by the individual advertisers, so they vary, but generally the commission is around the 5% mark.

Some of the best companies to work with on the LinkShare website are:

- American Express
- Macy's
- Avon
- 1-800 Flowers.com

- AT&T
- Apple iTunes
- Lego
- Office Depot
- Toshiba
- Walmart

## *Payments*

The different merchants on the site set their own commission rates for their own programs, meaning that you have to choose wisely when deciding which ones you will promote. The payment threshold is incredibly low – at just $1 – but you do have the option of changing this so that you receive cheques only when you reach a reasonable figure. All payments come through LinkShare directly, meaning that you do not have to collate the money earned from every affiliate program separately. Payment is in the form of a cheque or direct deposit – affiliates from outside the US have to set up an international direct deposit account.

## *Advantages*

- They are a fast-growing company.
- They work with a number of extremely large companies, so the products are easy to sell.
- The payment threshold is very low.
- Very good reporting features.

## *Disadvantages*

- They do not offer a great selection of payment options and those outside the US need to work out how to set up international bank transfers.

## Google Affiliate Network Program

Google seems to have its hand in nearly every aspect of the internet, and the world of affiliate marketing is no exception. With its massive scope and ability to place merchants' adverts in all the right places, it is the company of choice for the vast majority of the world's biggest online retailers. This means that it is a great company to sign up with, whether you are a new or experienced affiliate marketer, as it can guarantee access to the best companies and the best forms of online advertising. It must be noted that Google Affiliate

Network is not the same as the Google AdWords scheme; AdWords works on a pay-per-click basis, while the Affiliate scheme rewards affiliates in a cost-per-action way.

### About the Google Affiliate Network Program

Google was started by Larry Page and Sergey Brin in 1998 and since then has gone on to become the world's number one search engine and arguably the most important brand online. Google has a huge number of different strings to its bow, and the Google Affiliate Network is just one of them. The Affiliate Network was set up in 2007, when Google purchased DoubleClick for $3.1billion, thereby taking on all their clients in the process. It is now one of the biggest affiliate networks in the world.

### Merchants & Products

Due to the power that Google has in the online world, it has been able to attract many of the world's top companies to its Affiliate Network, meaning that you can benefit from the great products that are offered for you to promote. As with the majority of the larger affiliate marketing networks, the commission is set by the individual advertisers and you can expect to receive commissions of around 5% in most cases.

Some of the best of the large companies working within the Google Affiliate Network's framework are:

- Barneys
- K-Mart
- Verizon
- Red Envelope
- Nike
- Target
- Fossil
- Capital One
- Netflix
- United

### Payments

Google pays directly on behalf of the companies that it partners with, and payment is made into your Google AdSense account (this is free to set up). You can choose to receive your payments in one of over 40 different currencies, but money cannot be withdrawn until the balance of your AdSense account reaches $50 or its equivalent.

### *Advantages*

- Google is a company you can trust, with a massive annual turnover.
- Google work with some of the world's best-known companies, so promoting their products is very easy.
- Reporting on your performance is of the highest level, using Google's specialist software.

### *Disadvantages*

- There is strong competition for some of the more profitable merchant offers.

## ShareASale

ShareASale is not one of the biggest players in the world of affiliate marketing, but despite this it has earned the reputation of offering great products and fantastic customer service to all its affiliates – perhaps the two most important factors that any affiliate network can offer. ShareASale is expected to keep on growing in the future as affiliate marketing is adopted by more and more companies around the world. It is a great company for newcomers to the industry to ally themselves with, as it guides you through the whole affiliate marketing process.

### *About ShareASale*

ShareASale is an American company, founded in April 2000 by Brian Littleton and currently based in Chicago, Illinois. It has won a number of different awards over the past few years, such as the "Best Affiliate Network" award and the "Best Affiliate Program" award, thereby underlining its credentials within the industry. It allows you to make your own decisions about which merchants to promote and how you will promote them (within ShareASale's rules and regulations), and also ensures that the interface of the site is intuitive, meaning that you can spend less time there and more time building your profitable sites instead!

### *Merchants & Products*

ShareASale currently offers all affiliates the choice of over 2,500 different merchants, all of who are engaged in different areas of business. This means that any affiliate will be able to find a company to work with that suits their own requirements and expertise – as well as one that meets their financial expectations! Some of the major areas within which ShareASale merchants work are finance, media, health, technology and gambling, although there are many others as well. Some of the best performing companies to work with on ShareASale are:

- Office Playground
- XSitePro.com
- Raven Internet Marketing Tools
- Diet Direct
- Xylitol
- Keyword Competitor
- LicensePlates.tv
- Busted Tees
- Hostel World
- Unique Article Wizard

### *Payments*

Since there are so many different companies advertising with ShareASale, it would be impossible to apply a standard commission rate across the board. For this reason, all the different advertisers are able to set their own commission rates, meaning that you have to do some research to find out which are the most profitable. Payment occurs on the 20th of each month and is paid directly by ShareASale. You are only paid once your account has reached $50 – amounts less than this are rolled over to the next month.

You can also make extra money directly from ShareASale by referring friends to the site and getting them to sign up as an affiliate. For every person that you get to sign up, you receive $1 but, more importantly, you also receive 5% of their future earnings on the site – which can make you a lot of money if your referrals turn out to be successful affiliates.

### *Advantages*

ShareASale is a great website for all affiliate marketers and therefore we could produce a massive list of the advantages that it has! We have limited ourselves to only the important points below.

- They have a massive portfolio of different merchants.
- All payments are made directly from ShareASale, meaning that you do not have to keep track of earnings from multiple merchants yourself.
- They provide plenty of advertising resources, such as banners and widgets.
- Their site is easy to use.

### Disadvantages

It would be dishonest to claim that there are no bad points to this site. The couple of negatives that we found are listed below.

- The site is slightly dated and will not inspire confidence in some of the bigger merchants.
- Some of the merchants have products that would be very difficult to sell.

# Plimus

Companies like Commission Junction and Google Affiliates are very much at the top of the affiliate marketing tree, but just under them are a number of other great companies, led by Plimus. When it comes to selling purely digital products, it is rivalled only by Clickbank and is narrowing the gap between them on a monthly basis. Its catchphrase of "Sell More" is simple, but it acts as a great reminder what affiliate marketing is all about.

### About Plimus

Plimus was founded in 2001 and is based in the heart of the dot com boom territory – Silicon Valley. Plimus has survived the test of time and has consistently improved its services over the last 10 years. The sole focus of Plimus is on digital products – products that can be sold and received over the internet – and for this reason it represents an easy way to get into affiliate marketing, as you don't have to be concerned with the merchant delivering items or with the items being faulty or otherwise damaged.

### Merchants & Products

Since the products sold on Plimus are all informational, they are delivered to buyers either through email or through a download link. These informational products can come in a number of different guises, such as ebooks, videos, audio files and reports and do not usually have a massive price tag on them. To make up for the small sales prices, the commission is usually very high and it is not unusual to find products with commissions of over 50%. There are over 5,000 different merchants affiliated with Plimus selling in a variety of niches, including:

- Software
- Online games
- Downloadable games
- Videos
- Music
- Photographs
- Subscriptions to online services

### *Payment*

Plimus offers a wide choice of different payment methods to all of its affiliate members, including bank transfer, e-cheque, wire transfer and PayPal. Affiliates usually receive their payments on the 15$^{th}$ day of the month through their preferred payment method, although you must have $35 in your Plimus account in order to qualify for a payout. If you do not have $35 in earnings, the amount is carried over to the next month. You must be aware that buyers can generally receive refunds on items for 6 months after they purchase the item; if this happens, Plimus automatically takes the commission earned back out of your account.

### *Advantages*

- It has an absolutely massive number of different merchants, providing a huge amount of choice.
- The interface is simple and allows you to see the details of every product without any hassle.
- The tracking systems used are extremely effective and allow you to keep a constant check on your conversions and commissions.

### *Disadvantages*

- Informational products are harder to sell than products sold by established companies, such as those found on LinkShare.
- Refunds can vastly reduce commission earned.

# LinkConnector

LinkConnector is an incredibly well-trusted affiliate marketing brand and the network of choice for many new affiliates in this highly lucrative industry, as well as being long-standing favourite for some of the longer serving affiliate marketers. Its catchphrase of "redefining affiliate marketing one technology at a time" is extremely apt, as the company is well known for the innovative approach that it brings to all its merchants and affiliates, through both great customer service and incredibly effective new concepts.

### *About LinkConnector*

LinkConnector is an American company with offices based in North Carolina, Colorado, Florida and Maryland. It has been trading for a number of years and therefore is certainly not the new kid on the block, meaning that it has heaps of experience to fall back on, as well as a fantastic range of clients. Many of the technologies that are available to affiliates on LinkConnector are unique and highly innovative which allow you both to generate revenue more effectively and to monitor conversions and traffic.

### *Merchants & Products*

There are hundreds of different merchants that an affiliate can choose to work with, ranging from those offering online services to those offering actual physical products. Each affiliate is able to pick and choose the merchants that they want to work with, but it is the merchant who has the final say over whether they accept the affiliate's application. Most of the merchants offer cookies that stay live for around 30 days and they also provide different promotions for you to use to help increase the sales that you make. LinkConnector provides a list of their current top 10 merchants which, at time of going to press, are:

- Air Trekkers
- Luxor Linens
- Morris 4x4 Center
- Toktumi
- It's Just Lunch
- Black Forest Décor
- TV Ears
- Writers' Store
- Richard Petty Driving Experience
- Calphalon

*Payments*

There is absolutely no cost to joining up with LinkConnector and becoming an affiliate. There are currently only two ways that you can receive any money earned, however, via cheque and through PayPal. They are working on a system to allow direct deposit payment as well, which will make things a lot more flexible. Any earned commission is paid directly by LinkConnector to affiliates on the 20th of each month, providing they have reached a balance of $100 in their account. If this is not the case, the balance rolls over to the following month.

*Advantages*

- It is completely free to join.
- Many of the merchants offer very high commission rates.
- They use something called Naked Link Technology, which means that affiliate links are not long and off-putting to the customer.
- They have a vast array of reporting tools, such as merchant performance and affiliate tracking tools.

*Disadvantages*

- The $100 threshold for payment is quite high.
- There are not many methods you can use to withdraw your earnings.

# Avangate

Avangate is more than just an affiliate program – it also provides e-commerce solutions and marketing for companies throughout the world. As a result it attracts some of the largest companies in the software industry – Avangate is a site specifically aimed at software sales, which means that selling the products there is quite an easy task, even for those new to the affiliate marketing scene. It offers everything that an affiliate could want from an affiliate network, so you should definitely take a look at Avangate if software is your main area of expertise and interest.

*About Avangate*

Avangate was founded in 2006 and, unlike most of the top affiliate marketing companies, is not headquartered in the USA. Its base is in Amsterdam and it also has offices in Bucharest and Canada, such is its global reach. As previously mentioned, Avangate concentrates solely on software. The company is recognized and certified by a number of large organizations, such as the PCI Security Standards Council, VeriSign and the Better Business Bureau, showing just how trustworthy it is.

### Merchants & Products

Avangate has some of the biggest names in the software industry as clients. This is great for you, as software is known to have one of the highest profit margins in the industry and therefore you can make large amounts of sales with a minimal effort! The site also has over 11,000 different products for you to market, providing something to suit absolutely everyone, regardless of their area of expertise. When it comes to the top companies working with Avangate, the following are some of the most respected and easiest to promote:

- DVDFab
- Kaspersky
- Bitdefender
- IsoBuster
- Fusion Charts
- HHD Software
- Lavasoft
- Movavi
- Axigen
- IObit

### Payments

Avangate offers its affiliates a wide range of different payment options. These include wire transfer, PayPal, cheque and even their own prepaid Mastercard! Payment can be up to twice every month, although the minimum amount for cashing out is €100, which is quite high compared to the industry as a whole. Commissions on sales can also be high, however, with some merchants offering up to 75% for every product sold.

### Advantages

- A huge number of different merchants to work with.
- High commissions on many different types of software.
- Payments available twice each month.
- Wide variety of payment methods.

- The company is trusted by a number of regulatory bodies and watchdogs.

### Disadvantages

- Affiliates need to have €100 in their account before they are allowed to make a withdrawal.

## Virgin Games

Virgin Games is of course part of Richard Branson's Virgin Group. The Virgin brand is held in high regard all around the world so is an easy brand to promote. Virgin Games comprises Virgin Bingo, Virgin Casino & Virgin Poker. Although Virgin is an extremely well-known brand, Virgin Games is underexposed especially when compared to market leaders such as Jackpotjoy, Ladbrokes and William Hill.

### About Virgin Games

Virgin Games was formed in 2004 and at first only consisted of casino and poker platforms, although bingo was added in 2005. In real terms Virgin Games is amongst the smaller gambling brands although many affiliates, myself included, rate the actual affiliate support the best there is.

### Virgin Games Products

Virgin Games is not tied to one particular games provider so the range of games you find at Virgin Games is second to none. Virgin Games simply cherry-picks the best games from the best providers, which means that the games lobbies are amongst the best you, find online. Virgin Games is also renowned for its innovative promotions, with a new promotion launched each week. Another great feature of Virgin Games is their cash back scheme, which offers players a percentage of their losses back in the form of Vpoints, which are earned from every pound spent.

### Virgin Games Payments

Virgin Games pay affiliates either through online wallets such as Neteller or by cheque or bank transfer. Affiliates are paid on or before the 10th of the month like clockwork. The threshold for payment release is £50.

### Advantages

- First Class Affiliate Support
- Great range of games, so easy to promote

- The brand has great trust and respect worldwide
- No worries about late payments
- 50% commission for new affiliates for 3 months

### Disadvantages
- Limited media exposure compared to leading gambling brands

# Market Ace

Most affiliates sign up to Market Ace so that they can promote Jackpotjoy. Market Ace has grown into a mini-network in recent years and now offers affiliates several well-known gambling programs such as:

- JackpotJoy
- Caesars Bingo
- Caesars Casino
- The Sun Bingo
- Fabulous Bingo
- Heart Games

Market Ace offers affiliates either revenue share or CPA or even in some cases hybrid deals comprising of both. The threshold for cash out is just £25 with commission starting at 30% and CPA starting at £25 per sign-up.

### About Market Ace

Market Ace has become one of the leading gambling affiliate programs and is especially popular with online bingo affiliates. Marketing materials in the form of banners, landing pages and even free play games are classed by many affiliates as the very best in the industry. Market Ace also has a great range of promotional material in foreign languages, which gives affiliates the option of cashing in on lucrative unexposed markets.

### Market Ace Products

As Market Ace offer affiliates several well-known brands, affiliates are spoiled for choice. Everybody in the UK must by now have heard of Jackpotjoy due to the heavily promoted TV commercials featuring Barbara Windsor. The recent addition of Caesars Casino with perhaps other casino operators set to follow makes Market Ace a must for any gambling affiliate.

## *Market Ace Payments*

Payments to affiliates are made on or before the 15<sup>th</sup> of the following month. Payments are made to the well-known online wallets, by cheque or even bank transfer.

## *Advantages*

- Saturated TV Promotion Increases Conversions
- Low payment threshold of just £25
- Choice of several different affiliate programs
- CPA, revenue share or even hybrid deals available

## *Disadvantages*

- None!

# Chapter 20 – Affiliate Software Tools

Everybody, no matter what their profession is, needs tools to carry out their daily work. You too, working as an online affiliate, need tools in the form of software applications. For example, your main tool for creating content is a word processor equipped with a spell checker. Ideally you will have Microsoft Word or the excellent free clone Open Office. Other tools you require include keyword tools, so that you can ensure that the articles you create will generate traffic from in-demand search phrases. Webpage analysis tools, so that you can check how search engines see the quality of your pages. Rank checking tools so that you can quickly check where your pages rank in popular search engines. The good news is that you can fill your virtual toolbox for free!

## Google Keyword Tool

Everyone in the business of SEO will tell you the same golden rule – if you want to succeed online, you absolutely must ensure that you select the correct keywords from the very start. After all, keywords are going to be the absolute lifeblood of the whole campaign – the primary way that you get people to come to your site and, you hope, spend their money on the products or services that you offer.

Before we go any further, it is probably prudent to spend a few minutes going over exactly what a "keyword" is, just in case you are not aware of the term. To put it simply, a keyword is the word or phrase that someone types into a search engine when they are looking for something. When they type in this word or phrase, they are presented with a list of all the sites that Google – or any other search engine – deems to be the most relevant to the query. This can amount to millions of different sites, but regardless of how many results there are, one thing remains the same; getting onto the first page of results is the only way to ensure that you get traffic from that keyword. It is estimated that 80% of people never go further than the first page of results, so not being there means that you are already missing out on 80% of your potential traffic.

Now that we have gone over the basics of what a keyword actually is, we should get back to the matter at hand – how to research them using the free Google Keyword Tool. There are a number of different things that need to be covered in this chapter regarding this, but the first thing that we will look at is why you should use this tool – after all, there are many others out there.

There are two main reasons why the Google Keyword Tool is one of the best in the business for those starting out in the world of keyword research. The first reason is simple and boils down to pure economics – the Google Keyword Tool is completely free, whereas the use of other keyword tools, such as Market Samurai, usually requires a fee. For those who have not yet made any money online, spending non-existent cash on services that they can actually do for free seems to be a waste of money.

The other reason to use the Google Keyword Tool revolves around the fact that it is made by Google, and of course Google will in most cases become your biggest traffic source. When you think about it, there is no company better placed to tell you the specifics of the keywords that are found on Google than Google themselves! After all, Google wants you to find out which keywords are best for your business, so that they can create a stronger and more useful community for everyone searching online through their search engine.

Now that you have some background on why to use this service from Google, let's dive in and start talking about how you can use the Google Keyword Tool to the best of its abilities. You can use this superb tool for free by simply going to the Google Tools page (http://www.googlekeywordtool.com/) and clicking the Google Keyword Tool link. You can also access this tool by simply searching for "Google External Keyword Tool" using Google or any other search engine. Once you have done this, you are then faced with a screen looking like this:

# Chapter 20 – Affiliate Software Tools

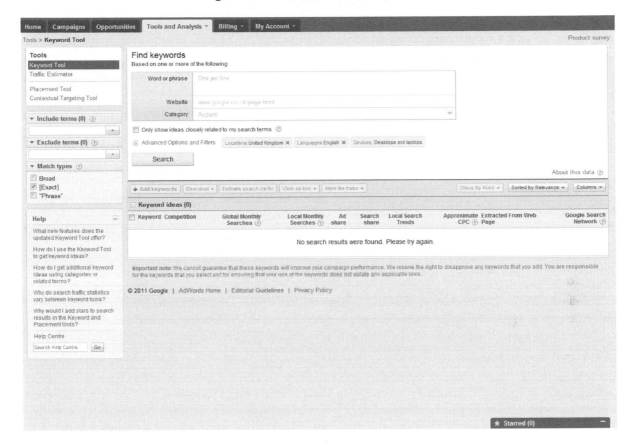

Now this screen might look a little scary at first, as it is covered with different sections that all seem a little confusing. There are only two areas that you need to be concerned with at the moment, however: the areas called "word or phrase" and "match types", which you find on the left hand side column.

"Match types" is where you can specify what type of result you want displayed: 99% of the time it should be left on "exact". This is because leaving it on "exact" ensures that you only see the search volumes for the exact phrase shown and not for related phrases as well, which makes for a much more accurate representation when conducting your research.

The other area you need at present is the box entitled "word or phrase" as this is the area into which you type your initial phrase. One thing that should be mentioned is that you should try to have a few different basic words or phrases noted down before you start, just to provide you with a good starting point. So, let's go ahead and type in your first phrase –

leaving the "match types" box selected to "exact". In the examples from here on, I will research keywords for a website that teaches people to speak French, but obviously you should look for keywords pertaining to your own site!

Okay, so I am going to type in "learn French" as my first keyword to research. Let's see what comes up (I've cropped into the screenshot so that you can see the results clearly, but I've made no changes to the default settings that you can't see)...

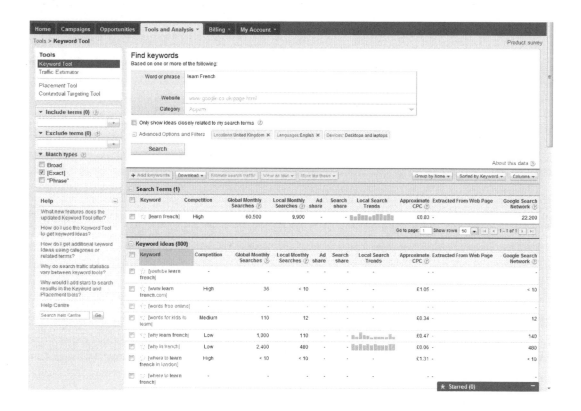

I suggest that to get an understanding of how this tool functions, you turn on your computer, load the tool and simply enter a few phrases. As you can see, when you type in our original word or phrase, you get results for more than just that one word or phrase. For the moment however, we shall concentrate on the results we have been given for "learn French", which appear at the top of the list. Also note that we can select a desired location and language, although for now we will just leave the tool on its default settings, which are United States and English.

The columns that you will be interested in are:

- Competition
- Global Monthly Searches
- Local Monthly Searches

These three columns tell you all that you need to know about your keyword, so let's start with the competition column. This basically tells you how many other sites out there are also competing for this keyword. Obviously high competition means that there are many sites looking to rank highly, while low competition means that it should be reasonably easy for you to climb into the higher reaches of Google's rankings on this term. In my case the competition reads "High", which means that I should probably steer clear of using that keyword for my site.

The next column is "Global Monthly Searches" which, as the name suggests, provides you with a figure of how many people search for that keyword every month. This is important, as optimizing for a keyword with only 100 searches a month is ultimately going to be pointless, as it will make you no money. A keyword with 100,000,000 searches per month, however, is probably equally pointless because – even if it says competition is low – you are likely to be faced with a huge number of other sites competing against you, many of whom will be established names in the industry. This might see strange and contradictory, but competition is worked out in conjunction with the number of searches, so low competition on a high number of searches still means that there is a lot of competition.

"Local Monthly Searches" only applies to you if you run a website that targets local people, such as a store or a service. If you run a 100% online business then you do not need to worry about this. All it does is tell you the number of people in your state/country who search for that term every month.

Therefore, what we can glean from this initial search is that the phrase "learn French" is going to be far too competitive, especially for a new website. This is not a problem, however, as this is only the beginning of our keyword research. Underneath you see a huge number of other suggestions that are related to the original search term. Now you just need to work your way down this list and pick out keywords that you like, all the while trying to pick ones with low competition and a reasonable number of searches per month. Once you have done this, you should have a few good ideas for potential key phrases to target.

This isn't the end of the task, however; in fact, this is only the beginning! As I mentioned at the beginning of the chapter, keyword research is the most important part of any SEO strategy, so you should be prepared to spend rather a long time on it. After you have gone through the process once, you should start with another word, typing it in and then going down all the suggestions that come up. Really you want to try to gather a list of a few hundred different possible keywords to target, exporting your results to a spreadsheet, and detailing the competition and searches for future reference.

It is really quite simple to carry out keyword research using the Google Keyword Tool, but it takes patience and time to complete! You will be more than happy that you took the time to do it properly, however, when the keywords that you picked drive huge amounts of traffic to your site.

## Rank Tracker

Rank Tracker is a powerful tool used by many SEO professionals throughout the world, as well as some of the biggest brand names in business, such as Microsoft, Disney and Audi. I am sorry to say that this tool is not free although there is I believe a free limited-use version available to download. As a new online affiliate you should look to purchase this tool as soon as you start to generate income.

Although Rank Tracker has a number of different features, without doubt the most often used is the ability to find quickly the position of your target key phrases in numerous search engine results. As you develop your SEO skills, you will find that the process of searching through pages and pages of results just to find your site can become a real chore – and a real time-wasting exercise – so this application will be worth its weight in gold.

Before we go into detail about how to use the rank-checking tool, let's just take a quick look at what it does and why this is important for your online business. As we know already, keywords are the lifeblood of any SEO campaign, so tracking them is absolutely vital. After all, if you do not know how your keywords are performing, you will not be able to prioritize which ones to work on! There is nothing worse than neglecting a keyword because you assume it is doing well, only to find out that it isn't.

Not only can you see your own results, but you can also see the SEO results for all your competitors, thereby gaining some absolutely vital information that you can use to your advantage. The information is not only current, but can also be looked at historically, so you can see how well you and your competitors are progressing.

The rank-tracking aspect of this application won't actually help you to increase your SERP rankings directly, but the information that it gives ensures that you always stay on top of the SEO on your site. Basically, it can be seen as a very handy administrative aid that takes the work away from you and allows you to spend more time on what you really want to be doing – making money! So, let's get on with finding out how to use this aspect of the Rank Tracker software.

## Downloading and Setting Up an Account

There are two different versions of Rank Tracker – the free version and the paid version. Both need to be downloaded to your computer, which takes just a few minutes. Go to http://www.link-assistant.com/rank-tracker/ and click on the "Download FREE" or "Order now" button. Depending on which option you choose, you are taken to another screen. Fill in your details and then download the product – it's as easy as that!

Once you have downloaded Rank Tracker, simply follow the instructions on the screen to install the software onto your computer. It is completely safe and won't harm your computer in any way.

## Getting Started on Monitoring Keywords

The first thing that you have to do is to create a new project for your website. If you want the whole site monitored, enter the URL of the homepage, but if you want to monitor a single page, fill in the exact URL of that page.

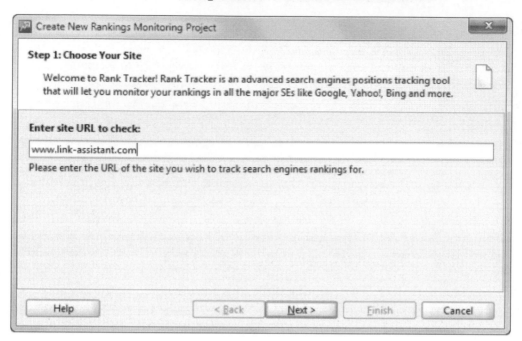

Once you have done this first step, you are then asked to choose the search engines that you want to monitor. Although there are a very wide variety of different search engines available for selection, you should ensure that you tick the big three – Google, Yahoo! and Bing. You should also make sure that you select the regional versions of these should your business be based in a specific geographical location, such as Google.co.uk for users in the United Kingdom.

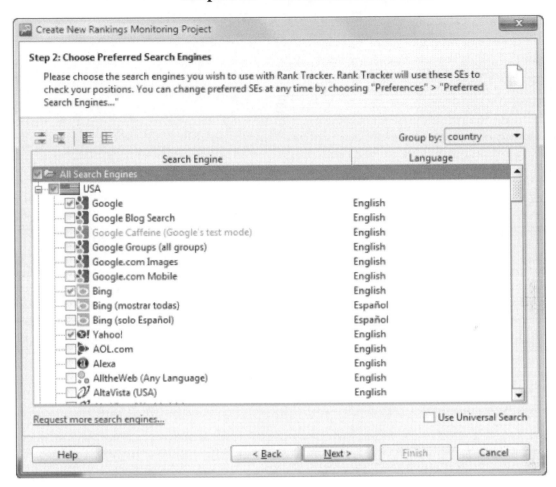

Now that you have chosen your search engines and specified the site to monitor, you can get down to the business end of proceedings and enter the keywords that you want to monitor into the next box. Every time you enter a keyword or phrase, hit "enter" so that the next is written on a new line. There is no limit to the number of keywords that you include in this list, so put in as many as you want!

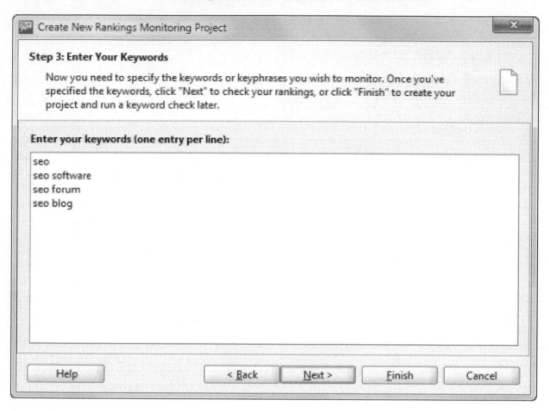

After this, the Rank Tracker software goes through a process whereby it finds the rankings for all the keywords that you have entered in relation to your site. This might take some time but you have to remember that creating this data takes an enormous amount of work! The fewer keywords and the fewer search engines you specify, the less time the process takes. When it finishes, however, the first step of your project is complete.

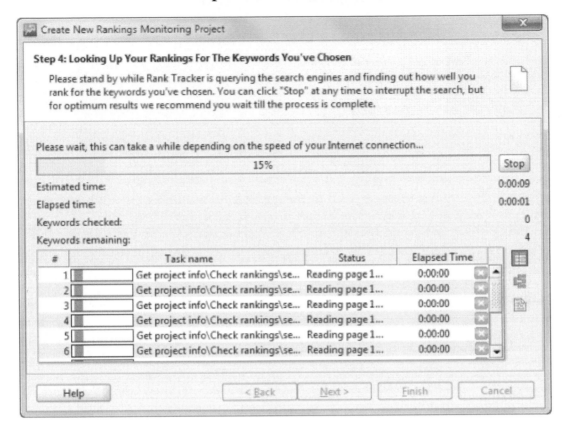

## Analyzing the Results

When you have created a project, you are presented with a screen that has two different tabs on it – "Keywords" and "Reports". Although there is a host of other features that you can also use, these two sections are the ones that we are going to focus on, as they are extremely important. So first off, let's get straight to the core of the whole process and look at the keywords tab.

## Keywords Tab

When you click on the keywords tab, you see a page that looks something like this:

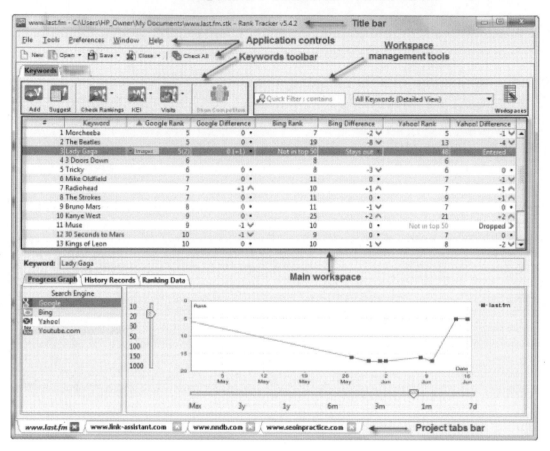

As you can see, there is a main workspace that shows you all the pertinent results for each of your keywords, and also a workspace underneath that brings up a detailed analysis of any specific keyword that you have selected.

The main workspace is very simple to understand, but let's just take a quick look over it. As you can see, it is ordered by default to display the most successful keywords at the top and then to work down. By most successful, I mean the keywords that come highest in Google's rankings, as this is the most important search engine for the majority of people.

Scrolling across, you see details of where the keyword currently ranks on Google and then the amount of movement that it has gone through since the last check was made. This is then repeated for the other search engines that you have used. A little hint would be to make sure that Google, Bing and Yahoo! are the first ones selected, as these are the only ones that you really care about – all the others fall into place as you optimize for these three.

The box underneath the main workspace shows you more details about a specific keyword on a specific search engine. Simply click on the keyword in the main workspace and the details for it are displayed in the bottom workspace. Then click on the relevant search engine in the box to the right to bring up the details.

There are three different tabs on this second workstation:

- **Progress Graph** – This is a simple graph that allows you to visualize just how well that keyword is doing on a search engine over a period of time. In an ideal world this always continues on an upward trend, but don't be downhearted if it dips sometimes – Google works in mysterious ways and it rights itself after a while!
- **History Records** – This tab shows you data relating to the keyword and the search engine, but in a table format instead of in a graph like the progress graph. It also shows you the URL that it found on the search, as this can change between different pages of your site occasionally.
- **Ranking Data** – This displays detailed statistics of a specific keyword across all the different search engines.

## *Report Tab*

The report tab is important but is a lot simpler to understand and use than the keywords tab, due to the fact that it has only one purpose – to generate reports. This comes in three different forms, which are:

- Saving a report to a pdf or html file;
- Emailing a report or uploading it remotely;
- Regenerating a report to get fresh data.

All these are quite self-explanatory, so there is no need to go into them in any more depth.

I suggest you set up Rank Checker to auto update each and every day so that you have a detailed history of each key phrase progress.

## Traffic Travis

There are a number of different features offered by Traffic Travis, all of which will be invaluable to you in your efforts to take your SEO activities to the next level. Perhaps the most important is the on-page SEO analysis that the software performs – an area that many people often neglect in favour of off-site SEO. This is risky as the search engines are placing more and more emphasis on the on-site aspect, so Traffic Travis can help you get this right. In a nutshell, this part of the software analyzes your website and lets you know where you are strong and where you are weak through the use of a star rating system. It also gives you information on how you can improve your on-site SEO quickly.

Another great feature of this software is the level of competition research that it can deliver. As the old adage says, you should "know thy enemy" and this is very true in the world of SEO. Using the competition research option, you can see what keywords are worth pursuing and which ones competitors have already dominated. It will come back with a star rating for a specific keyword in a matter of seconds to show how easy it is to optimize for – something that would take hours to do manually.

Researching the competition does not just stop there, however, as there are a few other tricks up this piece of software's sleeve – most notably the ability to seek out the different backlinks that competition websites have going to their page. This is important because once you know this, you can get links from exactly the same place, therefore increasing your online presence. It is also possible to spy on the keywords that your competitors use for their PPC campaigns. Even if you don't plan on running one yourself, looking for campaigns on one keyword that have run for a long time shows you some great keywords for optimizing your SEO.

Other than the features mentioned, there is also a whole bunch of other more standard features that this piece of software has, such as the ability to track your rankings within search engines and create lists of keywords to analyze and possibly use. Basically, this piece of software has everything from the basics to the advanced SEO tools that you will need as you try to take your online business to the next level.

The best thing about Traffic Travis is that it is completely free to use – simply visit their website at www.traffictravis.com and enter your name and email address. You are then able to download this software for no charge whatsoever! There is also a paid version, although in my opinion purchasing the Rank Checker software described in the previous section is a much better option.

## Majestic SEO

Majestic SEO has a massive number of different features, the availability of which are dictated by the subscription package that you choose. All the features in some way or another contribute towards a more effective SEO strategy for your site.

Although there are a number of different features included within this package, the flagship one seems to be the Site Explorer feature, which is an application that allows you to gather detailed information pertaining to a specific URL. Only those with Gold, Silver or Platinum memberships can use it to its full extent. When used to its full extent, members are able to generate reports on other sites apart from their own, therefore enabling them to gather important information about their competition.

Another excellent feature of this application is the Backlink History tool, which can be used to find out the number of backlinks going to a specific site, or your own website. Free users can use this tool but only to find information on one specific URL, whereas paying registered users are able to compare up to five different domains at the same time, thereby benefiting from a great way to analyze the competition across the board. It is also possible to use the Bulk Backlink Checker, which quickly returns a count of the backlinks for a number of sites in a record amount of time.

The final aspect of this application to mention is the feature that they call "Neighbourhood Checker". Many people first starting out in the world of SEO don't realize that the sites hosted on the same IP address as yours by the hosting company can often play a role in the success of your site, as having a bad "neighbour" can make the search engines penalize your site through no fault of your own. This tool allows you to check the credentials of the other sites hosted on the same IP and, should one of them come back as having a problem, you can contact your host and request that they place you on a different IP address. The process should be repeated on a regular basis, as new sites are added to IP addresses on a regular basis.

When it comes to the cost of this tool, there are four different tiers, with the first of these being free.

- The free option, however, really does restrict what you can do with the tool, as it only allows you to generate reports and does not give access to features like the Site Explorer and API access.

- The Silver membership costs £29.99 per month and gives access to all the features bar API access, with a limit of 60 reports per month and 5,000,000 backlinks reports.
- The Gold Package, priced at £99.99 per month, gives the same features but the number of reports is increased to 300 and the number of backlink reports rises to 25,000,000.
- The final level is Platinum which costs the user £250.00 per month, although for this price you get API access and are able to get 950 reports a month, and 100,000,000 backlink reports.

# Raven Tools

Raven Tools provides a comprehensive selection of different tools for those engaged in SEO, social media and advertising. As there are many different tools available, this section simply gives a brief rundown of each category and its tools. For a better description of each of the tools, head to www.raventools.com, where you will find all the information that you need. It must be noted that membership of the site gives access to all the tools and not just to one of the sections.

## SEO Tools

The first section to look at is that of the SEO tools, which is packed full of useful things to use for anyone interested in SEO. The main feature of the SEO tools is that you have a centralized location to view all of your data, instead of having to go to loads of different places and try to collate the data yourself. Raven also provides a central location for all the tools that you need, such as keyword research tools, backlink creation tools and website ranking tools. This means that you do not need to trawl the internet looking for each of these services separately – they are all included here! The philosophy of the site in respect to SEO is that "good decisions are educated decisions", and therefore it aims to provide you with as much data as possible for your campaign.

## Social Media Tools

The social media tools provided by Raven Tools aim to take advantage of this aspect of the internet – an aspect that has been proving to be more and more important in recent times. Perhaps the most impressive tool in this selection is the notification you receive whenever anyone mentions your website on a large number of different social media sites, such as YouTube, Facebook and Twitter, so that you can respond to the comments and massively increase the customer service that you provide. You can also set this up for specific keyword phrases, which obviously helps when researching keywords for your campaign.

The social media tools also generate regular reports on trends developing on the various sites that they cover, which is presented to you in the form of a graph and charts. This monitoring of trends means that you can be one of the first to capitalize on a new interest sweeping the internet, thereby gaining you vast numbers of new customers.

## Advertising Tools

The advertising tools are the final element of the tools provided by this site and they are absolutely essential if you want to run a cost effective campaign. They let you compare your paid advertising with the traffic that you generate through SEO and also allow you to make changes to your budget and focus with just one simple click. Essentially, the tools make it both simple and effective to run a paid advertising campaign.

The tools described here come in two different packages, called the Pro and the Agency plans.

- The Pro Plan costs $99 per month and includes 20 social monitor searches, 1,000 keyword rankings and 50,000 managed links, as well as the facility to have up to two users and an unlimited number of websites and Twitter/Facebook accounts.
- The Agency Plan offers all the features of the Pro Plan, but allows up to eight users, 50 social monitor searches, 2,500 keyword rankings and 150,000 managed links.

Before you sign up, there is a one-month free trial for all users, just so that you can see exactly what these tools can do for your company.

## Ozzu

Ozzu is actually a forum for webmasters to meet and discuss all the latest goings-on within their industry, but it also offers one incredibly useful tool to those engaged in the activity of SEO for their website. This tool is a PageRank checker that allows you to input your site's name – or another site's name – and immediately find out the PR (PageRank) of the site.

The PR of a site is something to which Google pays a lot of attention and is a large factor when it comes to SEO. Pages with higher PageRank are seen by Google to be more trustworthy as they provide relevant information and have also often been around for a number of years. It isn't just your own site's PageRank that you want to monitor, however; you also want to pay attention to the PR of the sites that you are getting backlinks from, as the higher the PR of that site, the stronger the links usually are.

To use this tool, all you have to do is simply enter the URL of the site that you want to check out and then hit the "Check PageRank" button. It is also possible to check a number of different sites at the same time, as long as you remember to press enter after each URL is input. After hitting the "Check PageRank" button, you are presented with the PR of the site – nothing more, nothing less.

Due to the simplicity of this tool, there is no way that the developers could get away with charging for it, so it is completely free for everyone to use. Just because it is simple, don't make the mistake of thinking that you don't need it – every site should keep a track of PR levels on a regular basis.

## URI

Uri is a product used by many internet marketers and, although it looks complex at first, it is in fact something that many people find to be absolutely essential! It has a number of different features, all of which are detailed in the following paragraphs.

What does this application actually do? Well, all that you need to do is visit the webpage – found at www.urivalet.com – and then input the address of any website that you want to investigate.

The results that URI generates are a mixture of highly technical components of the site – such as the types of encoding and the server used – and also more basic, yet nonetheless highly useful, statistics, which are the ones that most internet marketers find of interest. These stats provide an excellent rundown of a specific site and therefore enable you to analyze the sites belonging to you or even your competitors, so that you can learn from them and possibly use their own tactics against them when you rise higher in the rankings.

The first box that you will find incredibly useful is the one containing details on the meta description and meta keywords, which gives you a great insight into any website. Granted, it is possible to discover these by going through the code of a site, but for those with less technical knowhow, this is a much easier route. Looking at these aspects allows you to see which keywords the site is targeting and how well they are doing for each – spot a weakness and you will be able to exploit it. You can also use it to look at your own site, just to ensure that all of your meta data is displaying correctly.

Below this you find a section that shows the breakdown of the page that you have asked to be analyzed, which is very important, because a page without enough text and containing too many videos or Flash always performs badly in SEO. You can use these figures to work out where you are falling down in terms of SEO on this site and alter the layout accordingly. Looking at the more successful sites within your niche lets you know the rough percentages of different items you should have.

The final piece of really important information that this application shows is page load time. Many people do not realize that load time has an impact on SERPs. Google has stated that page load time is factored into its algorithm, although many place too much emphasis on it. It is fair to say, however, that Google sees faster sites as being more professional and providing a better experience for users. If you find that the download times for your site are above average, you really should look at the reasons why.

One of the things that you will notice when using this application is that, despite the amount of information provided, the looks are rather basic. This is fine, as it is completely free to use and therefore everyone should simply be grateful for the huge amount of information they receive. If you do find yourself benefiting from the work that this application does for you, you might want to consider donating to keep it running, although this is in no way mandatory.

## Xenu's Link Sleuth

When you first click on the webpage of Xenu's Link Sleuth – found at home.snafu.de/tilman/xenulink.html#FAQ – there is one thing that you will notice straightaway: it really does not look very professional or well-designed at all! If you can see past this, however, you will come face to face with a piece of software that makes searching for broken links on your website an extremely easy process – well, a lot easier than going through all of them by hand anyway!

Broken links are a disadvantage for any website, both in terms of the loss of profit made and in terms of SERP rankings. As you might imagine, if you have an affiliate link that doesn't work, you are losing out on revenue every time someone tries to click on it. It more than one affiliate link is broken, the amount of revenue you lose is even higher.

Broken links can also give a negative signal to search engines. Obviously if a site has broken links, Google and other search engines form the opinion that the site does not take care of the user and is probably outdated.

Xenu's Link Sleuth has no other features apart from finding broken links, but it ensures that your website manages its links in the best way possible and that you never again miss a sale thanks to a link being broken.

# Ranks

Ranks, (www.ranks.nl) brings a great number of tools to your disposal, all of which make the job of completing your SEO a much easier task. There are so many different features that it would be impossible to go over them all in detail in the short space available here, so below follows a brief rundown of the most useful tools that are provided on Ranks.

## *File Differences Tool*

Perhaps the most innovative tool that can be found on Ranks is known as the "File Differences" tool, which has the function to compare two different files and highlight the major differences found within them. Now this might seem like a pointless exercise, but imagine that you have just changed your homepage and suddenly you have dropped significantly in the SERPs – you are going to want to know why. This tool points you in the right direction, so that you can quickly find the reason. It can also be used to root out any mistakes that you might have made, simply by comparing a file you know is correct with a file that has just been created.

## *Page and Article Analyzers*

The tools provided by Ranks also include an extremely effective page analyzer, which shows a huge amount of different information regarding a specific webpage. It shows the keywords that are being used, how often they are being used and even a list of the page's outgoing links. You can also analyze articles in their HTML format before they are published online using the Article Analyzer tool, so that you can check for any mistakes and also make sure that the different aspects of the article – such as the keyword density – are correct before publication.

## *Compare Search Engine Tool*

The final tool that you will find extremely useful when conducting your SEO on a specific site is the "Compare Search Engine" tool, which, as the name suggests, allows you to compare your results in different search engines. Keeping track of where you rank is very important when trying to ascertain your overall SEO strategy, but it also takes an incredibly long time – especially if you haven't made it onto the first few pages yet! This tool displays all rankings in the blink of an eye and saves you hours in the process!

As you would expect from a site that offers this number of tools, they do not offer them for free – although you can currently have a week's free trial of the features. Any subscription that you take out covers you to use all the tools that they offer and the longer your subscription, the cheaper the price becomes per month. For a three-month pass, you pay $69, whereas the six-month pass costs just $112. A one-year pass is $182 and it is also possible to purchase a pass to use the tools for just one day, which costs $12.70. It is possible to pay in a wide variety of different ways, including PayPal.

## Screaming Frog

Screaming Frog, along with having the best name for any online tool, also has a fantastic tool for all website owners to use, named SEO Spider. This tool is downloaded through the link found at www.screamingfrog.co.uk/seo-spider/ and the "Lite" version is completely free to use, although it does have its limitations.

The Screaming Frog spider works in roughly the same way that Google's spiders function. For those of you not aware of what spiders are in the SEO sense, they are basically sent out by the search engines to gather information about different websites, which is then used to determine rankings given to pages for a specific keyword. Those with a good knowledge of SEO always try to optimize their site to make it as spider-friendly as possible, and using Screaming Frog SEO Spider gives you an invaluable insight towards where you want to improve your site.

What exactly does SEO Spider look at? Well, the software investigates all links, images, script, apps and CSS, before presenting its findings in an easy to read report that highlights the SEO issues that the site is facing. Many people seem to think that the majority of SEO is done offsite, but the reality is that SEO should begin at home and therefore a perfectly optimized website is essential.

The results that you receive from the SEO Spider also allow you to export the results straight into Excel, which is incredibly useful if you need to present your findings in an easy to read way to a third party. People also often use it so that they can print the results out and keep a handy reference as to how their SEO campaign is progressing.

SEO Spider is ideal for those with larger sites, as it is often impossible to keep on top of all the different aspects of SEO when you have hundreds of pages to work through. As already mentioned, the "Lite" version of SEO Spider is free to download, but only allows you to make 500 URL crawls, which for some people simply isn't enough. Should you want to upgrade, the full package only costs £99 per year and gives you access to unlimited amounts of URL. It is available to download for both Windows and Mac.

## GTmetrix

As mentioned previously, the speed of a web site is extremely important, both when it comes to the rankings that you gain in search engines, and for the experience that visitors gain when using your site. GTmetrix is a highly useful tool that allows you to see how quickly a page on your site loads and, should it take longer than expected, provides you with a number of different suggestions as to how to remedy this problem effectively.

The overall use of this tool couldn't be any easier – simply type in the URL of the site that you want to analyze, click on the "GO!" button and then wait for 30 seconds or so. When it has finished, you are presented with a huge amount of data of different facts and figures, all of which provide invaluable information on your site's load speed. What is even better is that it presents the results with the most important results right at the top of the page, so that you can easily identify the key areas that need action.

Many of the sections will seem completely alien to you when you first see them. 99% of the population are not going to know what "parallelize downloads across hostnames" means, or to what "minify CSS" refers. This is not a problem, however, as the site provides clear descriptions of each of the terms used. All you need to do is click on the action and then click the question mark to the right, where you are then given an easy to understand definition of what the process is and why it is important.

You will notice that there are two different sets of analysis for the website – one called "Page Speed" and another called "YSlow". This is because the site has realized that people try to optimize not just for Google, but for other search engines as well. "Page Speed" analyzes the site from the point of view of Google's own analysts, whereas "YSlow" works to provide information on your site that helps you to rank higher in Yahoo's results. You need to compare the results and decide what you want to change, ensuring that you do not damage the results for the other set at the same time. Generally people stick to optimizing for Google, as it is by far and away the most important search engine out there.

The other two tabs found at the top of the results box show the timeline of the page's loading time – something that allows you to pinpoint the exact parts of the page that are causing the slow load – and the history of the site. The history displays a graph of all the times that you have searched the specific site so that you can understand whether a slow load was a mere blip, or whether it is a constant problem that needs remedying ASAP.

Anyone looking to use this tool will be glad to know that it is 100% free, which is always a bonus when you have limited resources to spend on your SEO efforts. The tool can be found at www.gtmetrix.com and should be looked at by everyone serious about refining their SEO strategy.

## IntoDNS

At first glance, this tool seems extremely basic; after all, the homepage only has a box for you to input the website address and nothing else. Once you type in your website address, however, you find an impressive volume of data at your disposal.

All of this data looks incredibly technical and, to be honest, it is! As you are new to the world of online marketing and website creation you will find that the results IntoDNS generates will be far beyond your understanding. Don't worry! If you find errors, simply copy and paste each error into Google search and you will find many others who have encountered the same error. After researching specific errors, either take the advice found on Google or hire someone from Elance to sort it for you. The list reaches well down the page and gives a tick if the site is meeting specified standards and provides an alert if a specific element is below par. While you might not know exactly what to do with the information once you have it, it will be extremely useful if you are working with a professional, as they will be able to analyze this data and make the necessary adjustments.

You can be assured that all the information is correct as the program uses official documentation from across a number of different sources. There is no guesswork involved in the results that are displayed – they are fact and as such there is no room for interpretation. This means that if it shows up a problem with your site, there really is a problem and you must rectify it as soon as you can!

Although this highly useful tool provides a huge amount of information to those understanding how to analyze it, it is still provided 100% free by the developers – so even if you glean only one piece of helpful advice from it, you have something for nothing. Just because it is technical, don't let it scare you – after all, Google is there to help you understand the different terms that it uses!

# Chapter 21 – Browser Plug-ins

In addition to the standalone tools that were detailed in the previous chapter, also of great use to affiliates are other tools that simply "plug in" to the Firefox browser. If you are using another browser such as Internet Explorer or even Google Chrome, I strongly advise you to download Firefox (it's free) and download and install the following plug-ins.

## Blekko – Firefox Plug-in

Blekko is a search engine that is becoming increasingly popular with SEO experts, as it provides a great deal of information on internet marketing related activities, all at the click of a button. With the Blekko add-on for the Firefox browser, users of this far more popular search engine can also receive all the advantages that Blekko users get, but without having to sacrifice the other excellent features that Firefox contains. So what are the different SEO features that the Blekko add-on offers that makes it an indispensable tool for internet marketing professionals throughout the world?

### *Link Analysis*

Links are seen as one of the most important aspects of SEO, although in recent times in my opinion, on page SEO factors are now more important. It is, however, good SEO practice to keep an eye on the links that are directing to your website, as well as the links that are directing to your competitors' websites.

Blekko comes up with a useful table that shows the inbound and outbound links for any website that you select, but this is not all that it does. Both of these figures can be expanded to give specific information on every single link found, so that you can work out where your links are coming from and evaluate which types of link are contributing the most towards the success of your SEO campaign. It also means that you can look at the inbound links for your competitors and try to get links from the same places, so that you can match them in their efforts and stay competitive.

The link analysis does not stop there as it includes a number of other extremely helpful features. Perhaps the most impressive of these is the regional link distribution option that you can use, which shows you the links that come into your site from the different countries around the world. As you can imagine, most internet marketers target sales from more than one country, so it is imperative that they optimize their site to all different nationalities – which is why it is vital to know how your links are doing in the specific countries you are targeting.

Other useful information about links provided by this add-on include a number of different graphs to indicate performance of sites, the number of links and the best performing links, together with information on how different anchor words are performing when it comes to driving traffic to your site.

### Duplicate Content

Duplicated content is a massive no-no for anyone looking to gain free, targeted traffic from search engines. Duplicated content (content copied from other websites) more often than not results in websites being removed from search engine results listings altogether. This means that it is always important to make sure that you have unique content on your site and that other people are not stealing it and using it as their own.

The Blekko duplicate content checker reports all cases of duplicated content. You can quickly find any websites that have copied your content and can request that the "stolen" content is removed. There are other sites that already offer this service but to have it attached to an add-on, making it incredibly easy to access, is certainly a great aid.

### Other Blekko Features

Apart from those already mentioned – which are undoubtedly the most useful found within the Blekko add-on – there are a number of other features. Some of these additional features are very much geared towards Blekko's own search engine, which means that the stats that they provide, such as the crawl stats and the indexed pages, do not reflect the figures of Google or other major search engines.

In conclusion, Blekko is a tool that many SEO professionals find to be completely essential, if only for the link and duplicated content aspects of the add-on. It can be downloaded from http://blekko.com/ws/+/blekkogear.

## Firebug – Firefox Plug-in

Those with experience in the web development industry might possible be surprised when they see Firebug included as a great SEO tool, although I'm sure that those working in SEO already know that its inclusion is more than merited. This is because the worlds of web development and SEO really do go hand in hand, which means that how a web site is created is integral to creating a site that performs well in the search engines' rankings.

Firebug integrates seamlessly with Firefox to enable you to complete a large number of different tasks. Granted, most of these tasks can also be done through other programs online, but the fact that they are all in one place and just a click away on any webpage means that Firebug saves an enormous amount of time and even more hassle. It is also trusted by a massive number of people, and therefore you know that it works perfectly and gives you accurate representations of the results whenever you use it.

The most useful feature that Firebug has is the ability not only to view the HTML of a specific webpage, but also to edit it and see the results in a completely different page, without having to change the actual HTML of the website. As you can imagine, this opens up many possibilities for you as an SEO expert. Changing the HTML of a site provides an instant change to the way the site looks and feels and can provide you with a valuable insight into how visitors to your site could benefit from changes. It also allows you to insert new items into the webpage – all previously optimized of course – so that you can see how they look and whether they could be improved in any way.

The facility that allows you to monitor network activity is another one that you will find extremely useful in your SEO endeavours, as a website's loading speed is an important factor in its position within SERPs. This handy tool points you in the right direction when looking to make your page load faster, and analyzes whether you have failed to compress your images, or written too much JavaScript or whether the servers used by people placing ads on your site are not performing properly. Using this information you can then go ahead and remedy the problems, which in turn causes an upturn in your rankings across all the major search engines.

The final massive advantage that SEO professionals get when using this handy add-on for Firefox is the fact that it allows them to root out any errors within the website's code that could be causing the website to be malfunctioning in certain places. Errors really will upset search engines and your website's readers so should be sorted quickly. Remember search engines, especially Google will penalize websites, that do not give a good user experience. Firebug quickly searches for all the errors that the script has and points them out to you, making the need to trawl through the entire HTML a thing of the past.

As can be seen, Firebug really does make a difference when you are looking to make your on-site SEO and coding as good as it can possibly be. The web development aspect might be slightly scary to newcomers  but, as with everything else, you just need to forge ahead and start learning. With Firebug at your side the time it takes to become competent is a lot shorter than it otherwise would be! Download it from www.getfirebug.com.

## Foxy SEO – Firefox Plug-in

Despite its rather playful name, the reality is that the Foxy SEO Tool is something that every serious SEO professional should have on their toolbar. It is an add-on that provides a great deal of data on every single website online and can therefore be used for a massive array of different purposes. So, what are the main features that this tool offers and how do those in the SEO industry use them to further their optimization efforts?

Although there are many features, the one that really stands out in most people's minds is the Spider Simulator, which is an absolute must-have piece of kit for anyone engaged in SEO activities. This tool allows you to view a webpage in exactly the same way that a spider would see it, ordered with the HTML code of the page but without the layout code that gives the site its shape. This is massively important, as getting those spiders to index your site is the biggest priority for any new webpage out there and knowing exactly what they are looking at helps you enormously in this quest.

Another great element of this SEO tool is the amount of information that it provides on the data found about a specific site on both the most popular search engines – such as Google, Yahoo and Bing – and on the world's biggest traffic analysis sites, Alexa, Compete and Quantcast. You can even check the data about a site on directories like Dmoz and Yahoo Directory and Web 2.0 sites, with the most important of these being Digg and Technocrati. Essentially, if you want to find out how well a site is doing, there is no more comprehensive way than using the Foxy SEO Tool.

Apart from the tools that this Firefox add-on provides, it is also a source of inspiration for many looking to add a new dimension to their SEO because it has a number of different links to sites that are on the cutting edge of the SEO world. This can provide indispensable advice to you on how to diversify and, occasionally, on where you might be going wrong in your efforts. It also has links to a number of different keyword research sites, should your efforts in this vital part of SEO seem to be temporarily stalling.

One thing that many people often find annoying about Firefox is that the menu can quickly become overloaded with different toolbars and other additions, making the whole screen look messy and difficult to work with. When using the Foxy SEO Tool, however, the toolbar can be disabled and the tool can simply be used through its contextual pop-up menu instead. All you need to do to activate it is to right click and you have all the options available to you, without the hassle of having yet another addition to your menu bar.

## IE Tab – Firefox Plug-in

Despite the fact that a great many people throughout the world loathe it, the fact remains that Internet Explorer is the most popular browser on the planet, used by millions of people every single day for all manner of reasons. This means that it is massively important to take into consideration the people using this browser when optimizing your website, even if you happen to be using one of the "better" browsers, such as Google Chrome or Mozilla Firefox.

The IE Tab add-on is extremely simple in its premise, as it is simply a way for you to use Mozilla Firefox while switching quickly to the view that people get when using Internet Explorer, so that you can double check your site is working okay. Then you simply have to open up Google Chrome and check the site there, and you have ensured that the top three browsers are all functioning well for your site!

The IE Tab is displayed through a simple tab on the menu bar of your Firefox browser. There are no complex extras included – the whole add-on simply involves pressing the button to switch between the views of the two browsers. It is so simple that even people with a very basic knowledge of the internet can use it, although if you are conducting SEO, you are likely to be slightly more proficient than that!

Why exactly is it important to keep an eye on how your site performs in Internet Explorer from the point of view of search engine optimization? Well, SEO is not just about getting good rankings on the search engines and optimizing the code on your site, because if you have a terrible site, nobody ever wants to come back to it or buy from it. Making sure that the site looks good in Internet Explorer – which is the most popular browser in the world – adds that finishing touch to your SEO activities and allows the traffic that you have driven to turn into paying customers who know that they are buying from a professional website.

Now you might be thinking that there are a number of different Internet Explorer versions around, as people do not always stay up to date with the latest releases. The IE Tab add-on has the situation covered by providing support for all the versions of Internet Explorer from IE6 to the present day (IE9), so that you can test your site over all the platforms. Another great reason to use this add-on is that it allows you to use ActiveX controls and to ensure that they work well too.

IE Tab might not be as far-reaching an add-on as SearchStatus, but it is still extremely important – hence the reason it is used by SEO professionals the world over. It can be downloaded directly from the Mozilla Add-ons site at https://addons.mozilla.org/en-US/firefox/addon/ie-tab/.

## SearchStatus – Firefox Plug-in

SearchStatus is an add-on for Firefox that allows the user to see information on every single website in the world, regardless of how large or well known it happens to be. It does not just provide simple statistics but provides the facts and figures that those working professionals within SEO need to ensure that they do their job to the highest standard possible.

In addition to the fact that all the information provided is extremely useful, the information is also extremely easy to read and therefore makes life incredibly easy when using it. This even extends to the position of the results on a page, as this can easily be changed using the inbuilt options within the extension.

What exactly does SearchStatus show in its results? It shows:

- The Google PageRank
- The Google category
- The ranking the site has in Alexa
- The Compete.com ranking
- The site's mozRank
- All Alexa links
- The backlinks from Google, Bing and Yahoo.

This means that, along with SEO Nuke, this add-on provides more information on specific sites than any other add-on out there, and is therefore relied on by a huge number of people working in the SEO industry.

The aspects listed above are only a few of the different features; there are many more – far too many to list in the short space available here. One that is certainly worth mentioning is how this add-on, much like SEO Nuke, shows whether a link on a page is a no-follow or a do-follow one. You can make sure that those links you were promised from another site really are do-follow, like they said they would be, or whether they are trying to pull a fast one on you!

The other very handy tool on this excellent SEO-oriented add-on is the robots tool, which is extremely simple to use but essential to your SEO efforts. It is possible that code added into the HTML of your website prevents Google or other search engines from crawling the site and listing it in their rankings, which is something that you don't want to happen at all! The robots tool check the pages of your site and makes sure that it is set up to be crawled, which can save you many wasted hours promoting your site uselessly! It is possible to do this without the add-on, but in reality many people forget to, so it's nice to have a reminder occasionally in the form of this tool!

As can be seen there is a lot to be taken from the SearchStatus add-on, regardless of whether you are a seasoned SEO campaigner or a newbie starting out in the business. It can be downloaded through addons.mozilla.org/en-US/firefox/addon/searchstatus/ and is completely free for everyone to use.

## SEO Quake – Firefox Plug-in

SEO Quake is considered by many to be the most important tool for their SEO strategy, as the amount of information that it provides is absolutely staggering. In SEO, information is the key to getting things right, so it is great to know that a good portion of the info that you need can be gleaned straight from one simple Firefox add-on!

SEO Quake is completely free to use and can be downloaded from http://www.seoquake.com/. You will notice that there is also the option to install it onto Chrome, Opera and Safari, such is the popularity of this tool. In fact, there have been 2,000,000 downloads of this add-on, which just goes to show how vital many different people consider it. The installation only takes a few seconds and it appears on your browser as soon as it is restarted.

What exactly does SEO Quake do? Well, it integrates the results that are provided by most of the major search engines in order to provide you with a huge quantity of different stats on every website out there. It also displays these stats at the top of every website that you go onto. These stats cover a multitude of different things, such as the PageRank of the site, the number of internal and external links and the number of pages that the site has indexed on Google, Yahoo and Bing. It also provides the age of the site and the WHOIS of the site.

All these figures provide an invaluable insight into the way that your competitors work, as well as giving you a simple way to keep track of the stats of your own website. No longer do you have to root out a service online to find your PR – it is simply there at the top of the screen. No longer do you need to count manually the links on a specific page – just look at the results given by SEO Quake instead! As you can see, the timesaving potential that SEO Quake offers is enormous and those in the SEO business know that time is not usually on their side, so anything that they can do to speed up the process is a good thing.

Another great feature of SEO Quake is how it highlights all no-follow links on a specific site, which is useful in so many different ways. Firstly, it allows you to check if the links on your own site are at the correct settings, as you do not want to give away links for free to people, especially if they are competitors. It also allows you to check the inbound links to your site and make sure that people have kept to their promise and given you a do-follow link. As you probably already know, the impact that no-follow links have on SEO is negligible, whereas do-follow links are some of the best things that an SEO campaign can have, especially if they come from a well-respected website.

The final incredibly useful feature that SEO Quake has is the Keywords Density option, which, as the name suggests, brings up a list of all the different words and phrases used throughout a webpage. This allows you to check to see which phrases a competitor is targeting and also whether your own site is too light or too heavy when it comes to the density of the keywords. This part of SEO Quake also shows you the meta description and the meta keywords that a site uses, which is a feature that can save you a lot of time as you don't need to trawl through the site's code to find them.

Overall, the fact that SEO Quake is free is just a bonus, as even if they charged for it, most SEO professionals would still be willing to download it. With the information that it provides and the intuitive way that it does so, this tool is truly one that is indispensable if you are really serious about maximizing the SEO of your site.

# Chapter 22 - Action Plans

By now you should have a very good idea of what exactly is involved in building your very own online cash cow. For many of you reading this book, the actual technical aspects of getting your site up and running may seem a little daunting, but in reality the techniques required sound far more complicated than they really are. Remember that if you struggle with the actual building of your site, then you can simply use the services of those with the expertise you require at online freelance sites such as Elance. Once your website is up and running, it is basically just a matter of creating daily quality content.

This chapter simply details the basic processes you need to undertake to research, build, maintain, update and monitorize your affiliate site. The action plans cover the following processes:

- Self-Appraisal

- Niche research

- Domain research

- Building your cash cow

- Daily tasks – pre-launch

- Daily tasks – post-launch

- Weekly tasks

- Monthly tasks

- Audits

All you need to do is work through the action plans ensuring that you complete EVERY task specified. I will tell you now it is not going to be easy, but of course you should know that already!

## Self-Appraisal

There is no point in even trying to start this project if you do not have the time or if it is going to damage your relationships with those you cherish. When I started to venture into the world of online affiliating I was running a computer hardware business, so in real terms

I got very little done. I knew that it was going to be impossible for me to build a new career while I was working long hours running my other business. My wife had a decent job as an administrator at a local nursing home so we were doing OK financially; although we worked so hard we hardly had time to talk to each other. To be completely frank, I am one of those people that can't say no, so I knew that unless we moved away from the city we had lived in all our lives, I would always be building and repairing computers.

Can you imagine how my wife felt when I told her that I wanted to shut down my computer business and move out of the city where we had lived our whole lives, leaving all our friends behind? Can you imagine the look on her face when I told her that I wanted to try to build a new career as an online affiliate and the chances were high that I would not earn a penny in the first year?

In most cases you will not have to make the drastic lifestyle changes my family and I had to endure, although taking on such a project, especially with no initial financial reward, will not be easy. In my case, I persuaded my wife and children to move from the midlands to the north west of England, so that I could have one last shot of "making it big". It was far from easy for us, as we did not really like the place we moved to, which created a lot of friction between us. Worse still, as I mentioned right at the start of this book, the only job my wife could secure was that of a low-paid care assistant so, as I'm sure you can imagine, the pressure was on me to come good.

Now again, I am not saying that you have to make the drastic lifestyle changes I had to make. You should, however, give a great deal of thought as to how taking on this project will affect not only your life but also the lives of those around you. Before taking on this project, talk to those closest to you and tell them exactly what you are thinking of doing. From my experience most of them will think you are crazy and will simply not understand. To this day many of my friends do not understand exactly how I make money and do not think I have a proper job, which I used to find extremely frustrating, although now it amuses me. If you are currently holding down a steady job, it would be foolish simply to give it up, so you are going to have to assess your free time to determine if you really do have the time to take on this project. I know of many now successful affiliates who started building their online affiliate careers while holding down a 9-to-5 job, although they had to make sacrifices, which for many of them put a great strain on their relationships. If you are currently out of work, then perhaps in many cases you have an easier decision, although I still strongly suggest you talk to those around you. Getting the approval of your partner or family to pursue your new career should be your very first goal!

No matter your current situation, take the time to keep a diary for at least a week to record your free time so that you can determine the actual amount of free time you have. Remember, however, that those around you need you, just as much as you need them, so ensure you do "put aside" quality time for your family. Remember, all work and no play makes Jack a dull boy!

Once you have the backing of your family, and provided you can fit this project into your daily schedule, start by creating new accounts at Digital Point and Elance. Make at least a couple of quality posts a day at Digital Point, because soon you will be posting a logo contest. Digital Point T&Cs state:

*"You must have been a member for 14 days, not have an overall red reputation and have 25 total posts to post in the Buy, Sell or Trade sections."*

### Self-Appraisal Action Plan
Keep a "free time" diary for at least a week                                    [  ]

Talk to family and friends                                                       [  ]

Create accounts at Digital Point and Elance                                      [  ]


## Niche Research
Take the time to go back and read the "What's Your Niche Chapter". Start by jotting down your interests, hobbies and passions. Be realistic and honest about your knowledge of any potential niche you are thinking of targeting. Take the time to research thoroughly key phrases, to examine existing affiliate sites targeting the niche and to research affiliate programs that you can use to monetize the niche. If you are highly knowledgeable in a potential niche, then it should be easy for you to compose a list of 100 potential articles.

Also of prime importance at this stage is to seek out affiliate programs for your chosen niche. It is also beneficial to email affiliate programs that you are intending to promote, simply telling them that you are very interested in promoting their products and are in the process of building an affiliate website. Ask for advice regarding exactly what they are looking for from new affiliates. Whatever advice they give you, make sure you act on it! Do not put all your eggs in one basket! Think about what you are going to do if for some reason your application to the main affiliate program you want to promote is rejected.

It is essential that you formulate the structure of your site because you don't want to make major changes to your website's structure after it has been indexed by search engines. Simply take the time to plan your different sections and make a quick sketch of how the homepage of each section will look.

## *Niche Research Action Plan*

Write down your interests and hobbies                                        [ ]

Choose a niche in which you know you excel                                   [ ]

Carry out keyword research                                                   [ ]

Write down 100 article titles for your chosen niche                         [ ]

Research affiliate programs                                                  [ ]

Estimate earnings using a conversion rate of 1% & 100 visitors a day        [ ]

Plan the structure of your website listing all sections                     [ ]

Email the affiliate programs you are thinking of promoting                  [ ]

## *Domain Research*

Go to Godaddy Auctions and search for a brandable domain name. An aged domain will give your affiliate website a boost to some degree but is not the be all and end all. Try to find a brandable .com domain, preferably where the .net and .org is also free. If you can't find an aged domain, go to Namecheap.com to find an unregistered domain name. Ensure you find a name that is brandable, which does not contain hyphens and is preferably no more than two words. Take your time choosing your domain name.

## *Social Media Branding*

Also of great importance, once you have found a potential good brandable domain name, is to take the time to see if anybody is already using the name for either a Facebook Page or a Twitter account name. You really need to be able to use the same name for all your internet content which in turn, provided of course that the content you produce is informative and high quality will help to build your brand.

Once you find a domain you are completely happy with, buy it!

### *Domain Research Action Plan*

Brainstorm potential brandable website names [ ]

Go to Godaddy Auctions and/or Namecheap to seek a .com domain [ ]

Check that for the social media you intend to use the above name is free [ ]

Secure the .net and .org of your .com domain name (if possible) [ ]

Create a Facebook page using your brand name [ ]

Create a Twitter account using your brand name [ ]

## Building Your Cash Cow

Order your hosting from Hostgator. I suggest you keep your expenditure low at first so just opt for the "Baby Hosting Plan" as you can upgrade at a later stage, easily and painlessly. The reason I suggest Hostgator is that their support is very good, they have a large amount of video tutorials online and their hosting plans are good value. If you prefer to opt for another host, that's fine; at the end of the day the choice is yours.

Once you have ordered your hosting, you need to change the name servers of your domain, so that it becomes linked to your hosting account. Take a look at the Hostgator video, which walks you through the process.

http://www.hostgator.com/tutorials/dns/godaddy/changing-your-nameservers.htm.

### *Installing Wordpress*

Now the time has come to start actually creating your affiliate website. Simply log in to your hosting account and use Fantastico to install Wordpress.

http://www.hostgator.com/tutorials/wordpress/2.7/installing-wordpress-via-fantastico.htm

### *Wordpress Settings*

After you have installed Wordpress, you must change a few of the default settings. Firstly, log in to your Wordpress administration by going to the URL, www.yoursitename.com/wp-admin, and entering your user name and password. Click "Settings", then "General" and you will see a screen similar to the one below:

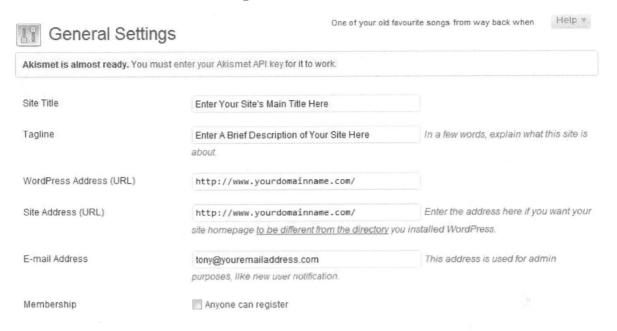

Enter your site information and ensure that you edit both the "Address URL" and "Site Address" URL so that it includes "www." Also ensure that you set the date format and time zone and then click the "Save changes" button.

## *Wordpress Permalinks*

Again click "Settings", then "Permalinks" and you should see the screen below.

## Common Settings

⊙ Default

⊙ Day and name

⊙ Month and name

⊙ Numeric

⊙ Post name

⊙ Custom Structure                    /%postname%/

Simply click the "Custom Structure" option, then enter /%postname%/ in the Custom Structure field, and then click the "Save Changes" button.

### Wordpress Privacy

Now you need to block search engines from crawling your site because, of course, it is going to go through great changes before it is ready for visitors. Again click "Settings" and then "Privacy" to load the screen below:

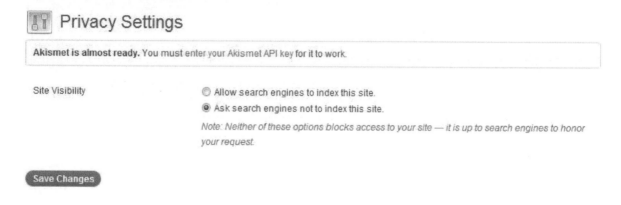

Simply click the "Ask search engines not to index this site" option, and then click the "Save Changes" button.

### Additional Wordpress Installs

Remember your website should be made up of more than one Wordpress install. Use Fantastico to install Wordpress for your other sections. For example if your domain name was www.bluewidgets.com and you were installing Wordpress for a news section, the actual folder would be www.bluewidets.com/news/. For each additional Wordpress install you must ensure you change the settings as detailed for your main Wordpress install. If you lack experience, keep things simple at this early stage of your affiliate career and just start with one Wordpress install, although it is of great importance that other sections are added as soon as you feel confident enough to do so.

### Install Wordpress Plug-ins

For each Wordpress install you will now need to load and activate the plug-ins specified in the Wordpress Plug-ins section of this book. To install a plug-in, again on the Wordpress admin page select "Plug-ins", then "Add New" and type in the name of the plug-in you want to install. You will then see the screen below:

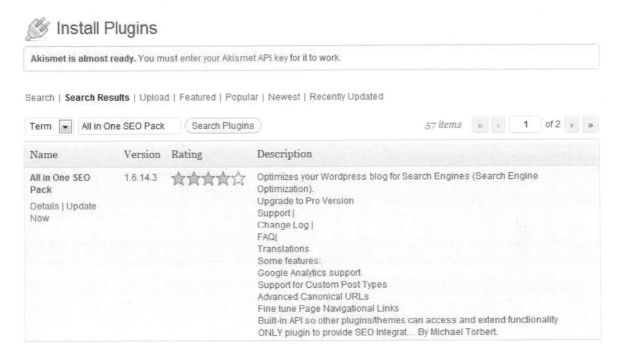

Simply seek the latest version of the plug-in you want to install and load and activate it. Repeat this procedure for all the required plug-ins. Remember that if you struggle to get your website installed, you can seek help by posting a job on Elance.

## Choosing Themes

The next stage is of course to choose a theme, since your Wordpress sections will look a little "naked" in their current state. Take the time to visit Theme Forest or even seek out other premium Wordpress theme sites using Google. Please ensure that you buy Wordpress themes and not pure HTML or other CMS themes such as Drupal. Before buying any theme ensure it looks professional and meets your exact requirements. Also, of prime importance, check that the theme has received good feedback from previous buyers. Buy the themes you require and download them to your home computer.

## Loading Themes

Each theme now needs to be loaded into the "Themes" folder of each Wordpress install. If you are familiar with FTP programs, simply use your FTP client to upload each theme. If not, watch these videos:

http://www.hostgator.com/tutorials/wordpress/2.7/managing-themes-in-wordpress.htm

If you don't already have an FTP client, download FileZilla from - http://filezilla-project.org/, and learn how to use it by viewing the Hostgator FileZilla tutorials you will find at http://www.hostgator.com/tutorials.shtml

## *Logo Design*

If you are building your site on a tight budget, provided you have been registered at Digital Point for 14 days and have made 25 posts, post your logo contest at http://forums.digitalpoint.com/forumdisplay.php?f=94. Ensure you post your exact requirements including general concept, size and colour scheme. If your budget allows, you could post a contest at a dedicated design site such as Design Crowd.

## *Loading your Logo*

Most premium Wordpress themes have a backend option that allows you to upload a logo. Once your logo is completed, upload it to all your Wordpress installs. If you struggle with this process, simply post a job at Elance. Adding a logo to a header is a job any competent coder can complete in just a few minutes.

## *Theme Styling & Categories*

All premium Wordpress themes have options so that you can in effect choose exactly where your content appears on your website. In most cases you simply set up categories, and then select which category appears in which section. Create the categories you require, create some test articles and play around with the theme's options so that you have a great understanding of how the theme actually functions. This will also let you have a feel of how you want your website to look, BEFORE you start adding quality articles to your site.

## *Building Your Online Cash Cow - Action Plan*

Order web hosting from Hostgator                                            [  ]

Change the name servers of your domain                                      [  ]

Install Wordpress                                                          [  ]

Change Wordpress default settings                                          [  ]

Install Wordpress plug-ins                                              [   ]

Purchase Wordpress Theme(s)                                            [   ]

Upload and activate Wordpress Theme(s)                                 [   ]

Post a logo design contest                                            [   ]

Upload logo                                                           [   ]

Setup theme options and categories                                    [   ]

# Pre Site Launch

Now your affiliate website should simply be waiting for you to add quality content. Your goal now should be to create around 50 quality articles, upload them to your website and then apply to the affiliate programs you already have researched. Start by writing a list of 50 potential articles that you need to get your website up and running. Writing three articles a day, this task is going to take you around 16 days.

### *Pre Site Launch – Action Plan*

Compile a list of 50 article titles                                   [   ]

Write 3 quality articles each day and upload them to your website      [   ]

Ensure that every article you produce is of the highest quality!      [   ]

# Get Ready For Launch

### *Change Privacy Settings*

Once you have 50 quality articles loaded onto your website, now is the time to let search engines take a look. Change your Wordpress privacy settings to allow search engines.

### *Create Your Google Accounts*

Now is a great time to create and activate your Google Analytics and Google Webmaster Tools accounts. Once both accounts have been activated and verified, log in to your

Wordpress backend and go to the settings of your Google analytics sitemap plug-in, run through the settings generating a sitemap and add the sitemap URL to your Google Webmaster Tools account. Next go to the settings of your Google Analytics plug-in and run the "Authenticate With Google" option. Check after 24 hours that both the sitemap and analytics data are being recognized by Google.

### *Apply to Affiliate Programs*

If you are 100% happy with the look of your site and the quality of your content, now is the time to apply to the affiliate programs you researched earlier. You will find that some affiliate programs will approve you instantly while for others you will have to wait at least a few days. If for some reason you find that your application is refused, simply reply with a polite email stating that you are new to the affiliate industry and ask for advice on how you can become approved. Once approved, log in to each of your affiliate program accounts to create affiliate links. Add these links to your sales pages ensuring that you test each link you add.

### *Get Ready For Launch - Action Plan*

Change Wordpress privacy settings to allow search engines                [ ]

Create Google Analytics and Webmaster Tools accounts                    [ ]

Add your site to both the above and complete the verification process   [ ]

Apply to affiliate programs                                             [ ]

Get links from the affiliate programs                                   [ ]

Test all the affiliate links you add to your site                       [ ]

## Daily Tasks

From other affiliates I have coached over the years, most take around a month to get their websites actually up and running. I would say that most new affiliates really enjoy the process of creating their own website, even those who are challenged by the technical tasks involved. Once your affiliate site is up and running, you now need to snap into a routine as quickly as possible. Creating and posting fresh quality content daily on your website is a must, as this not only generates a positive signal to search engines but also results in your readers frequently returning to your site to "check out" your newly published articles.

## Weekly Content List

At the start of each and every week, take the time to research article titles you aim to produce for the week ahead. This is a task I still religiously carry out so that I can ensure my sites continue to grow. As soon as each article is live, I simply tick off the title from my weekly content list. I have a rule that I NEVER break. At the end of each week, all articles must be live on my sites. During the early days of my affiliate career, following this rule meant that on many occasions at the end of the week I had to play catch up, which resulted in me having to work through the night. Keeping on schedule is of prime importance and in reality sorts out the wheat from the chaff!

The next few months are going to be extremely difficult, because most of you will see very little, if any, financial reward for all your efforts. Remember that those that stick it out for the long term, those who keep on keeping on, are the ones who prosper in the long term.

Give yourself a pat on the back for the initial shoots of success. For example to see how many of your pages are indexed by Google, simply type into Google search *site:www.yoursitename.com*. You will notice that little by little, more and more of your pages are indexed by Google. Also check your affiliate accounts once per day, keeping an eye on views, clicks and, if you are extremely lucky during your first few months, earnings. Also, of course, once a day check your daily traffic in Google Analytics and your Google Webmaster Tools account for any problems with your site's functionality.

Don't get obsessed with checking your website and affiliate stats as you will just be wasting time!

### *Daily Tasks – Action Plan*

At the start of each week create a weekly content list                    [  ]

Add three pages of quality content EVERY DAY!                           [  ]

Check the number of your websites pages indexed in Google            [  ]

Check your Google Analytics and Webmaster Tools Account             [  ]

Read blogs, forums & social media in your chosen niche                [  ]

Post at least one quality response to any of the above                  [  ]

## Weekly Audit

At the end of each week you should take the time to audit your website. At first it will seem like you are getting nowhere, with only a trickle of traffic and the odd click here and there on your affiliate pages. As you gather more data from increased traffic to your website, if you analyse your traffic by using Google Analytics, you will start to see which of your articles and sales pages are popular and which are not. In time you will start to understand which types of key phrase are driving traffic to your site, and, excluding search engine traffic, what other traffic sources are becoming valuable to you. Simply take action on the data you find!

Taking the time to analyse which banners and links, especially the anchor text you use for your affiliate links, are generating a high proportion of clicks is vital. If one of your sales pages is getting a decent number of views but very few clicks, you should experiment with either another banner or different anchor text. The name of the game is simply to replace poor performing banners and links with those that perform better. In time, the testing of different banners, links and anchor text will result in increased clicks, which of course will result in increased sales.

It is also vitally important that at least once each week you spend time examining your Google Webmaster Tools account. Ensure that the load time of your pages are not increasing, check that your sitemap is still active, check that Googlebot is still crawling your site and don't forget to check to see if there are any messages in your Google Webmaster Tools inbox. Putting time aside to spend a good 20 or 30 minutes a week examining all data in Google Webmaster Tools is simply good housekeeping.

### *Weekly Audit – Action Plan*

Analyse Google Analytics visitor and keyword data                    [  ]

Take action on the above                                             [  ]

Analyse sale pages views and clicks                                  [  ]

Take action on the above                                             [  ]

Analyse Google Webmaster Tools data                                  [  ]

If problems are found with the above, take immediate action          [  ]

# Monthly Action Plan

You must ensure that you take the time to examine clicks for all banners and calls to action at the end of each month. For sales pages with high views and low clicks change banners and anchor text, keeping a detailed history of the changes you make. Remember that the name of the game with banners and links is to replace those with a low ratio of clicks to page views with those with a high ratio of clicks to page views. For example, a link to a merchant product page with the anchor text "click here" will produce a lower number of clicks compared to the anchor text "click here for an exclusive discount".

If you have a product page that is producing a high number of page views and clicks but is not generating any sales, then you will need to investigate why. Is another merchant offering the product at a cheaper price? Is there another product that is outperforming the product you are promoting? A good affiliate will take the time to find products that are in demand as well as finding the merchant that offers the product at the best price. Tweaking sales pages, by means of changing banners and text or even switching to another product, is essential so that you can "squeeze" maximum revenue from your pages.

Also of great importance is to ensure that you continue to build a presence on social media sites and forums in your chosen niche. You should be making at least three posts a week on external sites. For month one simply concentrate on getting your affiliate website up and running. From month two onwards you MUST start to make quality posts on external websites. Remember not to spam!

A great ploy to increase traffic is to seek out key phrases that are not ranked highly in Google search results nor contained in your existing article titles and write a complete article targeting the key phrases. You should search for such key phrases each month.

Also take the time to find others that have linked to your affiliate website (external links) using Google Webmaster Tools. Find your website's popular pages and create more of them!

Each month carry out the following tasks.

## Monthly Action Plan – Tasks

Check external links in Google Webmaster Tools                                    [  ]

Tweak banners and calls to action                                                [  ]

Analyse product performance in page views, clicks and sales                      [  ]

Use Google Analytics to seek out new key phrases                    [  ]

## *Monthly Progress Schedule*

You simply have to keep on keeping on!  If you fall behind in any month, ensure that you catch up before the end of the next month!

### Month 1

Website built                                                       [  ]

Affiliate applications successful                                   [  ]

50 Articles loaded                                                  [  ]

### Month 2

140 Articles loaded                                                 [  ]

12 External Links                                                   [  ]

### Month 3

230 Articles loaded                                                 [  ]

24 External Links                                                   [  ]

### Month 4

320 Articles loaded                                                 [  ]

36 External Links                                                   [  ]

**Month 5**

410 Articles loaded                                            [  ]

48 External Links                                              [  ]


**Month 6**

500 Articles loaded                                            [  ]

60 External Links                                              [  ]


**Month 7**

590 Articles loaded                                            [  ]

72 External Links                                              [  ]


**Month 8**

680 Articles loaded                                            [  ]

84 External Links                                              [  ]


**Month 9**

770 Articles loaded                                            [  ]

96 External Links                                              [  ]

**Month 10**

860 Articles loaded                                                                         [   ]

108 External Links                                                                         [   ]


**Month 11**

950 Articles loaded                                                                         [   ]

120 External Links                                                                         [   ]


**Month 12**

1040 Articles loaded                                                                       [   ]

132 External Links                                                                         [   ]


# Onwards & Upwards!
Remember that this book simply gives you the basic concepts to set you on your journey to become a successful affiliate. The action plans included in this chapter list the bare minimum of tasks you need to complete to build your affiliate website. By reading this book you should be aware of many other ways to generate traffic to your website. Being honest I would say most affiliates do not harness other traffic sources as they rely solely on Google, which of course is a big mistake. Take the time to build multiple traffic streams and you will never have to worry about Google algorithm changes or indeed Google penalties.

### *Increase Traffic Sources Action Plan*
Build a list                                                                                  [   ]

Post quality unique content on your Facebook page                          [   ]

Post quality tweets                                                                       [   ]

Seek out quality forums in your niche and post helpful advice            [   ]

Seek out quality blogs in your niche and post informative advice     [   ]

Create a YouTube Channel, posting new videos each week     [   ]

Upload your videos on other video sharing sites     [   ]

Post quality informative articles on leading article directories     [   ]

Seek out addition online traffic sources     [   ]

Seek out offline traffic sources     [   ]

### *What You Should Not Do!*

Successful affiliates will tell you that if you want to succeed, you should not take shortcuts. If you do, perhaps by means of buying links, producing spun articles, key word stuffing, buying fans or followers or numerous other shady practices, then you are simply condemning your website to failure!

### *Need Extra Help?*

For those who intend to build their very own online cash cow I have some great news for you! On 1$^{st}$ September 2012 I will be launching a dedicated site (www.onlinecashcow.com), which will offer free advice and guidance for those attempting to build an affiliate website using the techniques detailed in this book. Unlike other such sites, access will be completely free!

# Glossary

**Above The Fold**

This phrase refers to the part of the webpage that is visible to the viewer as soon as the page opens, without scrolling. It is generally accepted that this part of the page is the most profitable and therefore it is imperative that all the important information relating to the page is contained "above the fold". Due to the layouts of different browsers, it is often the case that this section of the webpage cuts off in different areas, which is something you must be mindful of when creating your website.

**Advertiser**

The advertiser – also commonly known as the merchant – is the person looking to get traffic sent to their website through affiliate websites. Therefore, they are the ones who pay money to online affiliates, depending on the actions of the traffic sent, which can range from a set sum per click-through to a percentage of any purchases made. As an example, Amazon would be counted as an advertiser, as they pay their affiliates depending on the amount of money the customer spends on their website when coming through an affiliate link.

**Affiliate**

An affiliate is essentially the opposite to an advertiser, as they are the people driving traffic to another site in the hope of making commission from any sales made there. They are usually paid a percentage of the money that a referred customer spends on the advertiser's site, although occasionally they are paid per click or when people sign up to a mailing list.

# Glossary

## Affiliate Link

An affiliate link is a link that contains a code within it, therefore meaning that both the affiliate and the merchant can track the numbers of clicks that it receives. Basically it will ensure that different visitors can have their sources recognized, so that the person owning the website that referred them gets paid their affiliate commission. It is essential that your affiliate links are set up correctly, as without them you will not receive any money for your efforts.

## Affiliate Management Agency

This type of agency is there to manage affiliate programs for a merchant, so that they can concentrate on other aspects of their business. They basically work with all of the affiliates as well as recruiting new affiliates – in an effort to increase the amount of traffic that each site sends, and they also encourage the affiliates to operate in ways that benefit both the affiliates and the merchants. They can also handle occasional promotions in an effort to temporarily boost the performance of the merchant's site. Although they are not necessary for every merchant, they are often used by those with a lack of knowledge in the area of affiliate marketing and the fee that they charge is usually covered by the extra income that they bring in.

## Affiliate Marketing

Affiliate marketing refers to the practice of merchants getting other webmasters to promote their site and therefore drive traffic to them so that more sales/leads can be generated. For every predefined action that the referral completes – such as purchasing goods or submitting their details – the affiliate will receive payment, which is either a set amount or a percentage of the income from the specific customer.

## Affiliate Network

An affiliate network is a company that is neither associated specifically with the merchant or the affiliate. Instead, they provide services to both parties, such as the use of tracking tools, reporting services and the ability to process payments easily from merchants to their affiliates.

## Affiliate Program

An affiliate program is any scheme being run by a business that encourages webmasters to send traffic through to them in exchange for payment should the sent traffic perform a specific action, such as buying a product or subscribing to a mailing list. They are also commonly referred to as referral, partner, revenue sharing or associate programs in different areas of online business, although they all mean the same thing.

## Affiliate Program Manager

This person is essentially the person responsible for the day to day running of any affiliate program. They will ensure that affiliate partners are regularly communicated with, implement new marketing strategies and answer any questions from affiliates or sites looking to work within the affiliate program. They can either work directly for the merchant, or they can be employed by an affiliate management agency.

## Affiliate Reporting

This is the way that the affiliate program communicates all sales and commissions to the different affiliates that it works with, encompassing the number of referrals that the affiliate has provided and the amount of money that they have earned over a set period of time.

## Affiliate Software

This type of software is for merchants who do not want to use an affiliate network to start their affiliate program. It means that they have all the resources available to them to communicate with their affiliates, track conversions and send out different marketing methods to the affiliates. It also allows the merchants to keep figures relating to different campaigns, so that they can make educated decisions regarding their effectiveness.

## Affiliate Solution Provider

This is a type of company that works within the world of affiliate marketing, helping various merchants with the implementation and software needed to start up an affiliate program effectively.

## Affiliate Tracking

This is the technology needed in order to track all the different sales, conversions and payments generated from affiliate websites. It is essential for any affiliate business that wants to work properly and provide accurate figures and payments to all affiliates.

**Banner Ad**

This is a type of advertisement found on a webpage that displays a graphic, which when clicked leads to another webpage thanks to an embedded link within it.

**Blog**

The word itself is a shortening of "web log" and it is one of the most common sites on the internet nowadays. In layman's terms it is a type of journal that someone can keep on the internet, where they write about a subject that interests them. Those owning a blog are referred to as "bloggers" and when they write for the site they are said to be "blogging".

**Blogging Affiliates**

While many people use blogs simply as a way to talk about a subject close to their heart, the vast majority of popular blogs have some affiliate links in them. Therefore they are a specific type of affiliate known as "blogging affiliates". They use the social aspect of their blog and the trust that it has with readers to encourage the readers to click-through to an affiliate page, therefore making money for the blog owner and raising sales for the merchant.

**Click-Through**

A click-through occurs when someone clicks on a link provided on a website and is navigated to a different website, often one owned by a merchant. Some merchants offer payment for every click-through that they get, although most do not offer payment until the visitor completes a specific action on the site.

# Glossary

## Co-Branding

Co-branding occurs when both the affiliate and the merchant club include both of their logos together on a site, thereby forming a visible partnership between the two. This is best used in order to increase awareness of the sites, as visitors to either will be exposed to the logo on the other site as well, which should help to drive extra traffic.

## Commission

Commission is the money that an affiliate earns every time they meet a certain prerequisite with the merchant, such as sending through customers that purchase items or customers that turn out to be good leads. Commission can either be a percentage of the value of the sale or a set fee agreed beforehand by both parties.

## Contextual Link

A contextual link is a type of link that is found embedded into text, so that the highlighted word can be clicked on and the person clicking will be taken to the merchant's website.

## Conversion

When a visitor sent to a merchant site from an affiliate site buys something, they are regarded as a "buyer" and not a "visitor", therefore meaning that they were a successful conversion. The number of conversions that a site has usually impacts heavily on the amount of commission paid to the affiliate, as most commission is paid after a sale has been made.

## Cookie

Cookies have been the subject of much controversy in the past, but they are very important in the world of affiliate marketing. Basically they are a piece of information that a site sends to an individual's browser, which is then saved and passed back to the site whenever the browser is used to access the site. This means that the site can adjust itself to suit the user's preferences or, in the case of affiliate marketing, know that the person visiting was referred previously by an affiliate. As referrals can be valid for days, the cookie is vital in making sure that the affiliate gets paid for their work.

## Cost Per Acquisition (CPA)

This is the total amount of money that a merchant has to spend to get every sale on their site, either in the form of advertising, marketing or affiliate payments. Obviously the lower the cost per acquisition is, the better it is for the merchant.

## Cost Per Action (CPA)

This is a way to ensure that the merchant is never out of pocket, as it refers to the practice of only paying an affiliate when one of their referrals actually makes a purchase on the site (or occasionally when the visitor does something else that can lead to money, such as filling out a form or signing up for a list).

## Cost Per Click (CPC)

This refers to the practice of paying the affiliate a small amount every single time someone visits the merchant's website through an affiliate link on the affiliate's website. The money is paid regardless of the following actions of the visitor.

## Coupon and Voucher Affiliates

These are affiliates who target people who are looking for deals and money saving tips for certain items. They still try to drive customers to the merchant site in the same way as other affiliates, but obviously they use the extra tools of offering discounts and vouchers.

## Coupons

Coupons are offered by merchants in an attempt to entice more people into purchasing items or services from them. They are usually used by the visitors to the site to get a certain amount of money off their purchases, but can also come in the form of coupons offering free shipping or such like. Often the coupon codes are distributed to affiliates, so that they can advertise them on their site and drive more traffic to the merchant's site.

## Creative

This refers to the tools that affiliates use in order to encourage people to click on the links that take them through to the merchant's site. They can either be created by the affiliates themselves, or can be sent through to the affiliates by the merchant. Some examples of creatives most commonly used are text links, banner ads, email copy, pop-up advertisements, buttons and tower ads. New and innovative ideas are constantly being thought up as new and innovative creatives can vastly increase conversions.

**Deep Linking**

Most links to a merchant site will lead straight to their homepage, but this is not always ideal when it comes to affiliate marketing. Deep linking refers to the process whereby the affiliate places a link that will take the visitor onto a page other than the homepage – a page that could be far more relevant to the content on the affiliate's site and therefore lead to more sales.

**Domain Name**

The domain name is the unique name given to a website on the internet, such as www.amazon.com, or www.google.com.

**Download**

The process by which a file is taken from one computer or server and placed onto your own computer. The time that a download takes depends on a number of factors, such as the size of the file and the download speed allowed by the ISP.

**Dynamic Content**

Dynamic content is a type of content on a website that frequently changes to engage readers, hence the use of the word "dynamic". This is most commonly seen with animations and other graphics, but can also come in the form of videos, audio or even text.

## Email Affiliates

One of the best tactics that affiliates can use in order to drive visitors to a merchant is by means of emailing people who have an interest in the merchant's products or services. A link to the merchant's site is usually included in the emails that are sent out, therefore meaning that the link gets a great amount of exposure from targeted visitors.

## Email Marketing

Email marketing is used by businesses as a way of engaging with their customer base and encouraging extra sales. They also increase brand loyalty among customers, as they will appreciate the fact that the company values them as a customer.

## Exclusivity

Exclusivity is the premise that a specific service or specific goods are exclusive – i.e. unique to – a specific organization, and therefore cannot be found anywhere else for sale.

## Feed

Feeds are snippets of web pages that are syndicated to people who subscribe to the feed, therefore increasing their awareness of the new additions to a website. They are shortened so as to encourage people to visit the site to read the webpage in its entirety. One of the most popular feed services is FeedBurner by Google, as it is free, but there are a huge number of others as well.

## Forum

A forum is a place where internet users can gather and discuss a topic of common interest. They are also great places to advertise specific websites, as the users will already have an interest in the good or service being offered, and therefore there is a high chance of them converting to sales.

## Google AdWords

Google AdWords is without doubt the most popular Pay Per Click advertising network in the world. Adverts are placed on Google search results pages and websites of affiliates and they are tailored to the interests of the person visiting the site, therefore meaning that there is a high chance of them clicking on them. Every time a click is registered, the owner of the site gets a small sum of money.

## Hit

A hit is a request to load a web page on a server, although one web page would not always be counted as one hit. This is because hits take into account different aspects of the page, such as graphics. Therefore, a page with four graphics on it would count as five hits – four hits for the graphics and one for the page itself.

## HTML

HTML is a markup language and stands for Hyper Text Markup Language. It is commonly used to create many aspects of a web page, through structuring the way that various text and images are displayed to the visitor. Another huge use for HTML is in the creation of hypertext links, which link different pages together, either on or off the site.

## Impression

An impression is created when an advertising link is displayed. Thus if a link was displayed 30 times, it would be referred to as having had "30 impressions".

## Incentivized Affiliates

This refers to the practice of providing incentives to site visitors in order to get them to complete a certain action on the site, therefore resulting in the affiliate making more money. Using incentives often means that people think that they are getting "something for nothing", even if the incentive is not particularly valuable. Obviously however, the better the incentive is, the more people will complete the action.

## Keyword

Targeting the correct keywords is probably the single most important part of any search engine optimization strategy, as it will dictate how much of your future strategy pans out. A keyword is essentially the word or phrase that someone uses to find information in search engines: therefore it is extremely important that your site appears high in the SERPs for certain keyword phrases, especially since it is estimated that 80% of people never click past the first page on Google.

## Keyword Density

When creating content for your site, it is important to include the keywords that you have chosen a significant number of times. Keyword density refers to the percentage of the text on your site that is taken up by the keywords that you are targeting.

## Lifetime Value

Lifetime value refers to the expected amount of money that a single specific customer will spend with the company over the length of his or her life, although this can be hard to predict due to the constant changes in situations, both of the customers and of the industry the site operates within.

## Loyalty Affiliates

Loyalty affiliates are affiliates that promote such things as membership to a site or other long term endeavours, often for larger payouts. In fact, many loyalty affiliates will receive recurring payments from the merchant every time the user renews their membership or makes a purchase.

## Mailer

A mailer is a type of email that is one of the principle points of contact with a customer base, usually used with the intention of raising sales or generating income in another way. It can also be used very effectively in the fields of direct marketing and lead generation.

## Manual Approval

This refers to an affiliate program that individually screens all applicants for the program, thereby ensuring that only the most suitable are allowed to promote their product. It is the direct opposite to the practice of mass approval.

## Merchant

A business that operates online, that pays commissions to affiliates for every successful action that a referred customer completes on the merchant's site. These actions can be anything from simply clicking onto the site – known as a "click-through" – all the way to purchasing a certain amount of goods from the merchants. Merchants are also often referred to as "advertisers".

## Meta Tags

Meta tags refer to the information placed within the site's source code that cannot be seen by visitors to the site – it is purely there for the benefit of the search engines and can be used to great effect for search engine optimization.

## Mobile Affiliates

The phrase "mobile affiliates" can have two different meanings. It can either mean an affiliate who targets customers through the use of their mobile phones, or it can mean affiliates who work within the industry of mobile phones, i.e. selling accessories or other items to use with an iPhone or a BlackBerry.

## Network

A network refers to all of the merchants and affiliates who are managed by an individual affiliate management team. Networks can be hugely useful for both affiliates and merchants alike. For merchants, it means that they can connect with a large number of different affiliates very easily and that they can monitor all of their statistics without too much trouble. For affiliates, the advantage is that they can connect to merchants in a huge number of different industries, therefore meaning that they can cherry pick the ones in which they are primarily interested.

## Niche Market

A niche market is a very specific sector of a market, therefore meaning that it is easy to target and conduct search engine optimization for. An example of this is that mobile phones are a market, whereas Samsung chargers would be a niche market.

## Paid Search

This is very similar to Pay per Click advertising – if not identical – in that the merchant only pays the site host if their advert is clicked on. When doing this through search engines, different merchants will usually bid on specific keywords, with the more popular keywords therefore costing more every time they are clicked on. This method obviously means that merchants do not have to risk paying a fee and then finding out that their advert is completely ineffective.

## Pay Per Click (PPC)

As with paid searches, this is a type of advertising where the merchant pays only when the advert that they are displaying is clicked on. However, it can also refer to the practice of an affiliate being paid when they host an advert that is clicked on.

## Pixel

A pixel is a measurement of size and is an abbreviation of the term "picture element". The more pixels there are in an image, the better the image quality will be. On the reverse side, the more pixels in an image, the larger it will be and therefore the longer it will take to load on a webpage. In affiliate marketing, a common tactic is called "pixel tracking", whereby all transactions and leads are recorded by a virtually invisible image.

## Plug-In

A plug-in is an application that can be added to a larger application, therefore altering the way that all or part of the larger application works. One application that makes a lot of use of plug-ins is Wordpress.

## Portal

A portal is a type of website that is used by people to gain access to a larger number of websites, usually within the same niche. For example, a website with a number of links to different gambling sites would be described as a portal. Usually a portal will not contain a huge amount of information other than information pertaining to the links that it is promoting.

## PPC Affiliates

PPC (Pay Per Click) affiliates host different adverts on their website that lead to a merchant's site and are generally provided by a PPC engine, such as Google AdWords or Bing AdCenter. The PPC adverts displayed on an affiliate's page cannot be fully controlled by the affiliate, as they are tailored to meet the individual search patterns of the site visitor, through the use of the cookies stored on the visitor's browser.

## Profit

A term used in all walks of business, which refers to the amount of money that your business makes once you have deducted all the costs that the business incurs in the same time period as the income was created.

## Publisher

Publisher is a phrase that can be used interchangeably with the term affiliate and is used by some affiliate networks. There is no difference between a publisher and an affiliate.

## Referring URL

This is the URL of the website that provided the visitor to a website. For instance, when www.bbc.co.uk sends a visitor to www.amazon.co.uk, the BBC website will be the referring URL.

## Return on Investment

This is used within the world of affiliate marketing most commonly to work out whether a PPC campaign is working as well as the site hoped it would. It basically refers to the practice of subtracting the cost of the investment from the profit of the investment, and then dividing the resulting figure by the cost of the investment. Results showing a negative return on investment are not profitable, whereas those with positive figures are profitable.

## Revenue

The total amount of money that your business has earned over a certain period of time, before any costs and other expenditure are taken away.

## ROI

An abbreviation of "return on investment".

## Search Engine Optimization

This is the practice of optimizing a website or webpage so that it performs well within a search engine's rankings for a certain keyword. There are a number of different tactics used within search engine optimization including, but not limited to: on site optimization, optimization of meta data, article marketing, building backlinks and, most importantly, keyword research. It is almost universally agreed that a good command of search engine optimization is key to any successful online business venture, although there are SEO companies out there to help with this aspect of a business.

## Social Networking Affiliates

These are paid in exactly the same way that regular affiliates are and also have the same goal as all other affiliates – to drive traffic to a merchant's website. However, to do this they make heavy use of social media, such as Facebook and Twitter, to engage their followers and persuade them to visit the merchant's site.

## Super Affiliates

These are the elite affiliates within an affiliate program. Generally they only account for a very small percentage of all affiliates (1-2%), but usually generate about 90% of the total sales for a specific program.

## Targeted Marketing

Targeted marketing is an essential tool for any affiliate marketer. It refers to the process of breaking a customer base down into smaller denominations in relation to their purchasing habits and the most effective way that they can be sold to. By doing this, it is possible to create products and sales approaches that maximize the potential market by targeting each section differently.

## Text Link

A text link – as the name suggests – is a link that is purely made up of text and that does not contain graphics of any sort. They can be very effective when embedded within a larger body of text.

**Third Party Tracking Software**

This refers to any software located away from your own server that tracks the amount of visitors that your site receives. This is often preferred by both affiliates and merchants as it means that unbiased figures can be generated and that therefore there is no ambiguity regarding the number of visitors an affiliate has referred to a merchant's site.

**Tracking Method**

Simply put, this is the method that the affiliate program uses in order to track the number of sales, leads and other conversions that an affiliate sends through to a merchant. This means that the correct commission can be paid to the affiliate every time.

**Tracking URL**

A tracking URL is similar to a regular URL, but where it differs is in the fact that it has a small piece of code attached to it. This code can be used to track the behaviour of any visitors that arrive on the site, therefore meaning that any purchases or other actions that they complete are logged properly.

**Transparency**

Transparency means that a certain aspect of an affiliate marketing program is completely open for the public to see, instead of being hidden away. The more transparency a site has, the more trust it is able to build up. However, at the same time it also means that more details regarding the business are open to scrutiny. It can also be used to describe the amount of detail that a specific piece of affiliate software reports to its users.

**Two-Tier**

A type of affiliate program that allows affiliates to earn commissions on the sales made by people that they have referred the program to, as well as on their own sales. This means that the merchant gets more affiliates driving traffic, and the original affiliate has the chance to make more money.

**Unique Visitor**

A unique visitor is a single IP address that has visited the website and has then been identified and tagged by the tracking software. This is not the same as total visitors, as many people will come back to the site more than once.

**Upload**

The process by which you transfer a file from your own computer or server to another computer or server, therefore meaning that the file is shared between people.

**URL**

This is an abbreviation for Uniform Resource Locator and, in layman's terms, refers to the address of any site on the internet. For example, the URL of CNN's website would be http://www.cnn.com.

# Glossary

## Viral Marketing

Viral marketing is an online marketing technique that makes use of people's desire to share information that they have found particularly useful or humorous. Therefore marketers try to create content that is likely to catch people's interest and get them to share it with all of their friends. This is an extremely effective and cheap way for new businesses to make a massive splash when first entering their chosen industry.

## Web Host

A web host is a business that allows people to place their websites onto their servers, as well as ensuring that the webmaster has all the services necessary to keep their site running effectively. They are essential if you do not have the capability to host your own websites and, even if you do, they provide the peace of mind that your site will be active 99.99% of the time.

## White Label

A white label is a type of product that is owned by an individual, but which other companies are allowed to use and brand with their own identity. The name "white label" basically refers to the fact that there is no labeling (or branding) on the original product, therefore meaning that it is extremely easy to rebrand. They are generally quite cheap to purchase, but obviously the better the product, the more money they will cost. A great idea for anyone without the time or skills to create their own products.

# Index

5419489R00267

Printed in Great Britain
by Amazon.co.uk, Ltd.,
Marston Gate.